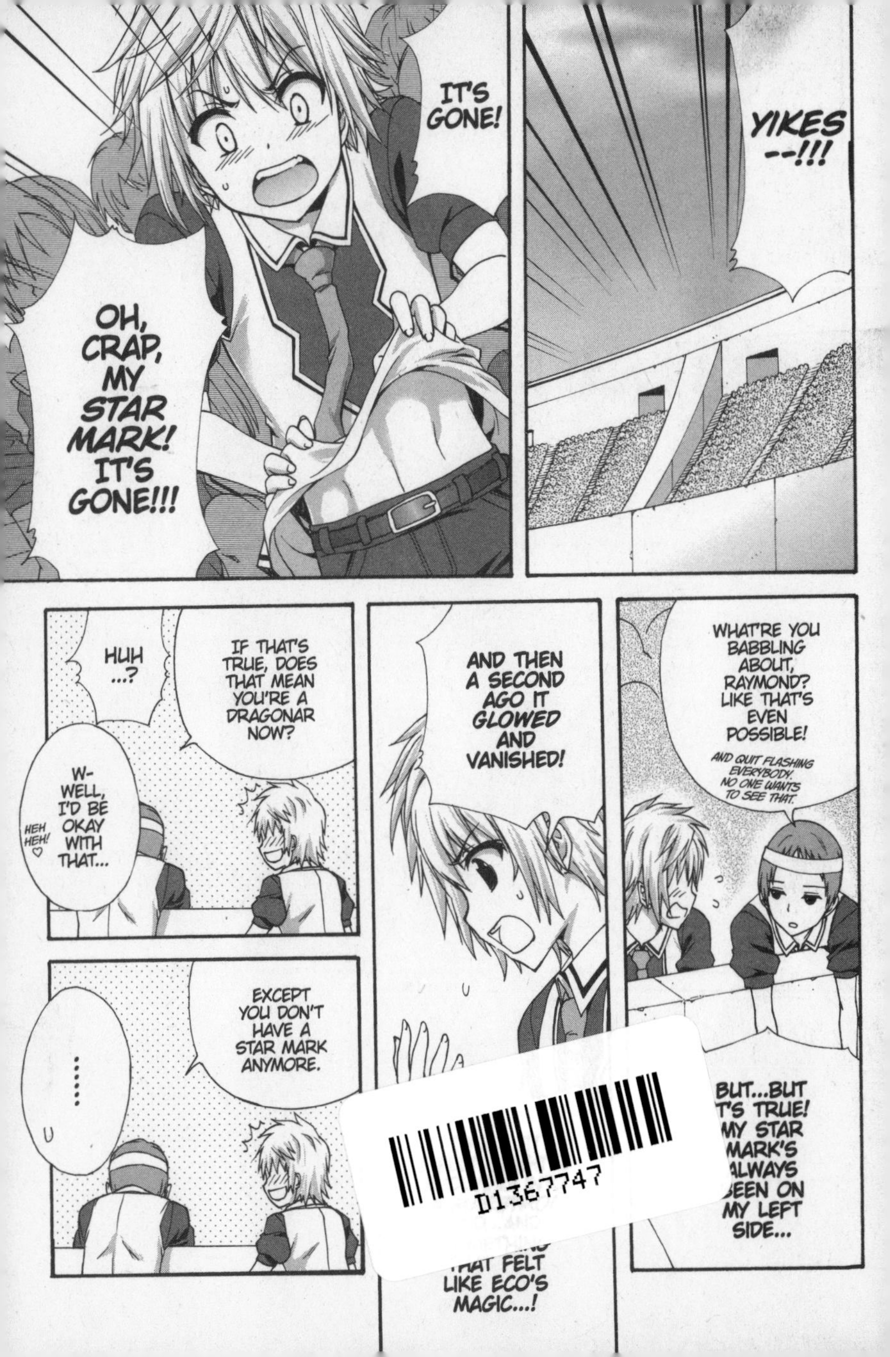
YIKES --!!!
IT'S GONE!
OH, CRAP, MY STAR MARK! IT'S GONE!!!
WHAT'RE YOU BABBLING ABOUT, RAYMOND? LIKE THAT'S EVEN POSSIBLE!
AND QUIT FLASHING EVERYBODY. NO ONE WANTS TO SEE THAT.
BUT...BUT T'S TRUE! MY STAR MARK'S ALWAYS BEEN ON MY LEFT SIDE...
AND THEN A SECOND AGO IT GLOWED AND VANISHED!
THING THAT FELT LIKE ECO'S MAGIC...!
IF THAT'S TRUE, DOES THAT MEAN YOU'RE A DRAGONAR NOW?
HUH ...?
W-WELL, I'D BE OKAY WITH THAT...
HEH HEH! ♡
EXCEPT YOU DON'T HAVE A STAR MARK ANYMORE.
......

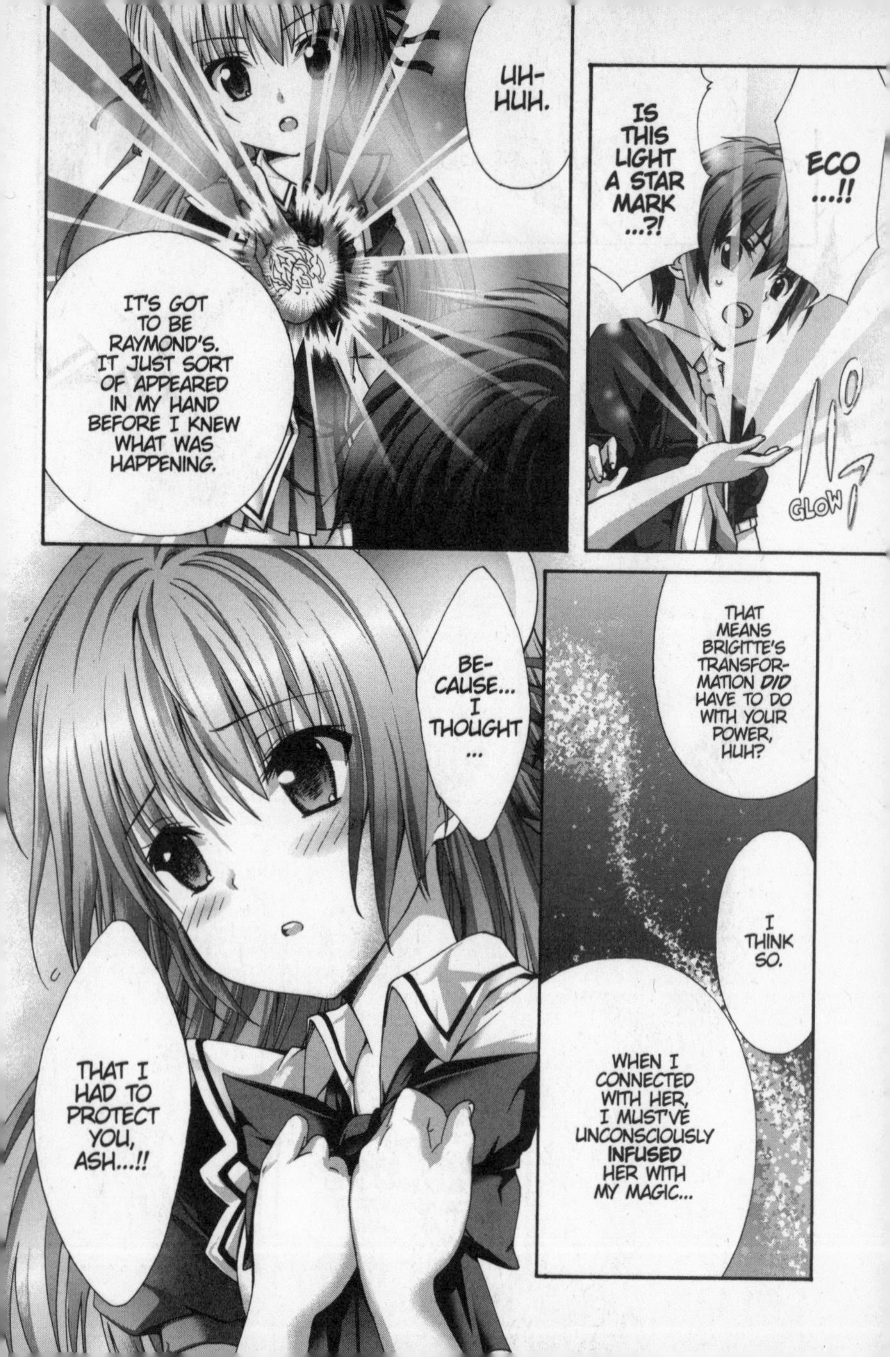
ECO ...!!
IS THIS LIGHT A STAR MARK ...?!
GLOW
UH-HUH.
IT'S GOT TO BE RAYMOND'S. IT JUST SORT OF APPEARED IN MY HAND BEFORE I KNEW WHAT WAS HAPPENING.
THAT MEANS BRIGITTE'S TRANSFORMATION *DID* HAVE TO DO WITH YOUR POWER, HUH?
I THINK SO.
WHEN I CONNECTED WITH HER, I MUST'VE UNCONSCIOUSLY INFUSED HER WITH MY MAGIC...
BE-CAUSE... I THOUGHT ...
THAT I HAD TO PROTECT YOU, ASH...!!

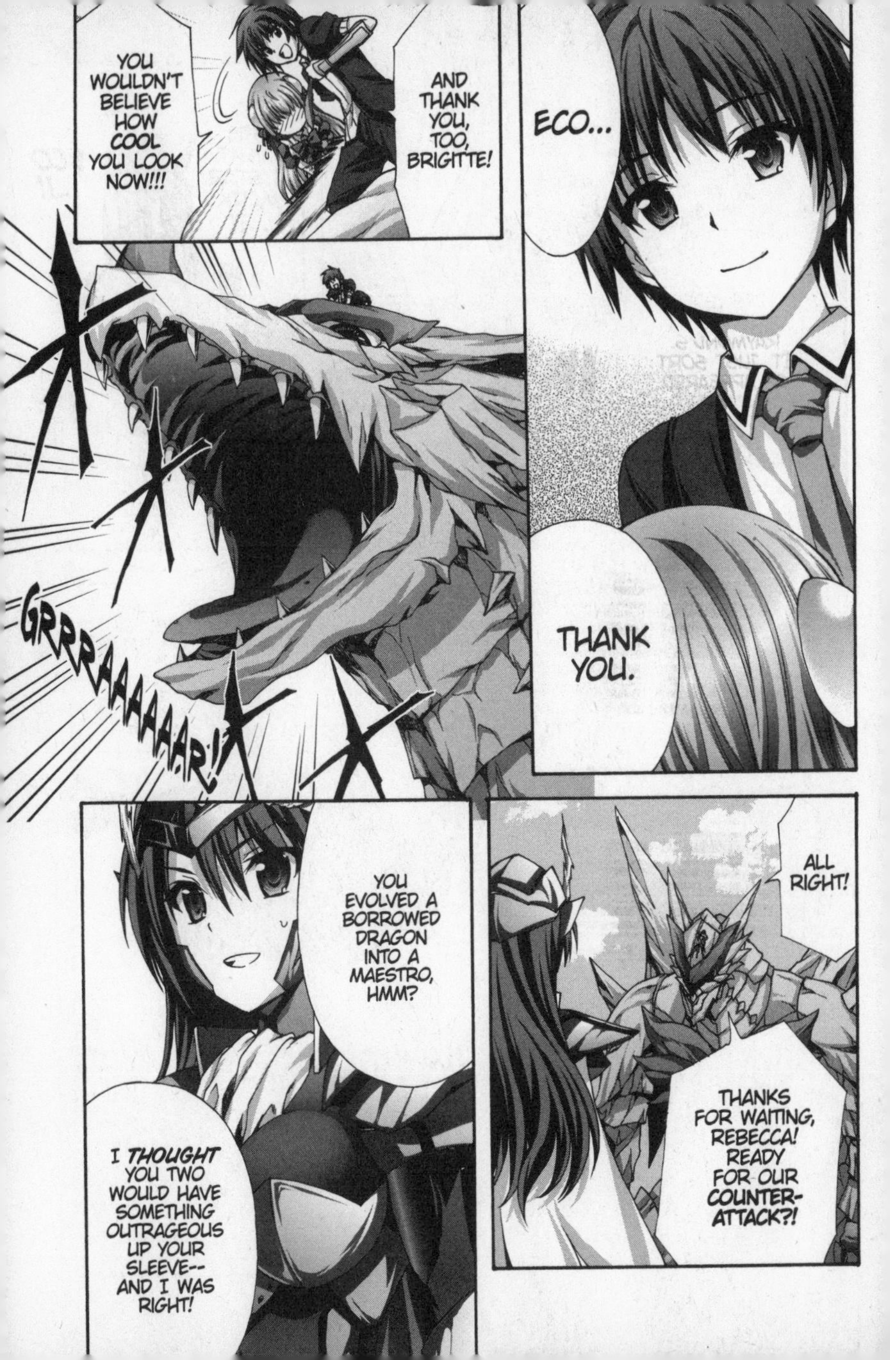
ECO...
THANK YOU.
AND THANK YOU, TOO, BRIGITTE!
YOU WOULDN'T BELIEVE HOW COOL YOU LOOK NOW!!!
GRRRAAAAAAAR!!
ALL RIGHT!
THANKS FOR WAITING, REBECCA! READY FOR OUR COUNTER-ATTACK?!
YOU EVOLVED A BORROWED DRAGON INTO A MAESTRO, HMM?
I *THOUGHT* YOU TWO WOULD HAVE SOMETHING OUTRAGEOUS UP YOUR SLEEVE--AND I WAS RIGHT!

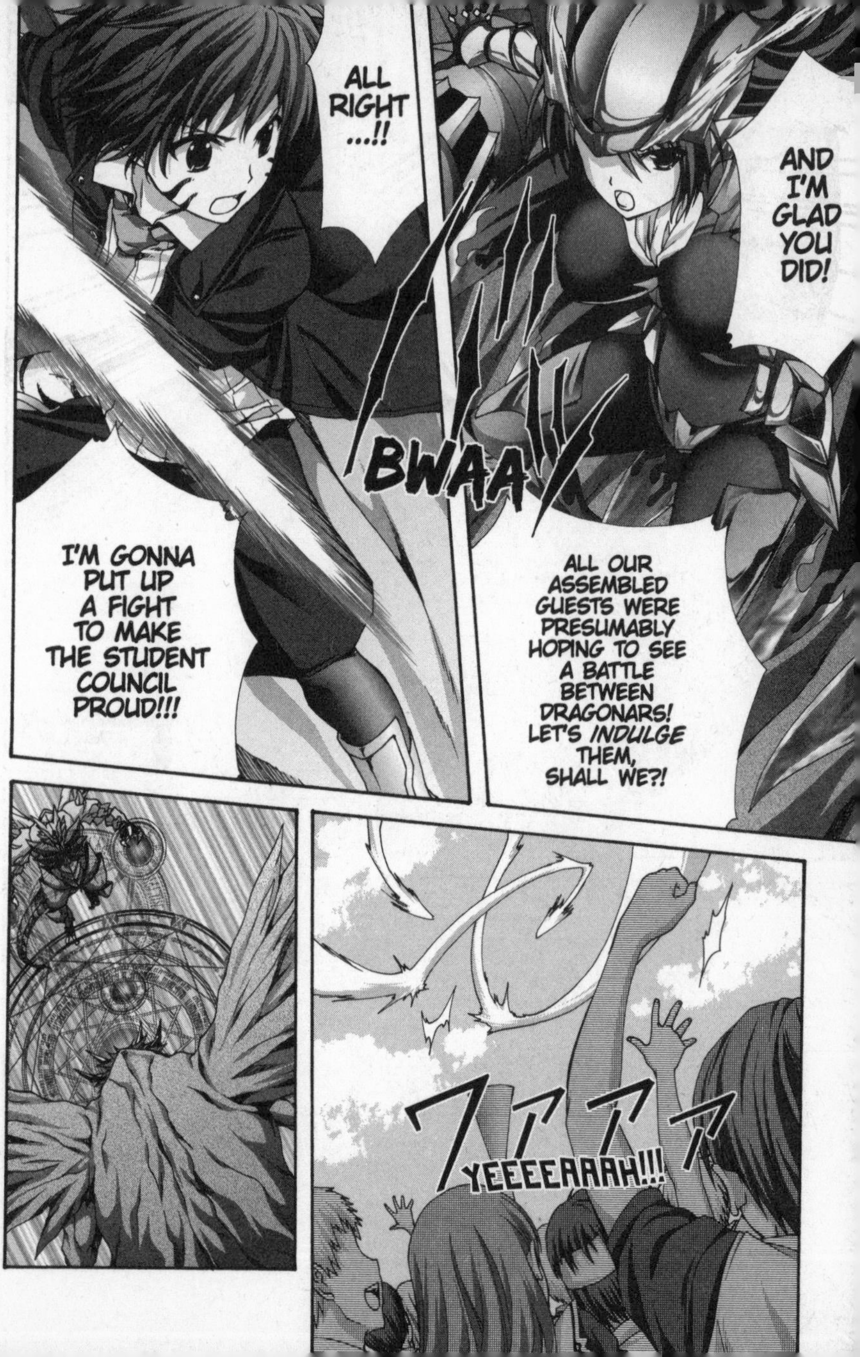
AND I'M GLAD YOU DID!
ALL OUR ASSEMBLED GUESTS WERE PRESUMABLY HOPING TO SEE A BATTLE BETWEEN DRAGONARS! LET'S INDULGE THEM, SHALL WE?!
BWAA
ALL RIGHT ...!!
I'M GONNA PUT UP A FIGHT TO MAKE THE STUDENT COUNCIL PROUD!!!
ワアアア
YEEEEAAAH!!!

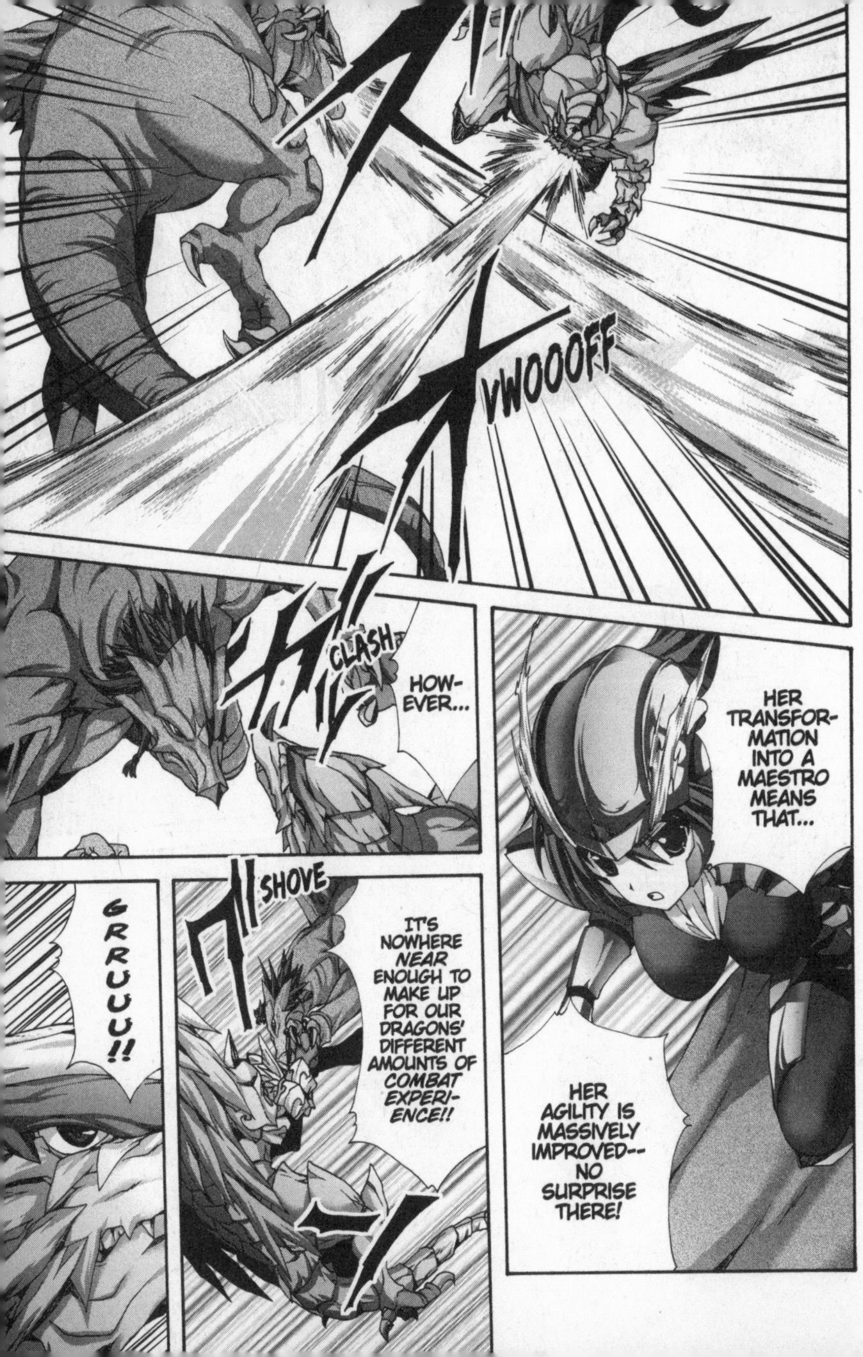
VWOOOFF
HER TRANSFORMATION INTO A MAESTRO MEANS THAT...
HER AGILITY IS MASSIVELY IMPROVED-- NO SURPRISE THERE!
CLASH
HOW-EVER...
SHOVE
IT'S NOWHERE NEAR ENOUGH TO MAKE UP FOR OUR DRAGONS' DIFFERENT AMOUNTS OF COMBAT EXPERIENCE!!
GRRUUU!!

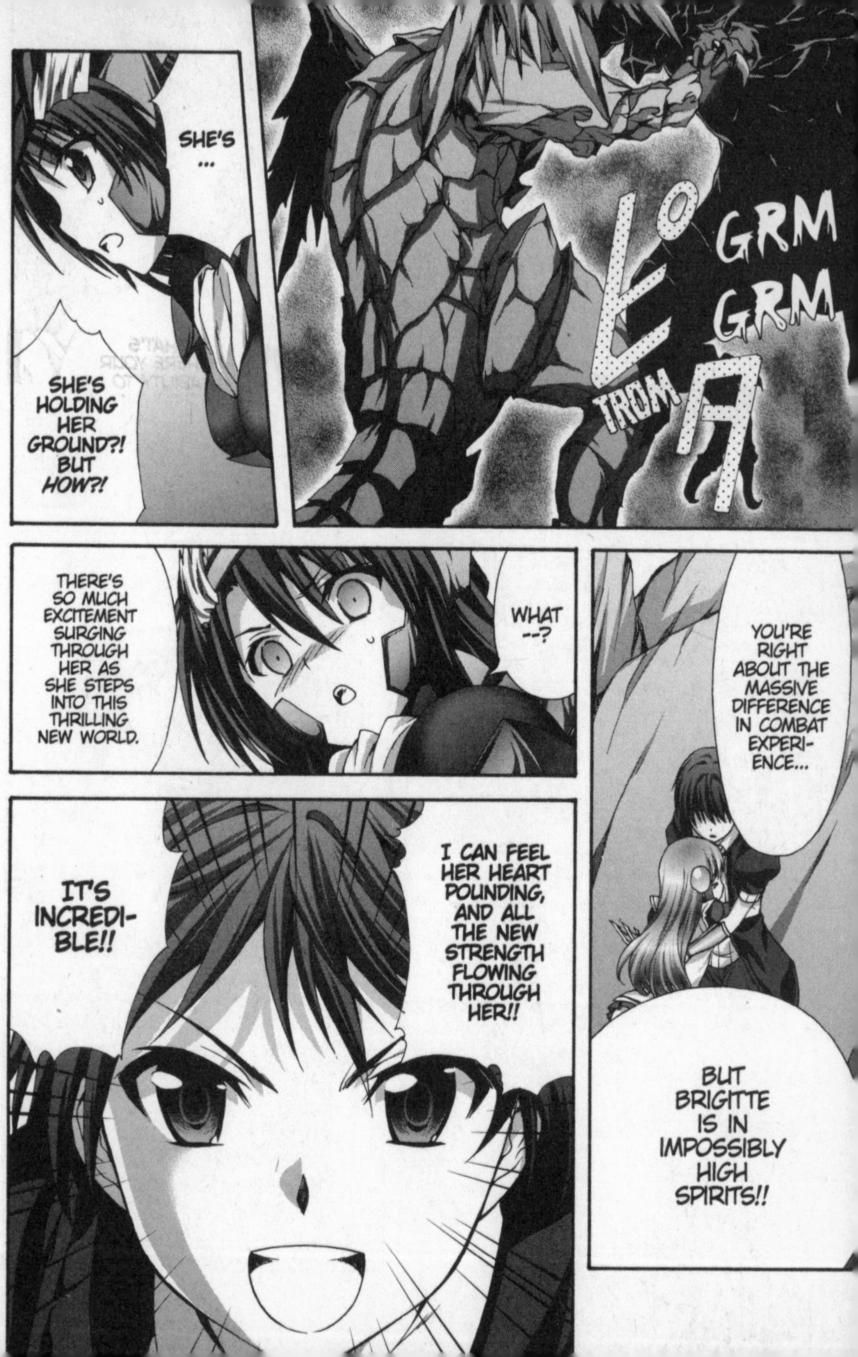
GRM GRM
TROM
SHE'S ...
SHE'S HOLDING HER GROUND?! BUT HOW?!
YOU'RE RIGHT ABOUT THE MASSIVE DIFFERENCE IN COMBAT EXPERI-ENCE...
BUT BRIGITTE IS IN IMPOSSIBLY HIGH SPIRITS!!
WHAT --?
THERE'S SO MUCH EXCITEMENT SURGING THROUGH HER AS SHE STEPS INTO THIS THRILLING NEW WORLD.
I CAN FEEL HER HEART POUNDING, AND ALL THE NEW STRENGTH FLOWING THROUGH HER!!
IT'S INCREDI-BLE!!

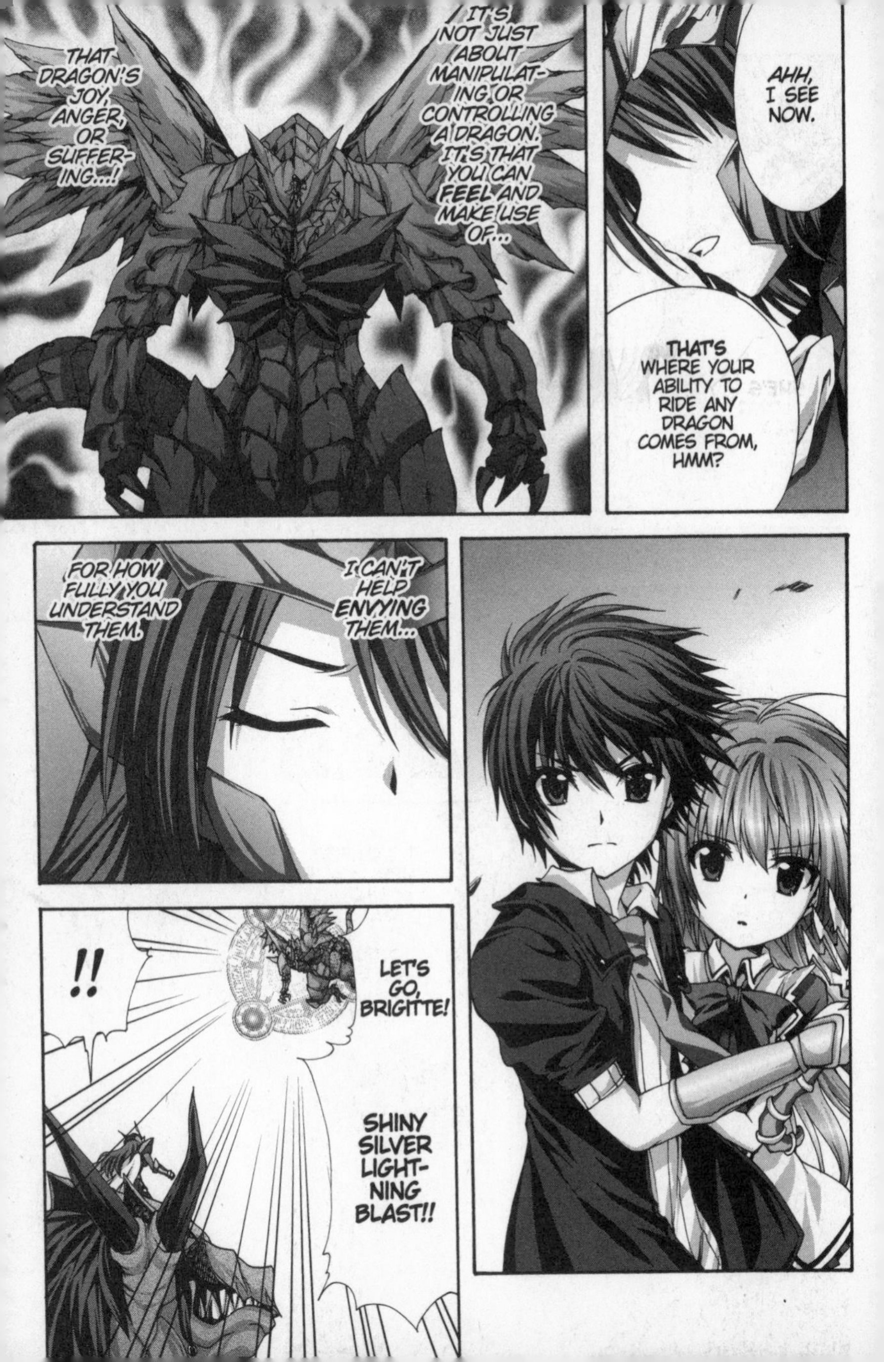
AHH, I SEE NOW.
THAT'S WHERE YOUR ABILITY TO RIDE ANY DRAGON COMES FROM, HMM?
IT'S NOT JUST ABOUT MANIPULATING OR CONTROLLING A DRAGON. IT'S THAT YOU CAN FEEL AND MAKE USE OF...
THAT DRAGON'S JOY, ANGER, OR SUFFERING...!
I CAN'T HELP ENVYING THEM...
FOR HOW FULLY YOU UNDERSTAND THEM.
LET'S GO, BRIGITTE!
!!
SHINY SILVER LIGHTNING BLAST!!

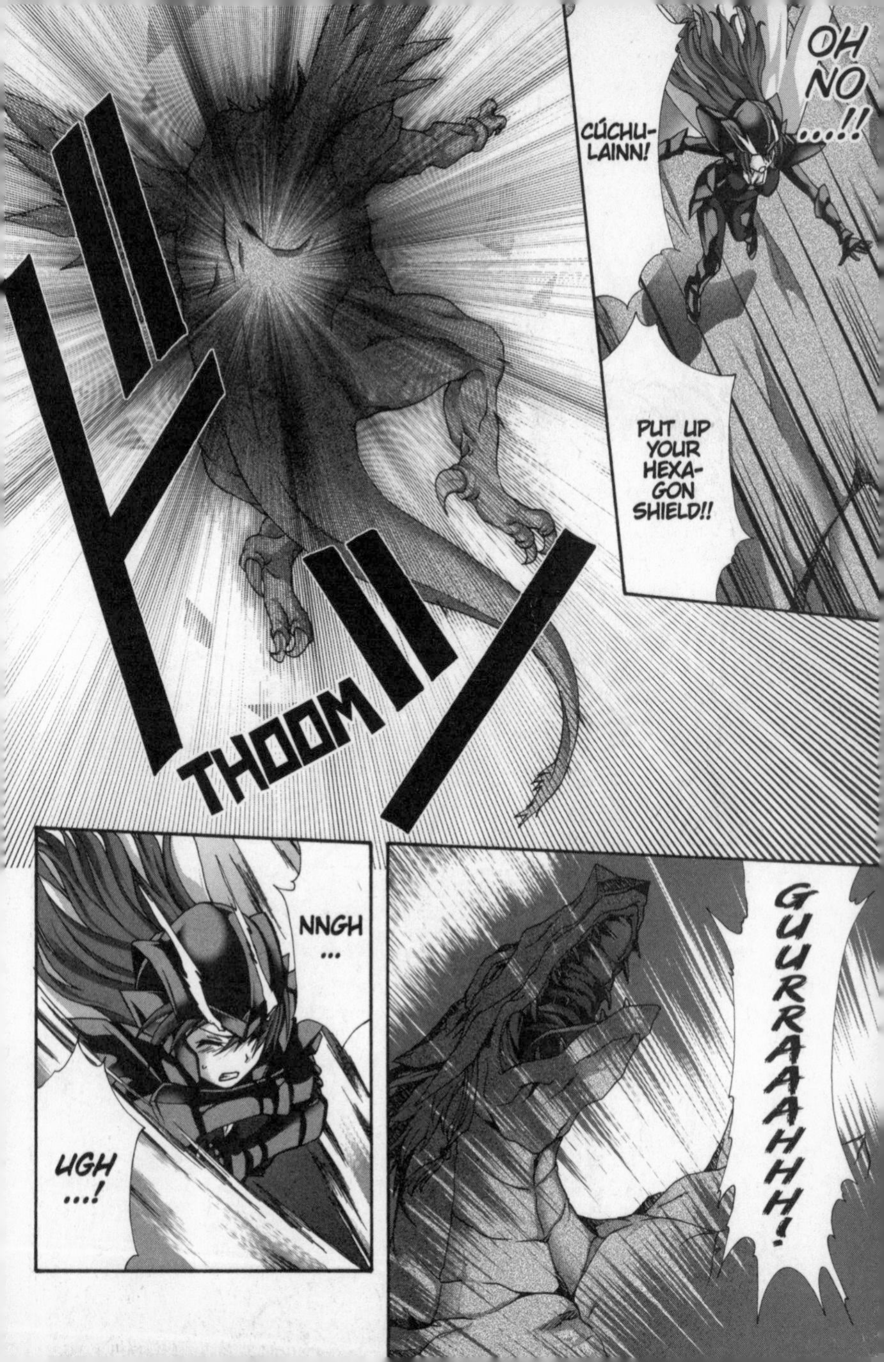
OH NO ...!!
CÚCHU-LAINN!
PUT UP YOUR HEXA-GON SHIELD!!
THOOM
GUURRAAAAHHH!
NNGH ...
UGH ...!

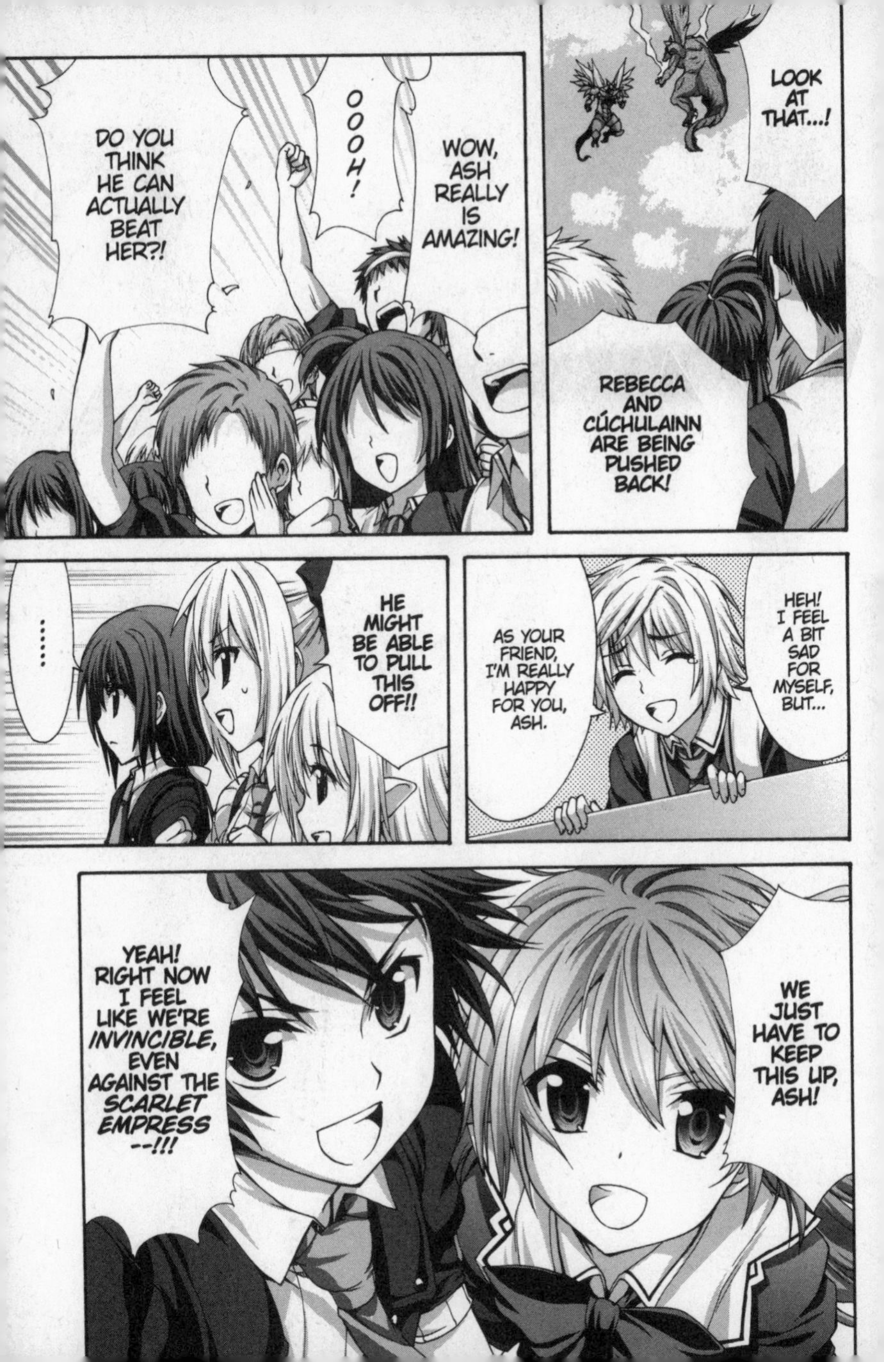
LOOK AT THAT...!
REBECCA AND CÚCHULAINN ARE BEING PUSHED BACK!
WOW, ASH REALLY IS AMAZING!
OOOH!
DO YOU THINK HE CAN ACTUALLY BEAT HER?!
HEH! I FEEL A BIT SAD FOR MYSELF, BUT...
AS YOUR FRIEND, I'M REALLY HAPPY FOR YOU, ASH.
HE MIGHT BE ABLE TO PULL THIS OFF!!
......
WE JUST HAVE TO KEEP THIS UP, ASH!
YEAH! RIGHT NOW I FEEL LIKE WE'RE *INVINCIBLE*, EVEN AGAINST THE *SCARLET EMPRESS*--!!!

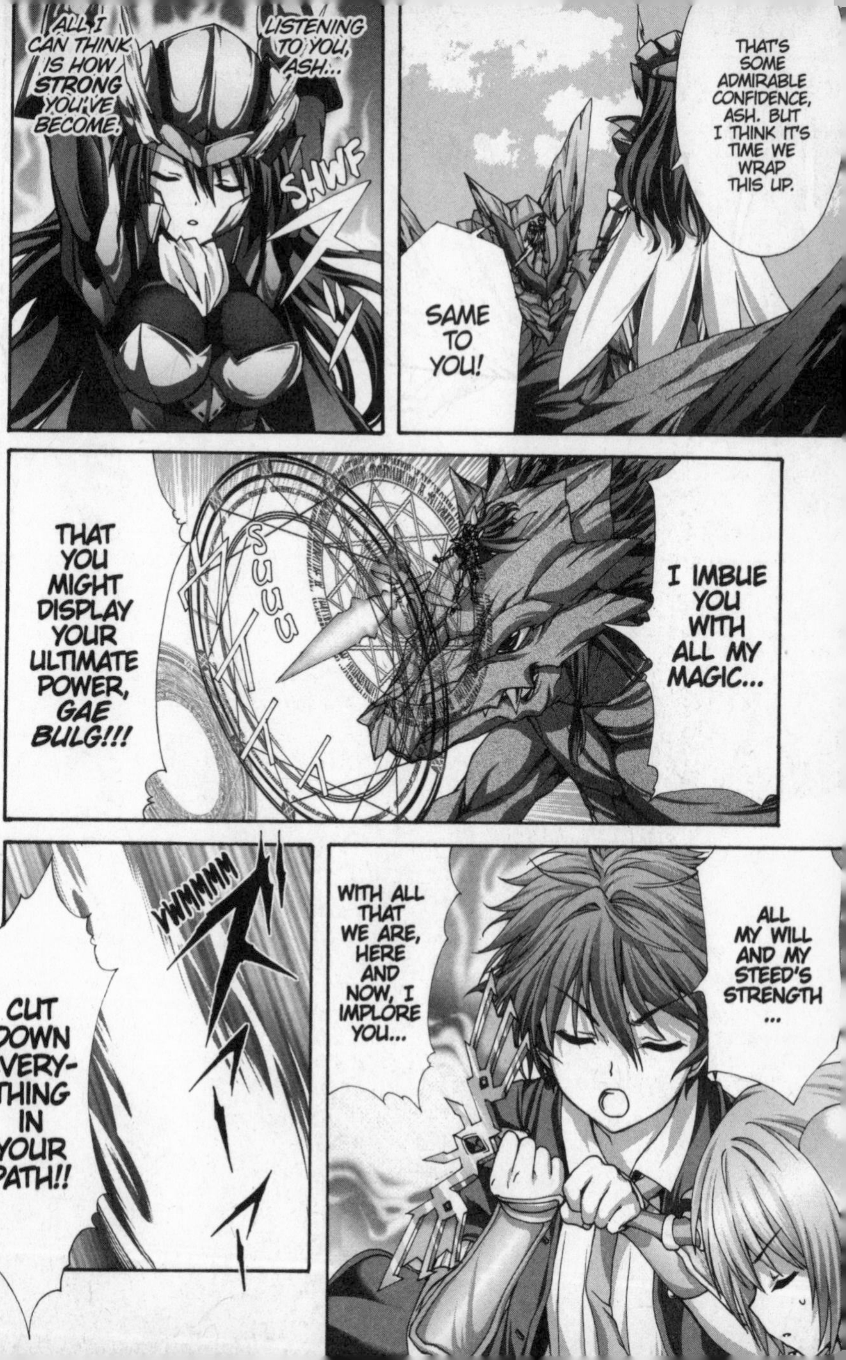
THAT'S SOME ADMIRABLE CONFIDENCE, ASH. BUT I THINK IT'S TIME WE WRAP THIS UP.
SAME TO YOU!
LISTENING TO YOU, ASH...
ALL I CAN THINK IS HOW STRONG YOU'VE BECOME.
SHWF
I IMBUE YOU WITH ALL MY MAGIC...
SUUUU
THAT YOU MIGHT DISPLAY YOUR ULTIMATE POWER, GAE BULG!!!
ALL MY WILL AND MY STEED'S STRENGTH ...
WITH ALL THAT WE ARE, HERE AND NOW, I IMPLORE YOU...
VWMMMM
CUT DOWN EVERY-THING IN YOUR PATH!!

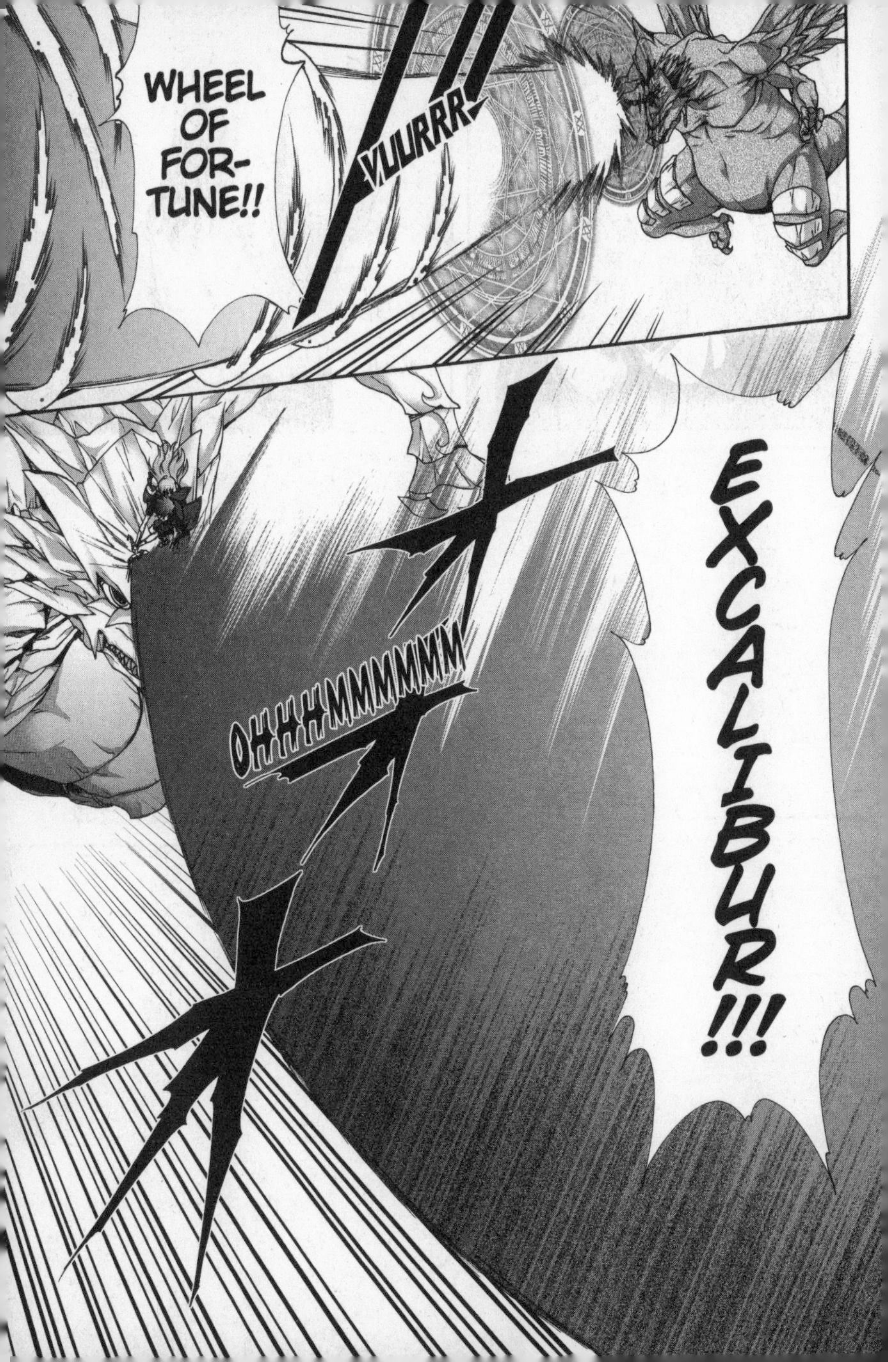
VUURRR
WHEEL OF FOR-TUNE!!
EXCALIBUR!!!
OHHHMMMMMMM

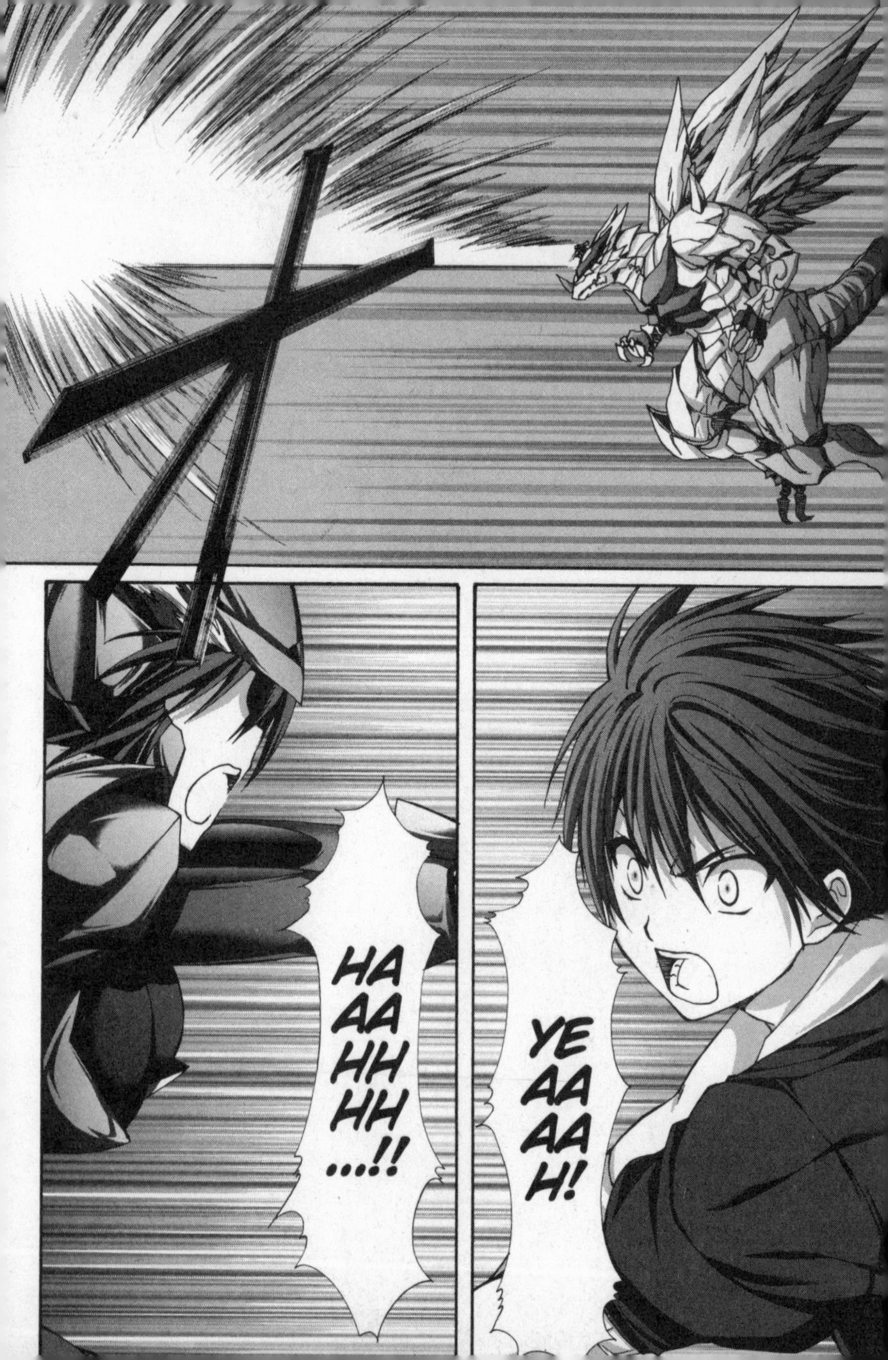
YEAAAAH!
HAAAHHHH...!!

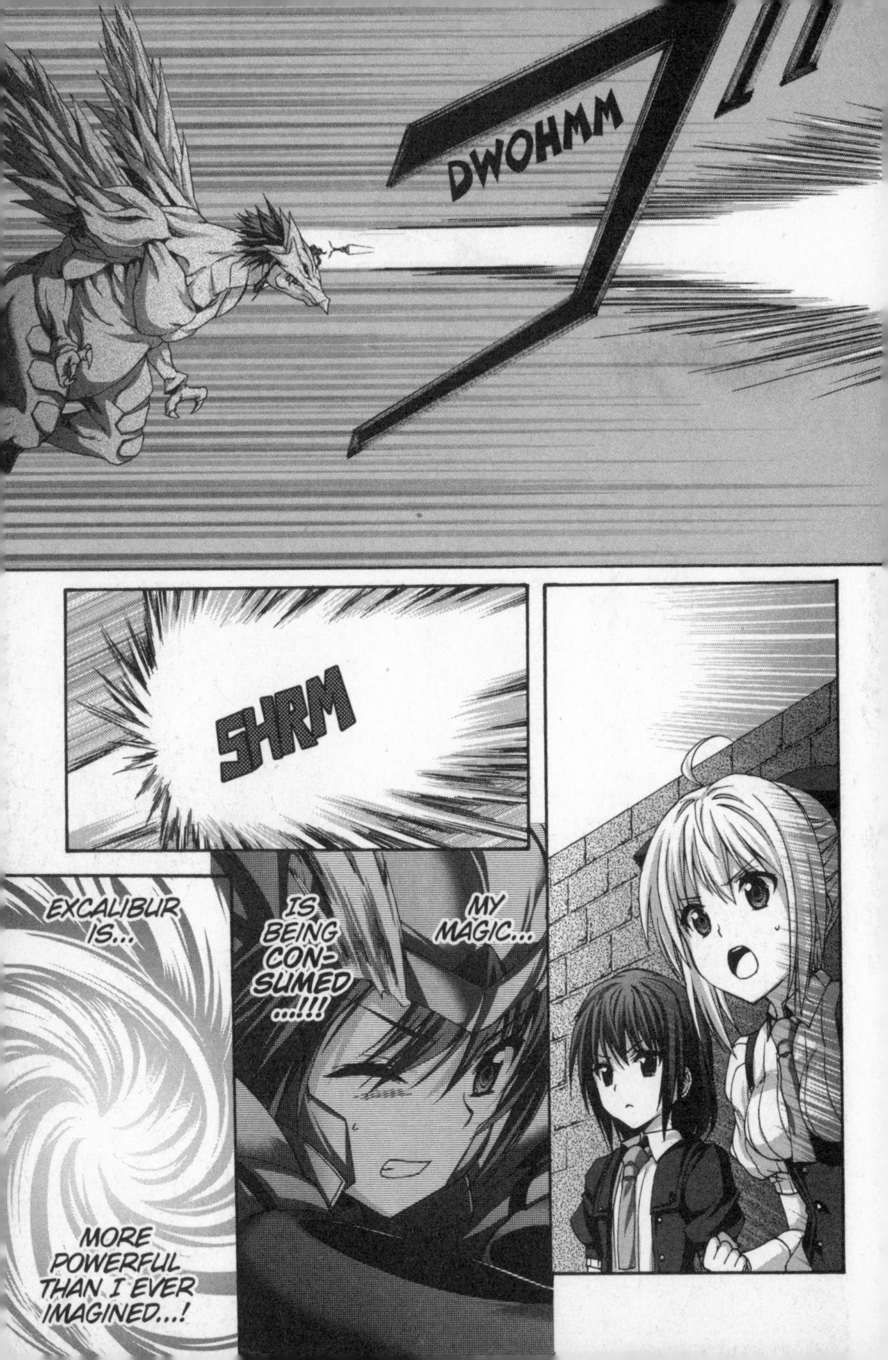
DWOHMM
SHRM
MY MAGIC...
IS BEING CON-SUMED ...!!!
EXCALIBUR IS...
MORE POWERFUL THAN I EVER IMAGINED...!

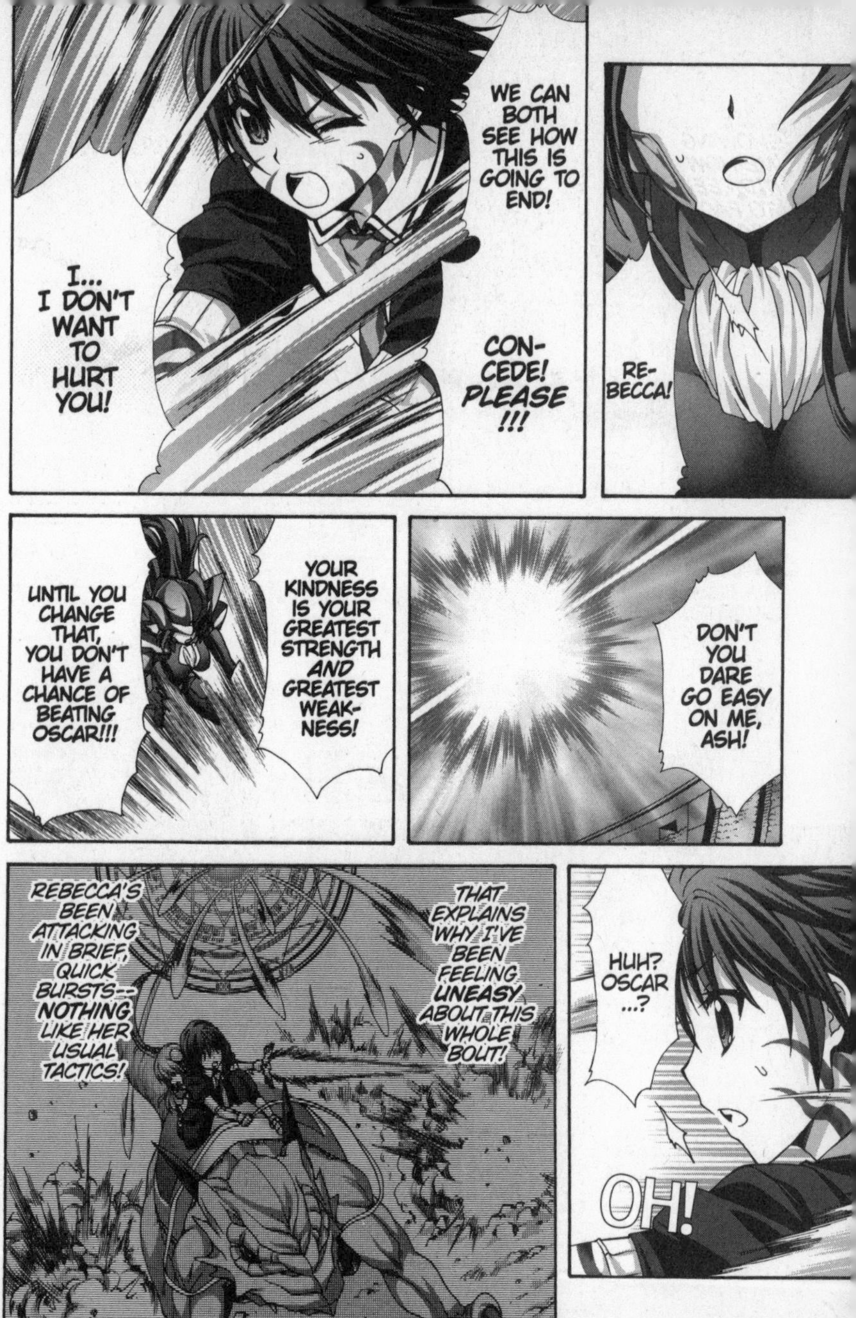
RE-BECCA!
WE CAN BOTH SEE HOW THIS IS GOING TO END!
CON-CEDE! PLEASE!!!
I... I DON'T WANT TO HURT YOU!
DON'T YOU DARE GO EASY ON ME, ASH!
YOUR KINDNESS IS YOUR GREATEST STRENGTH AND GREATEST WEAK-NESS!
UNTIL YOU CHANGE THAT, YOU DON'T HAVE A CHANCE OF BEATING OSCAR!!!
HUH? OSCAR ...?
OH!
THAT EXPLAINS WHY I'VE BEEN FEELING UNEASY ABOUT THIS WHOLE BOUT!
REBECCA'S BEEN ATTACKING IN BRIEF, QUICK BURSTS-- NOTHING LIKE HER USUAL TACTICS!

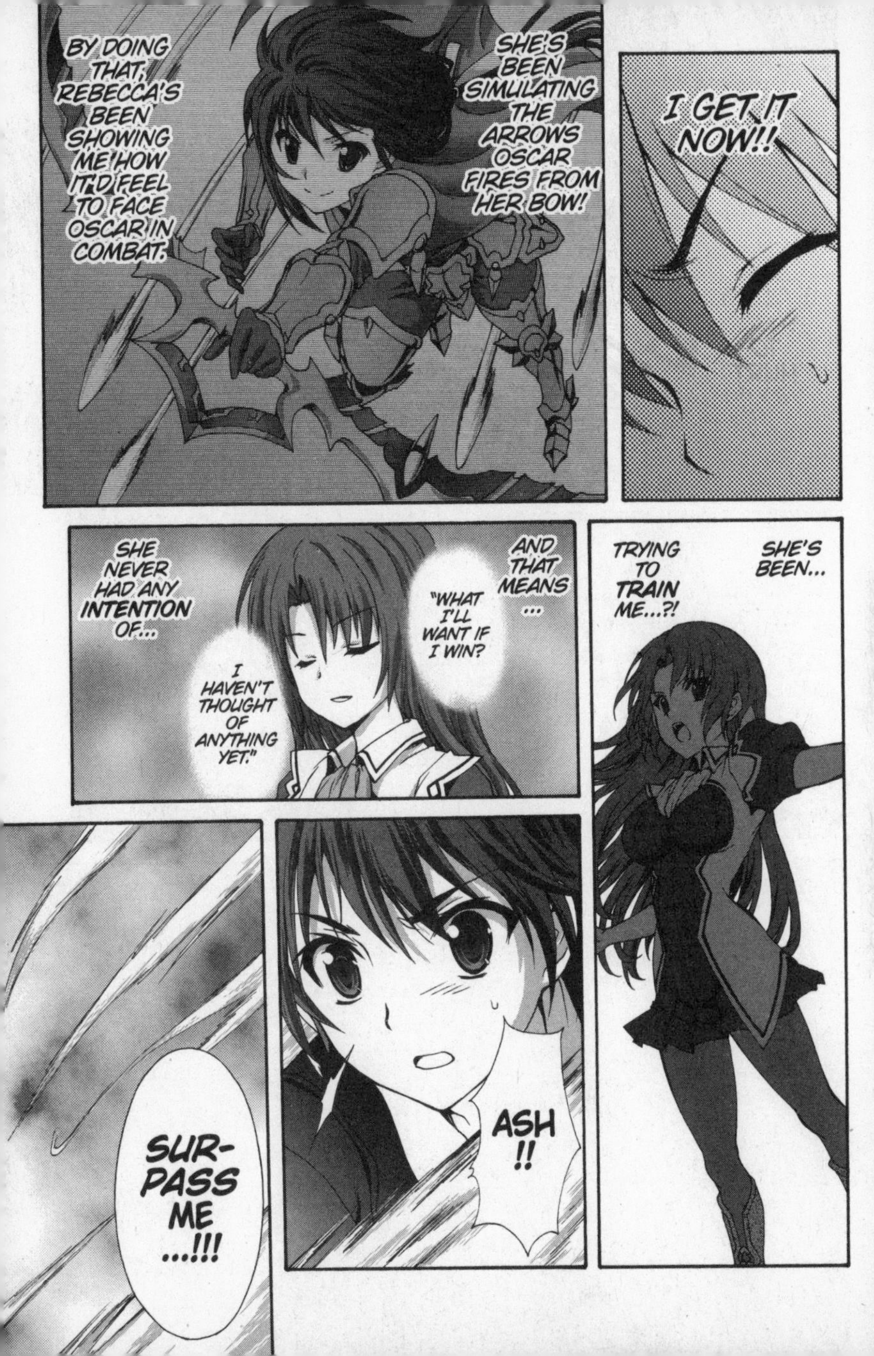
I GET IT NOW!!
SHE'S BEEN SIMULATING THE ARROWS OSCAR FIRES FROM HER BOW!
BY DOING THAT, REBECCA'S BEEN SHOWING ME HOW IT'D FEEL TO FACE OSCAR IN COMBAT.
SHE'S BEEN...
TRYING TO TRAIN ME...?!
AND THAT MEANS...
"WHAT I'LL WANT IF I WIN?
I HAVEN'T THOUGHT OF ANYTHING YET."
SHE NEVER HAD ANY INTENTION OF...
ASH!!
SUR-PASS ME...!!!

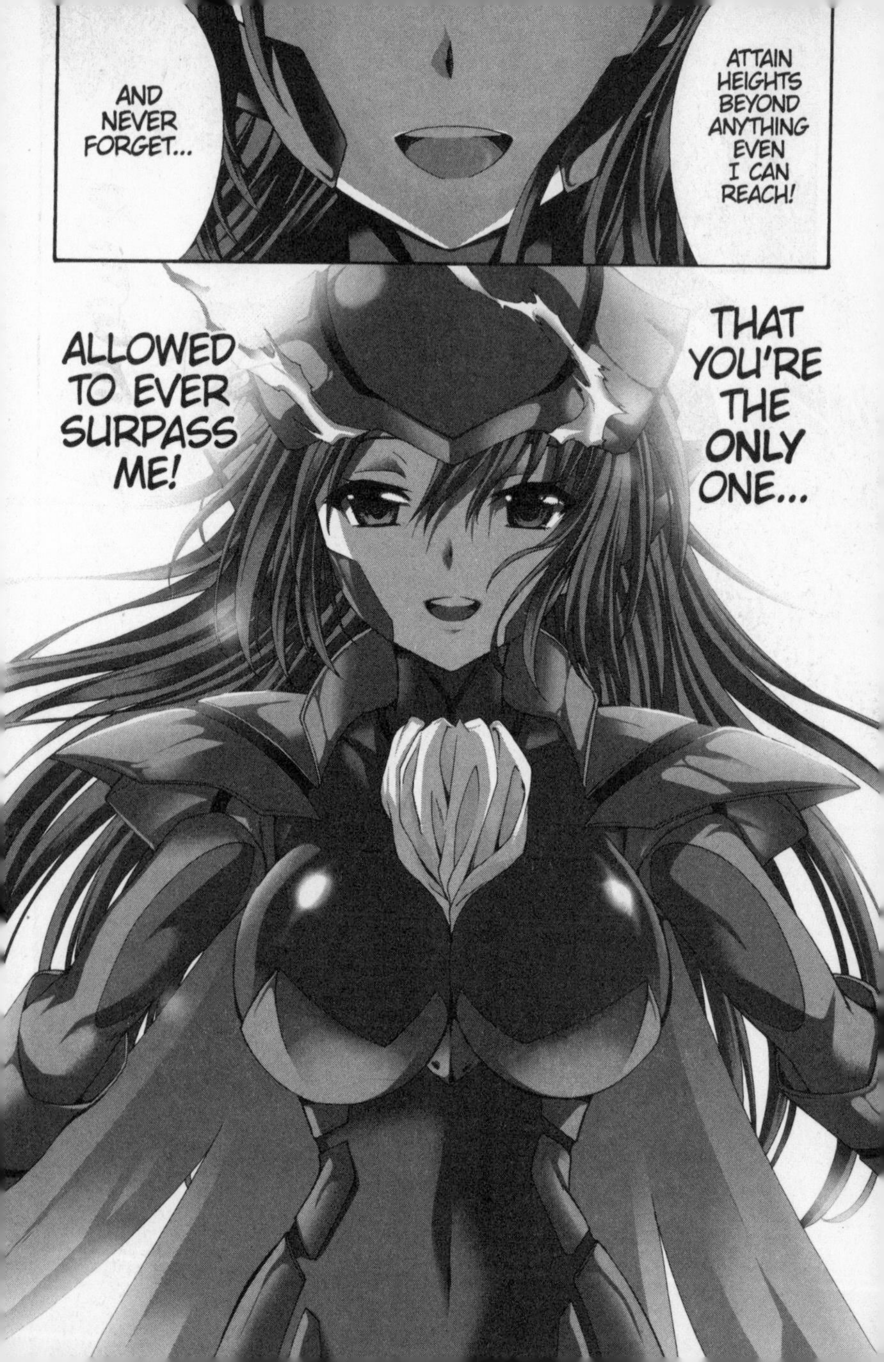
ATTAIN HEIGHTS BEYOND ANYTHING EVEN I CAN REACH!
AND NEVER FORGET...
THAT YOU'RE THE ONLY ONE...
ALLOWED TO EVER SURPASS ME!

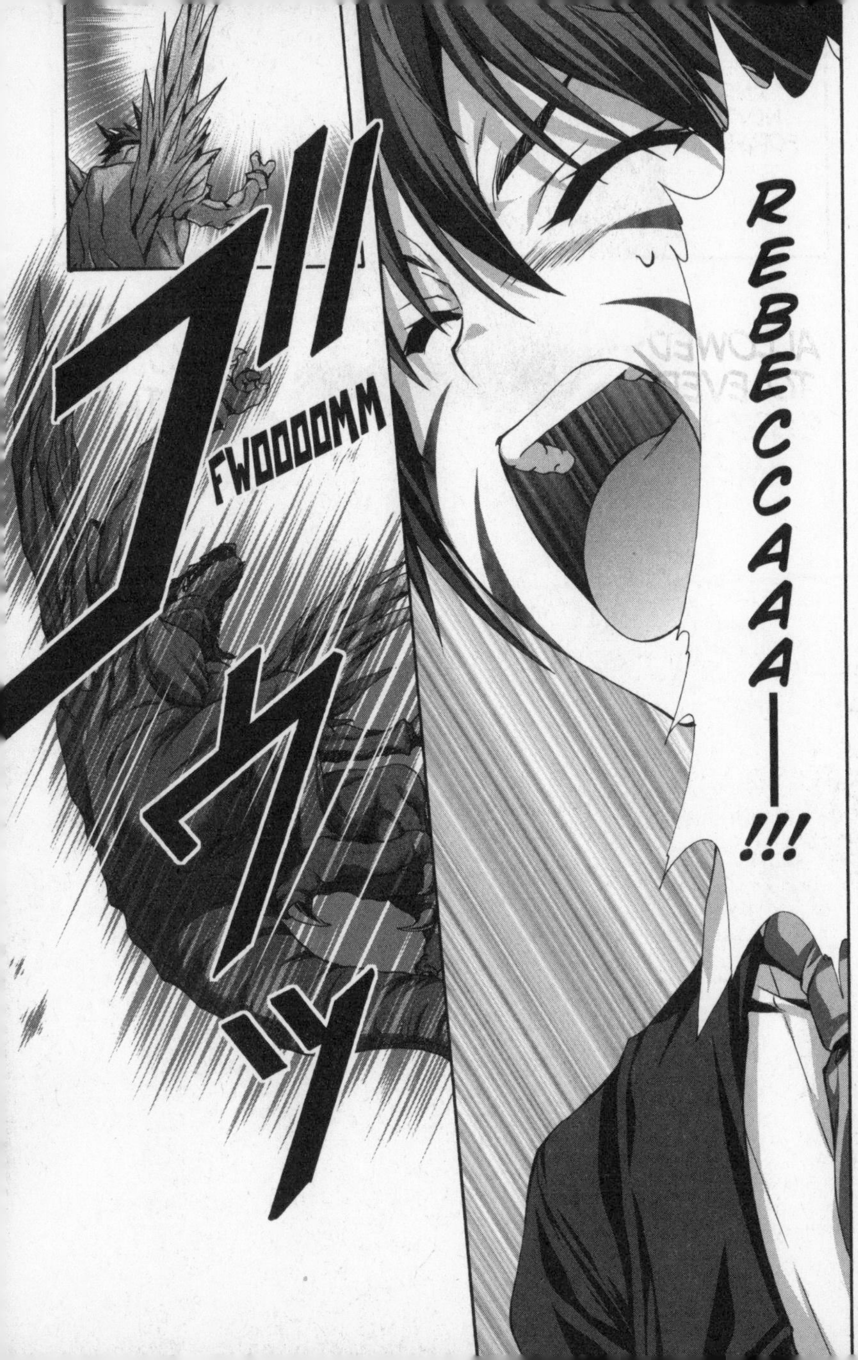
REBECCAAA—!!!
FWOOOOMM

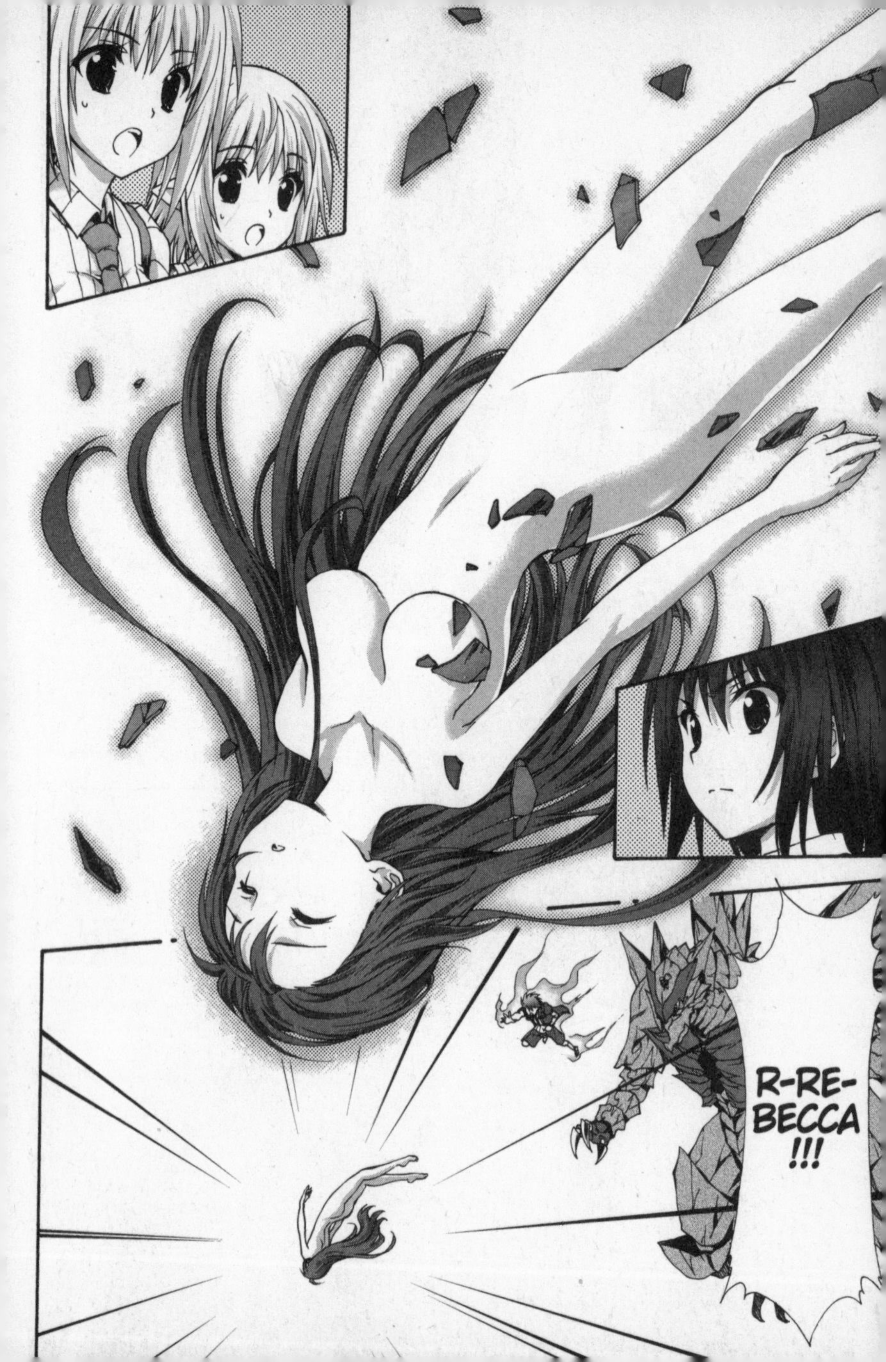
R-RE-
BECCA
!!!

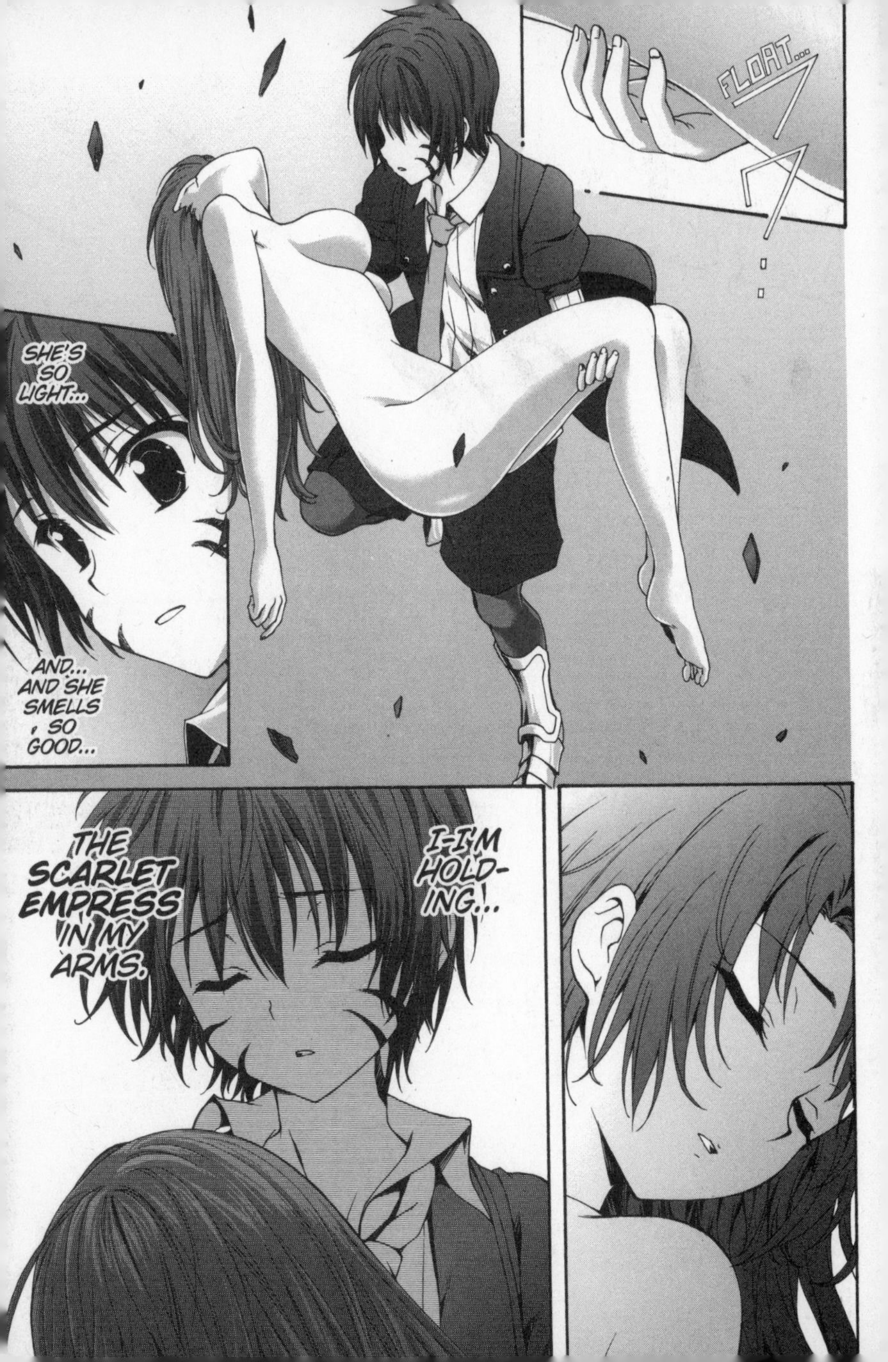
FLOAT...
SHE'S SO LIGHT...
AND... AND SHE SMELLS, SO GOOD...
I-I'M HOLDING...
THE SCARLET EMPRESS IN MY ARMS.

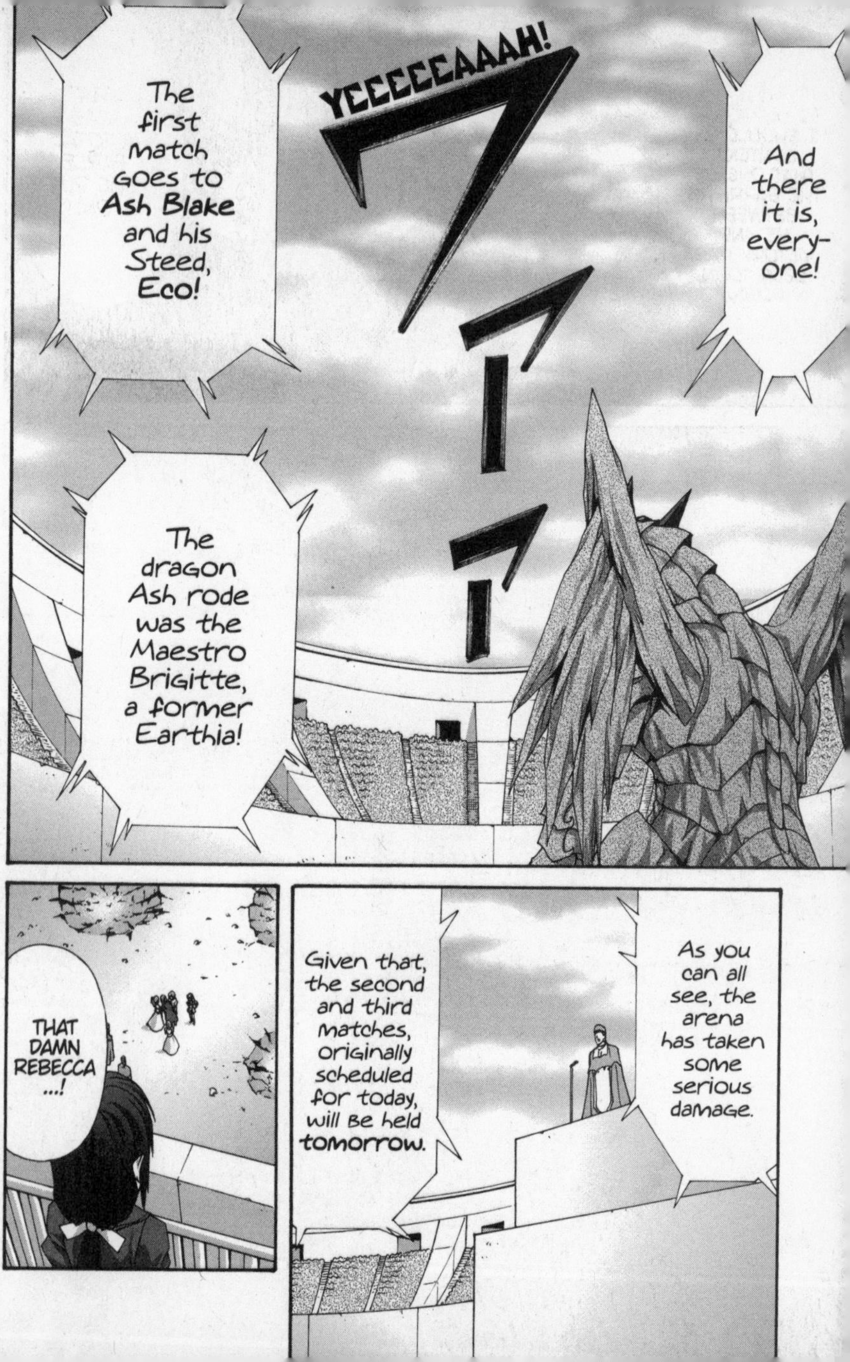
And there it is, everyone!
YEEEEEAAAH!
The first match goes to Ash Blake and his Steed, Eco!
The dragon Ash rode was the Maestro Brigitte, a former Earthia!
As you can all see, the arena has taken some serious damage.
Given that, the second and third matches, originally scheduled for today, will be held tomorrow.
THAT DAMN REBECCA ...!

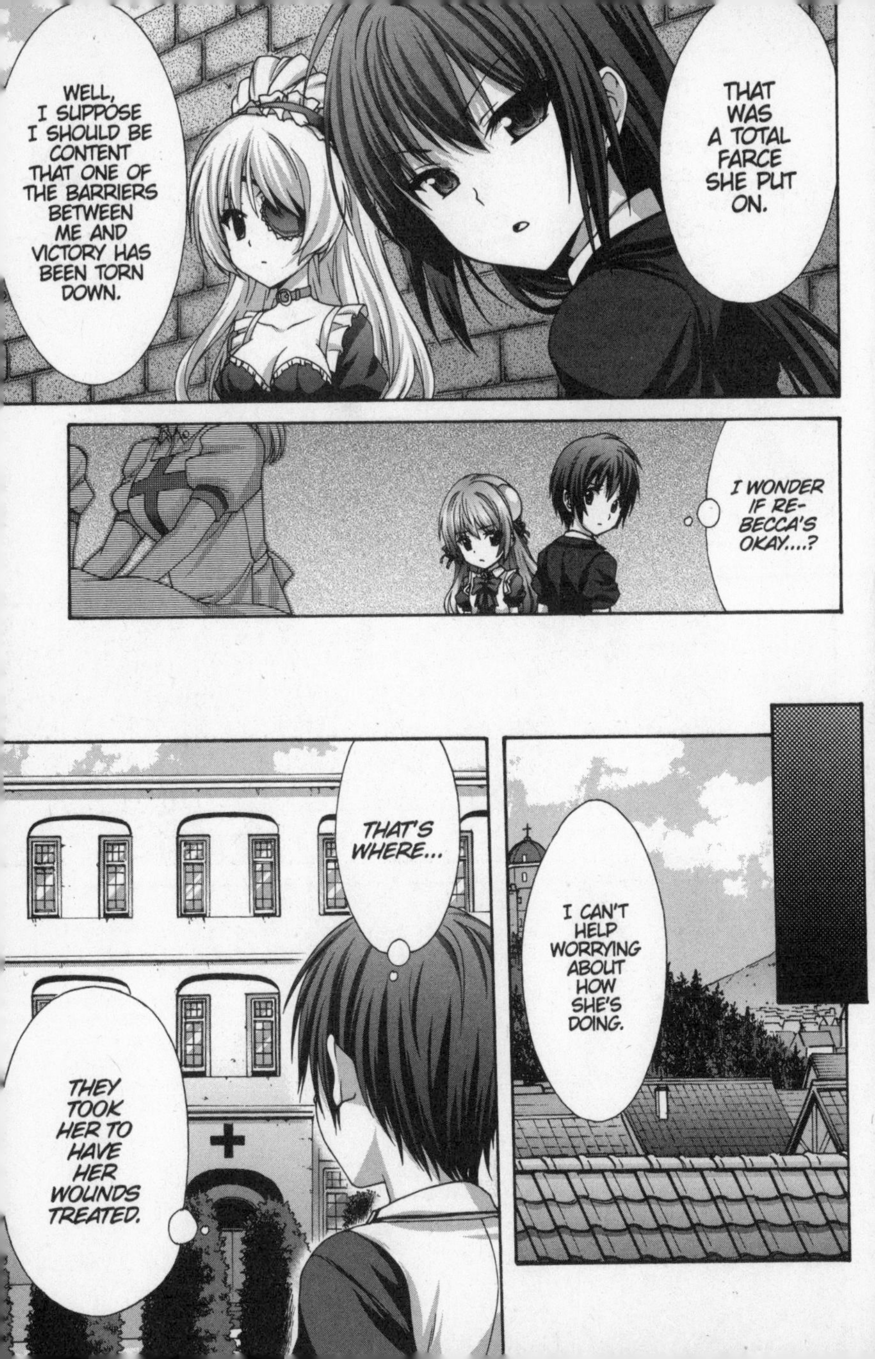
THAT WAS A TOTAL FARCE SHE PUT ON.
WELL, I SUPPOSE I SHOULD BE CONTENT THAT ONE OF THE BARRIERS BETWEEN ME AND VICTORY HAS BEEN TORN DOWN.
I WONDER IF RE-BECCA'S OKAY....?
I CAN'T HELP WORRYING ABOUT HOW SHE'S DOING.
THAT'S WHERE...
THEY TOOK HER TO HAVE HER WOUNDS TREATED.

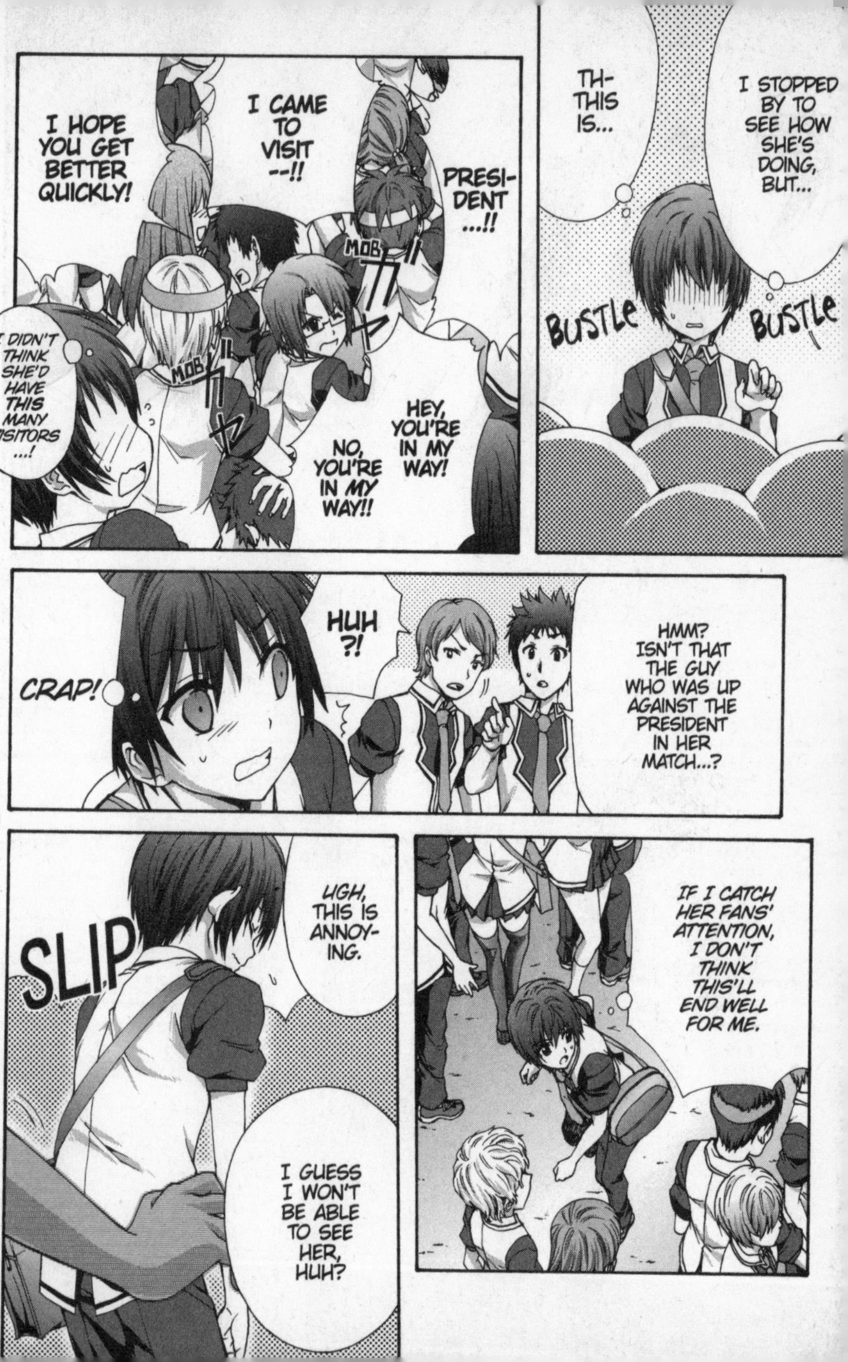
I STOPPED BY TO SEE HOW SHE'S DOING, BUT...
TH-THIS IS...
BUSTLE
BUSTLE
PRESI-DENT ...!!
I CAME TO VISIT --!!
I HOPE YOU GET BETTER QUICKLY!
MOB
MOB
HEY, YOU'RE IN MY WAY!
NO, YOU'RE IN MY WAY!!
I DIDN'T THINK SHE'D HAVE THIS MANY VISITORS ...!
HMM? ISN'T THAT THE GUY WHO WAS UP AGAINST THE PRESIDENT IN HER MATCH...?
HUH ?!
CRAP!
IF I CATCH HER FANS' ATTENTION, I DON'T THINK THIS'LL END WELL FOR ME.
UGH, THIS IS ANNOY-ING.
SLIP
I GUESS I WON'T BE ABLE TO SEE HER, HUH?

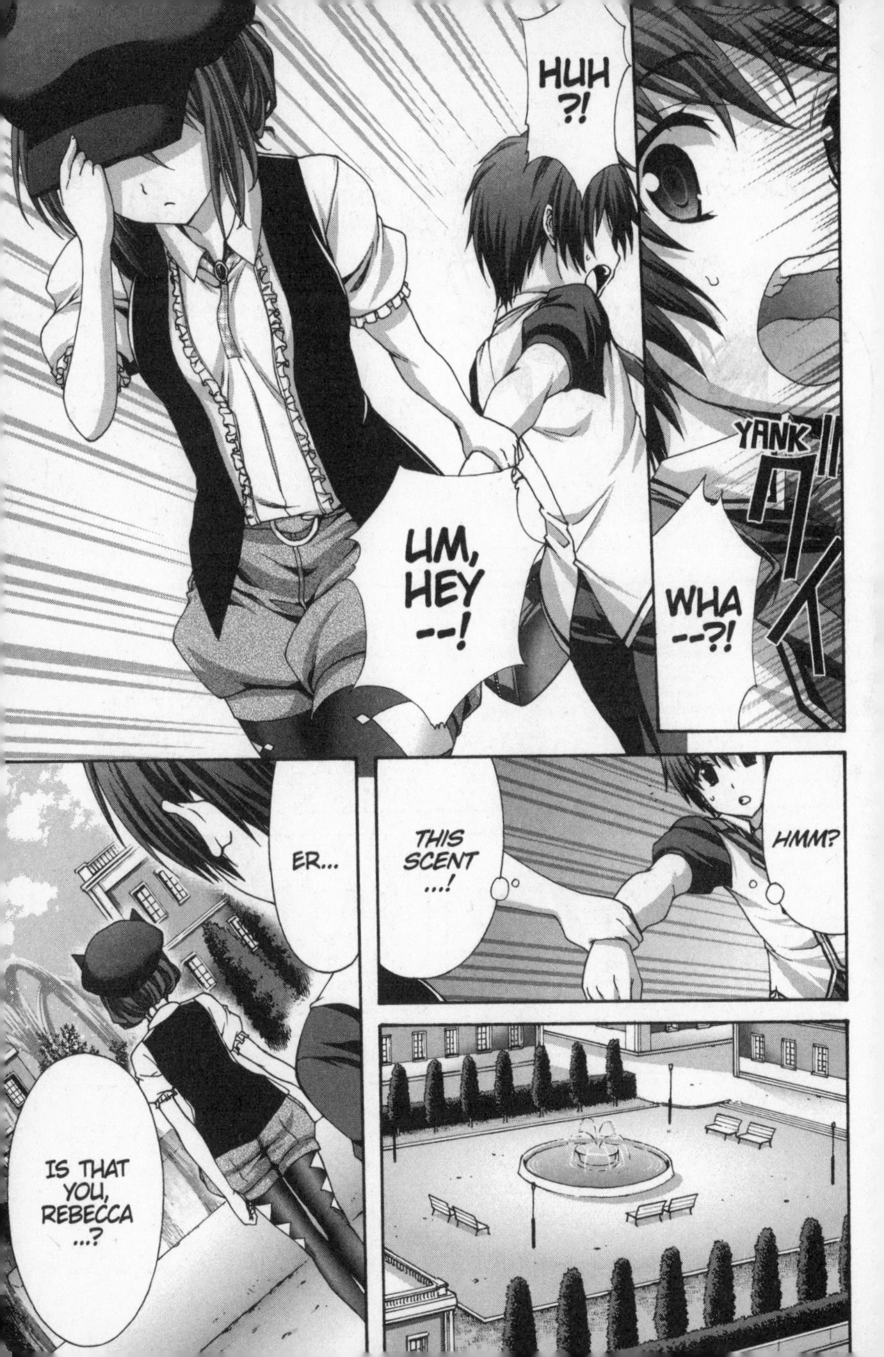
YANK
グイ
WHA --?!
HUH ?!
UM, HEY --!
HMM?
THIS SCENT ...!
ER...
IS THAT YOU, REBECCA ...?

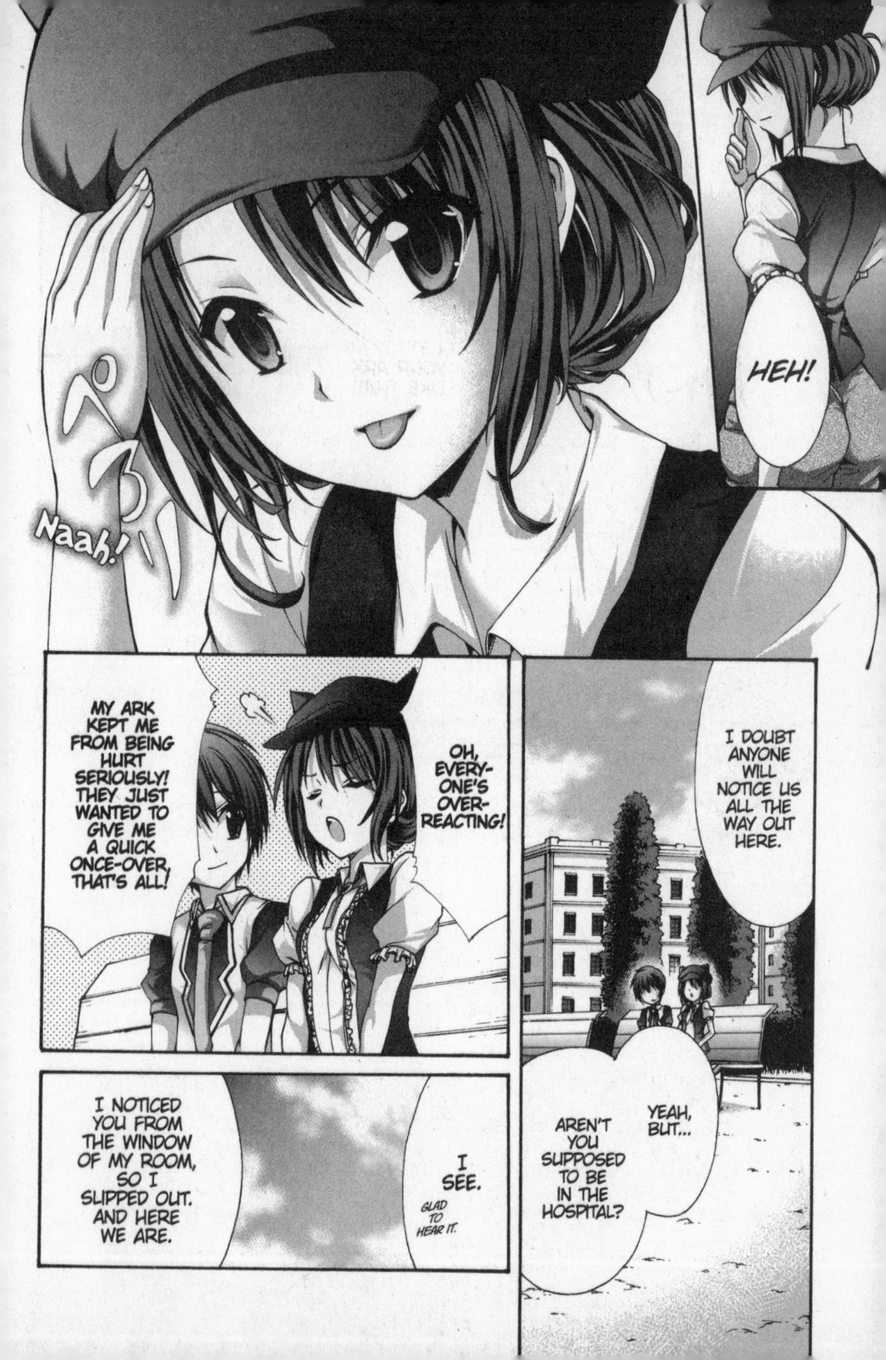
HEH!
ぺろ
Naah!
I DOUBT ANYONE WILL NOTICE US ALL THE WAY OUT HERE.
YEAH, BUT...
AREN'T YOU SUPPOSED TO BE IN THE HOSPITAL?
OH, EVERYONE'S OVER-REACTING!
MY ARK KEPT ME FROM BEING HURT SERIOUSLY! THEY JUST WANTED TO GIVE ME A QUICK ONCE-OVER, THAT'S ALL!
I SEE.
GLAD TO HEAR IT.
I NOTICED YOU FROM THE WINDOW OF MY ROOM, SO I SLIPPED OUT. AND HERE WE ARE.

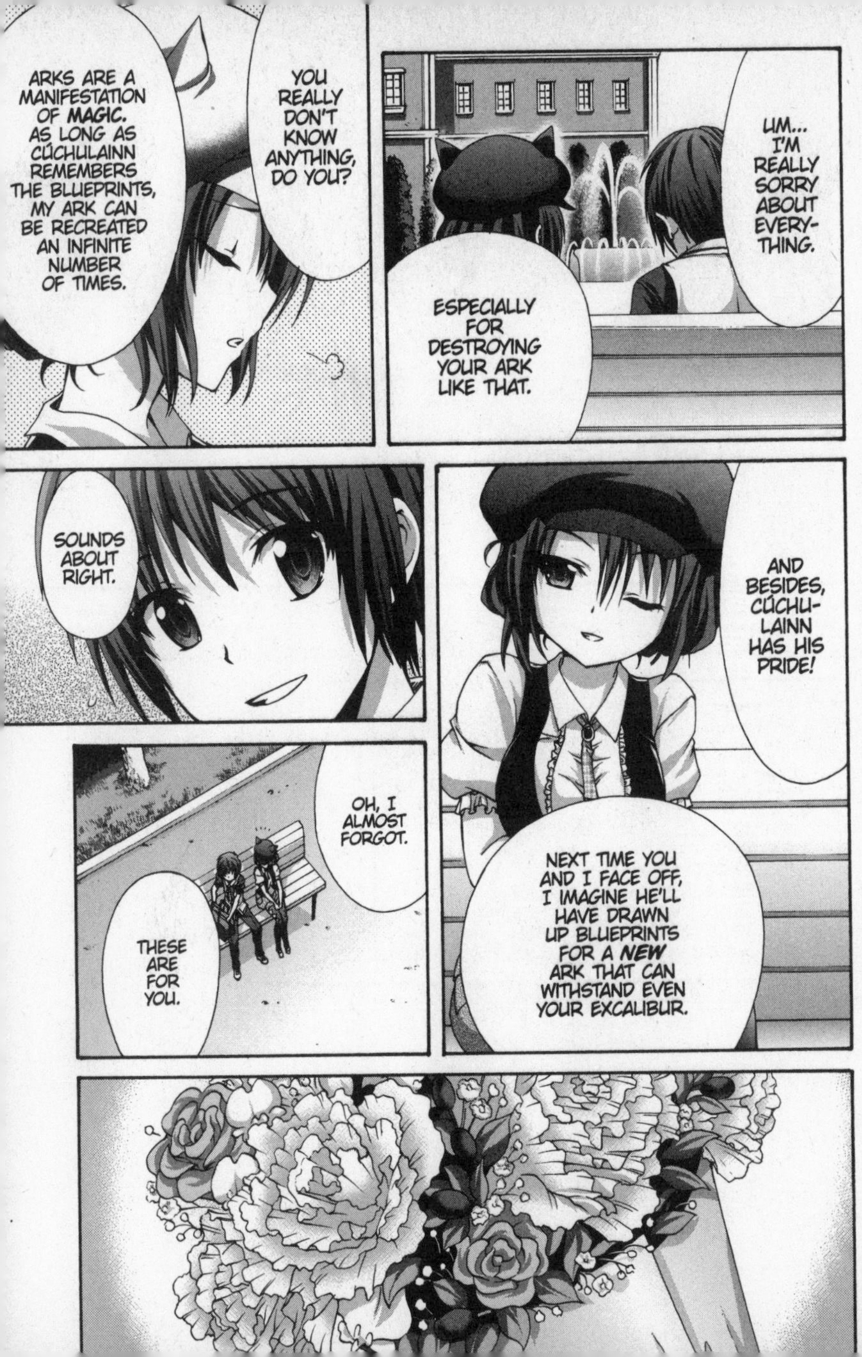
UM... I'M REALLY SORRY ABOUT EVERYTHING.
ESPECIALLY FOR DESTROYING YOUR ARK LIKE THAT.
YOU REALLY DON'T KNOW ANYTHING, DO YOU?
ARKS ARE A MANIFESTATION OF **MAGIC**. AS LONG AS CÚCHULAINN REMEMBERS THE BLUEPRINTS, MY ARK CAN BE RECREATED AN INFINITE NUMBER OF TIMES.
AND BESIDES, CÚCHULAINN HAS HIS PRIDE!
NEXT TIME YOU AND I FACE OFF, I IMAGINE HE'LL HAVE DRAWN UP BLUEPRINTS FOR A ***NEW*** ARK THAT CAN WITHSTAND EVEN YOUR EXCALIBUR.
SOUNDS ABOUT RIGHT.
OH, I ALMOST FORGOT.
THESE ARE FOR YOU.

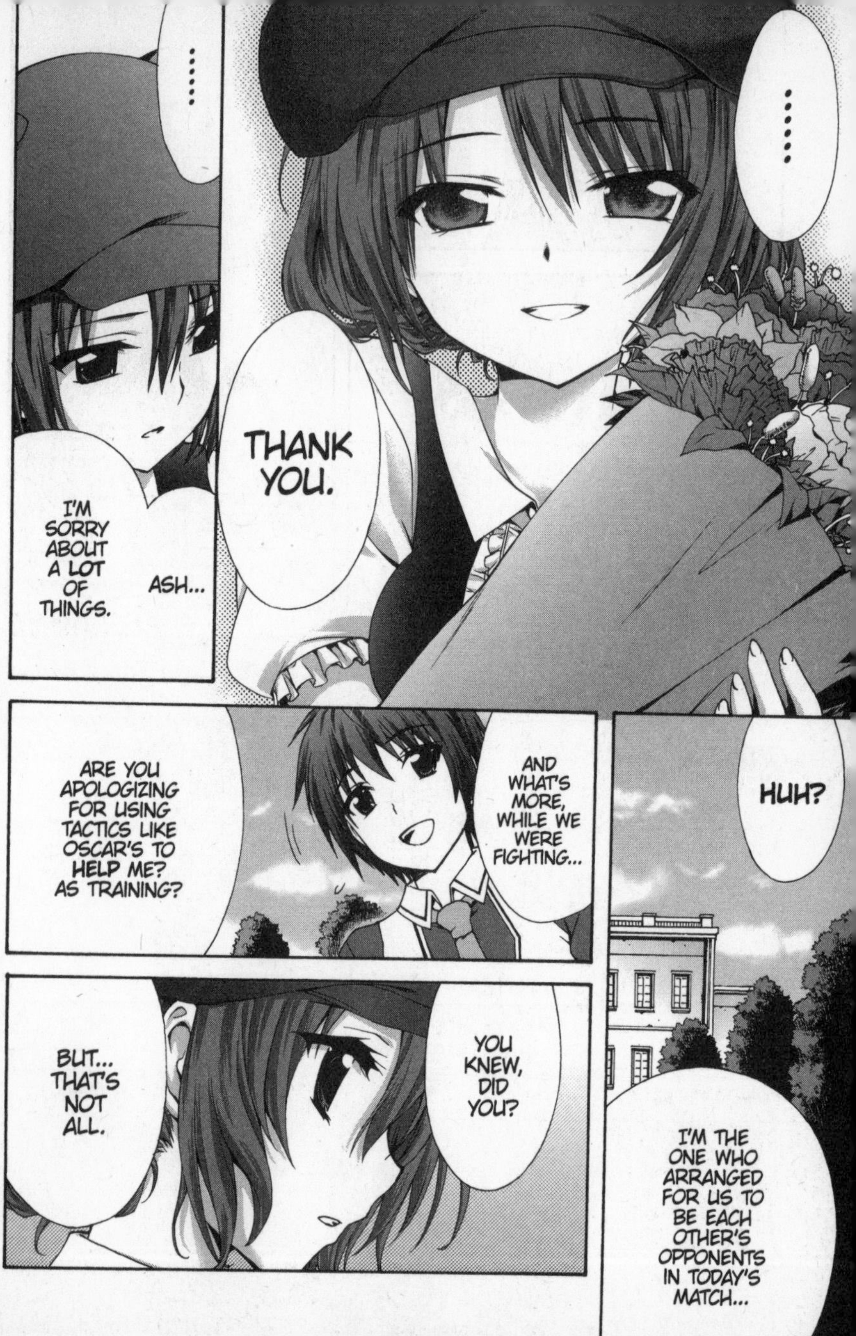
......
THANK YOU.
......
ASH...
I'M SORRY ABOUT A LOT OF THINGS.
HUH?
I'M THE ONE WHO ARRANGED FOR US TO BE EACH OTHER'S OPPONENTS IN TODAY'S MATCH...
AND WHAT'S MORE, WHILE WE WERE FIGHTING...
ARE YOU APOLOGIZING FOR USING TACTICS LIKE OSCAR'S TO HELP ME? AS TRAINING?
YOU KNEW, DID YOU?
BUT... THAT'S NOT ALL.

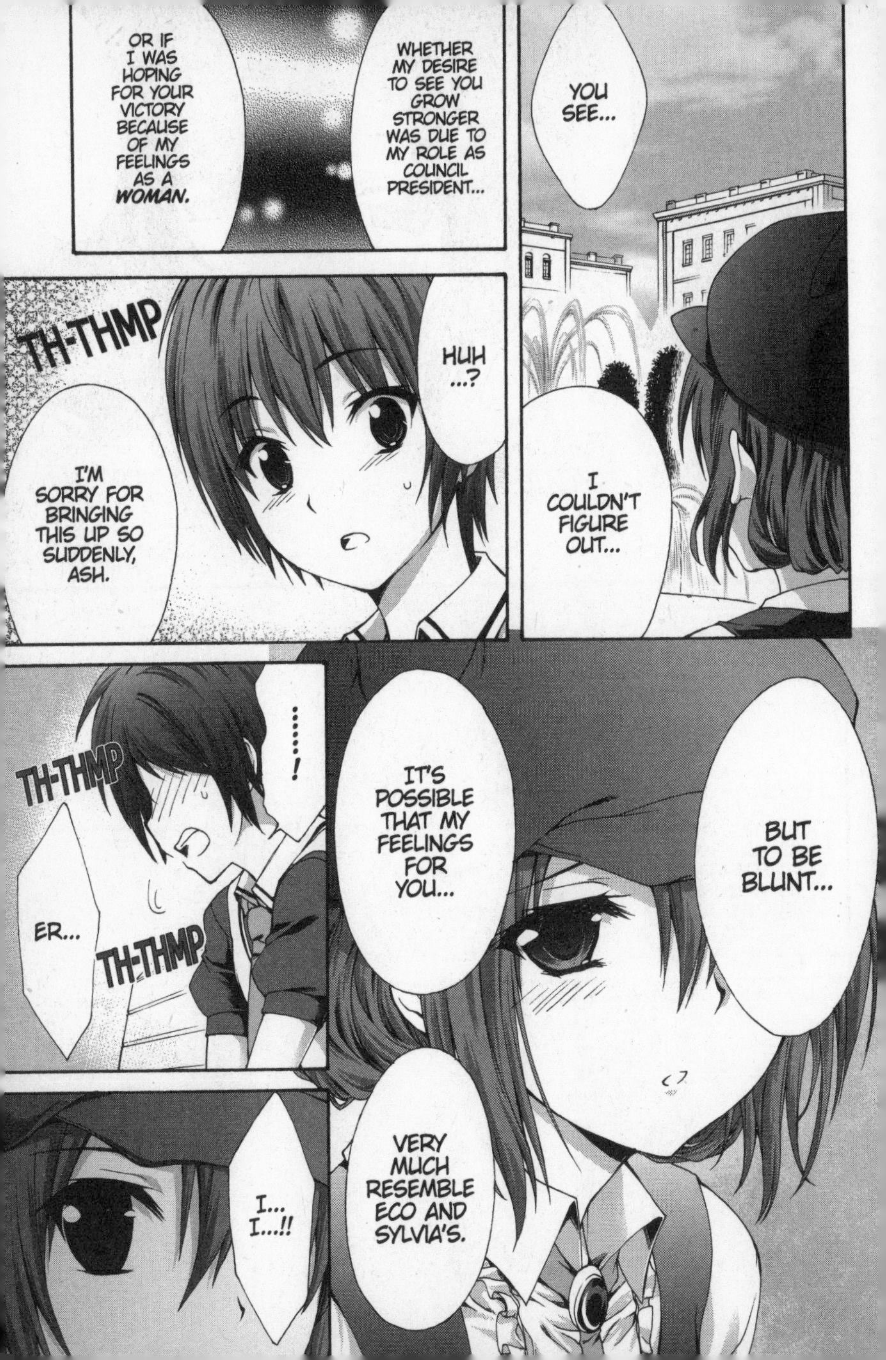
YOU SEE...
I COULDN'T FIGURE OUT...
WHETHER MY DESIRE TO SEE YOU GROW STRONGER WAS DUE TO MY ROLE AS COUNCIL PRESIDENT...
OR IF I WAS HOPING FOR YOUR VICTORY BECAUSE OF MY FEELINGS AS A *WOMAN*.
HUH ...?
TH-THMP
I'M SORRY FOR BRINGING THIS UP SO SUDDENLY, ASH.
BUT TO BE BLUNT...
IT'S POSSIBLE THAT MY FEELINGS FOR YOU...
VERY MUCH RESEMBLE ECO AND SYLVIA'S.
......!
TH-THMP
ER...
TH-THMP
I... I...!!

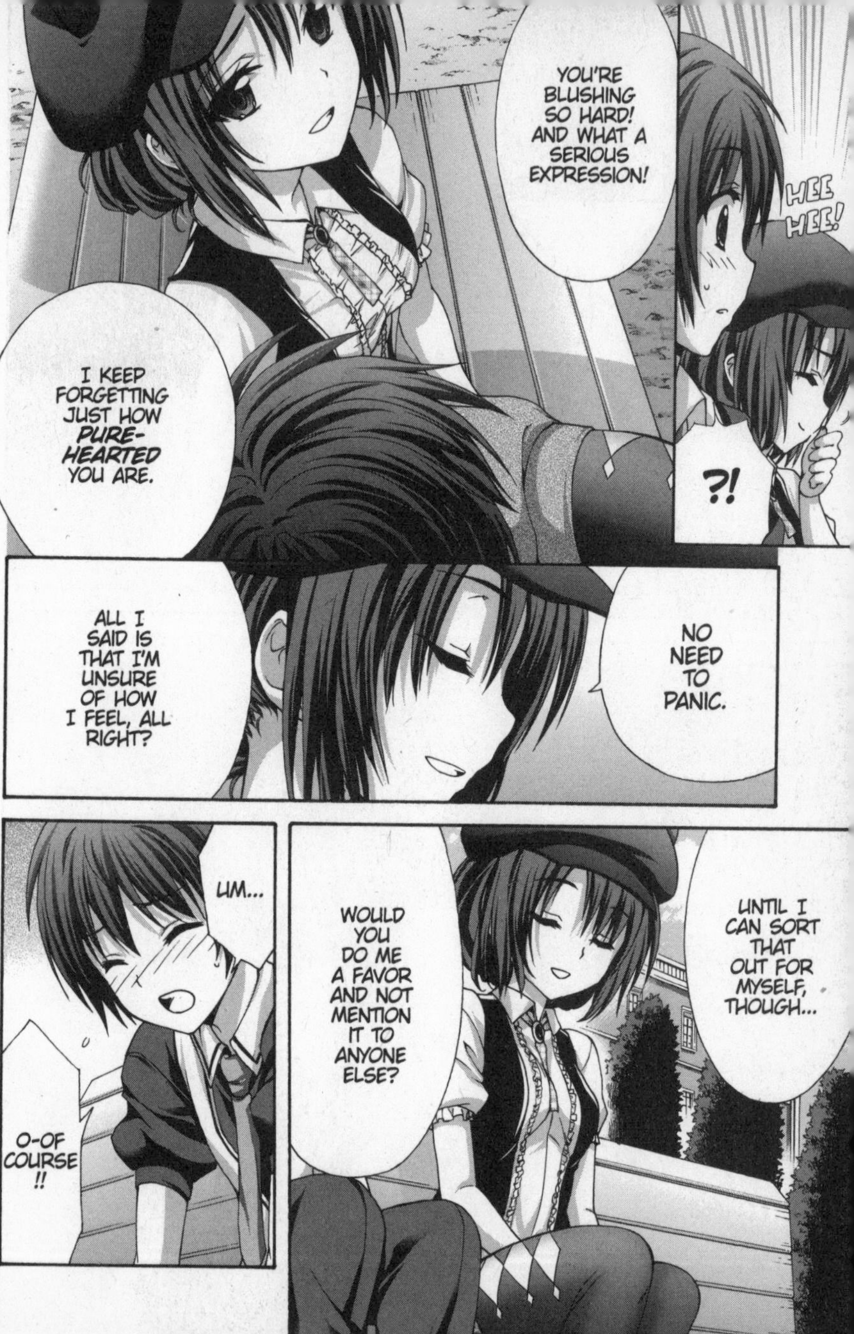
HEE HEE!
?!
YOU'RE BLUSHING SO HARD! AND WHAT A SERIOUS EXPRESSION!
I KEEP FORGETTING JUST HOW *PURE-HEARTED* YOU ARE.
NO NEED TO PANIC.
ALL I SAID IS THAT I'M UNSURE OF HOW I FEEL, ALL RIGHT?
UNTIL I CAN SORT THAT OUT FOR MYSELF, THOUGH...
WOULD YOU DO ME A FAVOR AND NOT MENTION IT TO ANYONE ELSE?
UM...
O-OF COURSE!!

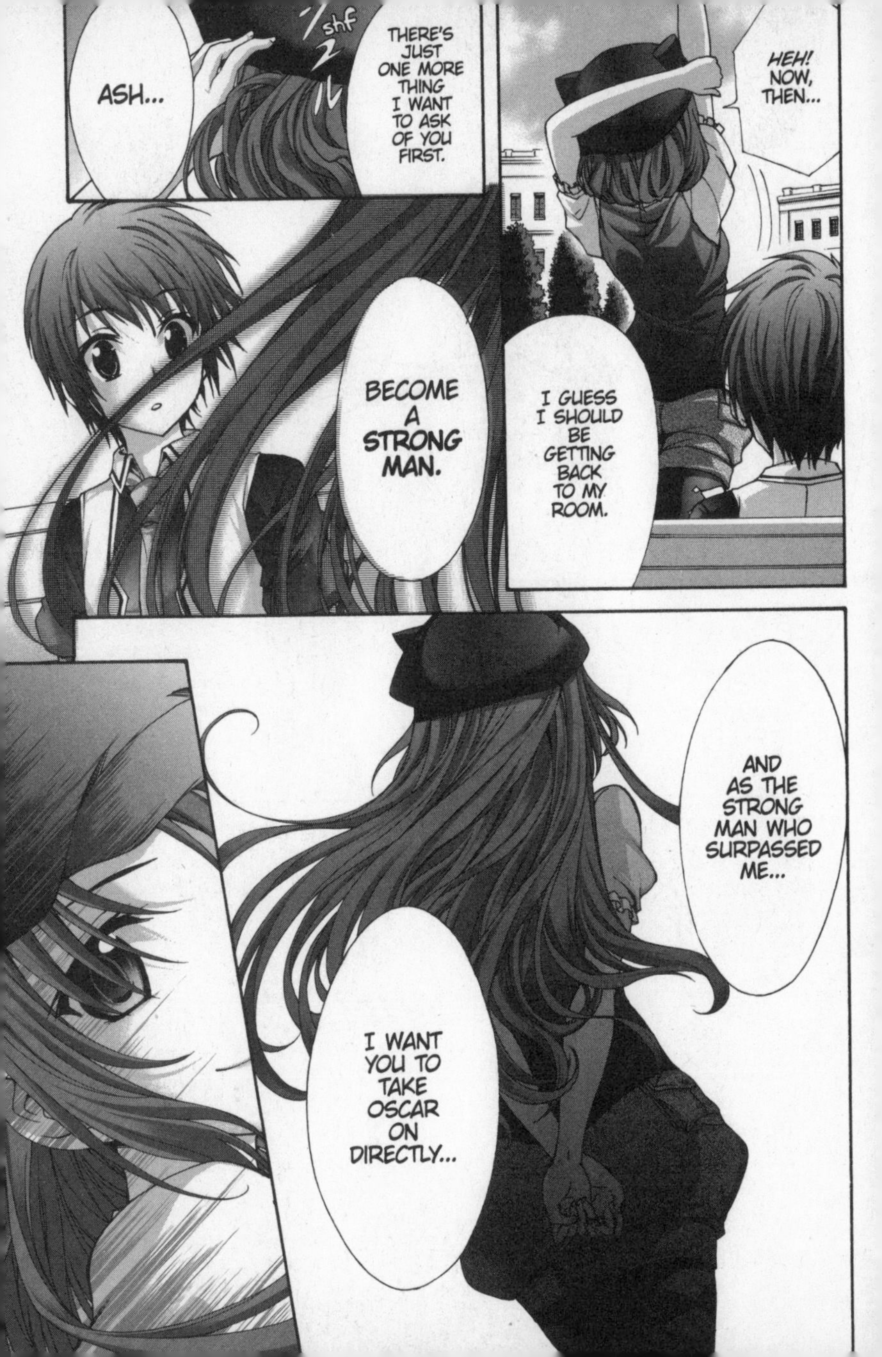
HEH! NOW, THEN...
I GUESS I SHOULD BE GETTING BACK TO MY ROOM.
shf
THERE'S JUST ONE MORE THING I WANT TO ASK OF YOU FIRST.
ASH...
BECOME A STRONG MAN.
AND AS THE STRONG MAN WHO SURPASSED ME...
I WANT YOU TO TAKE OSCAR ON DIRECTLY...

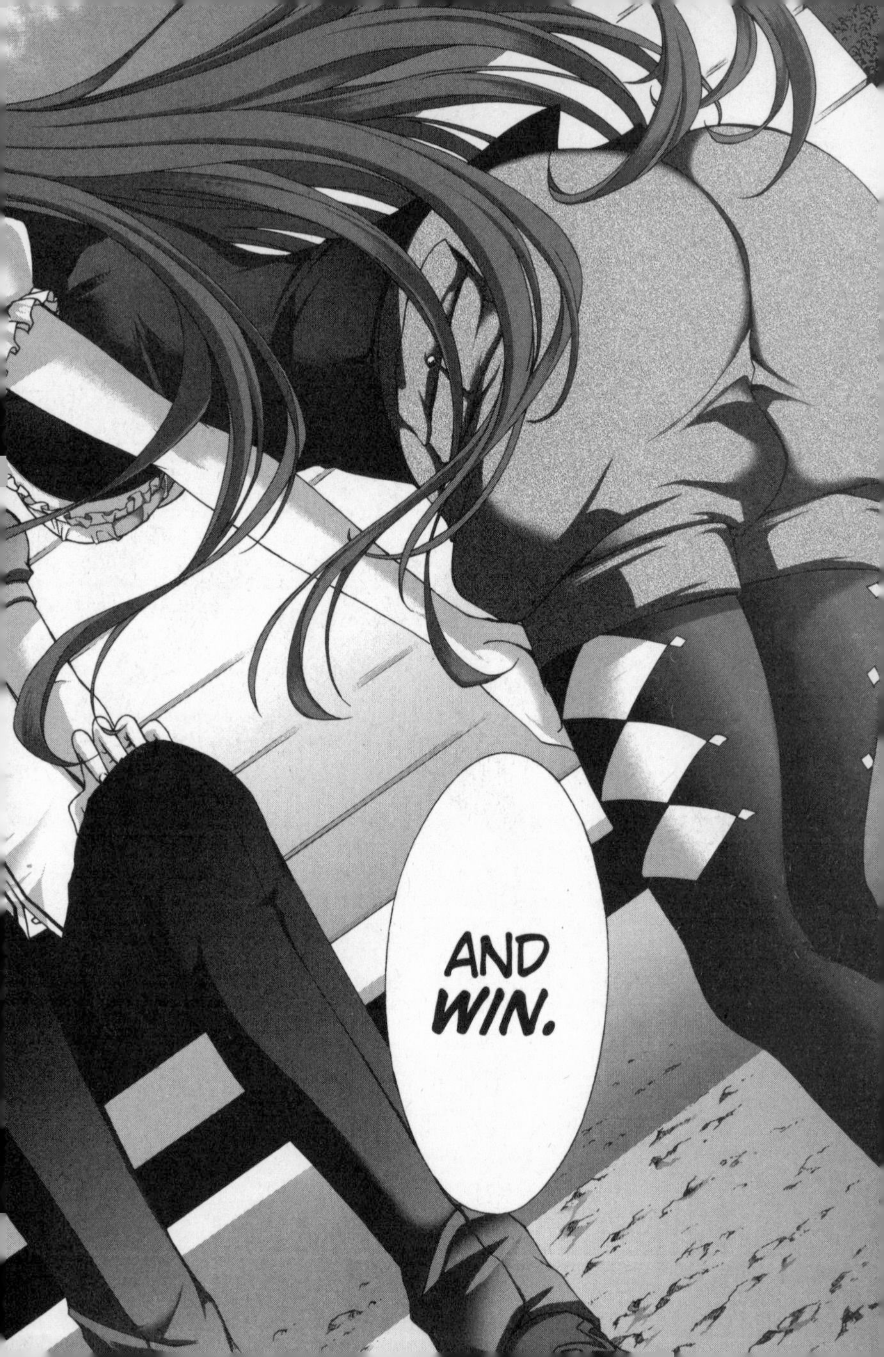
AND WIN.

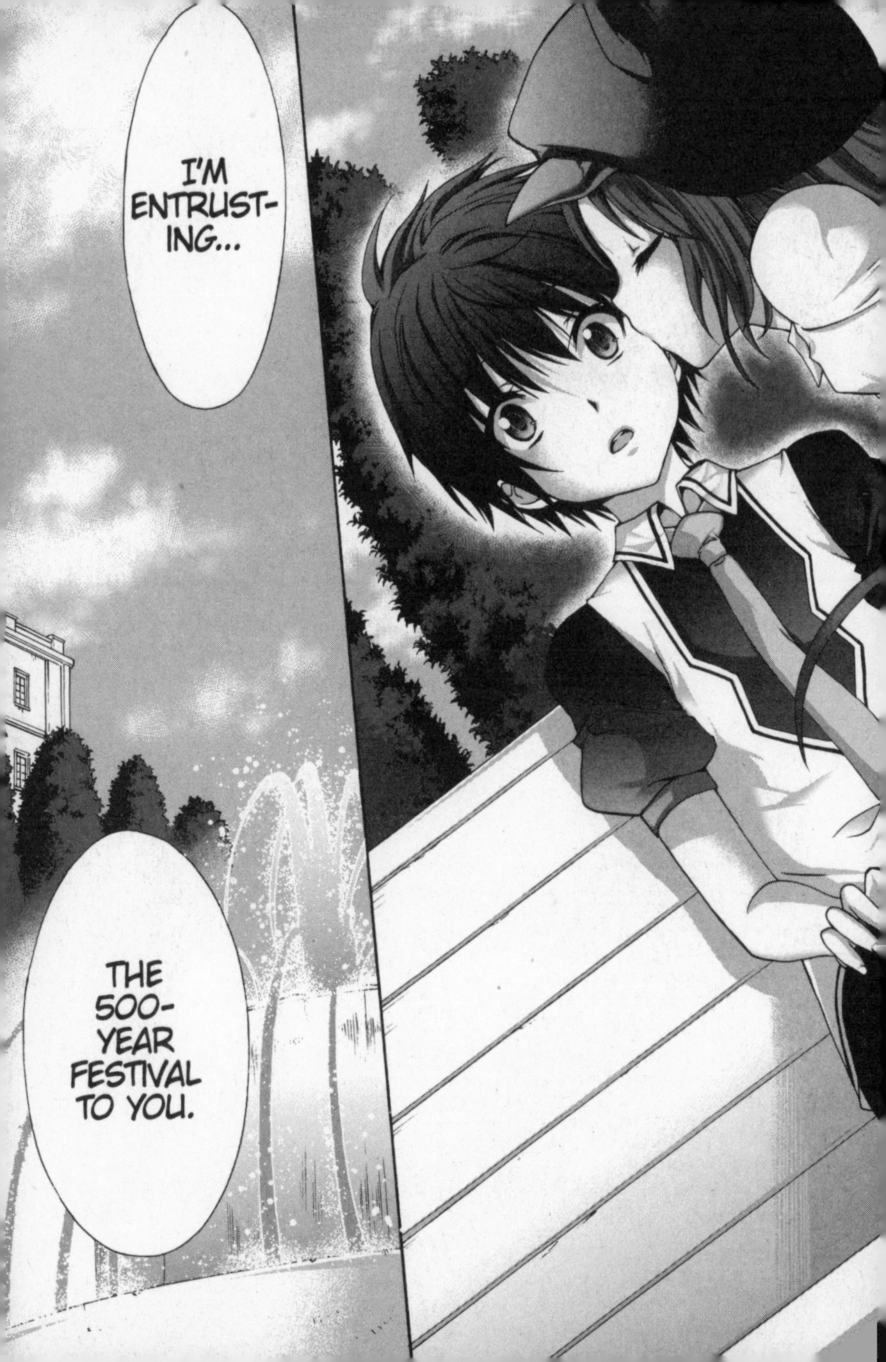
I'M ENTRUST-ING...
THE 500-YEAR FESTIVAL TO YOU.

DRAGONAR
ACADEMY

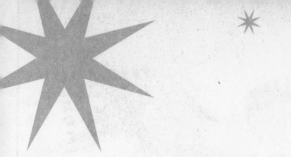

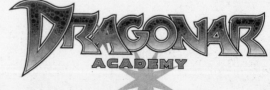

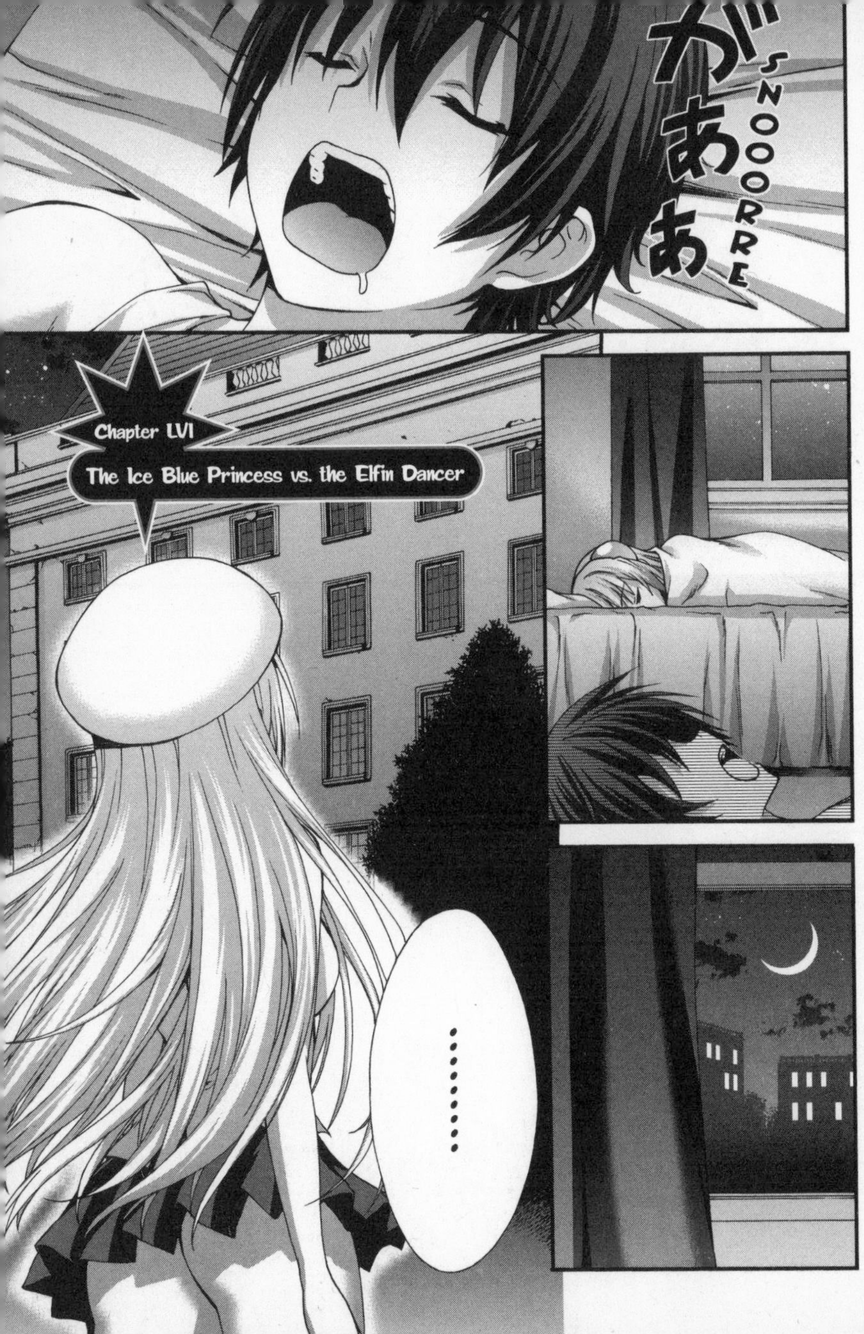
がああ
SNOOORRE
Chapter LVI
The Ice Blue Princess vs. the Elfin Dancer
....

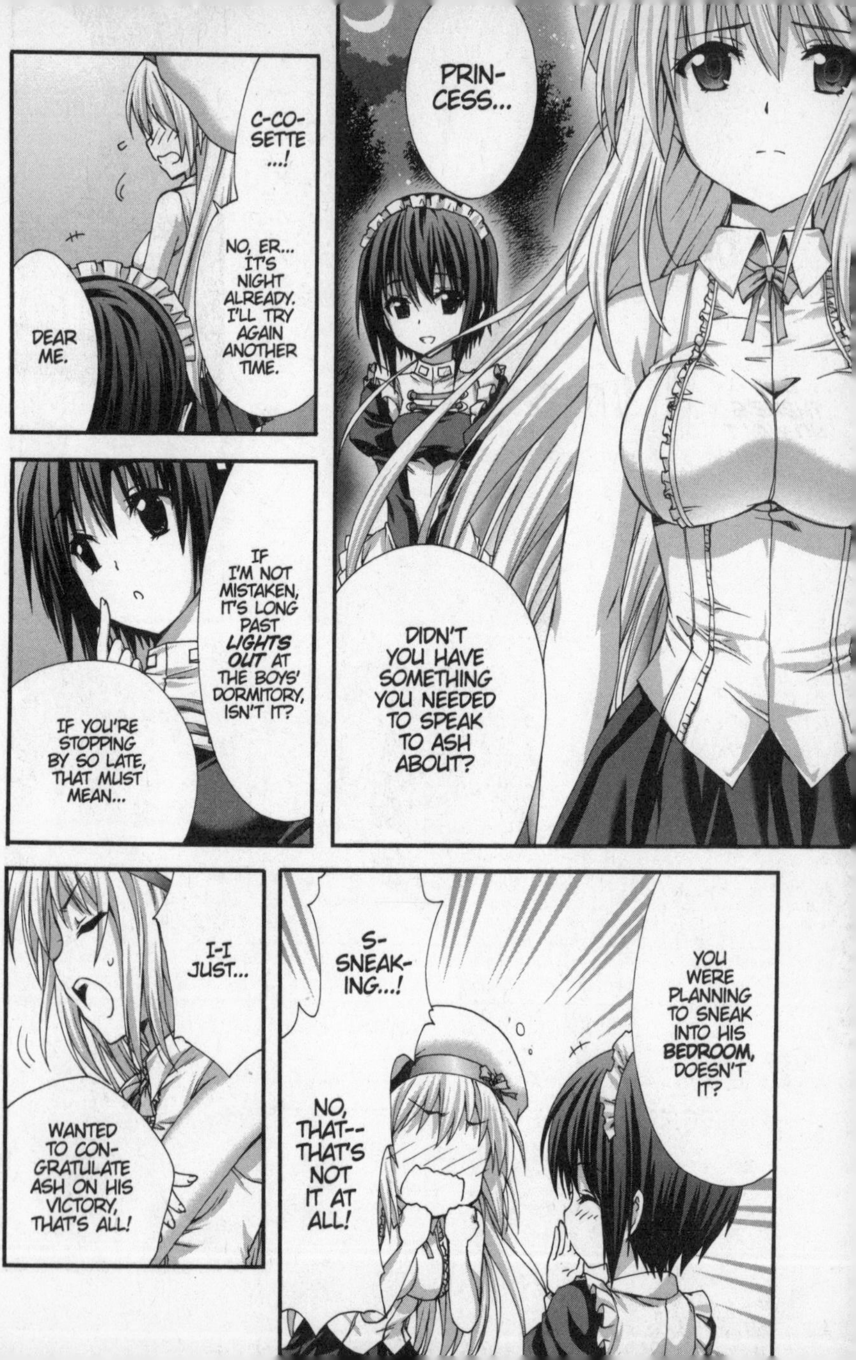
PRINCESS...
DIDN'T YOU HAVE SOMETHING YOU NEEDED TO SPEAK TO ASH ABOUT?
C-CO-SETTE ...!
NO, ER... IT'S NIGHT ALREADY. I'LL TRY AGAIN ANOTHER TIME.
DEAR ME.
IF I'M NOT MISTAKEN, IT'S LONG PAST **LIGHTS OUT** AT THE BOYS' DORMITORY, ISN'T IT?
IF YOU'RE STOPPING BY SO LATE, THAT MUST MEAN...
YOU WERE PLANNING TO SNEAK INTO HIS BEDROOM, DOESN'T IT?
S-SNEAKING...!
NO, THAT--THAT'S NOT IT AT ALL!
I-I JUST...
WANTED TO CONGRATULATE ASH ON HIS VICTORY, THAT'S ALL!

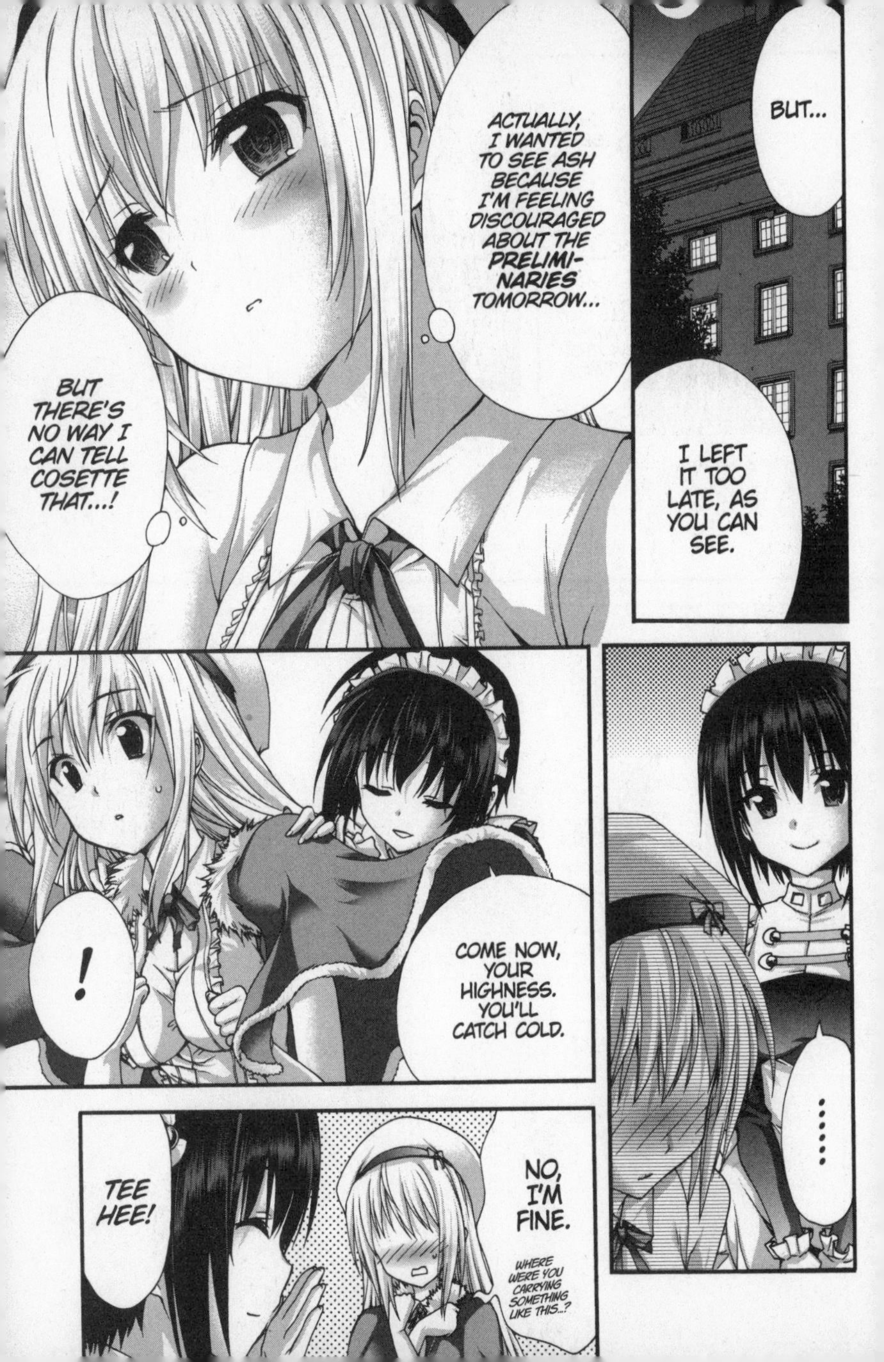
BUT...
I LEFT IT TOO LATE, AS YOU CAN SEE.
ACTUALLY, I WANTED TO SEE ASH BECAUSE I'M FEELING DISCOURAGED ABOUT THE PRELIMI-NARIES TOMORROW...
BUT THERE'S NO WAY I CAN TELL COSETTE THAT...!
......
COME NOW, YOUR HIGHNESS. YOU'LL CATCH COLD.
!
NO, I'M FINE.
WHERE WERE YOU CARRYING SOMETHING LIKE THIS...?
TEE HEE!

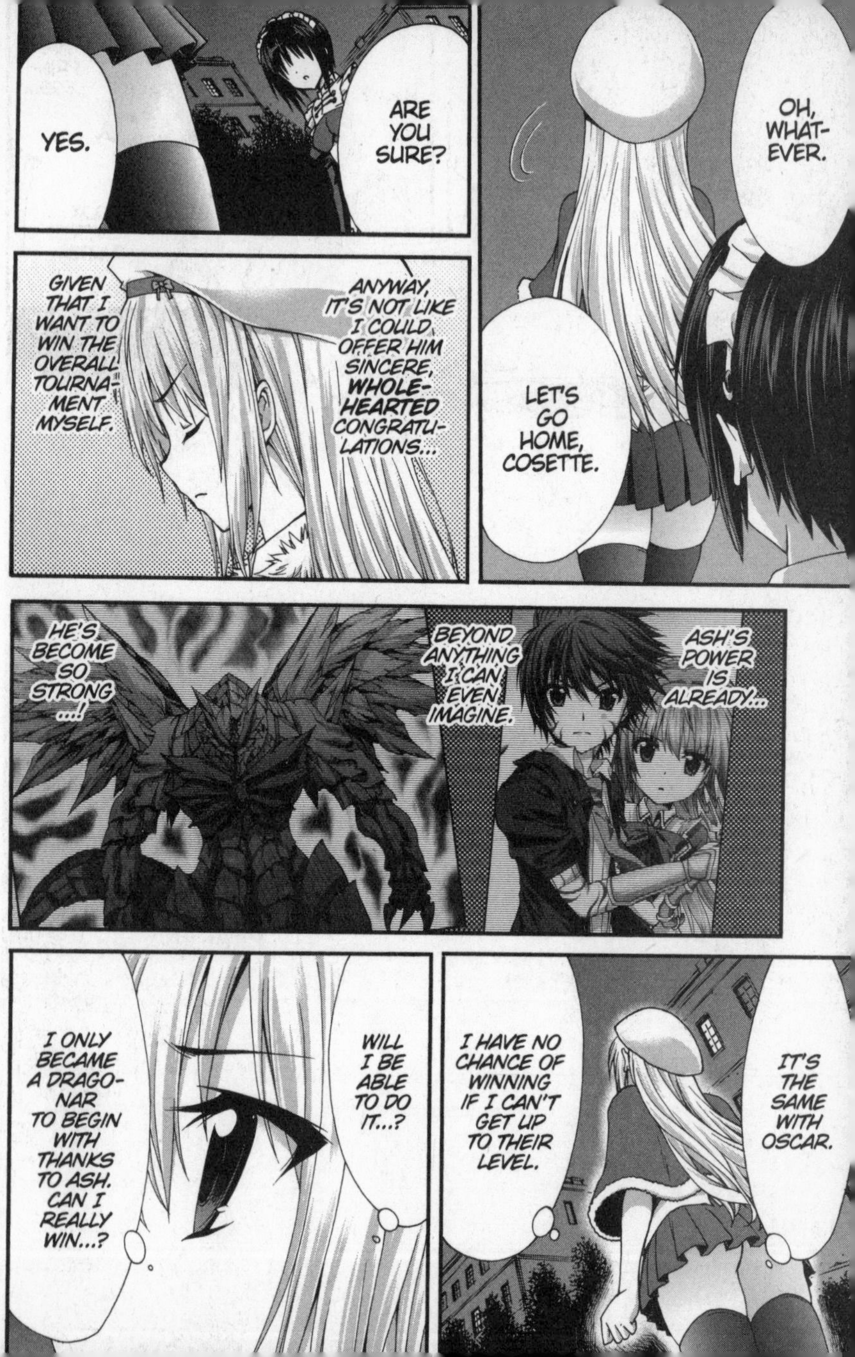
OH, WHATEVER.
LET'S GO HOME, COSETTE.
ARE YOU SURE?
YES.
ANYWAY, IT'S NOT LIKE I COULD OFFER HIM SINCERE, **WHOLEHEARTED** CONGRATULATIONS...
GIVEN THAT I WANT TO WIN THE OVERALL TOURNAMENT MYSELF.
ASH'S POWER IS ALREADY...
BEYOND ANYTHING I CAN EVEN IMAGINE.
HE'S BECOME SO STRONG...!
IT'S THE SAME WITH OSCAR.
I HAVE NO CHANCE OF WINNING IF I CAN'T GET UP TO THEIR LEVEL.
WILL I BE ABLE TO DO IT...?
I ONLY BECAME A DRAGONAR TO BEGIN WITH THANKS TO ASH. CAN I REALLY WIN...?

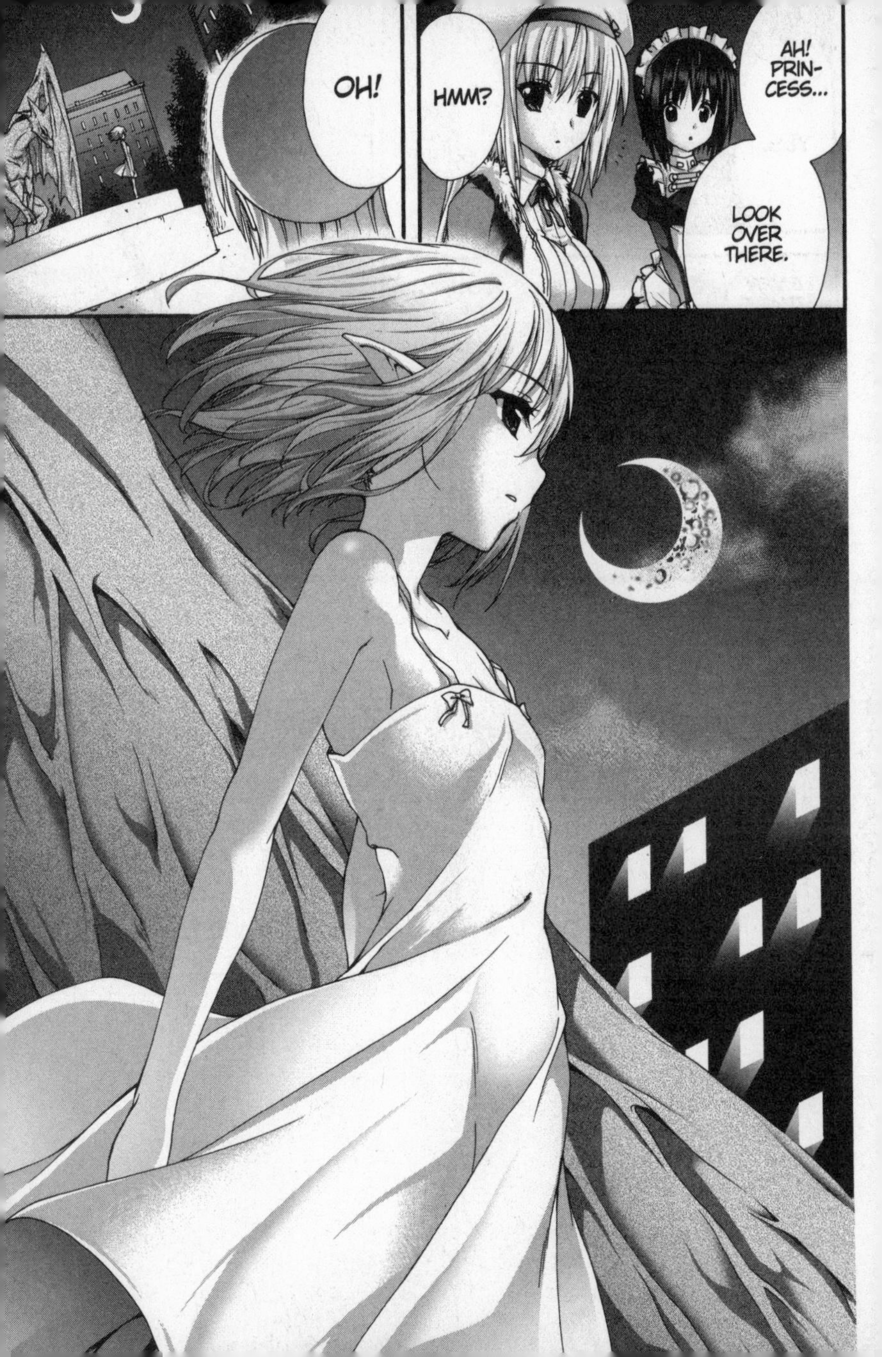
AH! PRIN-CESS...
HMM?
LOOK OVER THERE.
OH!

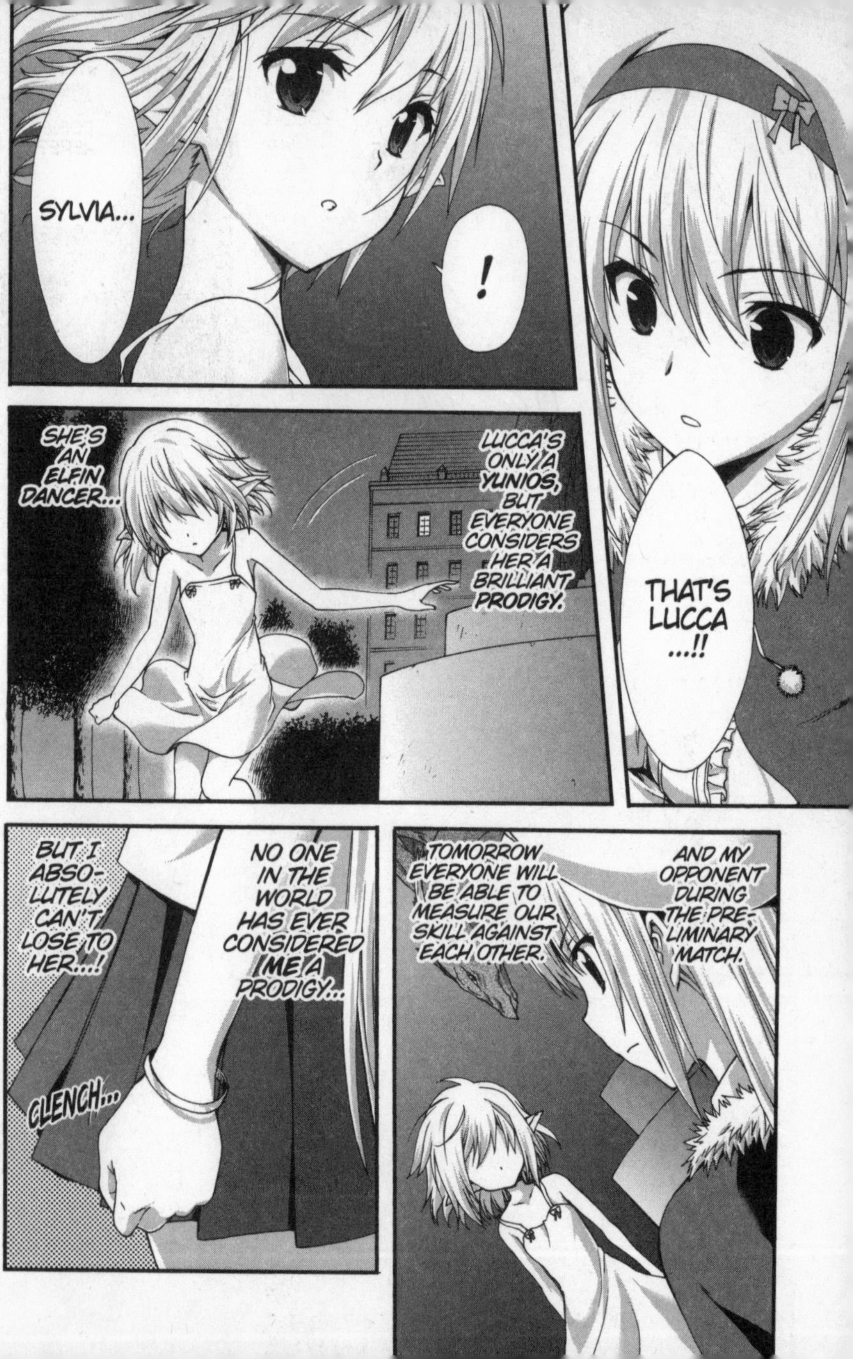
THAT'S LUCCA ...!!
!
SYLVIA...
LUCCA'S ONLY A YUNIOS, BUT EVERYONE CONSIDERS HER A BRILLIANT PRODIGY.
SHE'S AN ELFIN DANCER...
AND MY OPPONENT DURING THE PRE-LIMINARY MATCH.
TOMORROW EVERYONE WILL BE ABLE TO MEASURE OUR SKILL AGAINST EACH OTHER.
NO ONE IN THE WORLD HAS EVER CONSIDERED ME A PRODIGY...
BUT I ABSO-LUTELY CAN'T LOSE TO HER...!
CLENCH...

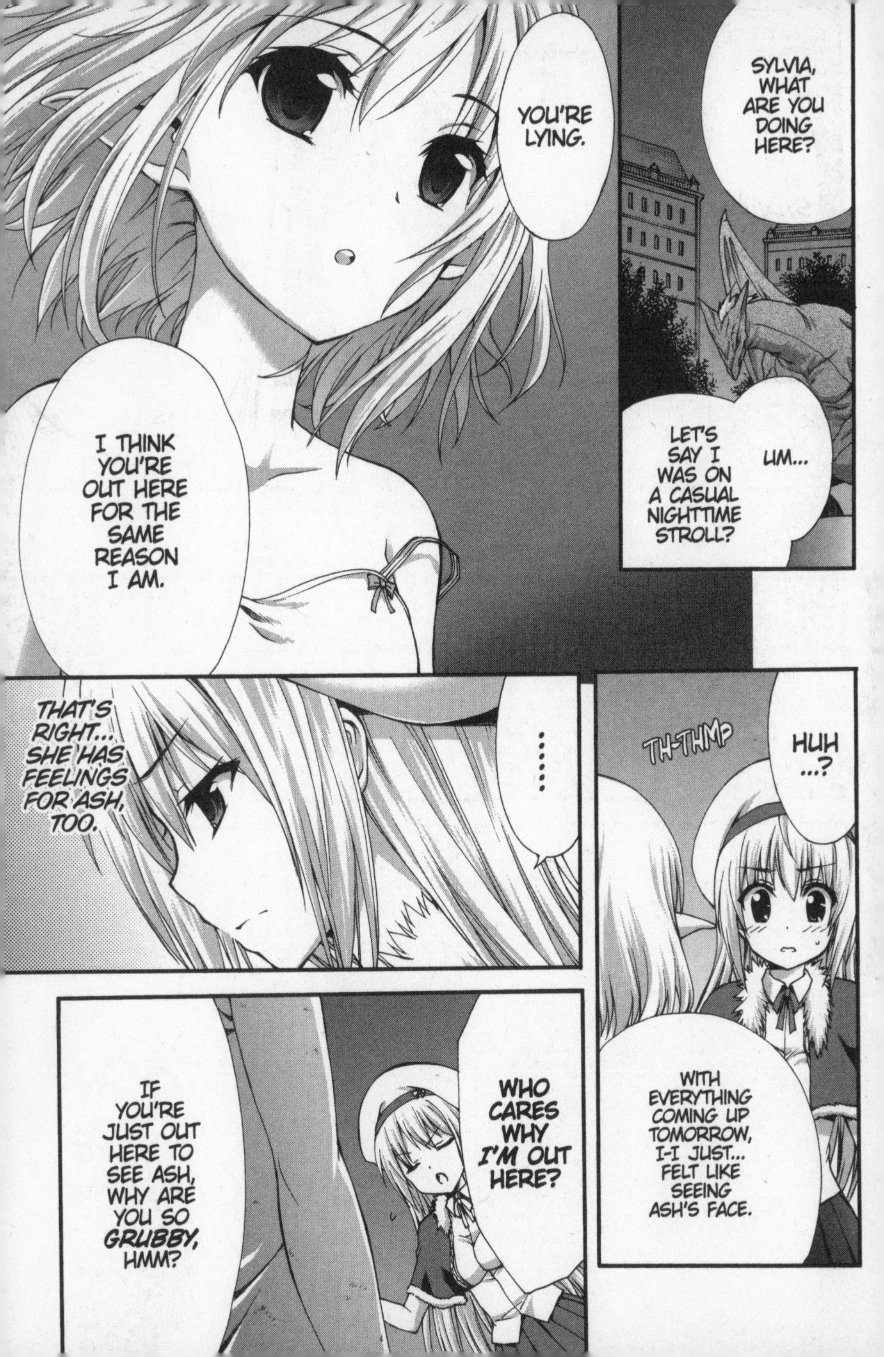
SYLVIA, WHAT ARE YOU DOING HERE?
UM...
LET'S SAY I WAS ON A CASUAL NIGHTTIME STROLL?
YOU'RE LYING.
I THINK YOU'RE OUT HERE FOR THE SAME REASON I AM.
HUH ...?
TH-THMP
WITH EVERYTHING COMING UP TOMORROW, I-I JUST... FELT LIKE SEEING ASH'S FACE.
......
THAT'S RIGHT... SHE HAS FEELINGS FOR ASH, TOO.
WHO CARES WHY *I'M* OUT HERE?
IF YOU'RE JUST OUT HERE TO SEE ASH, WHY ARE YOU SO ***GRUBBY,*** HMM?

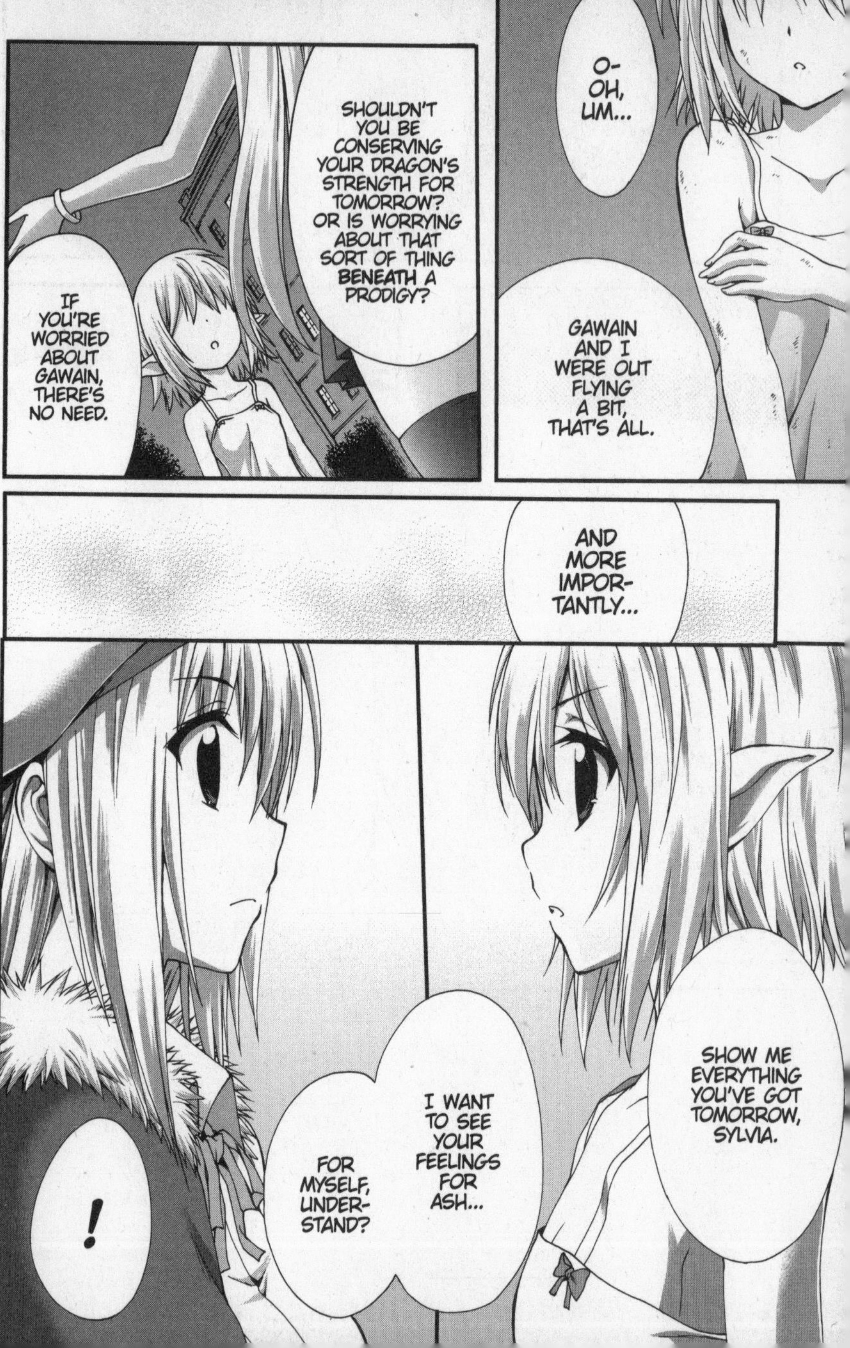
O-OH, UM...
GAWAIN AND I WERE OUT FLYING A BIT, THAT'S ALL.
SHOULDN'T YOU BE CONSERVING YOUR DRAGON'S STRENGTH FOR TOMORROW? OR IS WORRYING ABOUT THAT SORT OF THING BENEATH A PRODIGY?
IF YOU'RE WORRIED ABOUT GAWAIN, THERE'S NO NEED.
AND MORE IMPOR-TANTLY...
SHOW ME EVERYTHING YOU'VE GOT TOMORROW, SYLVIA.
I WANT TO SEE YOUR FEELINGS FOR ASH...
FOR MYSELF, UNDER-STAND?
!

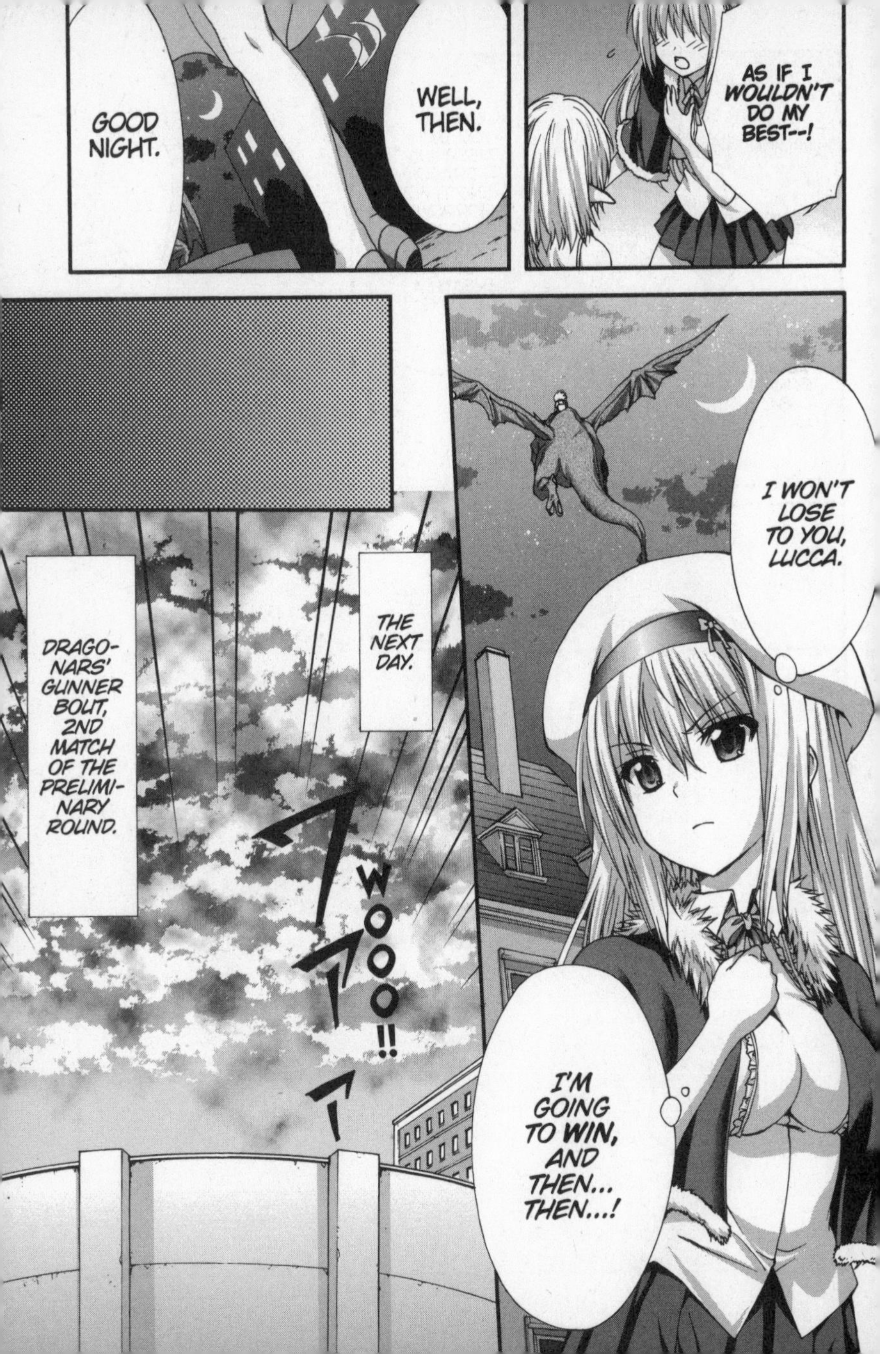
AS IF I WOULDN'T DO MY BEST--!
WELL, THEN.
GOOD NIGHT.
I WON'T LOSE TO YOU, LUCCA.
I'M GOING TO WIN, AND THEN... THEN...!
THE NEXT DAY.
DRAGO-NARS' GUNNER BOUT, 2ND MATCH OF THE PRELIMI-NARY ROUND.
WOOO!!

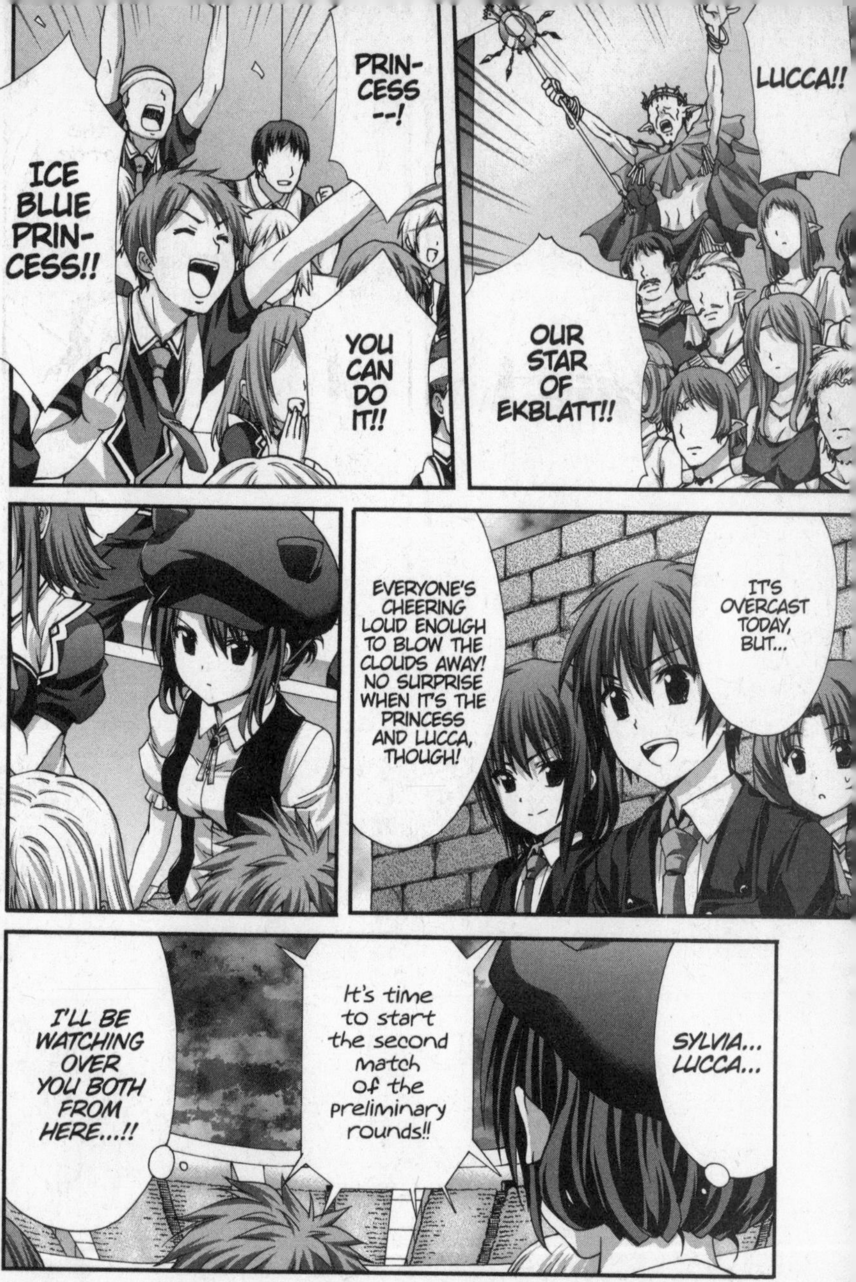
LUCCA!!
OUR STAR OF EKBLATT!!
PRIN-CESS--!
YOU CAN DO IT!!
ICE BLUE PRIN-CESS!!
IT'S OVERCAST TODAY, BUT...
EVERYONE'S CHEERING LOUD ENOUGH TO BLOW THE CLOUDS AWAY! NO SURPRISE WHEN IT'S THE PRINCESS AND LUCCA, THOUGH!
SYLVIA... LUCCA...
It's time to start the second match of the preliminary rounds!!
I'LL BE WATCHING OVER YOU BOTH FROM HERE...!!

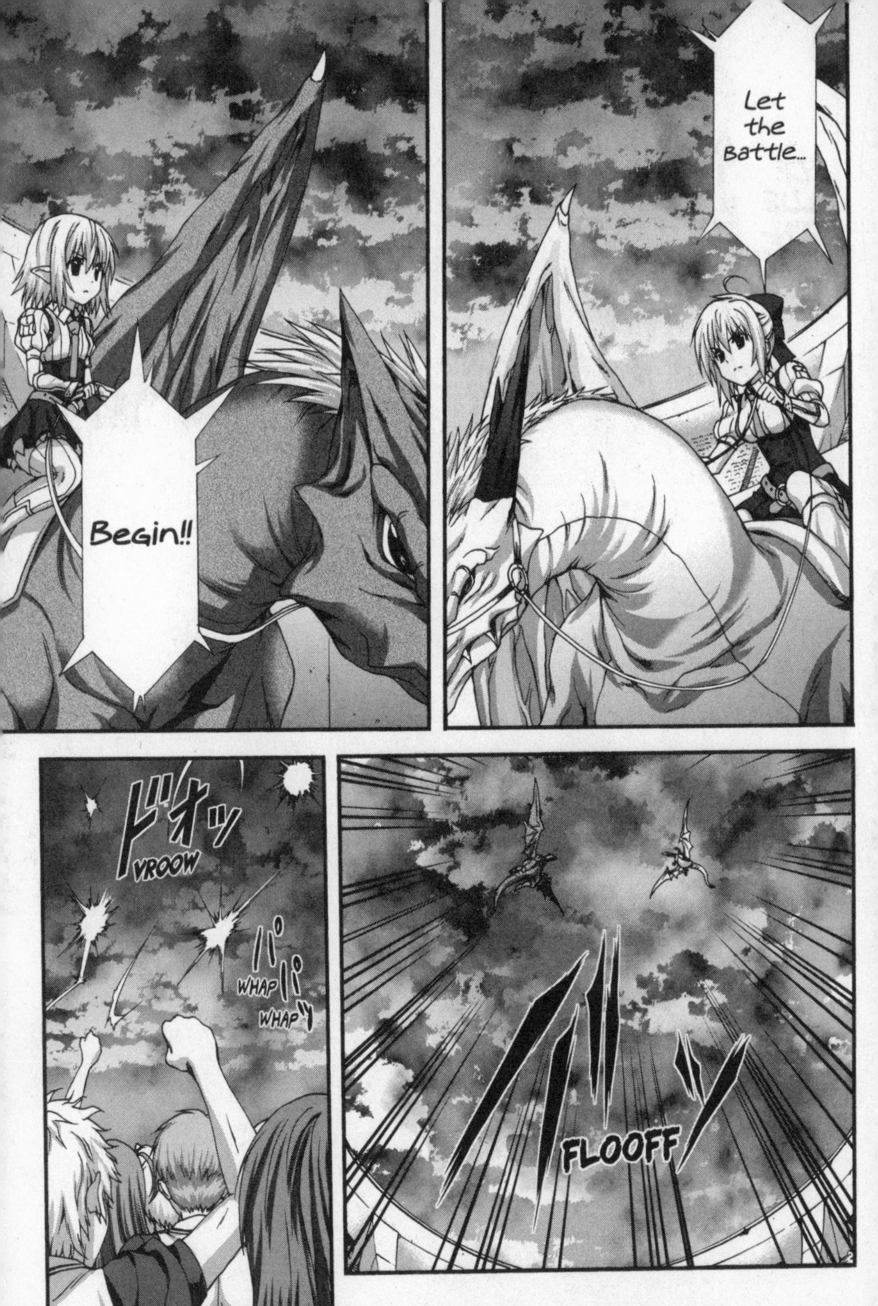
Let the Battle...
Begin!!
FLOOFF
ドオッ
VROOW
パパッ
WHAP WHAP

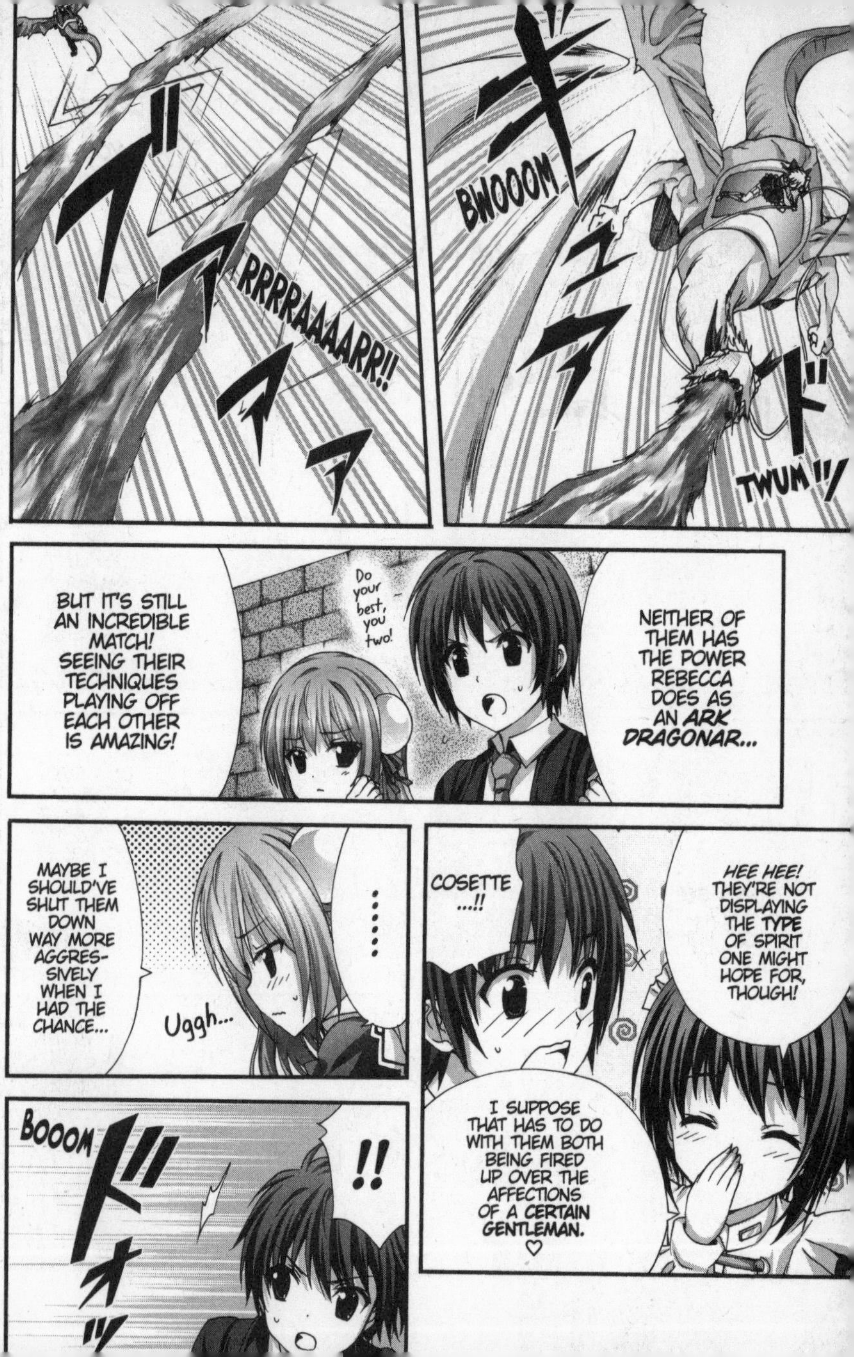
BWOOOM
TWUM!!
RRRRAAAARR!!
NEITHER OF THEM HAS THE POWER REBECCA DOES AS AN *ARK DRAGONAR*...
Do your best, you two!
BUT IT'S STILL AN INCREDIBLE MATCH! SEEING THEIR TECHNIQUES PLAYING OFF EACH OTHER IS AMAZING!
HEE HEE! THEY'RE NOT DISPLAYING THE **TYPE** OF SPIRIT ONE MIGHT HOPE FOR, THOUGH!
COSETTE ...!!
......
MAYBE I SHOULD'VE SHUT THEM DOWN WAY MORE AGGRES-SIVELY WHEN I HAD THE CHANCE...
Uggh...
I SUPPOSE THAT HAS TO DO WITH THEM BOTH BEING FIRED UP OVER THE AFFECTIONS OF A **CERTAIN GENTLEMAN.** ♡
BOOOM
!!

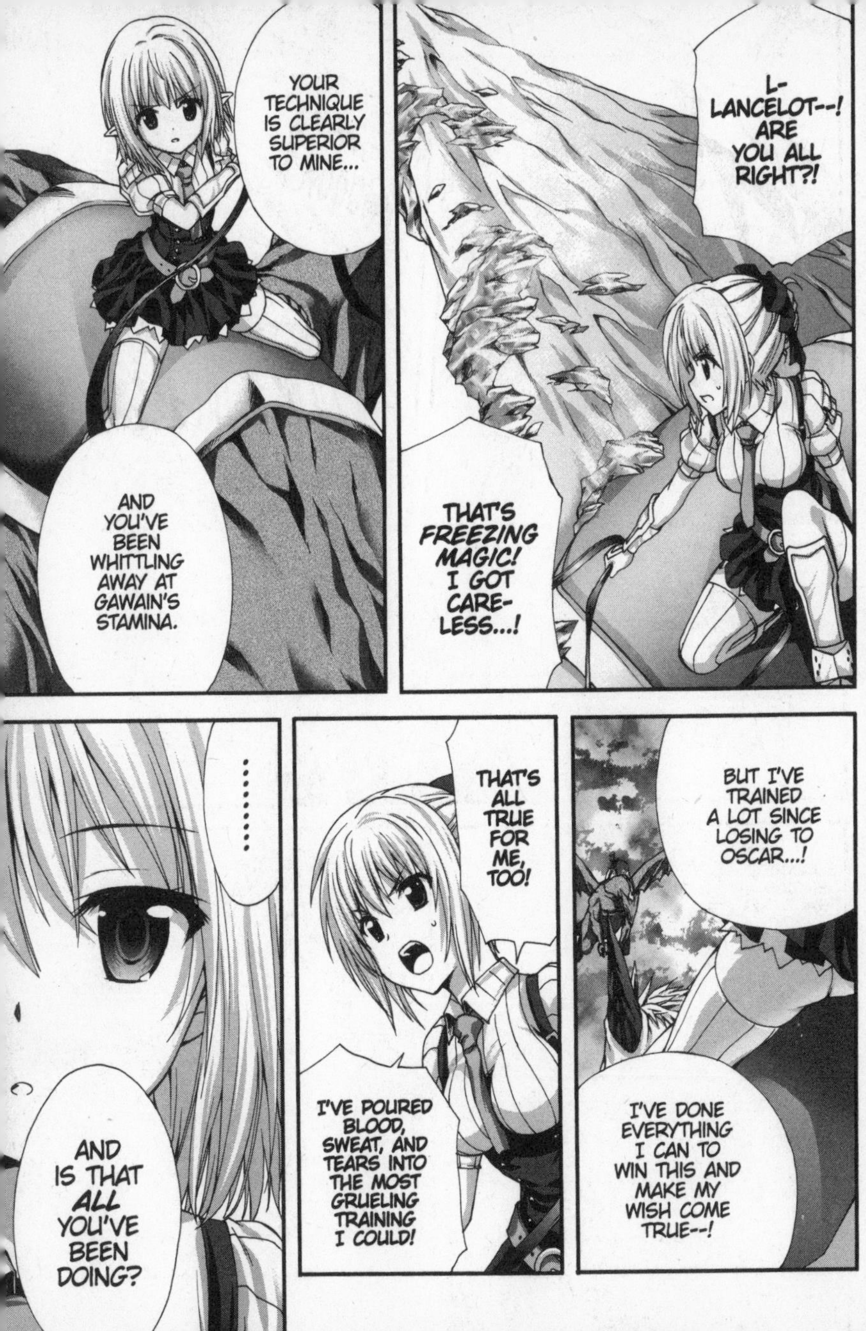
L- LANCELOT--! ARE YOU ALL RIGHT?!
THAT'S *FREEZING MAGIC!* I GOT CARE-LESS...!
YOUR TECHNIQUE IS CLEARLY SUPERIOR TO MINE...
AND YOU'VE BEEN WHITTLING AWAY AT GAWAIN'S STAMINA.
BUT I'VE TRAINED A LOT SINCE LOSING TO OSCAR...!
I'VE DONE EVERYTHING I CAN TO WIN THIS AND MAKE MY WISH COME TRUE--!
THAT'S ALL TRUE FOR ME, TOO!
I'VE POURED BLOOD, SWEAT, AND TEARS INTO THE MOST GRUELING TRAINING I COULD!
......
AND IS THAT ***ALL*** YOU'VE BEEN DOING?

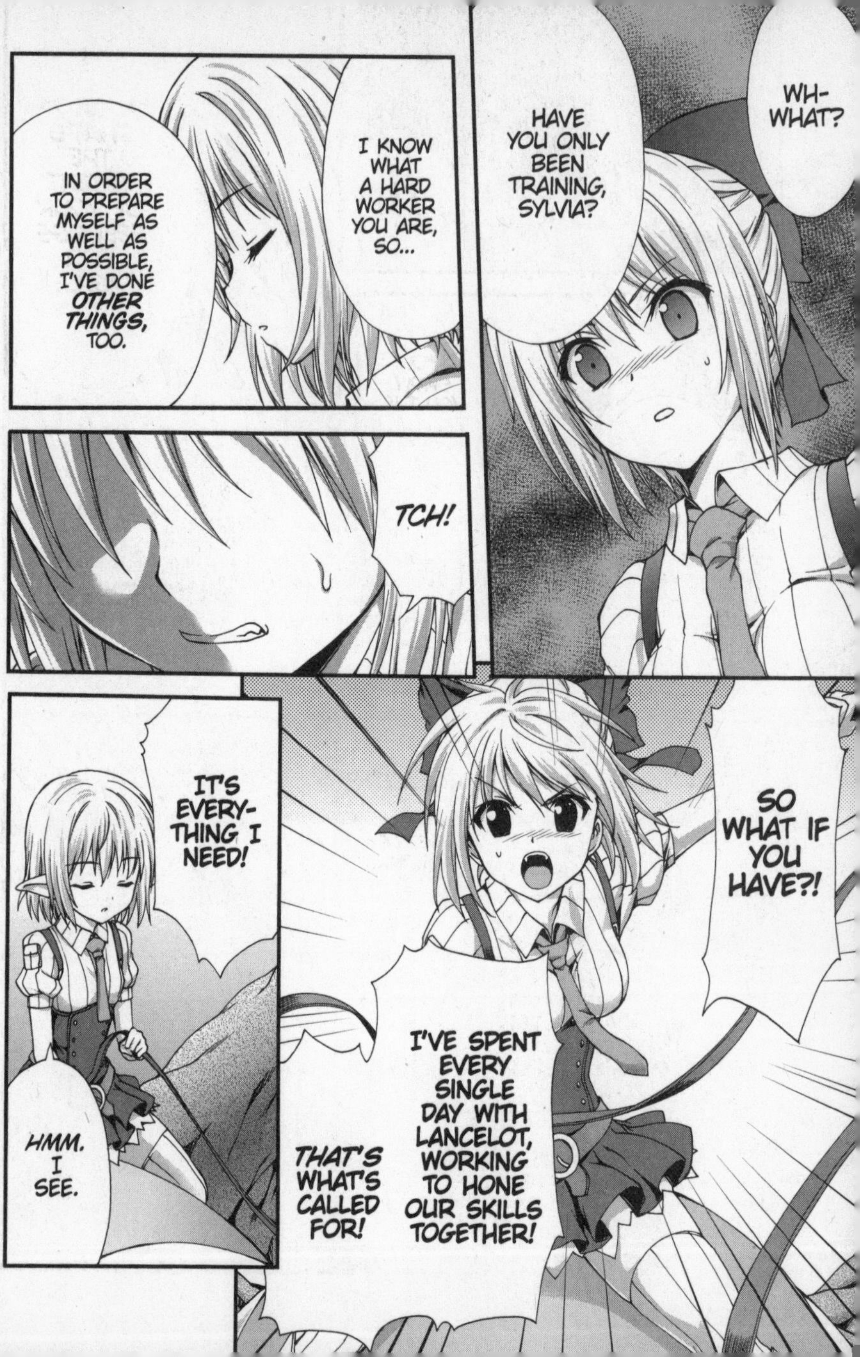
WH- WHAT?
HAVE YOU ONLY BEEN TRAINING, SYLVIA?
I KNOW WHAT A HARD WORKER YOU ARE, SO...
IN ORDER TO PREPARE MYSELF AS WELL AS POSSIBLE, I'VE DONE *OTHER THINGS,* TOO.
TCH!
SO WHAT IF YOU HAVE?!
I'VE SPENT EVERY SINGLE DAY WITH LANCELOT, WORKING TO HONE OUR SKILLS TOGETHER!
THAT'S WHAT'S CALLED FOR!
IT'S EVERY- THING I NEED!
HMM. I SEE.

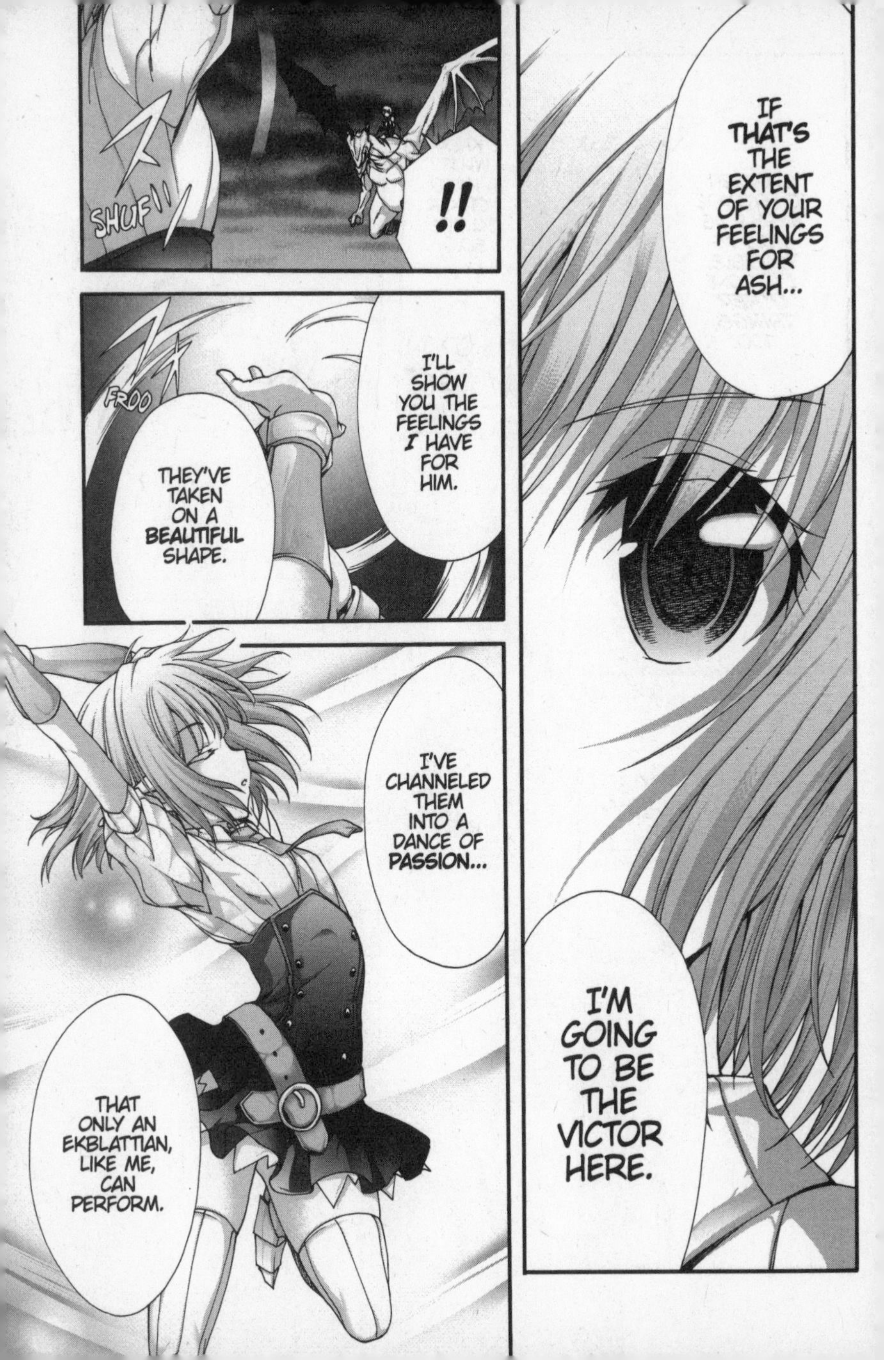
IF THAT'S THE EXTENT OF YOUR FEELINGS FOR ASH...
I'M GOING TO BE THE VICTOR HERE.
!!
SHUF!!
FROO
I'LL SHOW YOU THE FEELINGS *I* HAVE FOR HIM.
THEY'VE TAKEN ON A BEAUTIFUL SHAPE.
I'VE CHANNELED THEM INTO A DANCE OF PASSION...
THAT ONLY AN EKBLATTIAN, LIKE ME, CAN PERFORM.

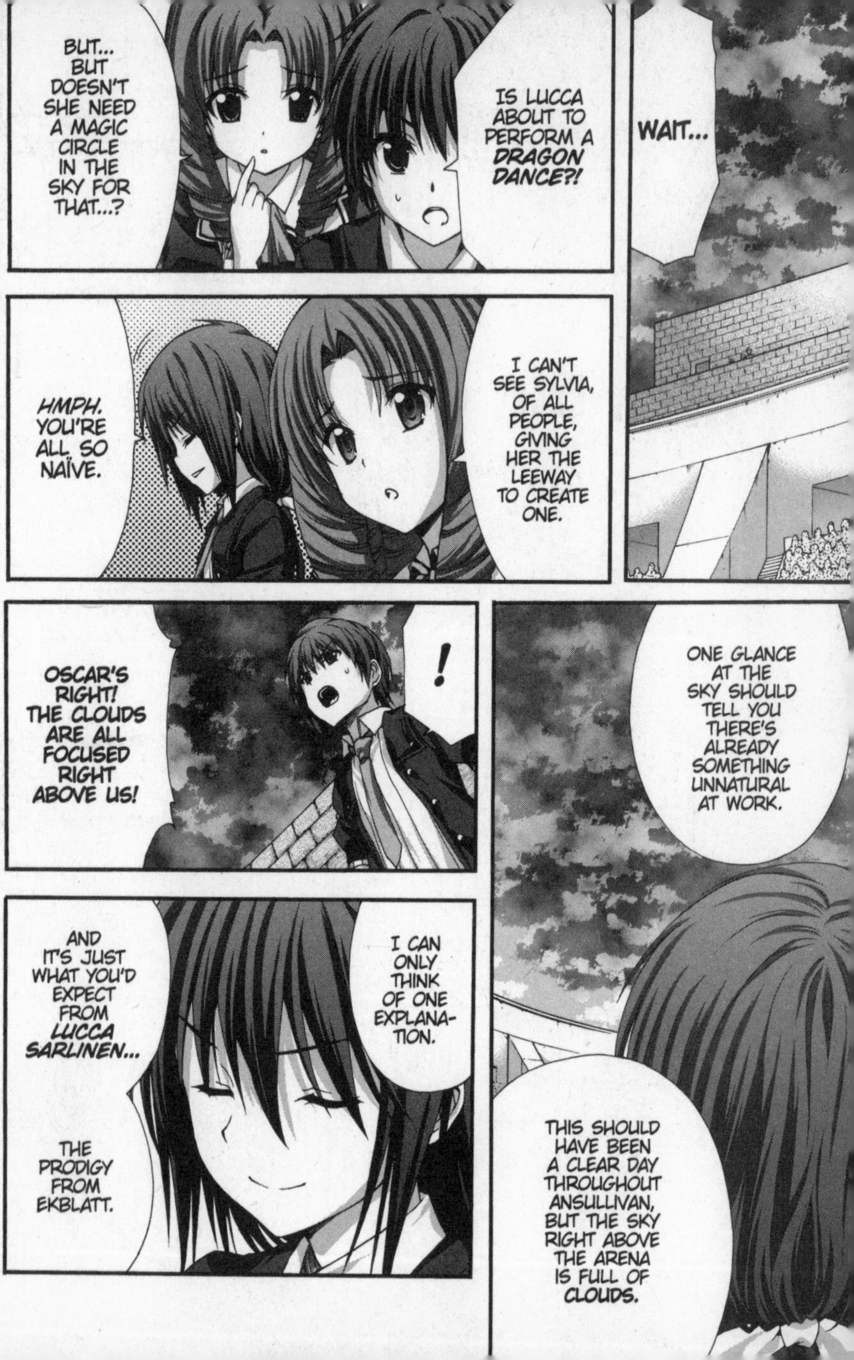

WAIT...
IS LUCCA ABOUT TO PERFORM A DRAGON DANCE?!
BUT... BUT DOESN'T SHE NEED A MAGIC CIRCLE IN THE SKY FOR THAT...?
I CAN'T SEE SYLVIA, OF ALL PEOPLE, GIVING HER THE LEEWAY TO CREATE ONE.
HMPH. YOU'RE ALL SO NAÏVE.
ONE GLANCE AT THE SKY SHOULD TELL YOU THERE'S ALREADY SOMETHING UNNATURAL AT WORK.
THIS SHOULD HAVE BEEN A CLEAR DAY THROUGHOUT ANSULLIVAN, BUT THE SKY RIGHT ABOVE THE ARENA IS FULL OF CLOUDS.
!
OSCAR'S RIGHT! THE CLOUDS ARE ALL FOCUSED RIGHT ABOVE US!
I CAN ONLY THINK OF ONE EXPLANATION.
AND IT'S JUST WHAT YOU'D EXPECT FROM LUCCA SARLINEN...
THE PRODIGY FROM EKBLATT.

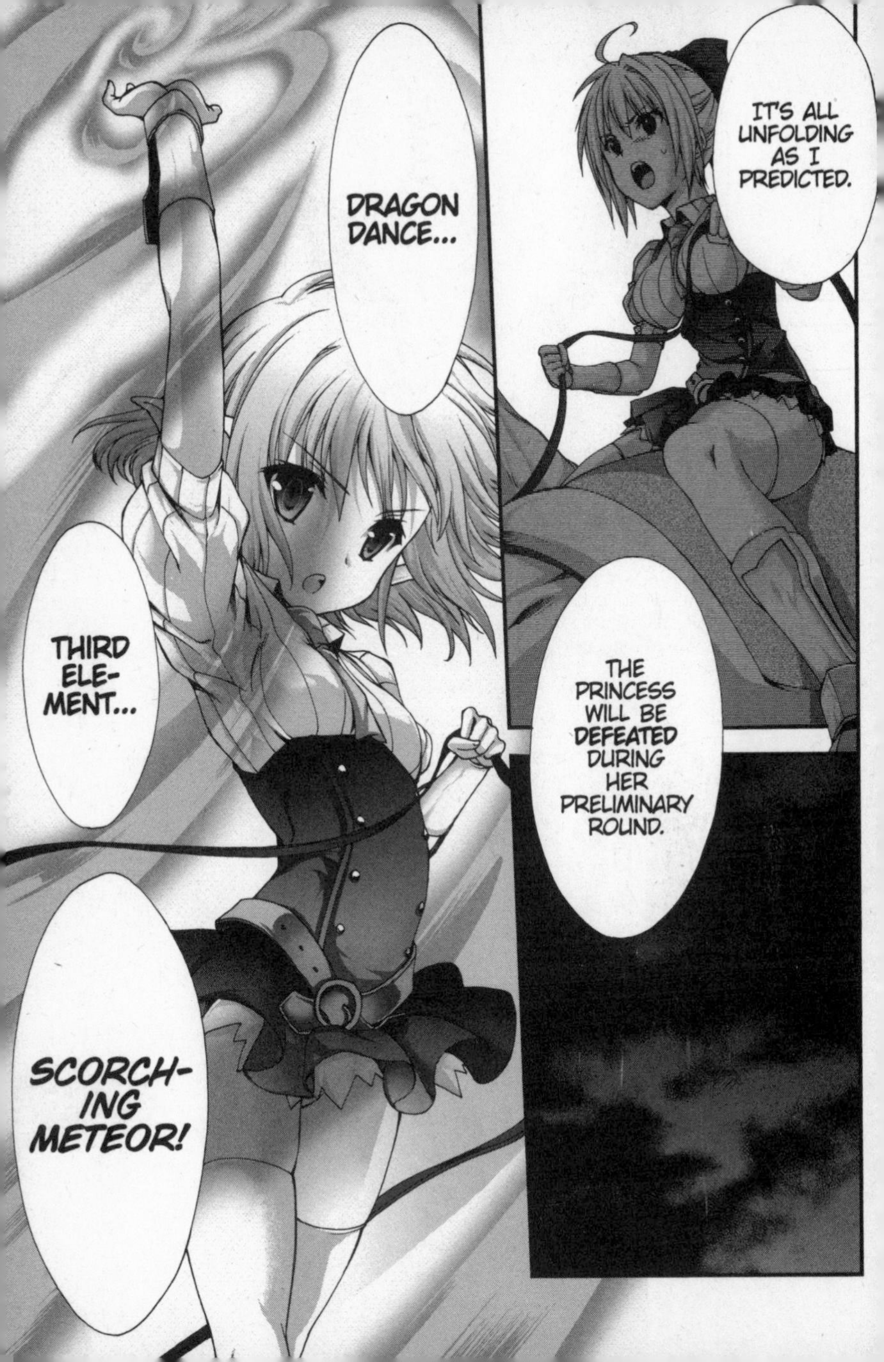
IT'S ALL UNFOLDING AS I PREDICTED.
THE PRINCESS WILL BE DEFEATED DURING HER PRELIMINARY ROUND.
DRAGON DANCE...
THIRD ELEMENT...
SCORCHING METEOR!

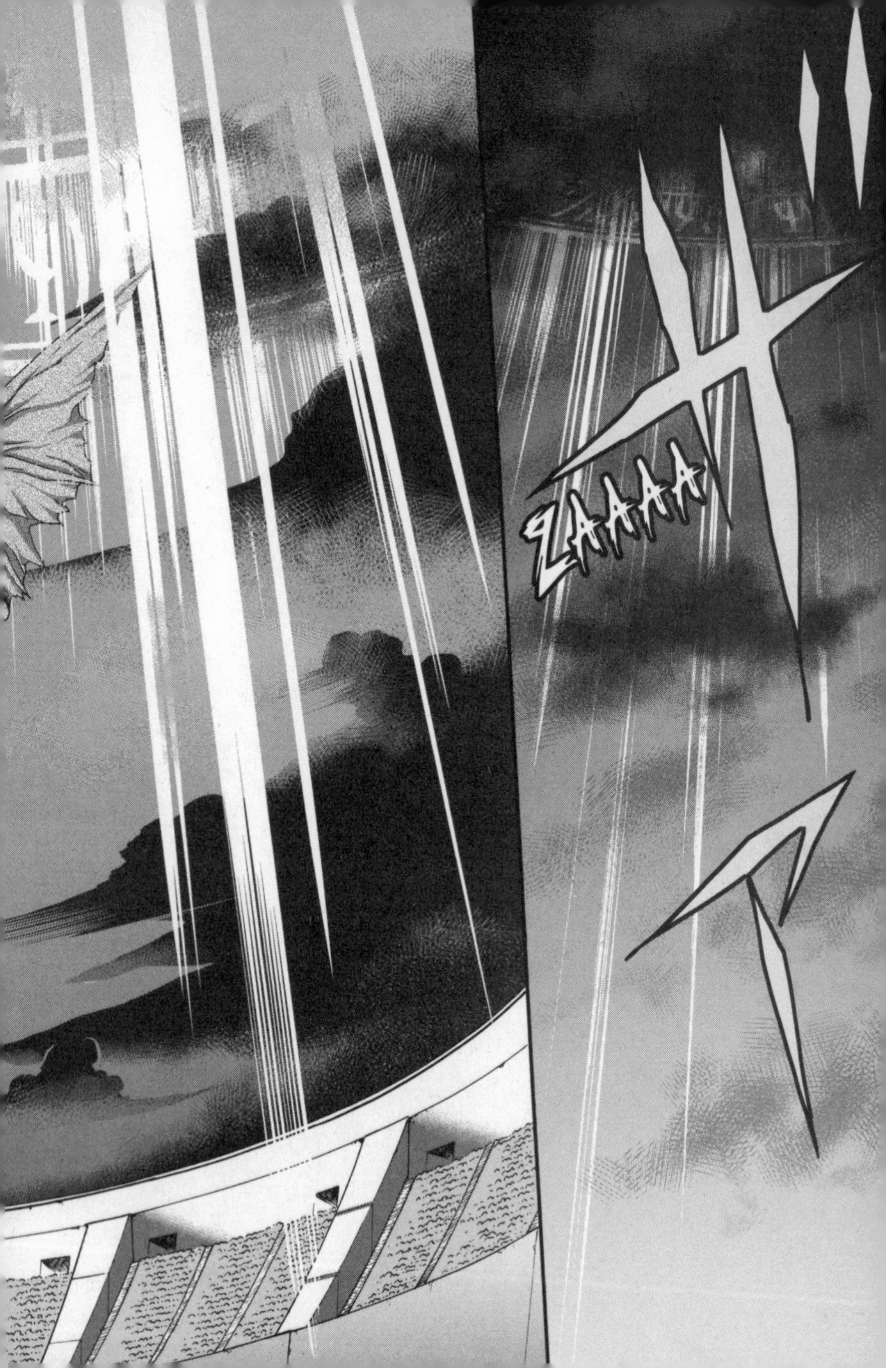
ZAAAA

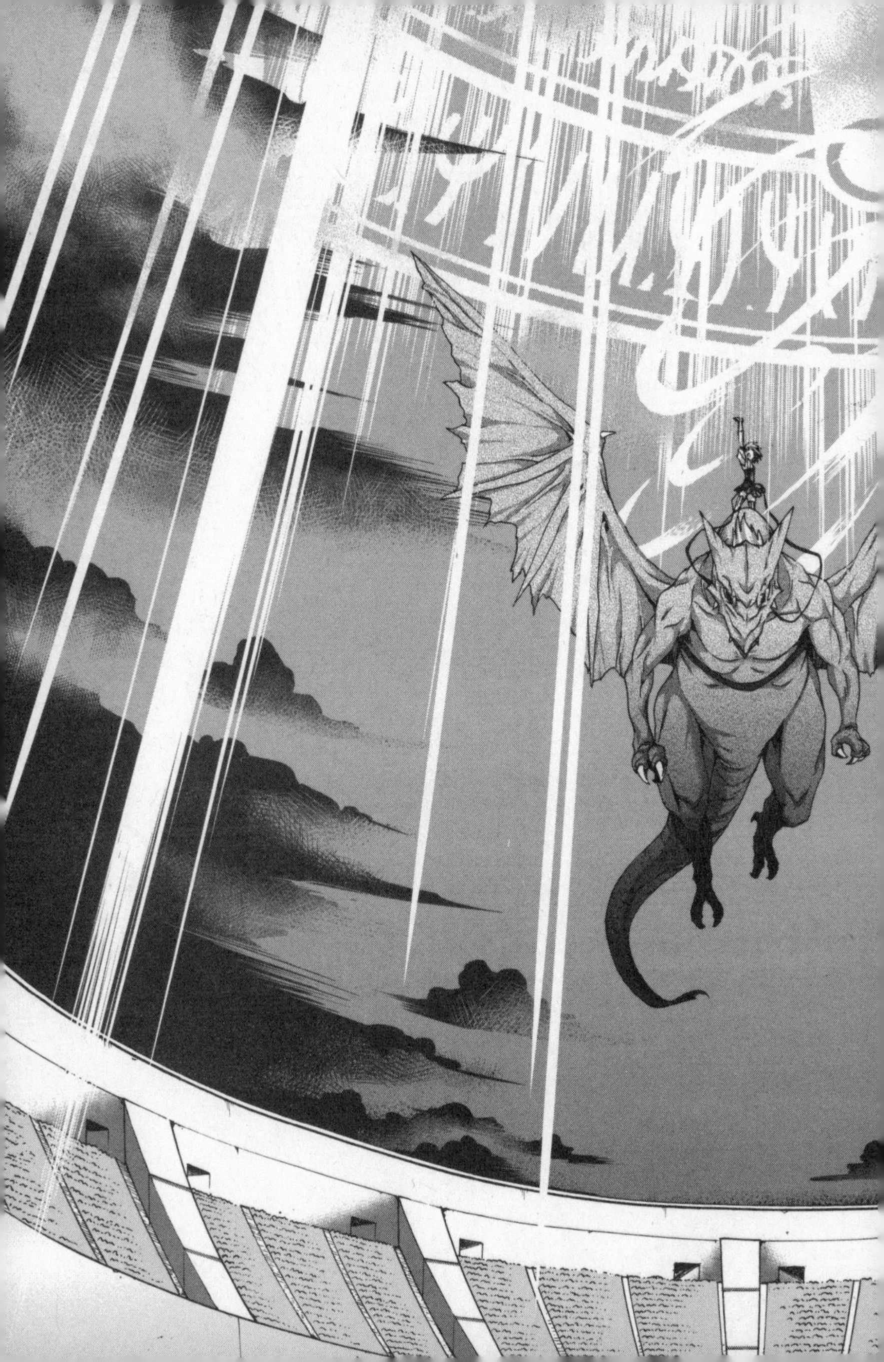

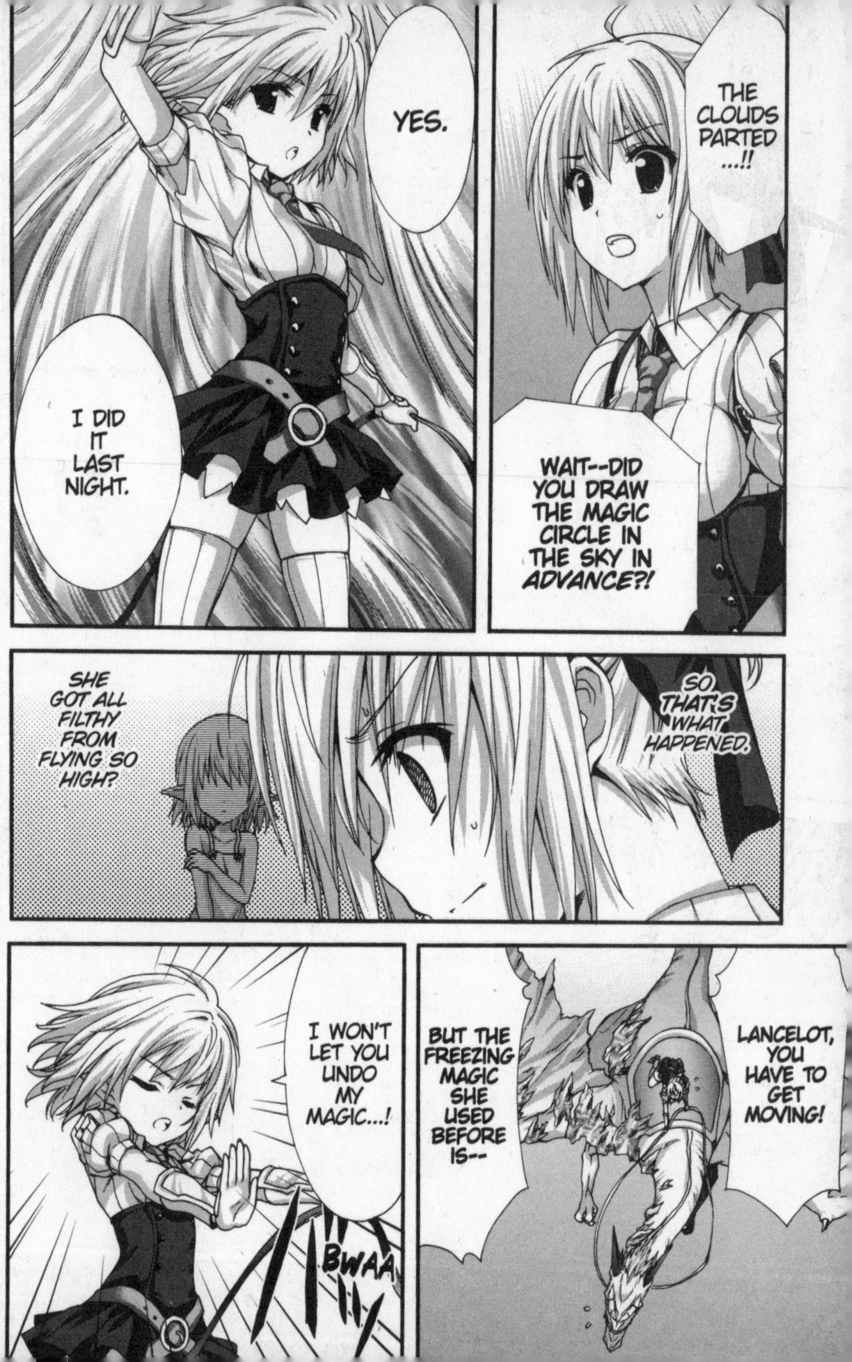
THE CLOUDS PARTED ...!!
WAIT--DID YOU DRAW THE MAGIC CIRCLE IN THE SKY IN *ADVANCE*?!
YES.
I DID IT LAST NIGHT.
SO THAT'S WHAT HAPPENED.
SHE GOT ALL FILTHY FROM FLYING SO HIGH?
LANCELOT, YOU HAVE TO GET MOVING!
BUT THE FREEZING MAGIC SHE USED BEFORE IS--
I WON'T LET YOU UNDO MY MAGIC...!
BWAA

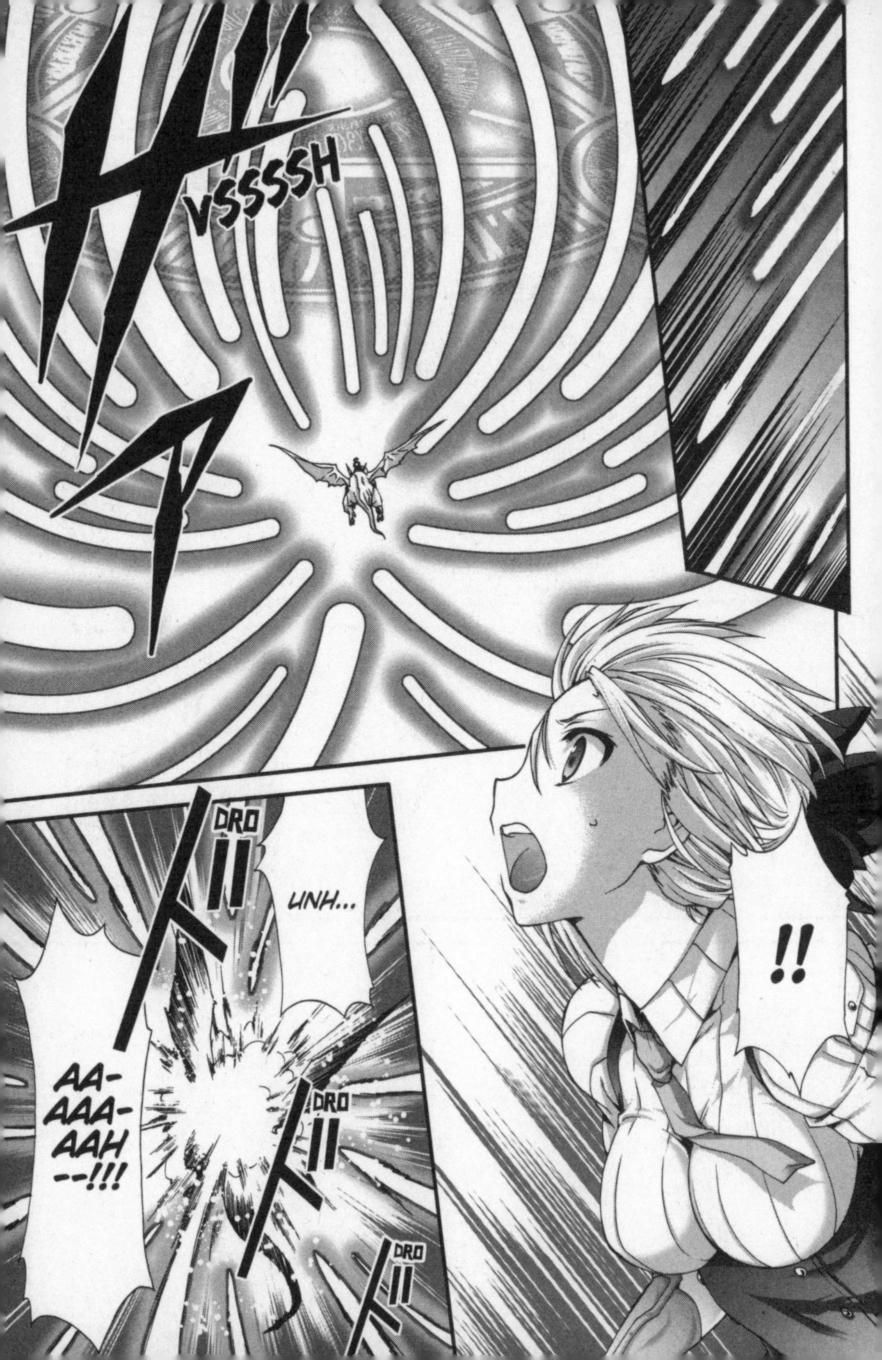
VSSSSH
!!
DRO
UNH...
AA-AAA-AAH--!!!
DRO
DRO

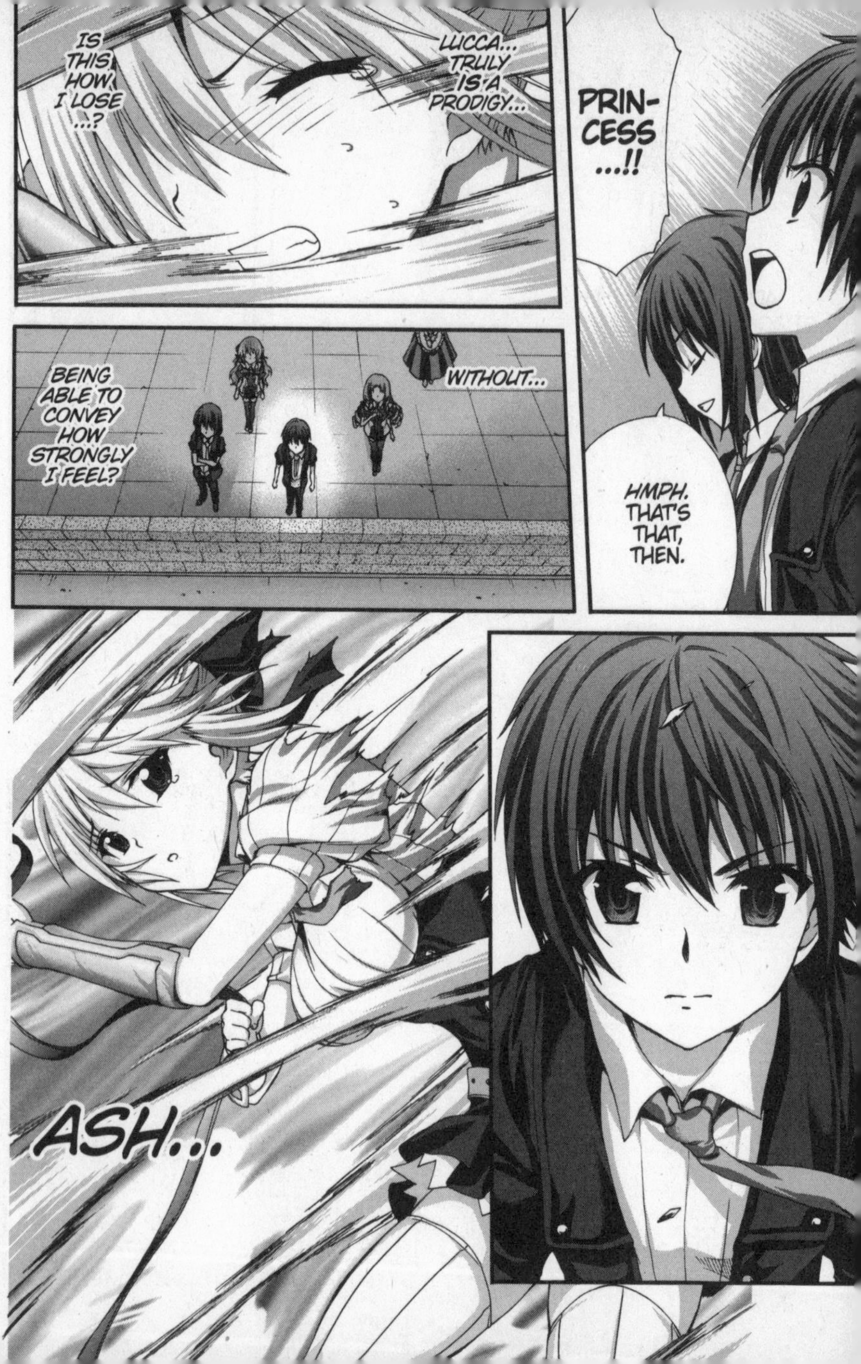
PRIN-CESS ...!!
HMPH. THAT'S THAT, THEN.
LUCCA... TRULY IS A PRODIGY...
IS THIS HOW I LOSE ...?
WITHOUT...
BEING ABLE TO CONVEY HOW STRONGLY I FEEL?
ASH...

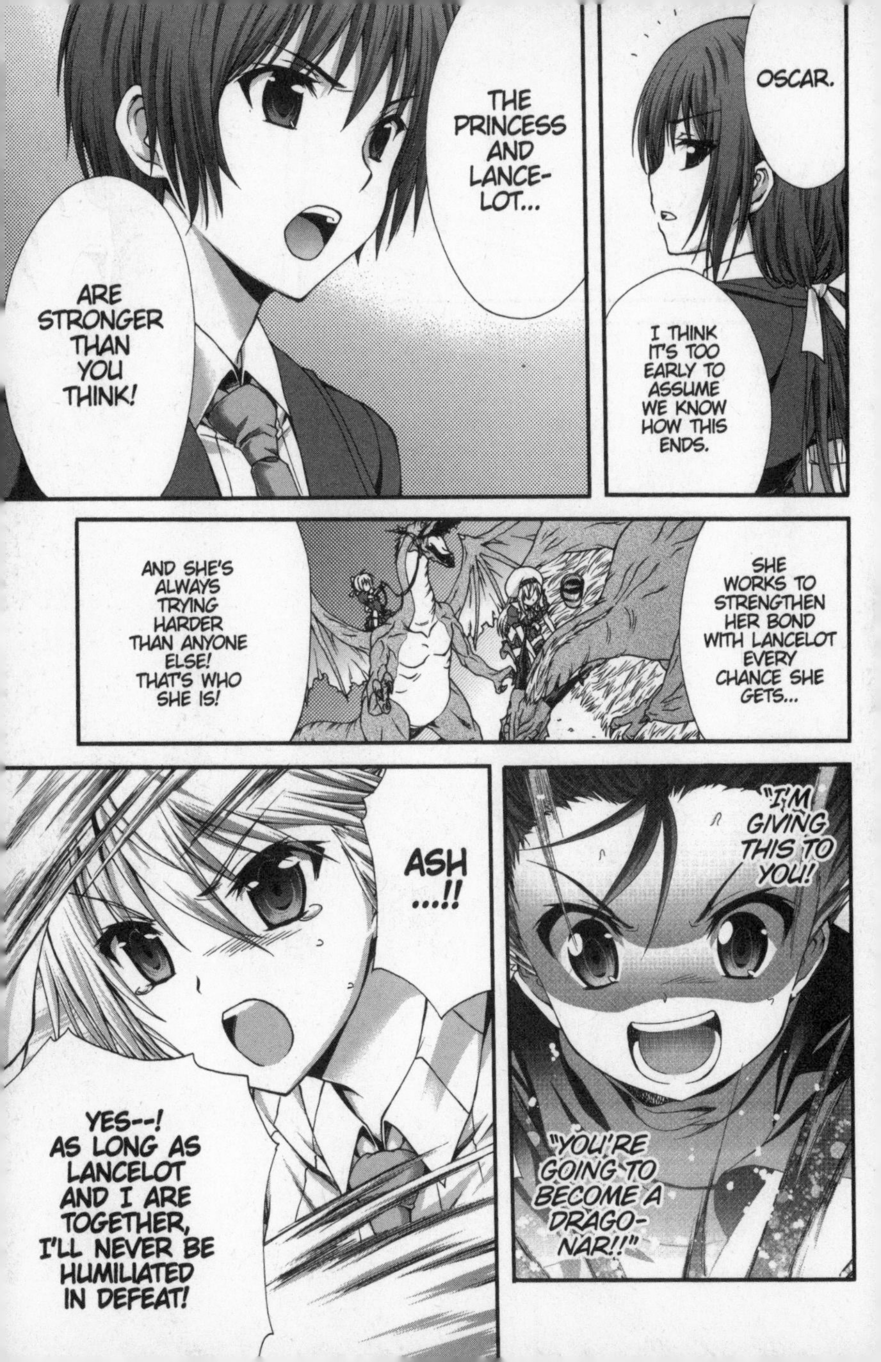
OSCAR.
I THINK IT'S TOO EARLY TO ASSUME WE KNOW HOW THIS ENDS.
THE PRINCESS AND LANCE-LOT...
ARE STRONGER THAN YOU THINK!
SHE WORKS TO STRENGTHEN HER BOND WITH LANCELOT EVERY CHANCE SHE GETS...
AND SHE'S ALWAYS TRYING HARDER THAN ANYONE ELSE! THAT'S WHO SHE IS!
"I'M GIVING THIS TO YOU!
"YOU'RE GOING TO BECOME A DRAGO-NAR!!"
ASH ...!!
YES--! AS LONG AS LANCELOT AND I ARE TOGETHER, I'LL NEVER BE HUMILIATED IN DEFEAT!

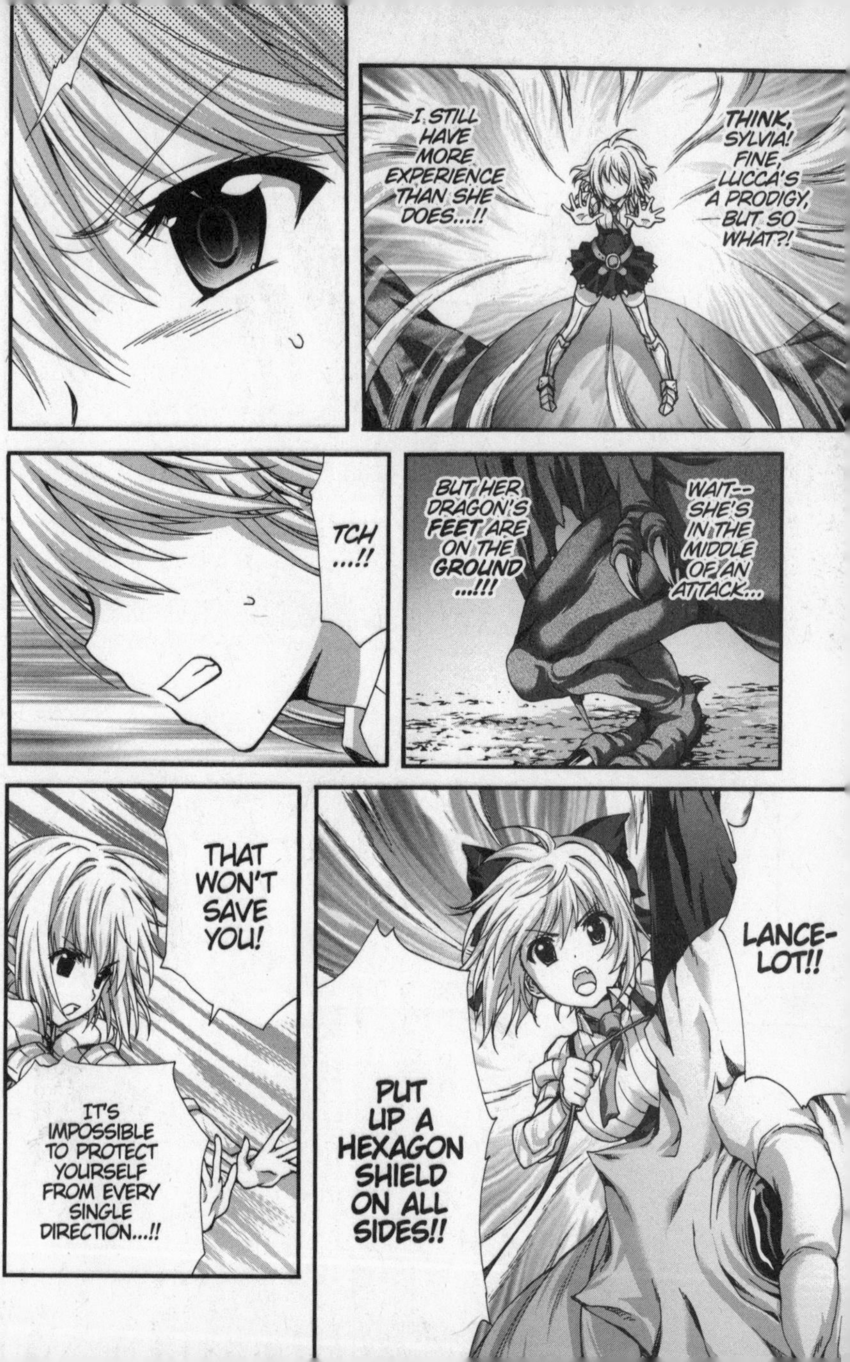
THINK, SYLVIA! FINE, LUCCA'S A PRODIGY, BUT SO WHAT?!
I STILL HAVE MORE EXPERIENCE THAN SHE DOES...!!
WAIT-- SHE'S IN THE MIDDLE OF AN ATTACK...
BUT HER DRAGON'S FEET ARE ON THE GROUND...!!!
TCH ...!!
LANCE-LOT!!
PUT UP A HEXAGON SHIELD ON ALL SIDES!!
THAT WON'T SAVE YOU!
IT'S IMPOSSIBLE TO PROTECT YOURSELF FROM EVERY SINGLE DIRECTION...!!

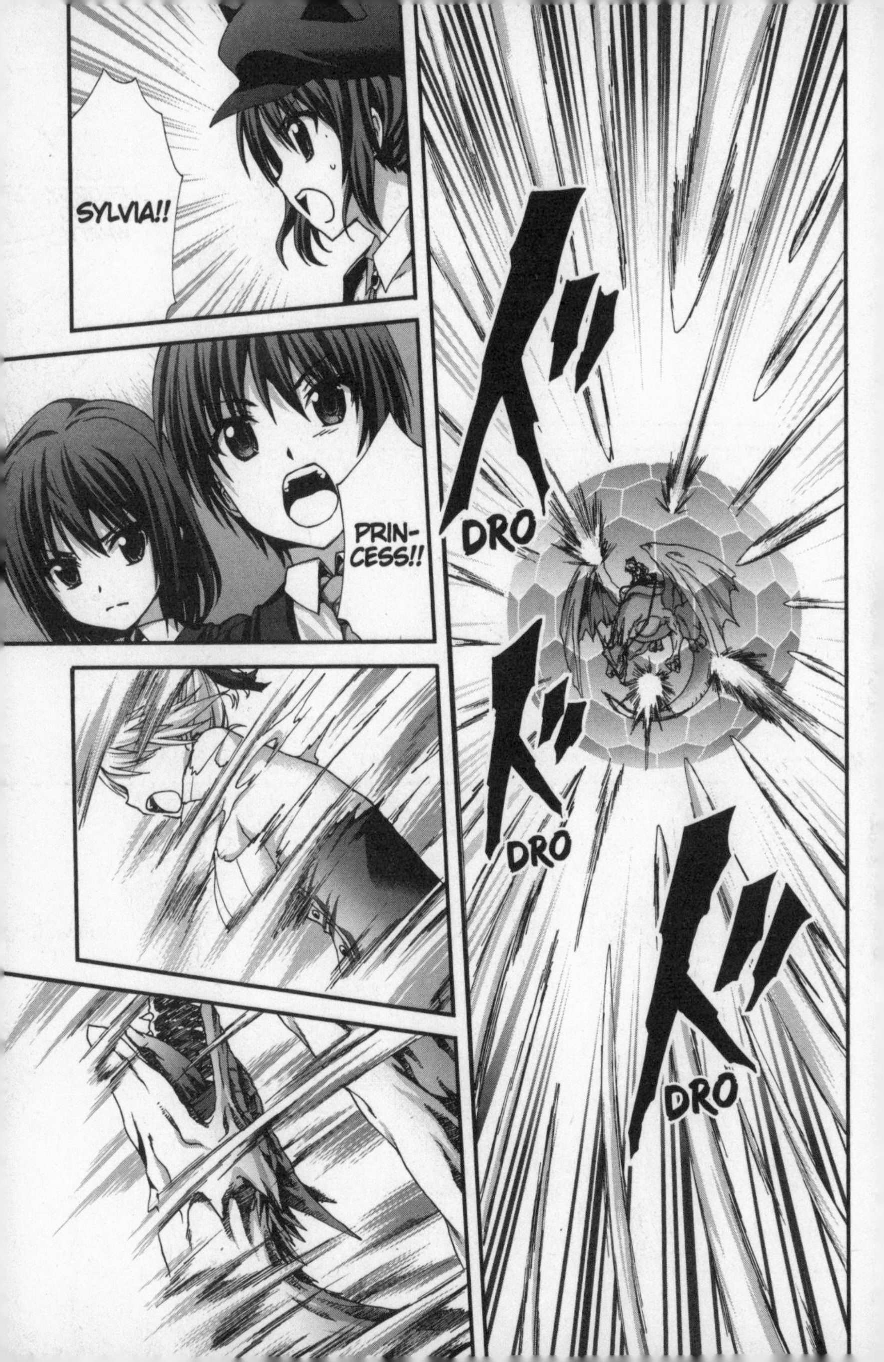
ド
DRO
ド
DRO
ド
DRO
SYLVIA!!
PRIN-
CESS!!

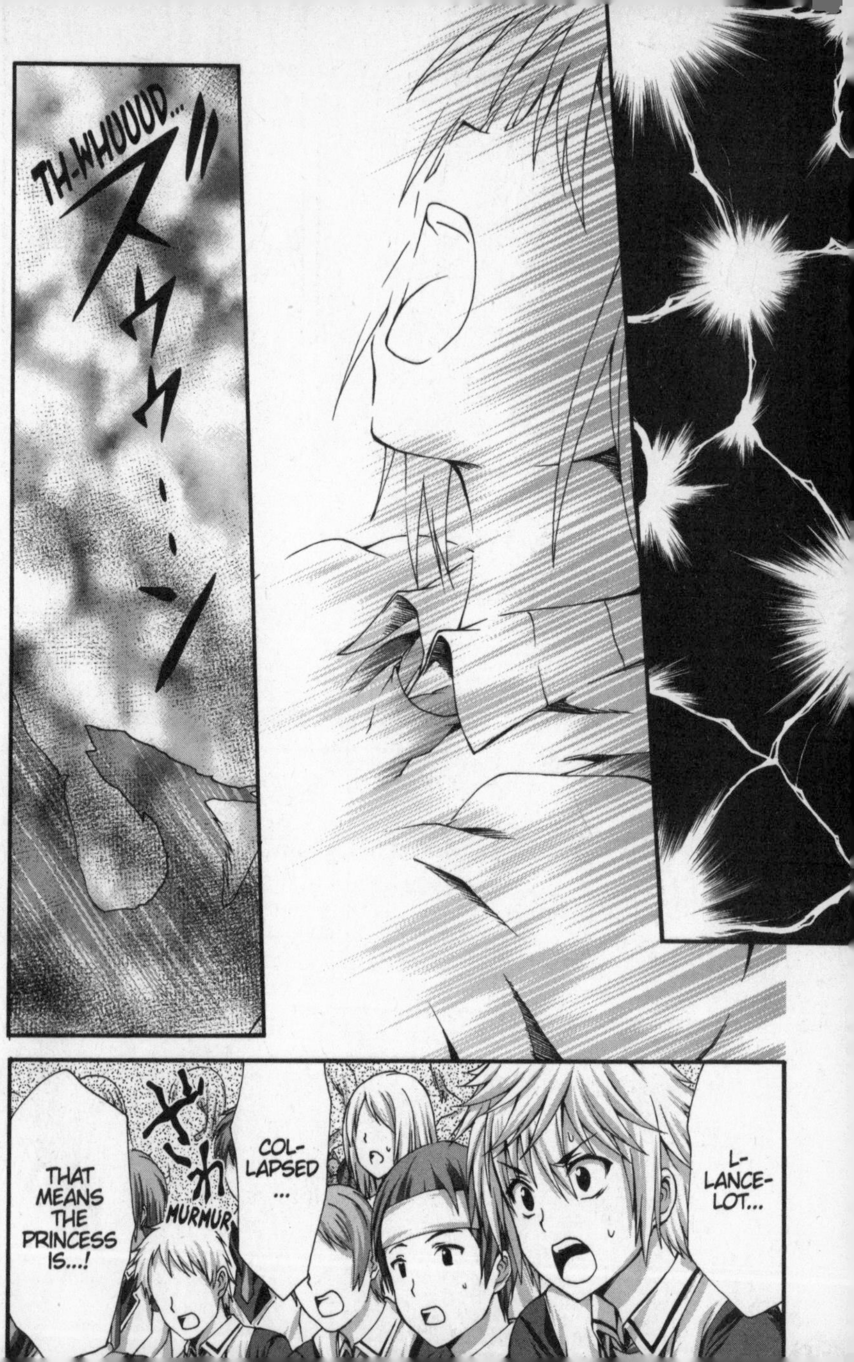

TH-WHUUUD...
L-LANCE-LOT...
COL-LAPSED...
MURMUR
THAT MEANS THE PRINCESS IS...!

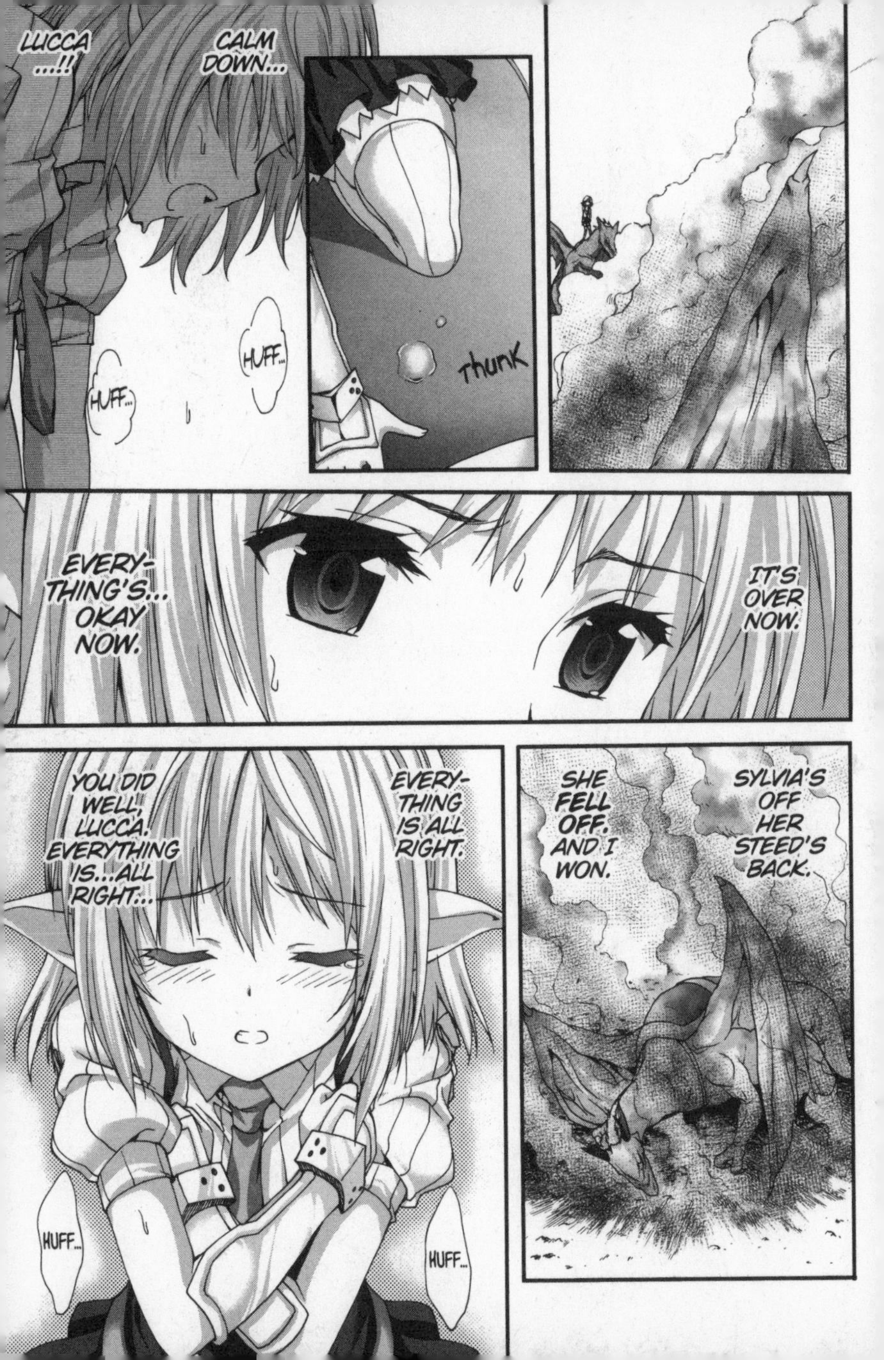
thunk
CALM DOWN...
LUCCA ...!!
HUFF...
HUFF...
IT'S OVER NOW.
EVERY-THING'S... OKAY NOW.
SYLVIA'S OFF HER STEED'S BACK.
SHE FELL OFF. AND I WON.
EVERY-THING IS ALL RIGHT.
YOU DID WELL, LUCCA. EVERYTHING IS...ALL RIGHT...
HUFF...
HUFF...

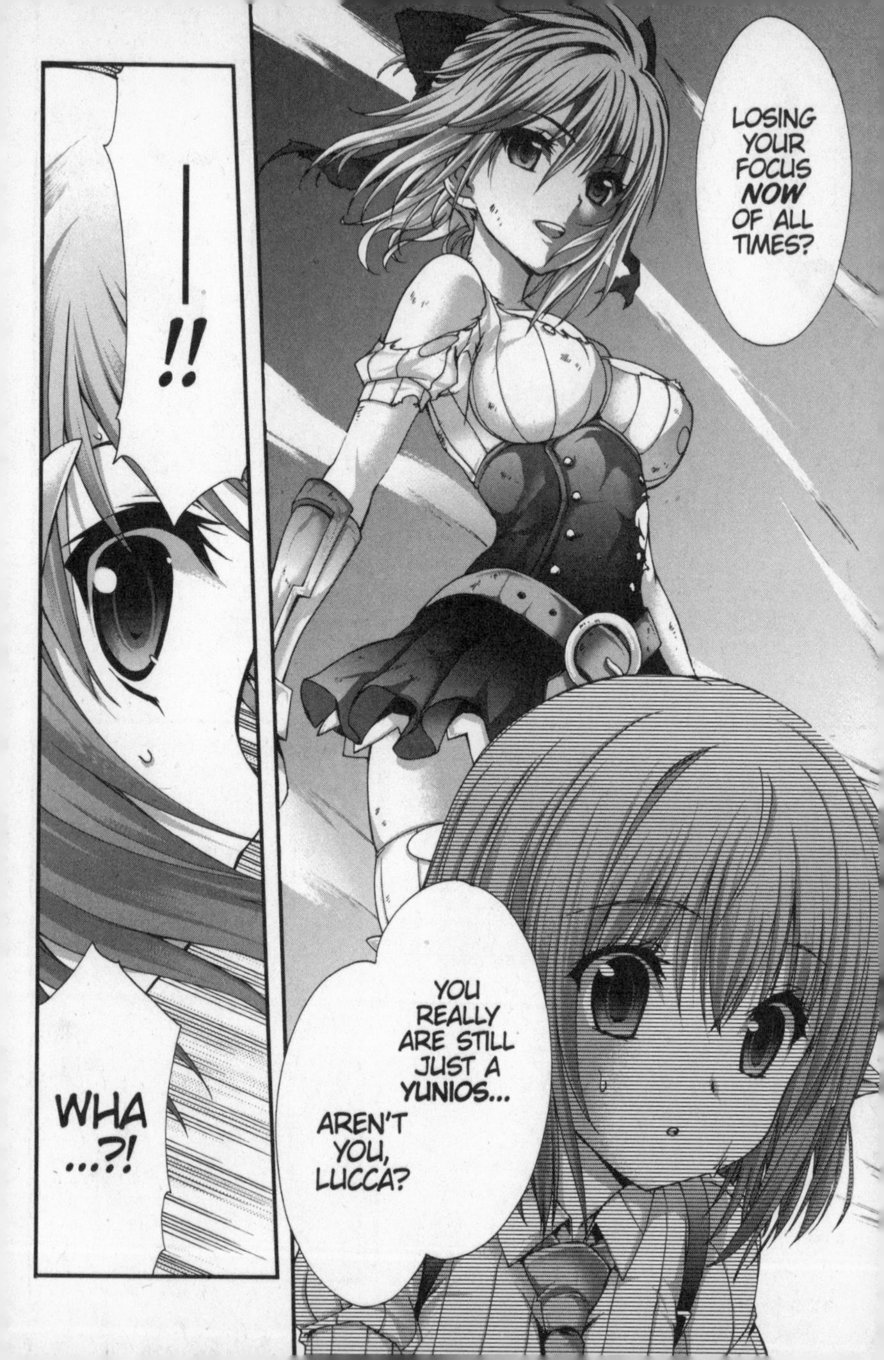
LOSING YOUR FOCUS *NOW* OF ALL TIMES?
YOU REALLY ARE STILL JUST A YUNIOS...
AREN'T YOU, LUCCA?
—!!
WHA ...?!

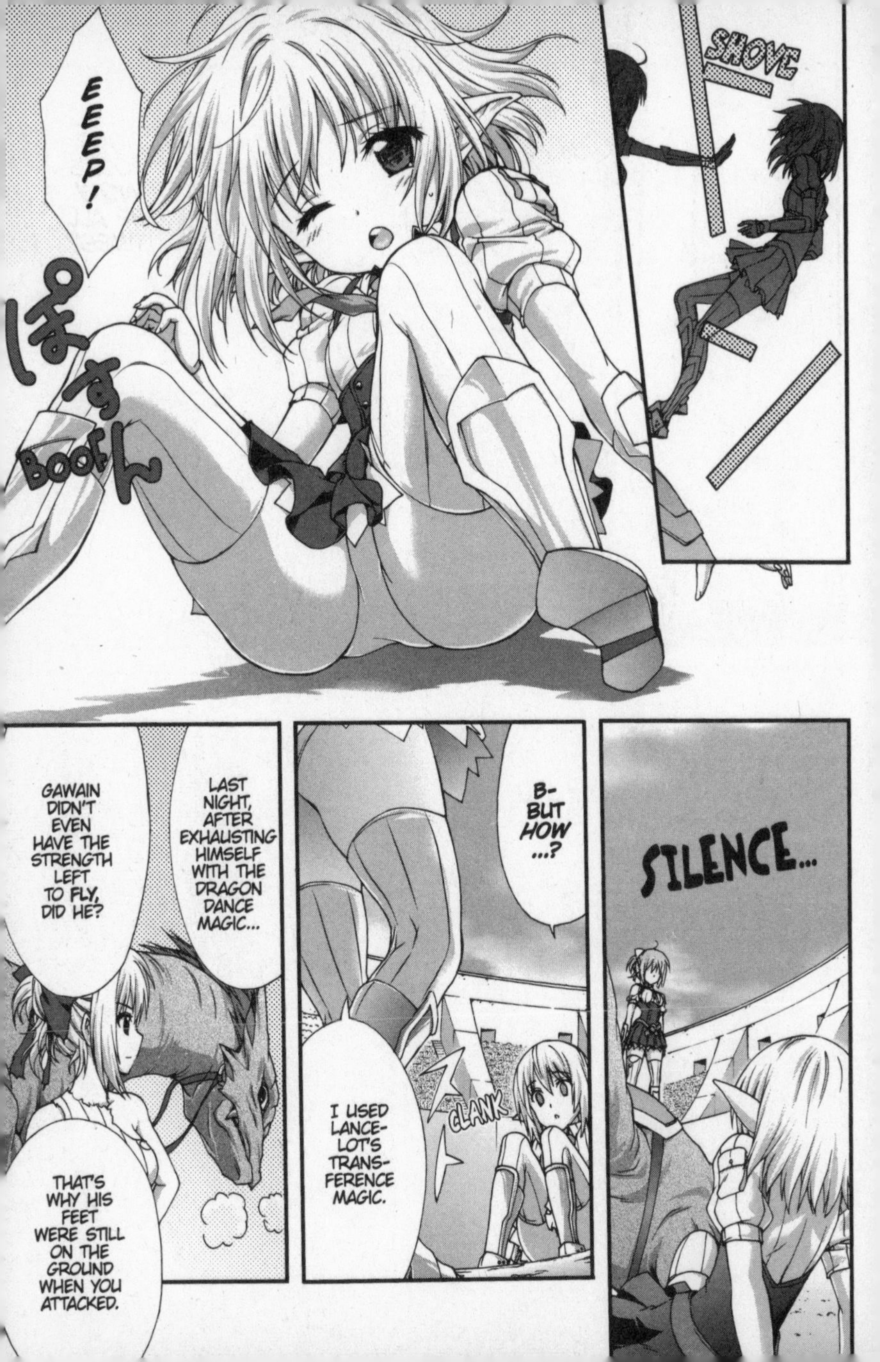
SHOVE
EEEP!
ぱすん
BOOF
SILENCE...
B-BUT HOW ...?
CLANK
I USED LANCE-LOT'S TRANS-FERENCE MAGIC.
LAST NIGHT, AFTER EXHAUSTING HIMSELF WITH THE DRAGON DANCE MAGIC...
GAWAIN DIDN'T EVEN HAVE THE STRENGTH LEFT TO FLY, DID HE?
THAT'S WHY HIS FEET WERE STILL ON THE GROUND WHEN YOU ATTACKED.

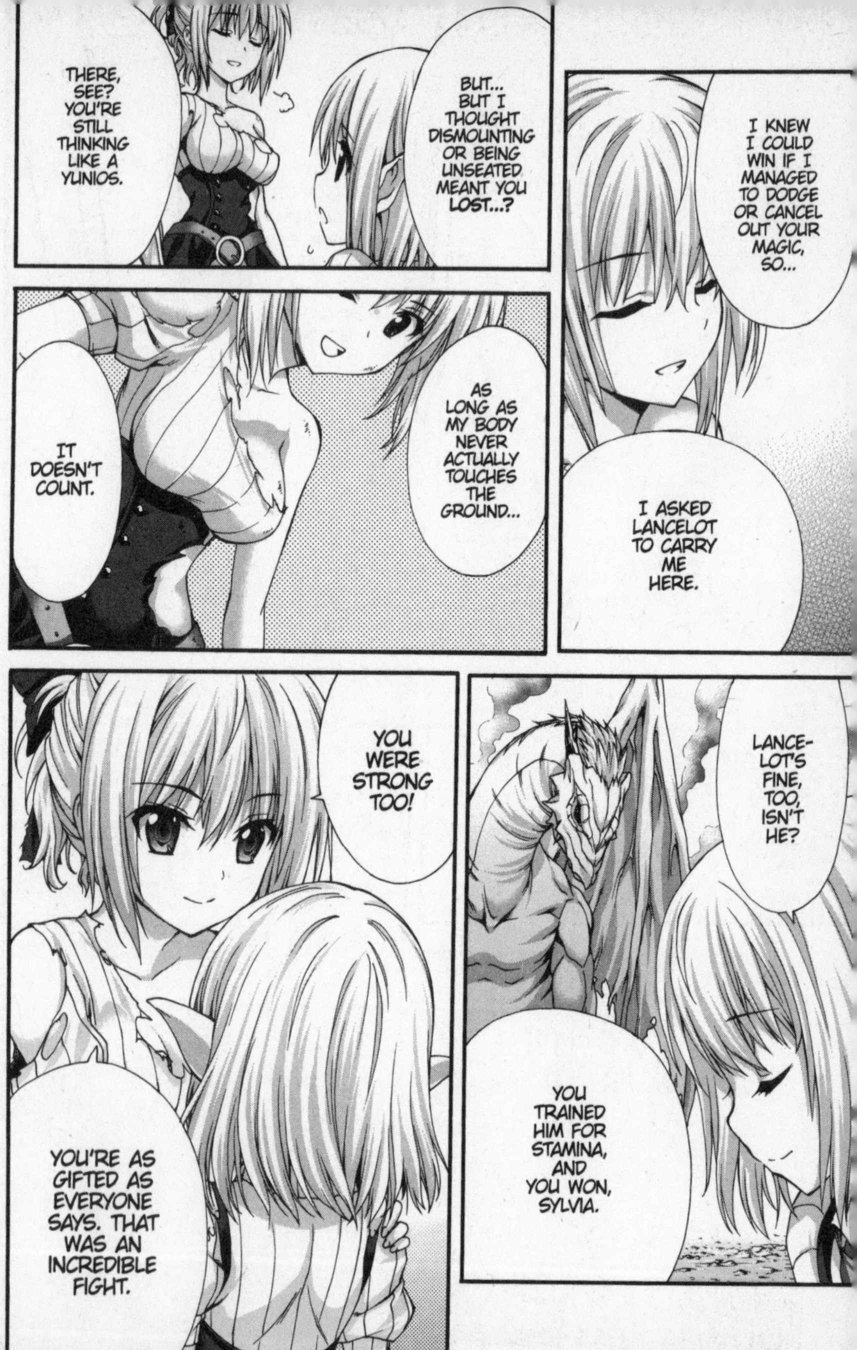
I KNEW I COULD WIN IF I MANAGED TO DODGE OR CANCEL OUT YOUR MAGIC, SO...
I ASKED LANCELOT TO CARRY ME HERE.
BUT... BUT I THOUGHT DISMOUNTING OR BEING UNSEATED MEANT YOU LOST...?
THERE, SEE? YOU'RE STILL THINKING LIKE A YUNIOS.
AS LONG AS MY BODY NEVER ACTUALLY TOUCHES THE GROUND...
IT DOESN'T COUNT.
LANCE-LOT'S FINE, TOO, ISN'T HE?
YOU TRAINED HIM FOR STAMINA, AND YOU WON, SYLVIA.
YOU WERE STRONG TOO!
YOU'RE AS GIFTED AS EVERYONE SAYS. THAT WAS AN INCREDIBLE FIGHT.

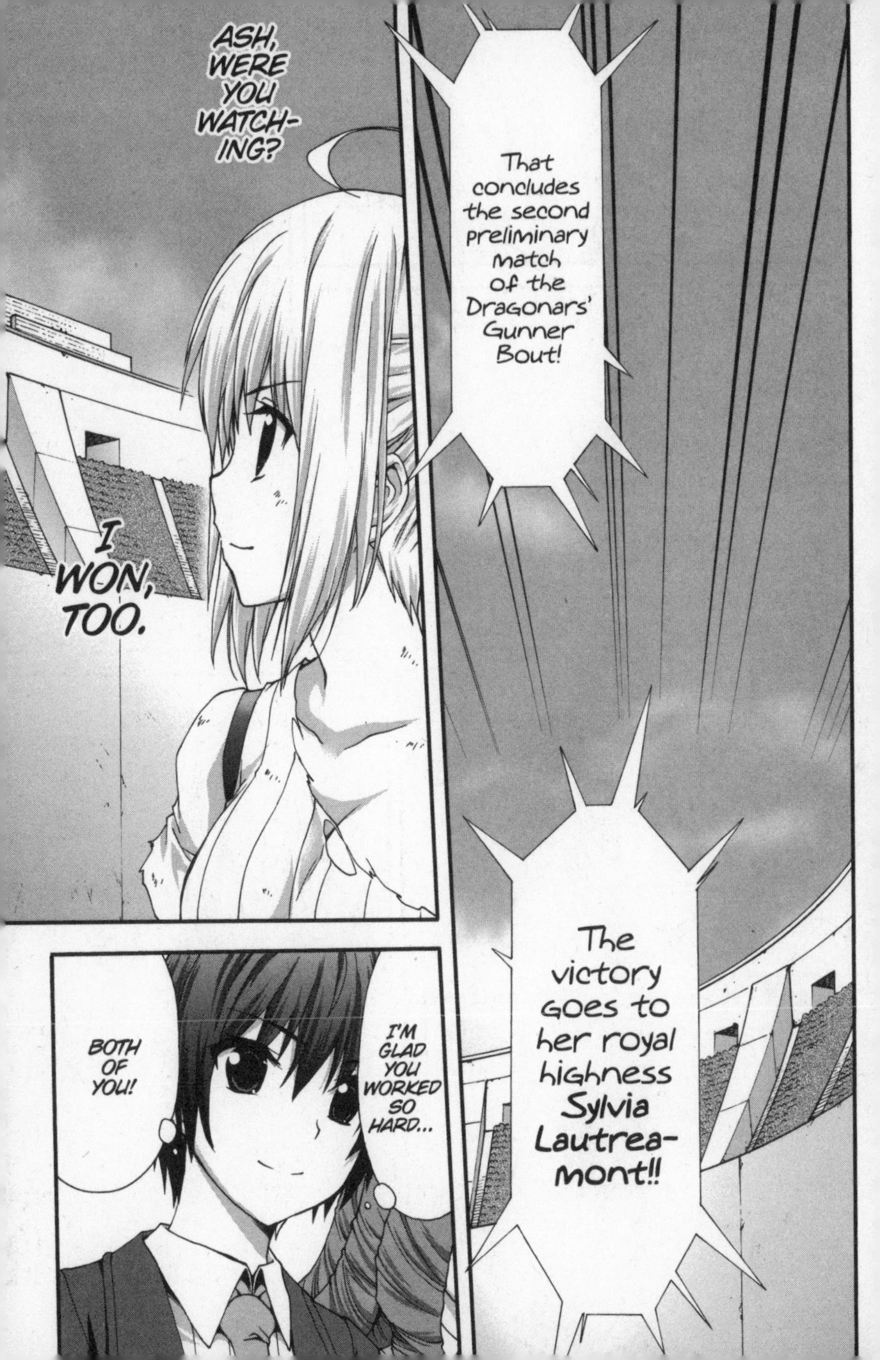
That concludes the second preliminary match of the Dragonars' Gunner Bout!
The victory goes to her royal highness Sylvia Lautrea-mont!!
ASH, WERE YOU WATCH-ING?
I WON, TOO.
I'M GLAD YOU WORKED SO HARD...
BOTH OF YOU!

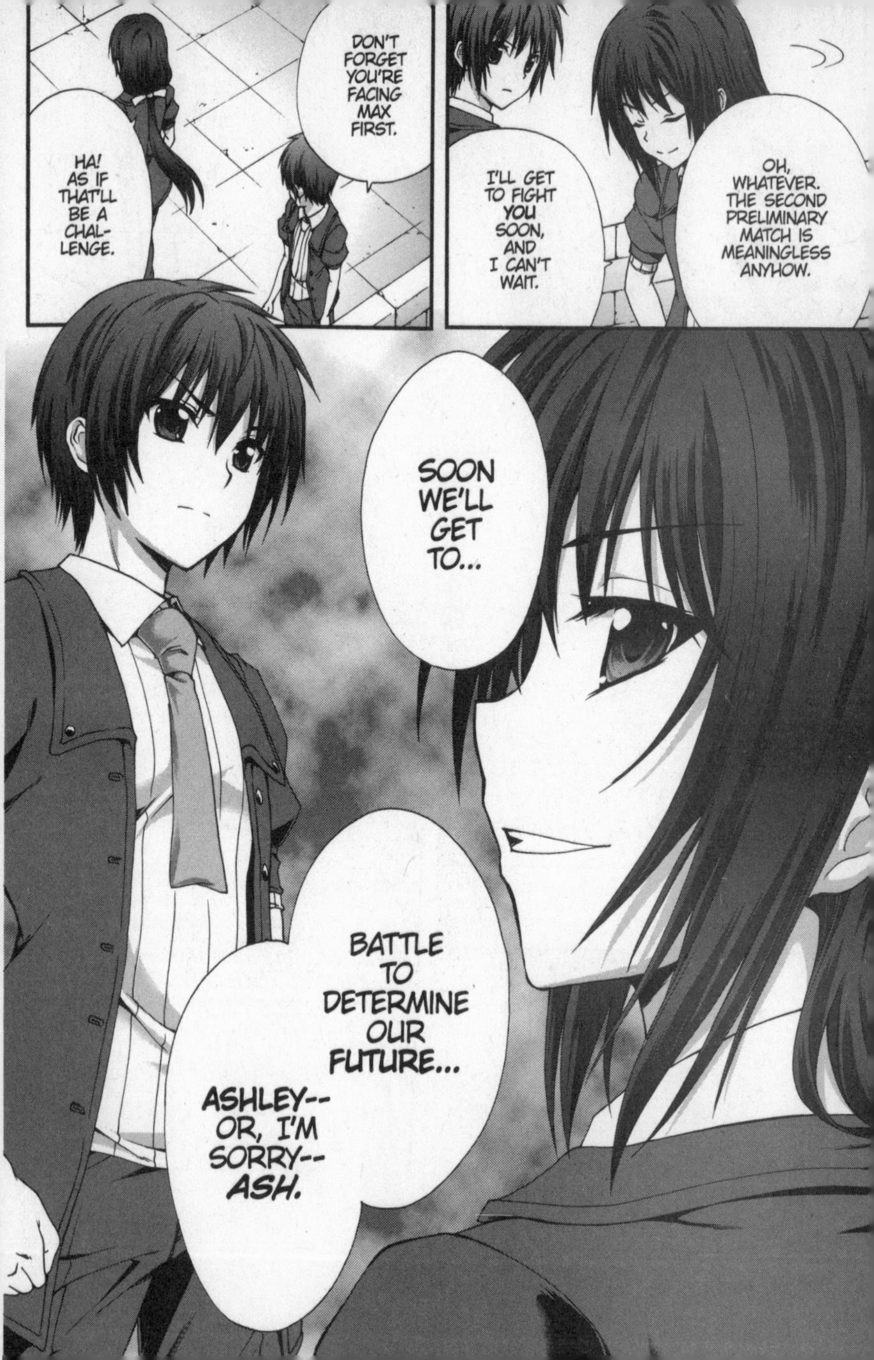
OH, WHATEVER. THE SECOND PRELIMINARY MATCH IS MEANINGLESS ANYHOW.
I'LL GET TO FIGHT YOU SOON, AND I CAN'T WAIT.
DON'T FORGET YOU'RE FACING MAX FIRST.
HA! AS IF THAT'LL BE A CHAL-LENGE.
SOON WE'LL GET TO...
BATTLE TO DETERMINE OUR FUTURE...
ASHLEY-- OR, I'M SORRY-- ASH.

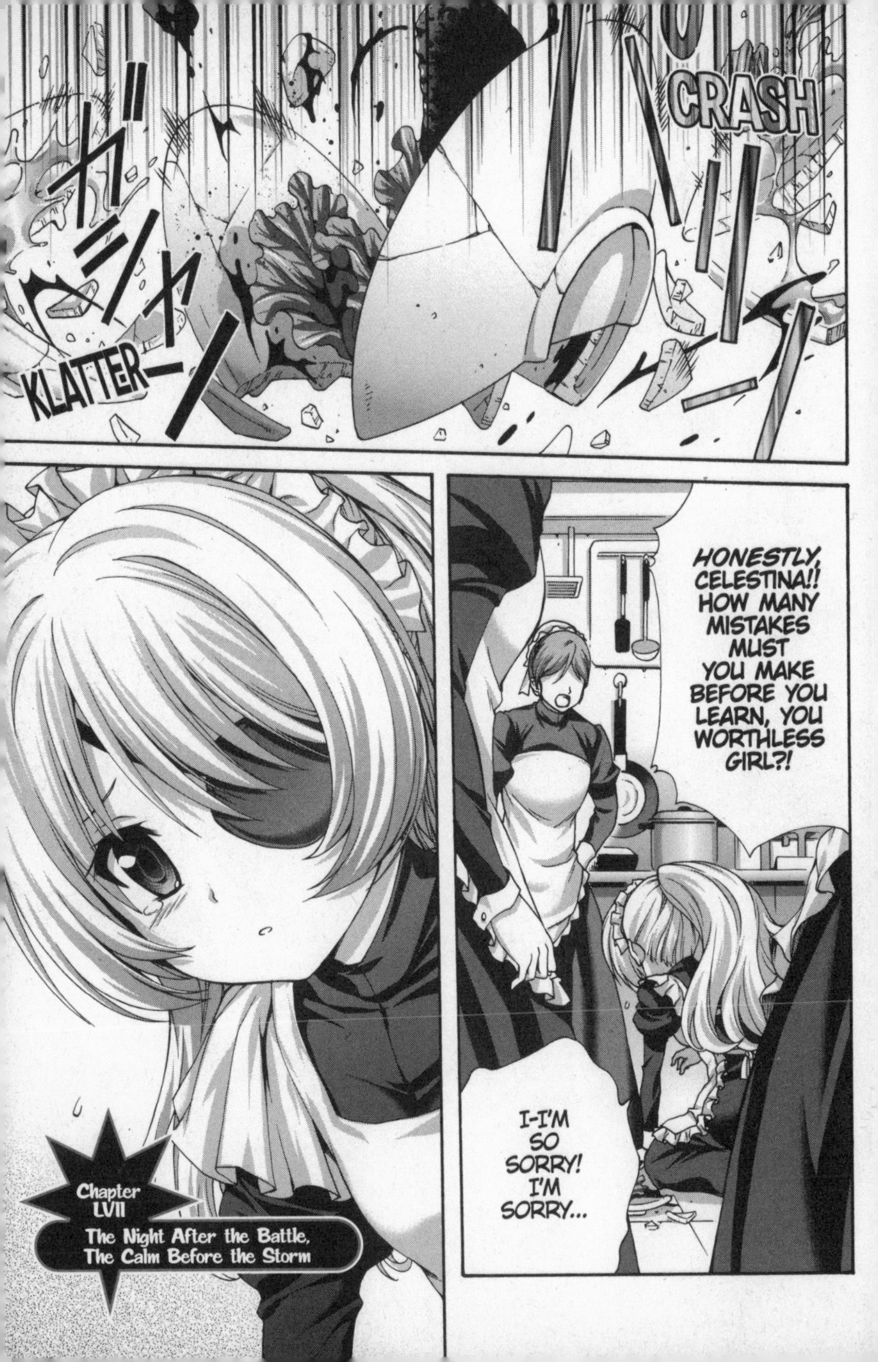
CRASH
ガシャン
KLATTER
HONESTLY, CELESTINA!! HOW MANY MISTAKES MUST YOU MAKE BEFORE YOU LEARN, YOU WORTHLESS GIRL?!
I-I'M SO SORRY! I'M SORRY...
Chapter LVII
The Night After the Battle, The Calm Before the Storm

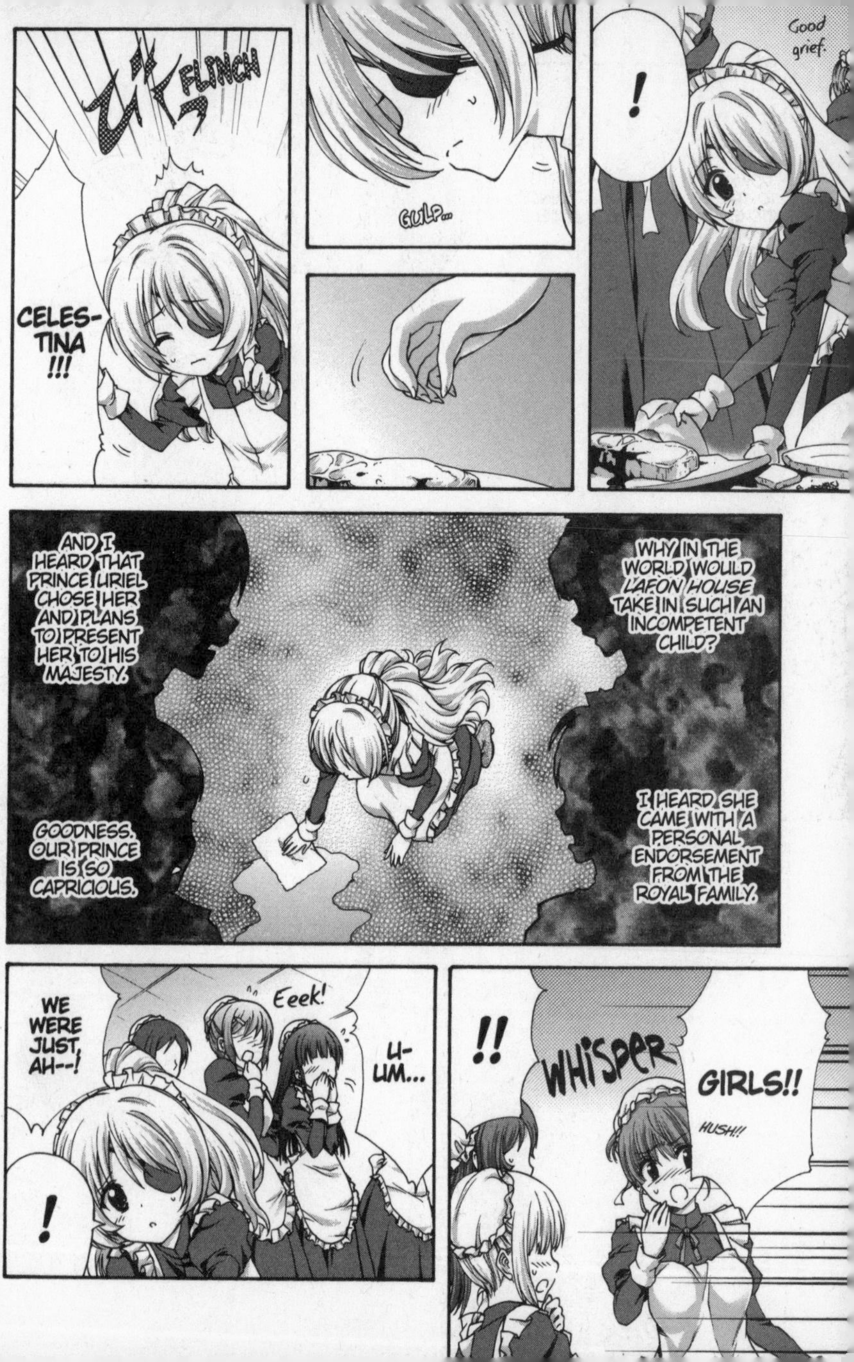
Good grief.
!
GULP...
FLINCH
CELES-TINA!!!
WHY IN THE WORLD WOULD LAFON HOUSE TAKE IN SUCH AN INCOMPETENT CHILD?
I HEARD SHE CAME WITH A PERSONAL ENDORSEMENT FROM THE ROYAL FAMILY.
AND I HEARD THAT PRINCE URIEL CHOSE HER AND PLANS TO PRESENT HER TO HIS MAJESTY.
GOODNESS. OUR PRINCE IS SO CAPRICIOUS.
GIRLS!!
HUSH!!
WHISPER
!!
Eeek!
U-UM...
WE WERE JUST, AH--!
!

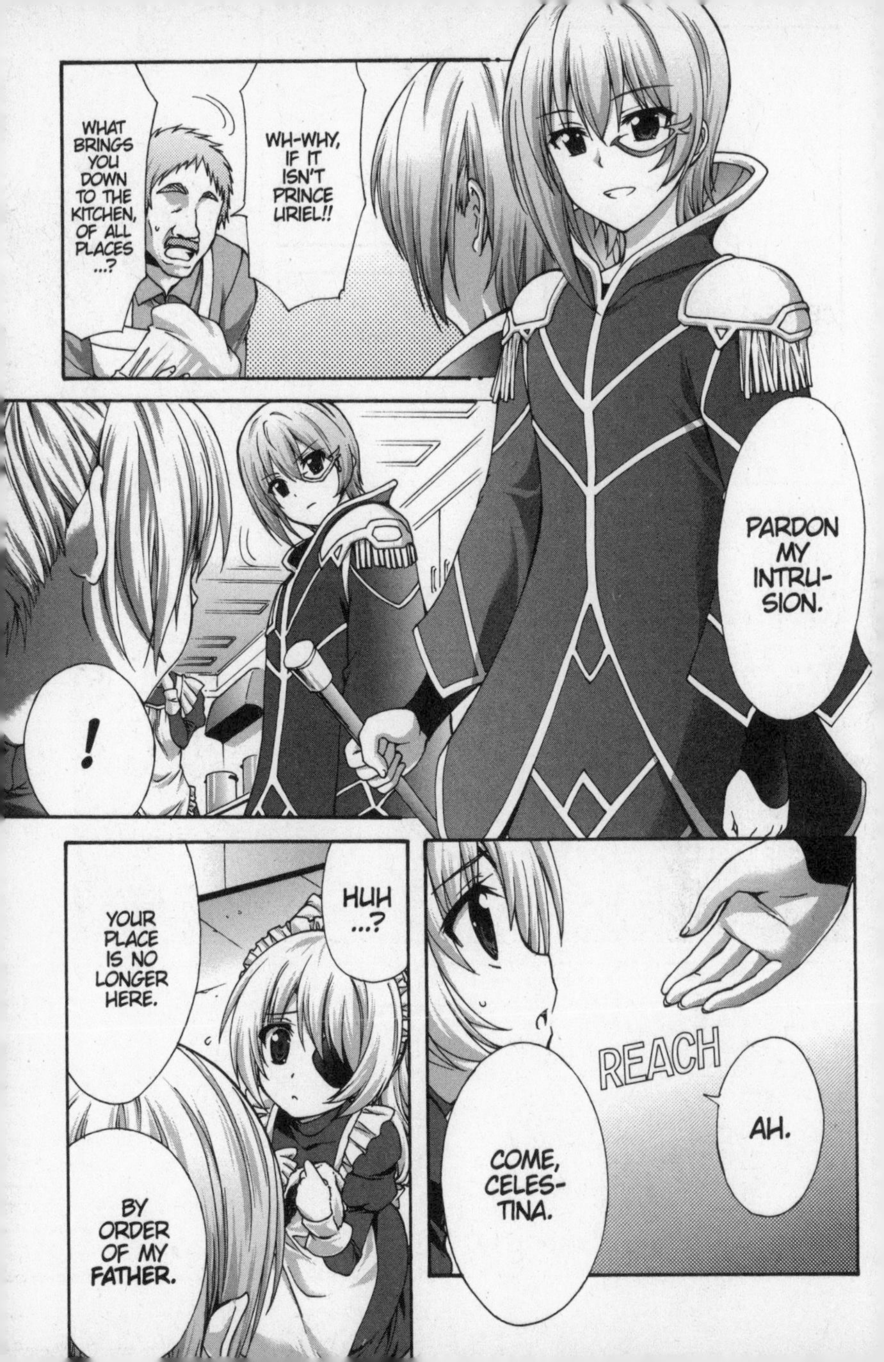
WH-WHY, IF IT ISN'T PRINCE URIEL!!
WHAT BRINGS YOU DOWN TO THE KITCHEN, OF ALL PLACES ...?
PARDON MY INTRU-SION.
!
AH.
REACH
COME, CELES-TINA.
HUH ...?
YOUR PLACE IS NO LONGER HERE.
BY ORDER OF MY FATHER.

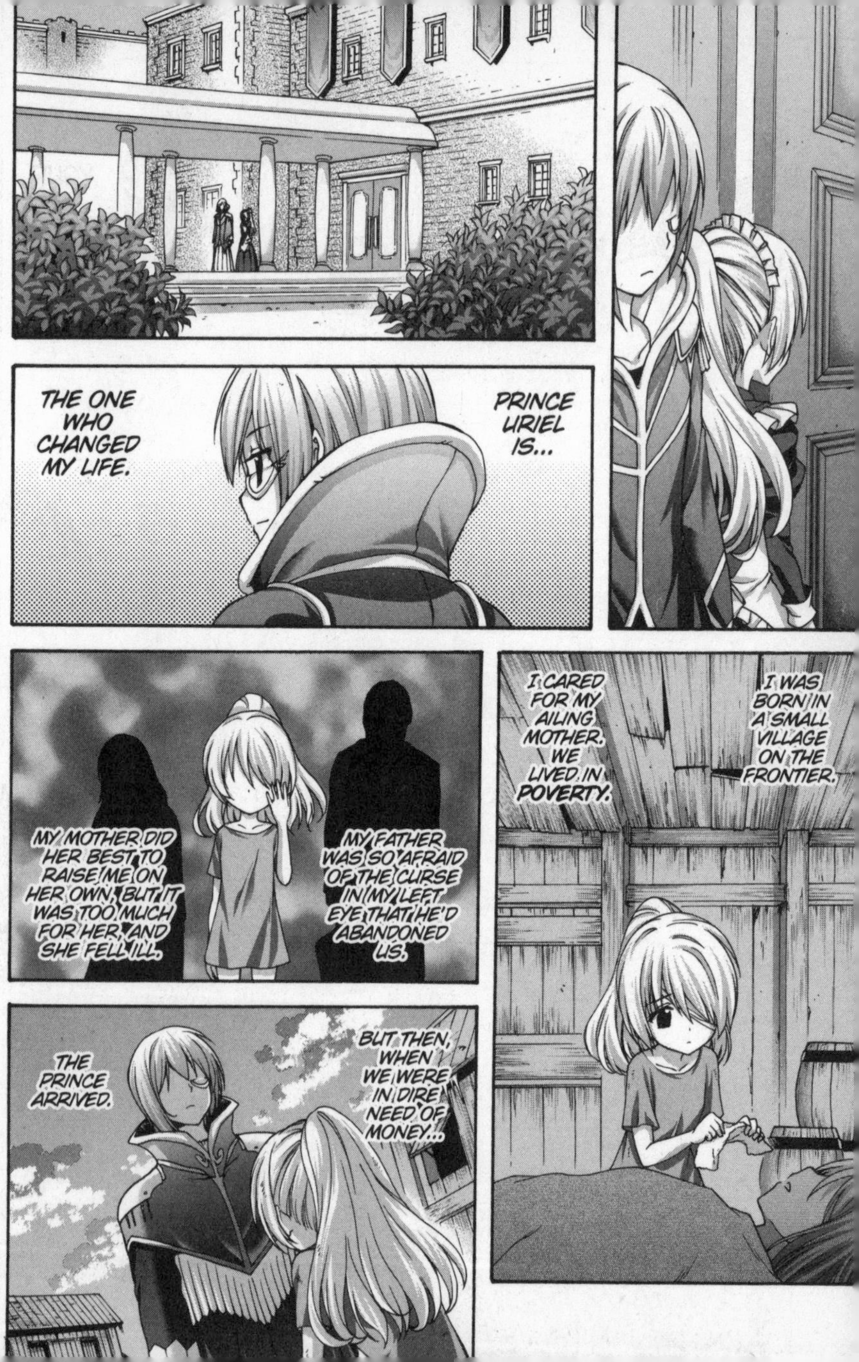
PRINCE URIEL IS...
THE ONE WHO CHANGED MY LIFE.
I WAS BORN IN A SMALL VILLAGE ON THE FRONTIER.
I CARED FOR MY AILING MOTHER. WE LIVED IN POVERTY.
MY FATHER WAS SO AFRAID OF THE CURSE IN MY LEFT EYE THAT HE'D ABANDONED US.
MY MOTHER DID HER BEST TO RAISE ME ON HER OWN, BUT IT WAS TOO MUCH FOR HER, AND SHE FELL ILL.
BUT THEN, WHEN WE WERE IN DIRE NEED OF MONEY...
THE PRINCE ARRIVED.

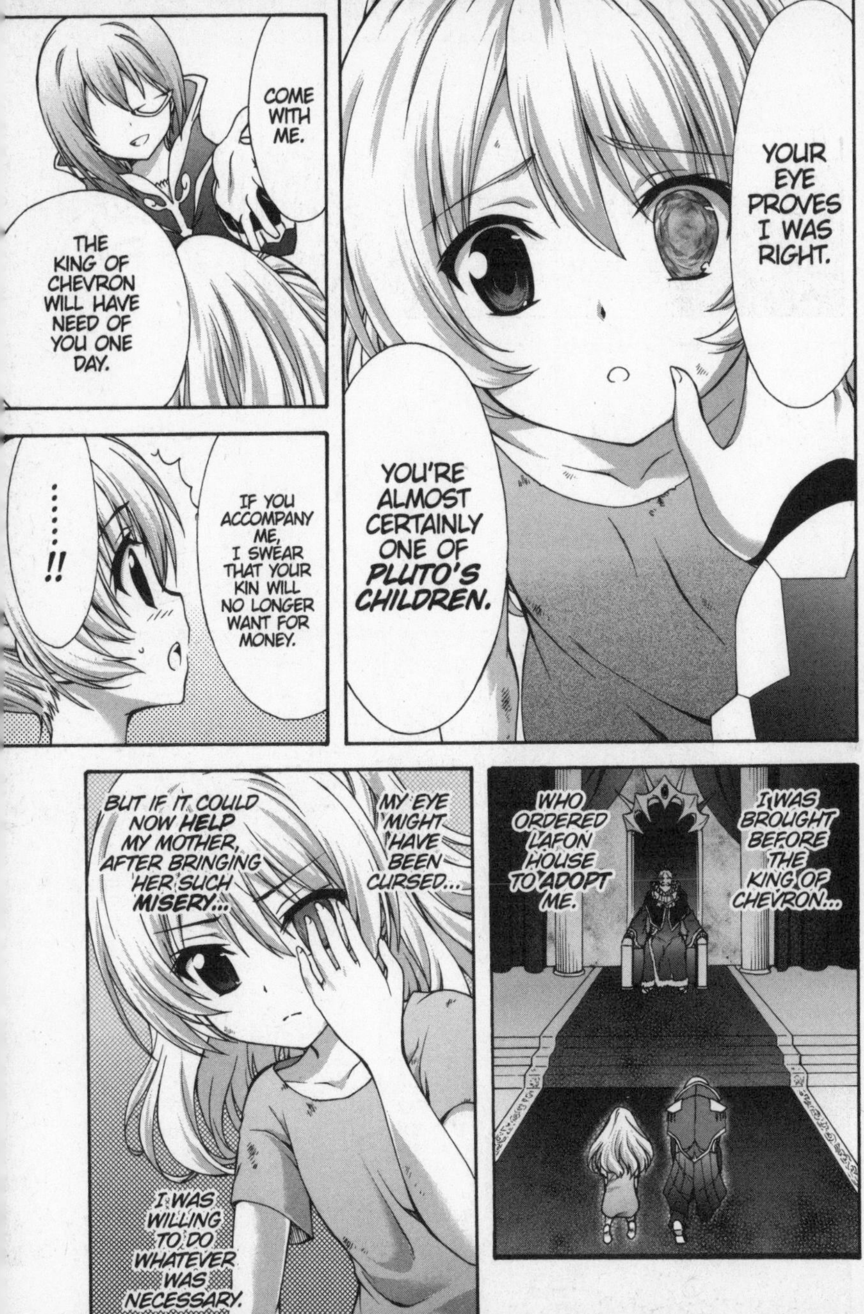
YOUR EYE PROVES I WAS RIGHT.
YOU'RE ALMOST CERTAINLY ONE OF PLUTO'S CHILDREN.
COME WITH ME.
THE KING OF CHEVRON WILL HAVE NEED OF YOU ONE DAY.
IF YOU ACCOMPANY ME, I SWEAR THAT YOUR KIN WILL NO LONGER WANT FOR MONEY.
......!!
I WAS BROUGHT BEFORE THE KING OF CHEVRON...
WHO ORDERED LAFON HOUSE TO ADOPT ME.
MY EYE MIGHT HAVE BEEN CURSED...
BUT IF IT COULD NOW HELP MY MOTHER, AFTER BRINGING HER SUCH MISERY...
I WAS WILLING TO DO WHATEVER WAS NECESSARY.

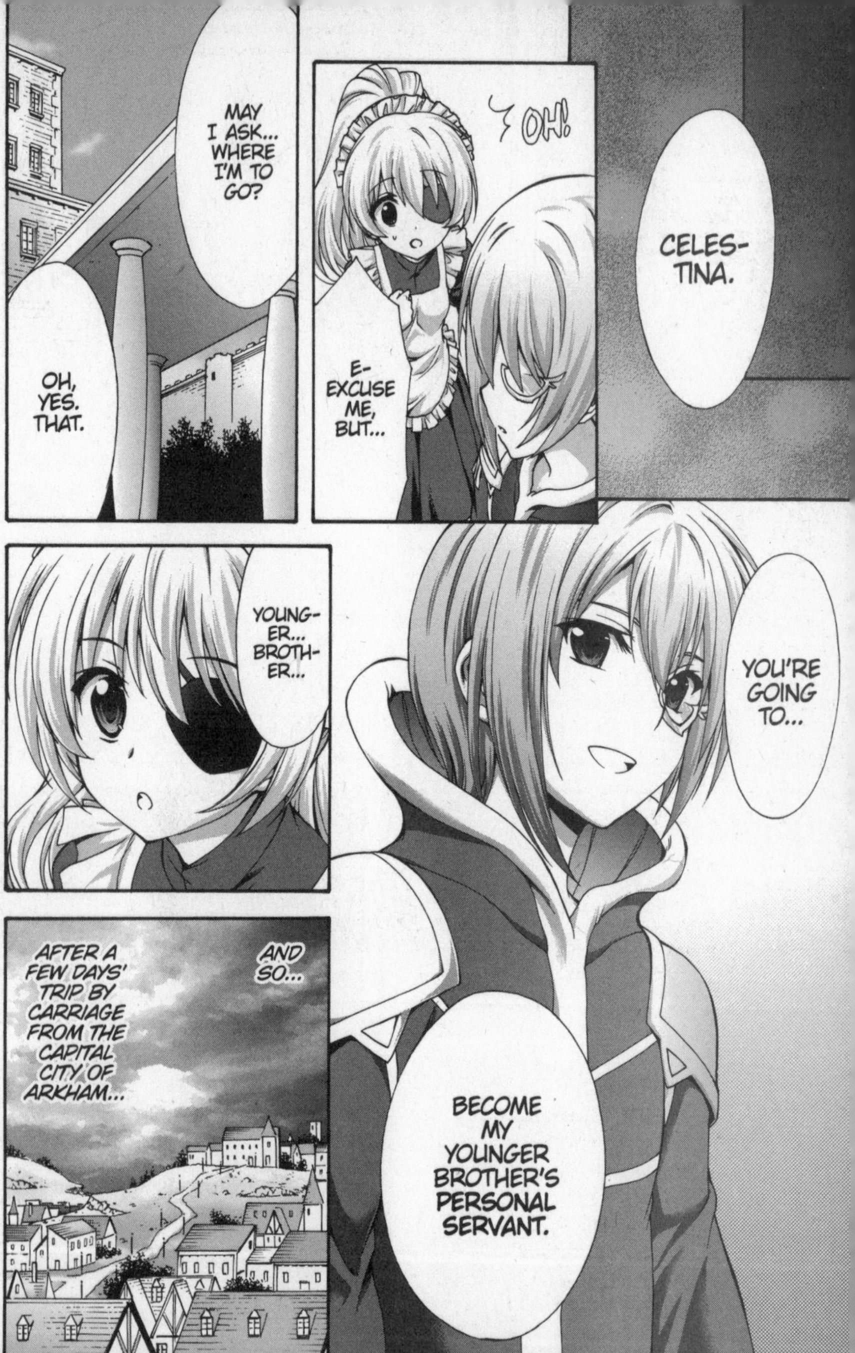
CELES-TINA.
OH!
E-EXCUSE ME, BUT...
MAY I ASK... WHERE I'M TO GO?
OH, YES. THAT.
YOU'RE GOING TO...
BECOME MY YOUNGER BROTHER'S PERSONAL SERVANT.
YOUNG-ER... BROTH-ER...
AND SO...
AFTER A FEW DAYS' TRIP BY CARRIAGE FROM THE CAPITAL CITY OF ARKHAM...

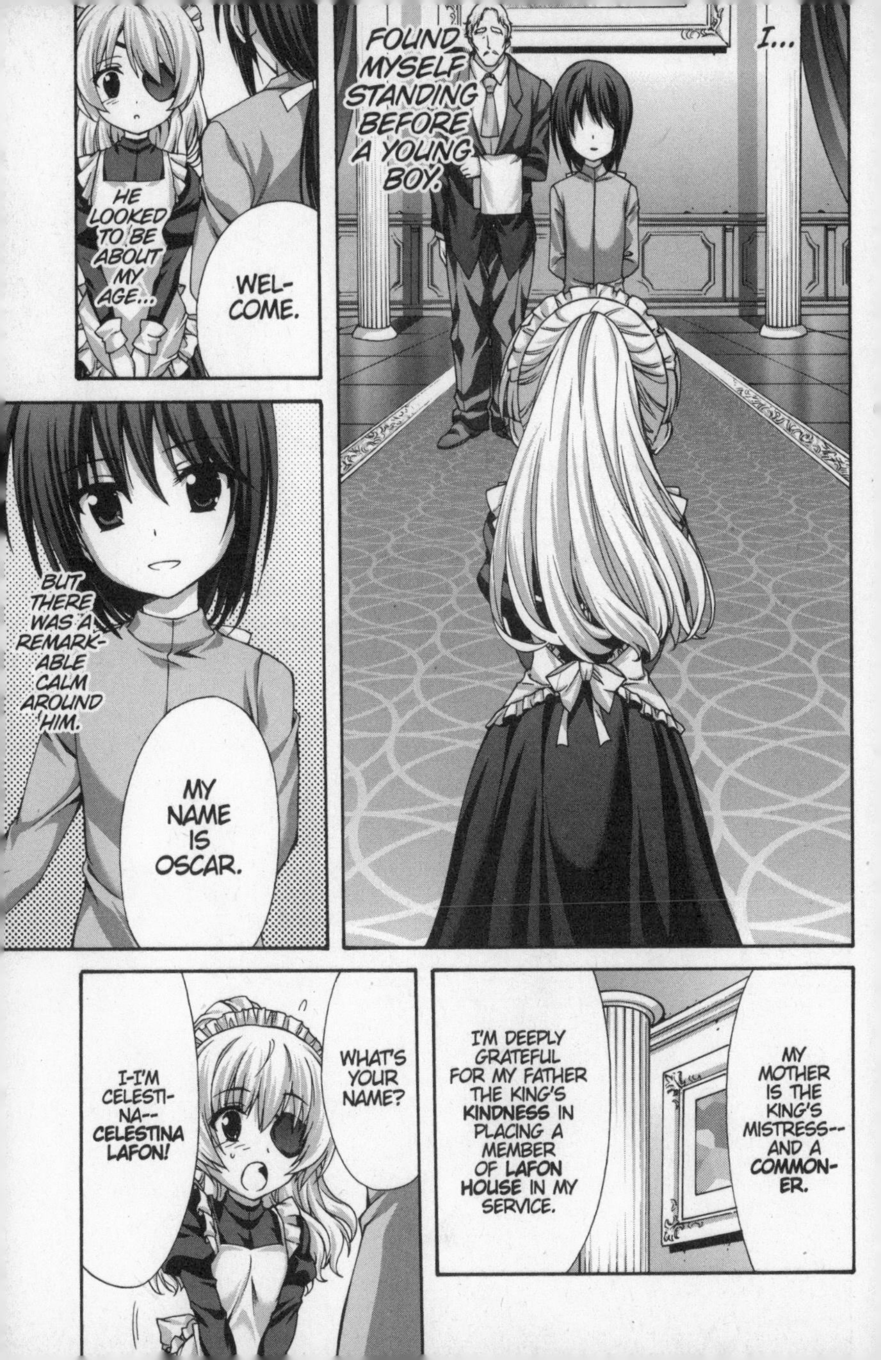
I...
FOUND MYSELF STANDING BEFORE A YOUNG BOY.
HE LOOKED TO BE ABOUT MY AGE...
WEL-COME.
BUT THERE WAS A REMARK-ABLE CALM AROUND HIM.
MY NAME IS OSCAR.
MY MOTHER IS THE KING'S MISTRESS-- AND A COMMON-ER.
I'M DEEPLY GRATEFUL FOR MY FATHER THE KING'S KINDNESS IN PLACING A MEMBER OF LAFON HOUSE IN MY SERVICE.
WHAT'S YOUR NAME?
I-I'M CELESTI-NA-- CELESTINA LAFON!

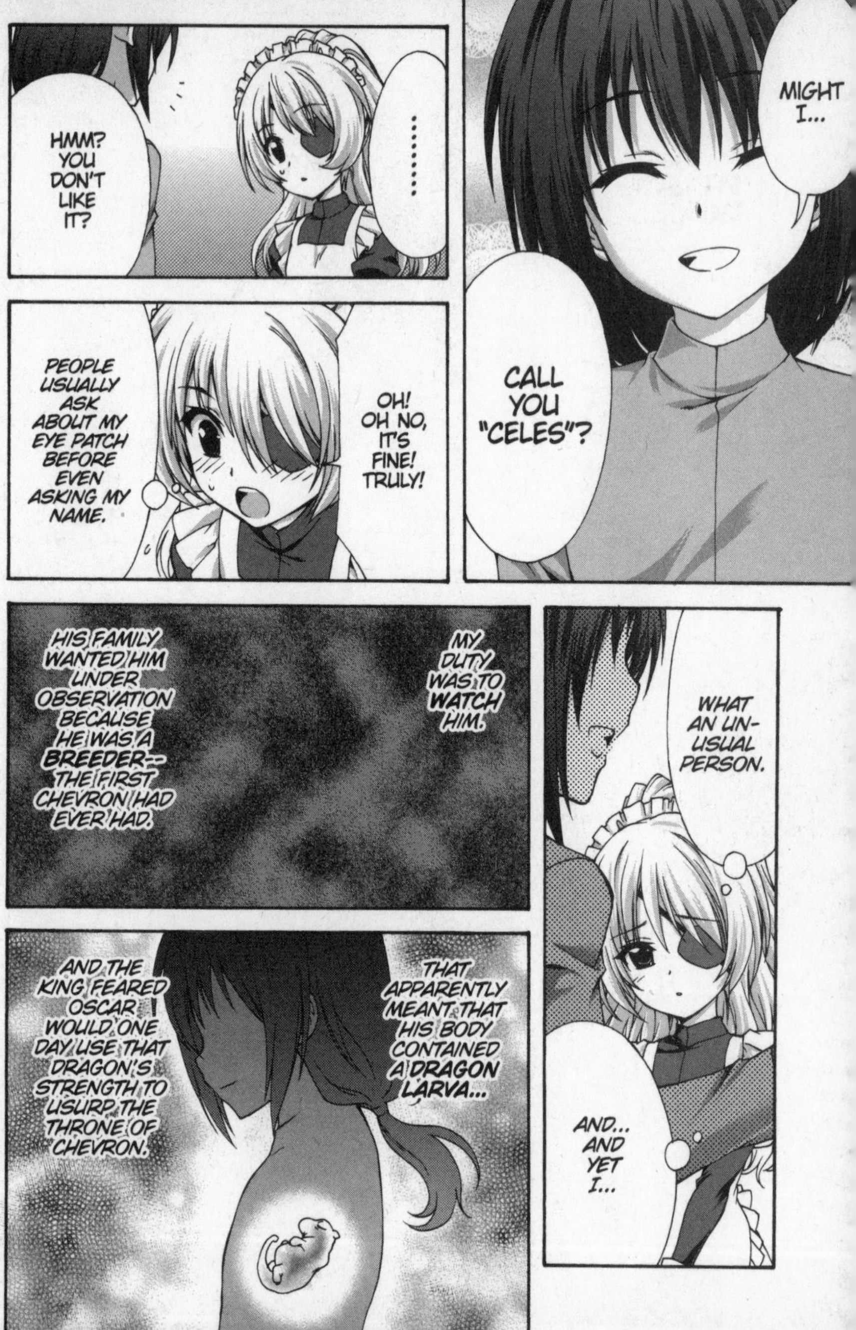
MIGHT I...
CALL YOU "CELES"?
......
HMM? YOU DON'T LIKE IT?
OH! OH NO, IT'S FINE! TRULY!
PEOPLE USUALLY ASK ABOUT MY EYE PATCH BEFORE EVEN ASKING MY NAME.
WHAT AN UN-USUAL PERSON.
AND... AND YET I...
MY DUTY WAS TO WATCH HIM.
HIS FAMILY WANTED HIM UNDER OBSERVATION BECAUSE HE WAS A BREEDER-- THE FIRST CHEVRON HAD EVER HAD.
THAT APPARENTLY MEANT THAT HIS BODY CONTAINED A DRAGON LARVA...
AND THE KING FEARED OSCAR WOULD ONE DAY USE THAT DRAGON'S STRENGTH TO USURP THE THRONE OF CHEVRON.

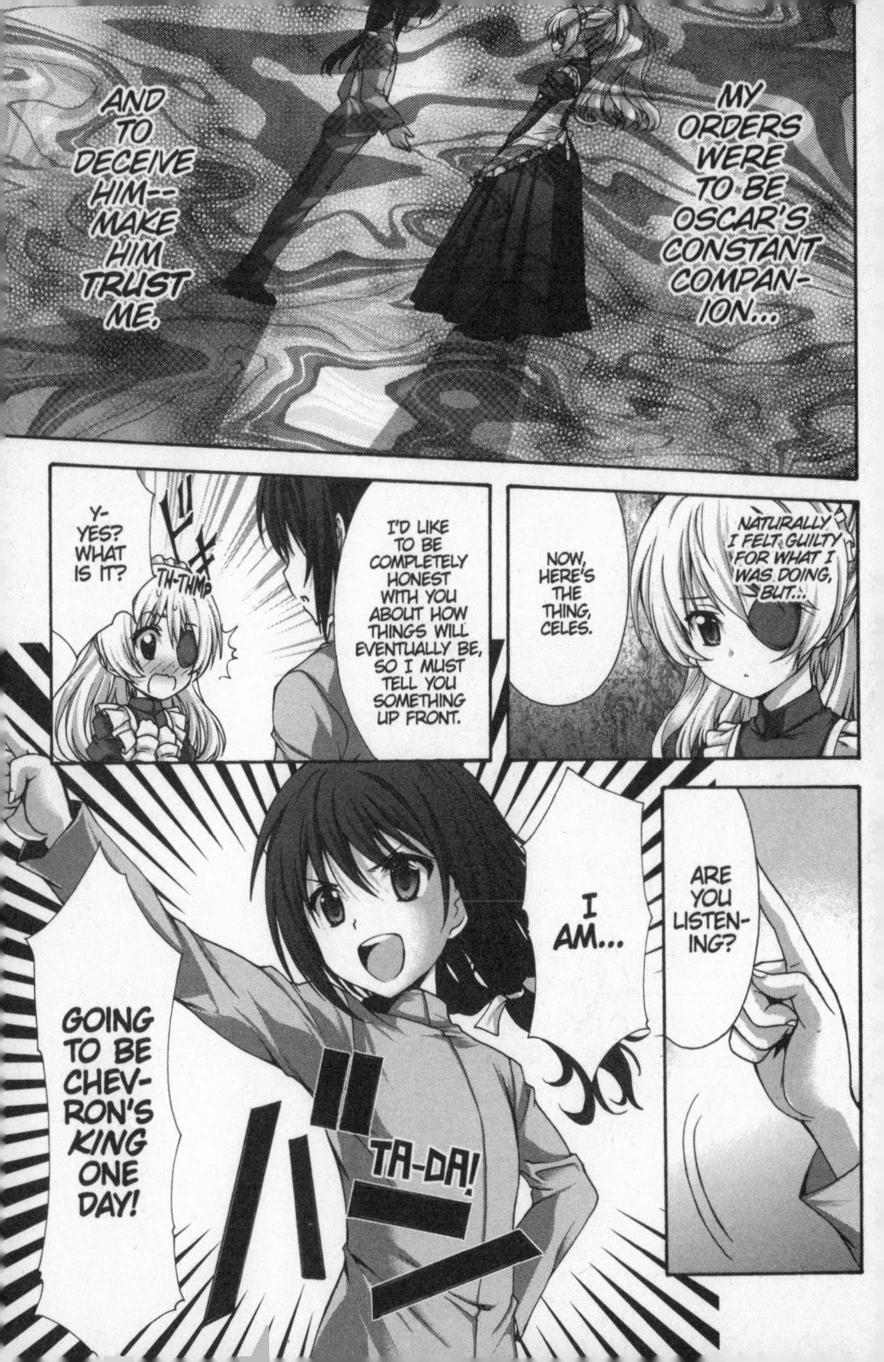
MY ORDERS WERE TO BE OSCAR'S CONSTANT COMPANION...
AND TO DECEIVE HIM--MAKE HIM TRUST ME.
NATURALLY I FELT GUILTY FOR WHAT I WAS DOING, BUT...
NOW, HERE'S THE THING, CELES.
I'D LIKE TO BE COMPLETELY HONEST WITH YOU ABOUT HOW THINGS WILL EVENTUALLY BE, SO I MUST TELL YOU SOMETHING UP FRONT.
Y-YES? WHAT IS IT?
TH-THMP
ARE YOU LISTENING?
I AM...
GOING TO BE CHEVRON'S KING ONE DAY!
TA-DA!

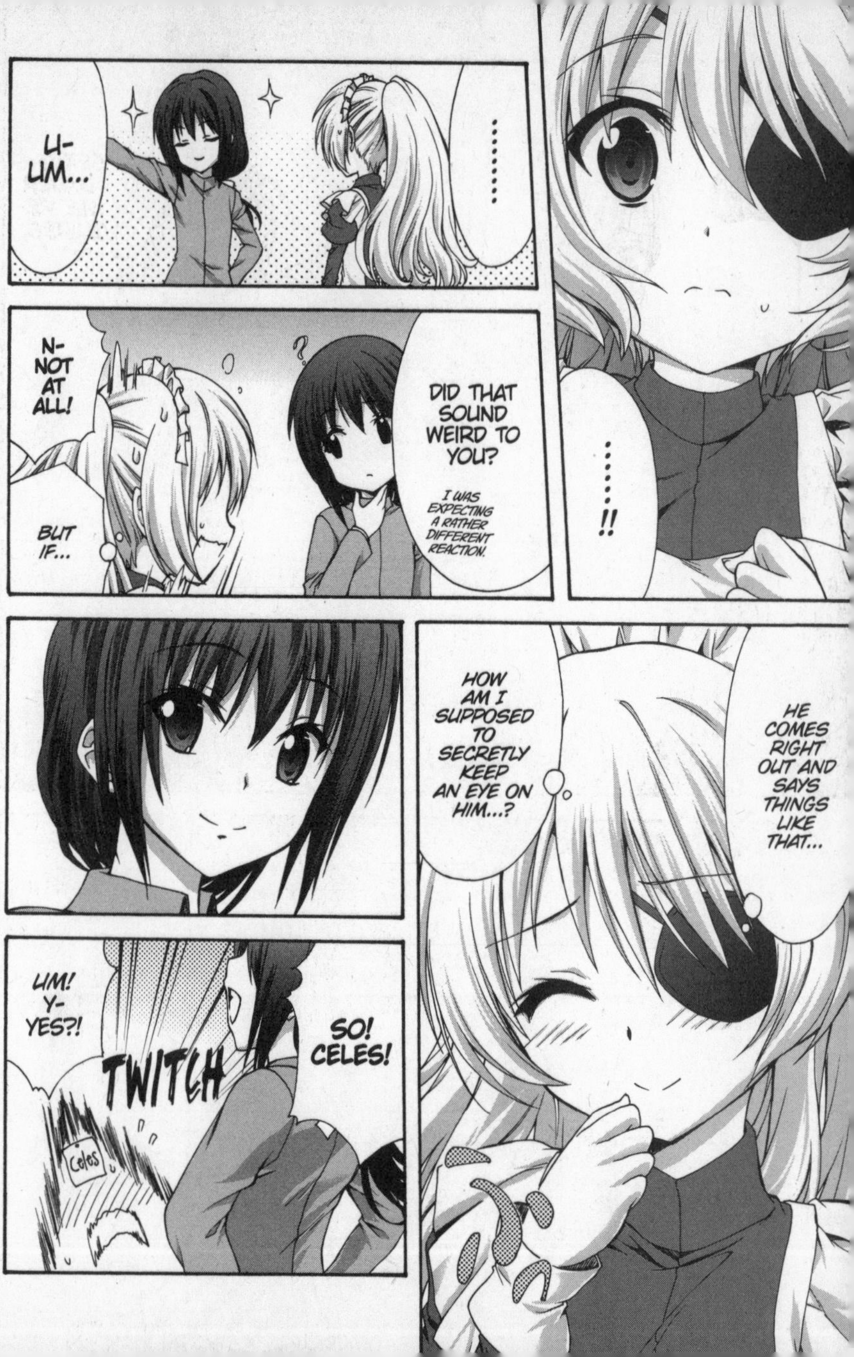
……!!
……
U-UM...
DID THAT SOUND WEIRD TO YOU?
I WAS EXPECTING A RATHER DIFFERENT REACTION.
N-NOT AT ALL!
BUT IF...
HE COMES RIGHT OUT AND SAYS THINGS LIKE THAT...
HOW AM I SUPPOSED TO SECRETLY KEEP AN EYE ON HIM...?
SO! CELES!
UM! Y-YES?!
TWITCH
Celes

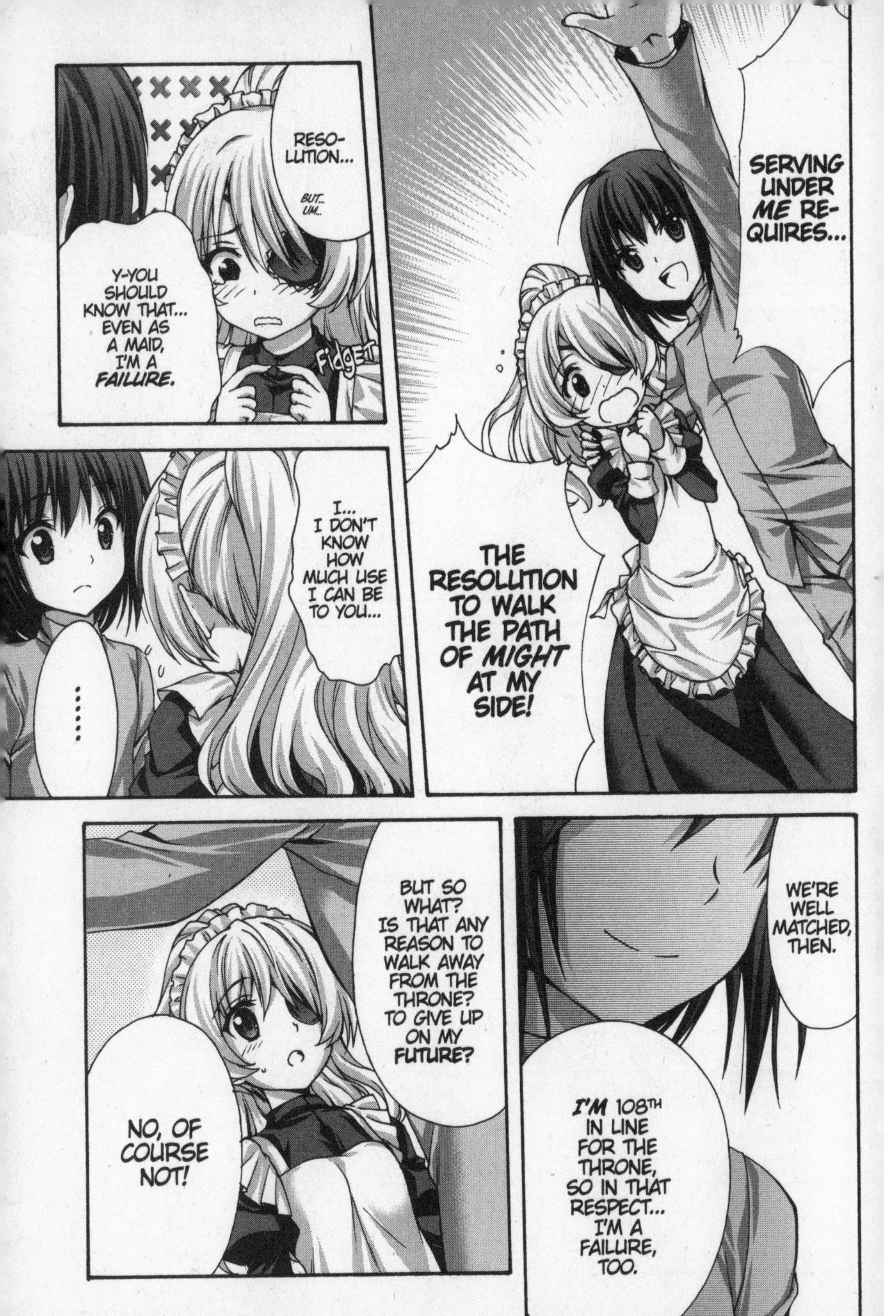

SERVING UNDER *ME* REQUIRES...
THE RESOLUTION TO WALK THE PATH OF *MIGHT* AT MY SIDE!
RESO-LUTION...
BUT... UM...
Y-YOU SHOULD KNOW THAT... EVEN AS A MAID, I'M A *FAILURE.*
FIDGET
I... I DON'T KNOW HOW MUCH USE I CAN BE TO YOU...
......
WE'RE WELL MATCHED, THEN.
I'M 108TH IN LINE FOR THE THRONE, SO IN THAT RESPECT... I'M A FAILURE, TOO.
BUT SO WHAT? IS THAT ANY REASON TO WALK AWAY FROM THE THRONE? TO GIVE UP ON MY *FUTURE?*
NO, OF COURSE NOT!

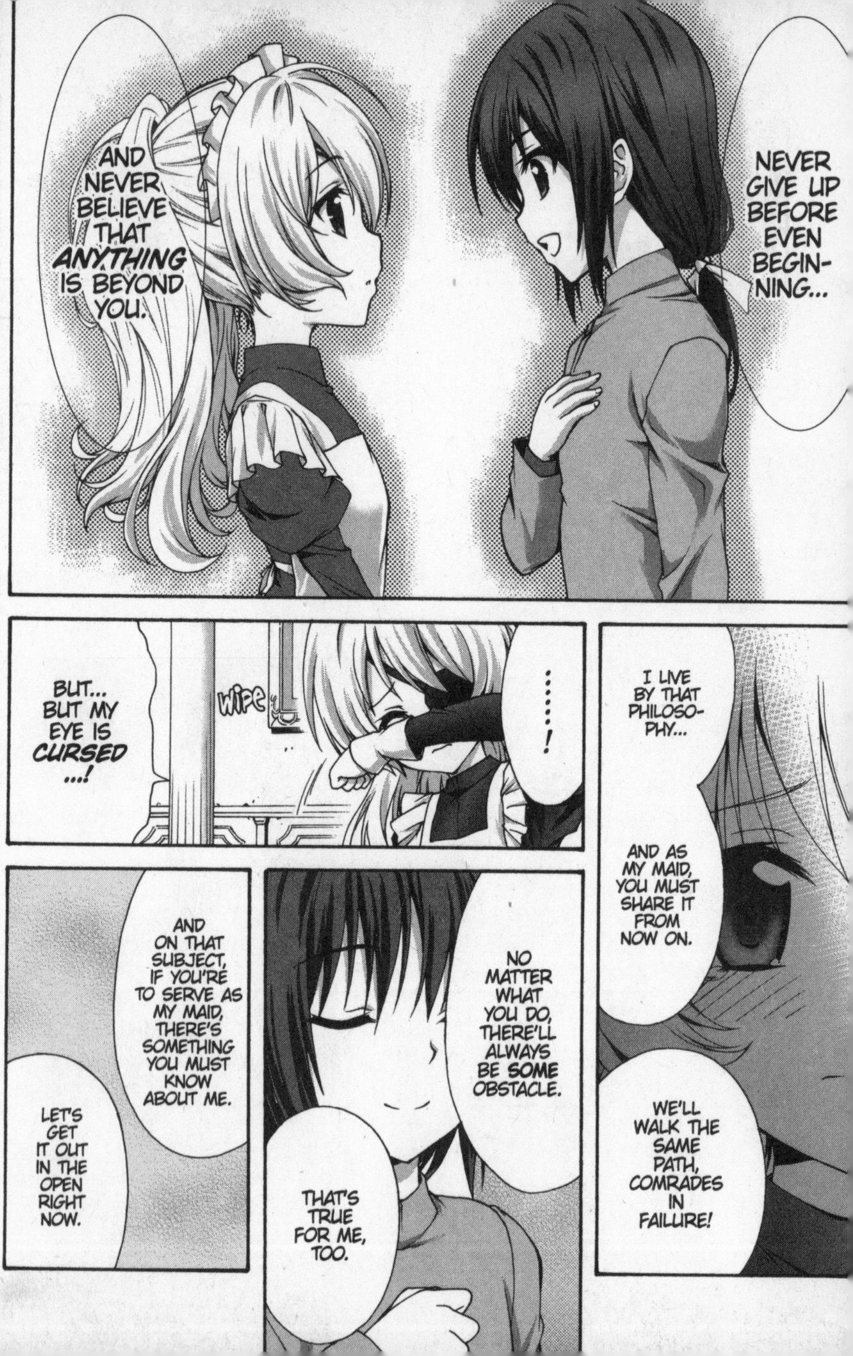
NEVER GIVE UP BEFORE EVEN BEGIN-NING...
AND NEVER BELIEVE THAT *ANYTHING* IS BEYOND YOU.
I LIVE BY THAT PHILOSO-PHY...
AND AS MY MAID, YOU MUST SHARE IT FROM NOW ON.
WE'LL WALK THE SAME PATH, COMRADES IN FAILURE!
......!
wipe
BUT... BUT MY EYE IS *CURSED* ...!
NO MATTER WHAT YOU DO, THERE'LL ALWAYS BE **SOME** OBSTACLE.
THAT'S TRUE FOR ME, TOO.
AND ON THAT SUBJECT, IF YOU'RE TO SERVE AS MY MAID, THERE'S SOMETHING YOU MUST KNOW ABOUT ME.
LET'S GET IT OUT IN THE OPEN RIGHT NOW.

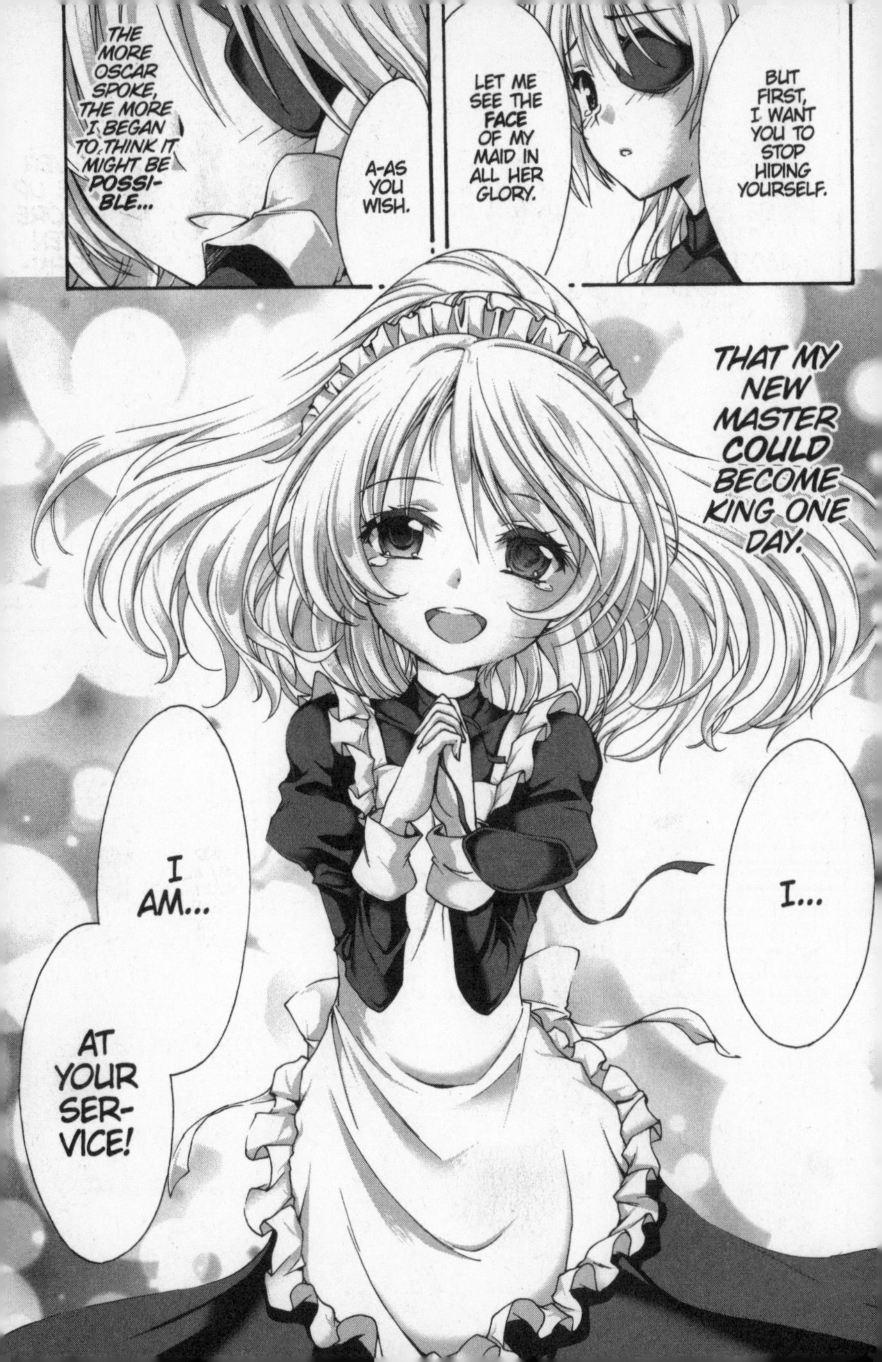
BUT FIRST, I WANT YOU TO STOP HIDING YOURSELF.
LET ME SEE THE FACE OF MY MAID IN ALL HER GLORY.
A-AS YOU WISH.
THE MORE OSCAR SPOKE, THE MORE I BEGAN TO THINK IT MIGHT BE POSSI-BLE...
THAT MY NEW MASTER COULD BECOME KING ONE DAY.
I...
I AM...
AT YOUR SER-VICE!

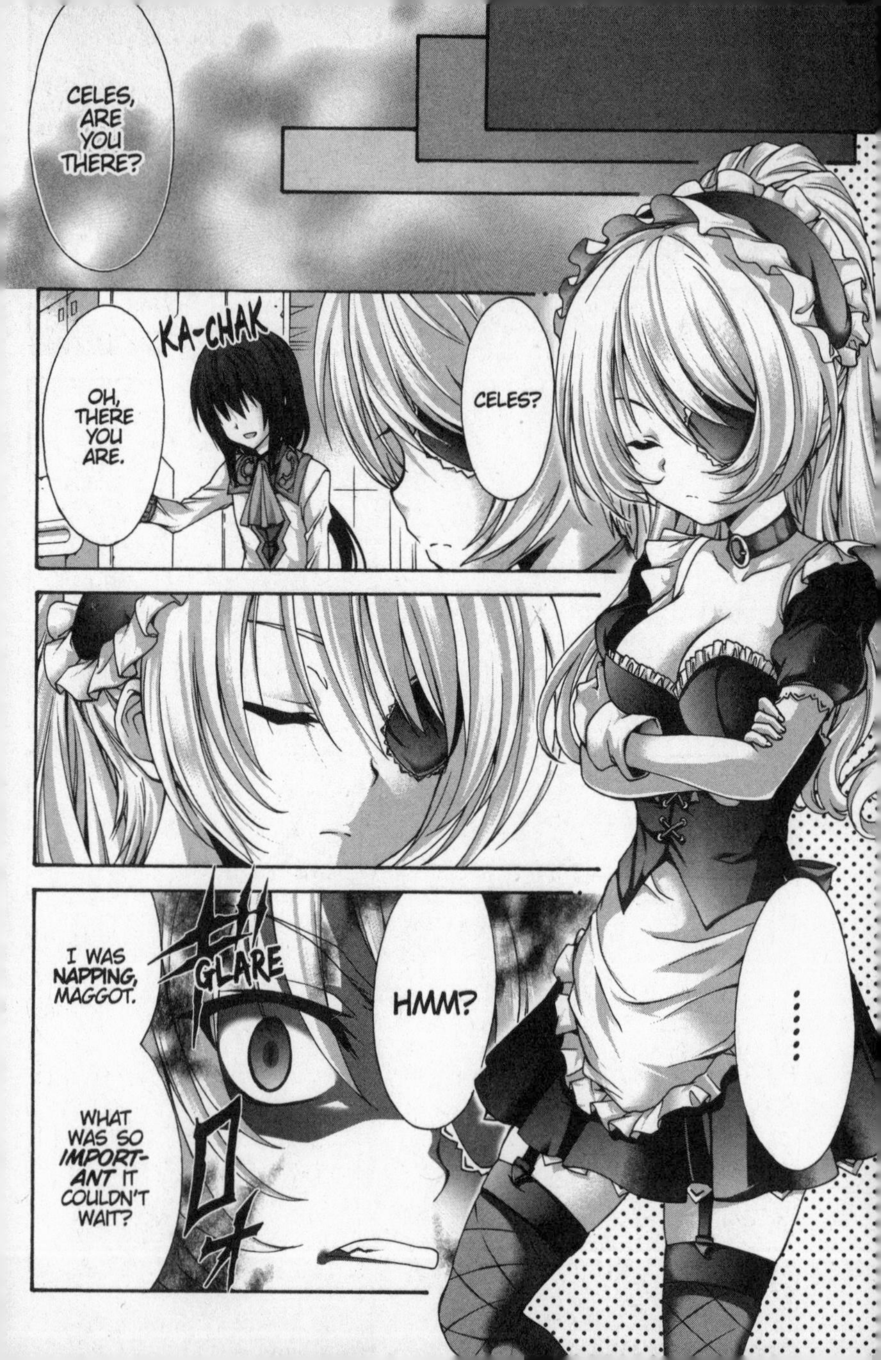
CELES, ARE YOU THERE?
CELES?
KA-CHAK
OH, THERE YOU ARE.
......
HMM?
GLARE
I WAS NAPPING, MAGGOT.
WHAT WAS SO *IMPORTANT* IT COULDN'T WAIT?

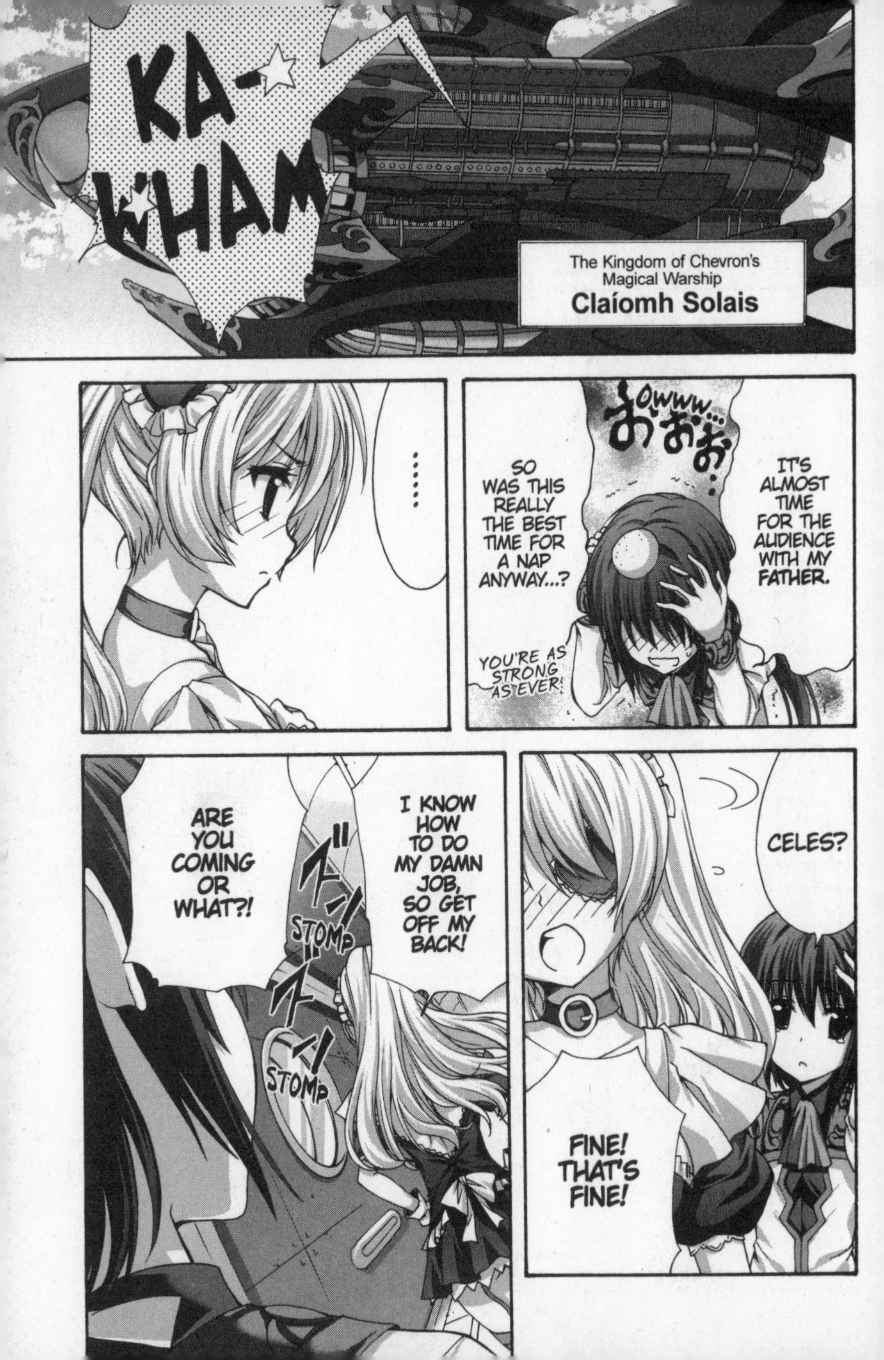
KA-WHAM
The Kingdom of Chevron's Magical Warship
Claíomh Solais
OWWW... おおお
IT'S ALMOST TIME FOR THE AUDIENCE WITH MY FATHER.
SO WAS THIS REALLY THE BEST TIME FOR A NAP ANYWAY...?
YOU'RE AS STRONG AS EVER!
......
CELES?
FINE! THAT'S FINE!
I KNOW HOW TO DO MY DAMN JOB, SO GET OFF MY BACK!
ARE YOU COMING OR WHAT?!
STOMP
STOMP

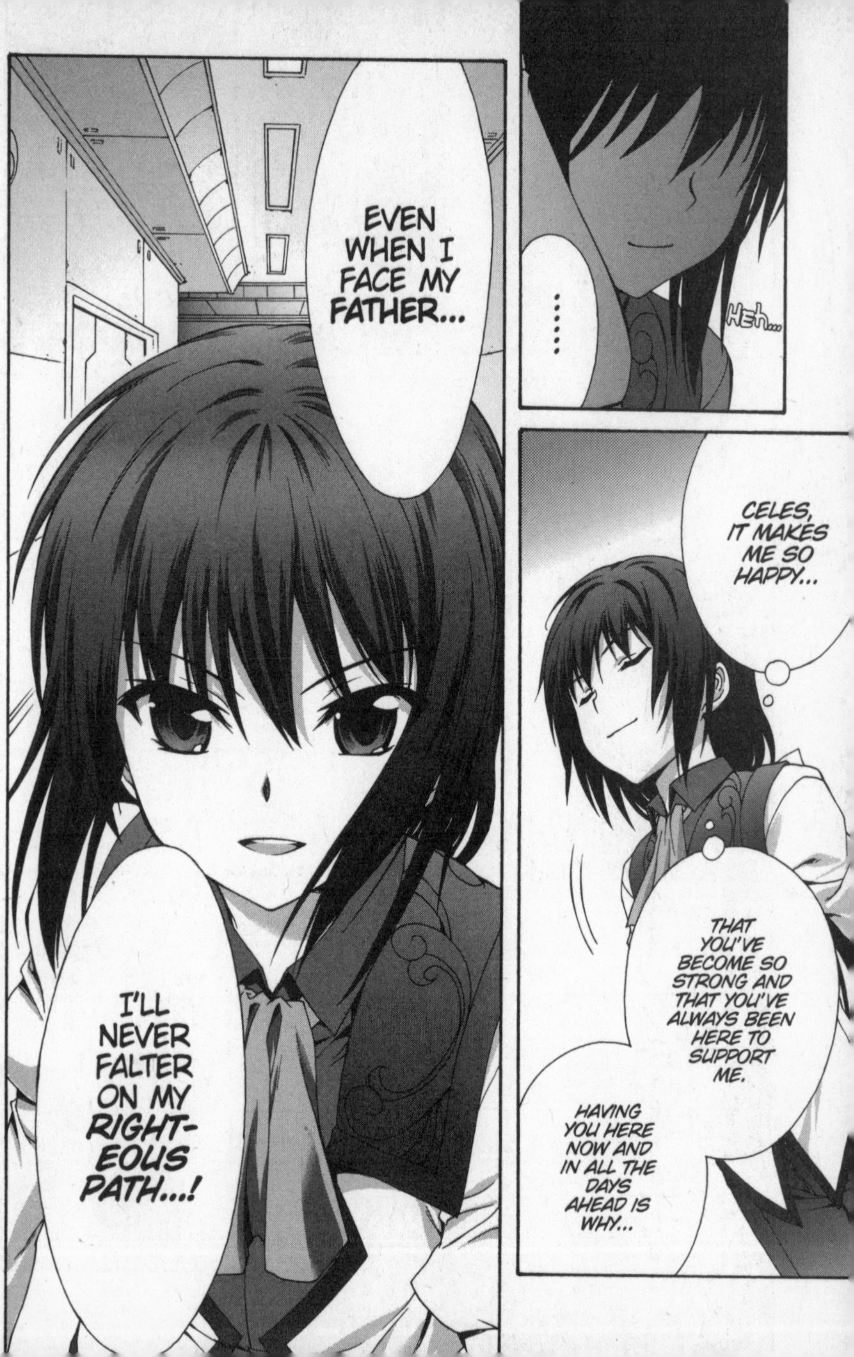
......
HEH...
CELES, IT MAKES ME SO HAPPY...
THAT YOU'VE BECOME SO STRONG AND THAT YOU'VE ALWAYS BEEN HERE TO SUPPORT ME.
HAVING YOU HERE NOW AND IN ALL THE DAYS AHEAD IS WHY...
EVEN WHEN I FACE MY FATHER...
I'LL NEVER FALTER ON MY RIGHTEOUS PATH...!

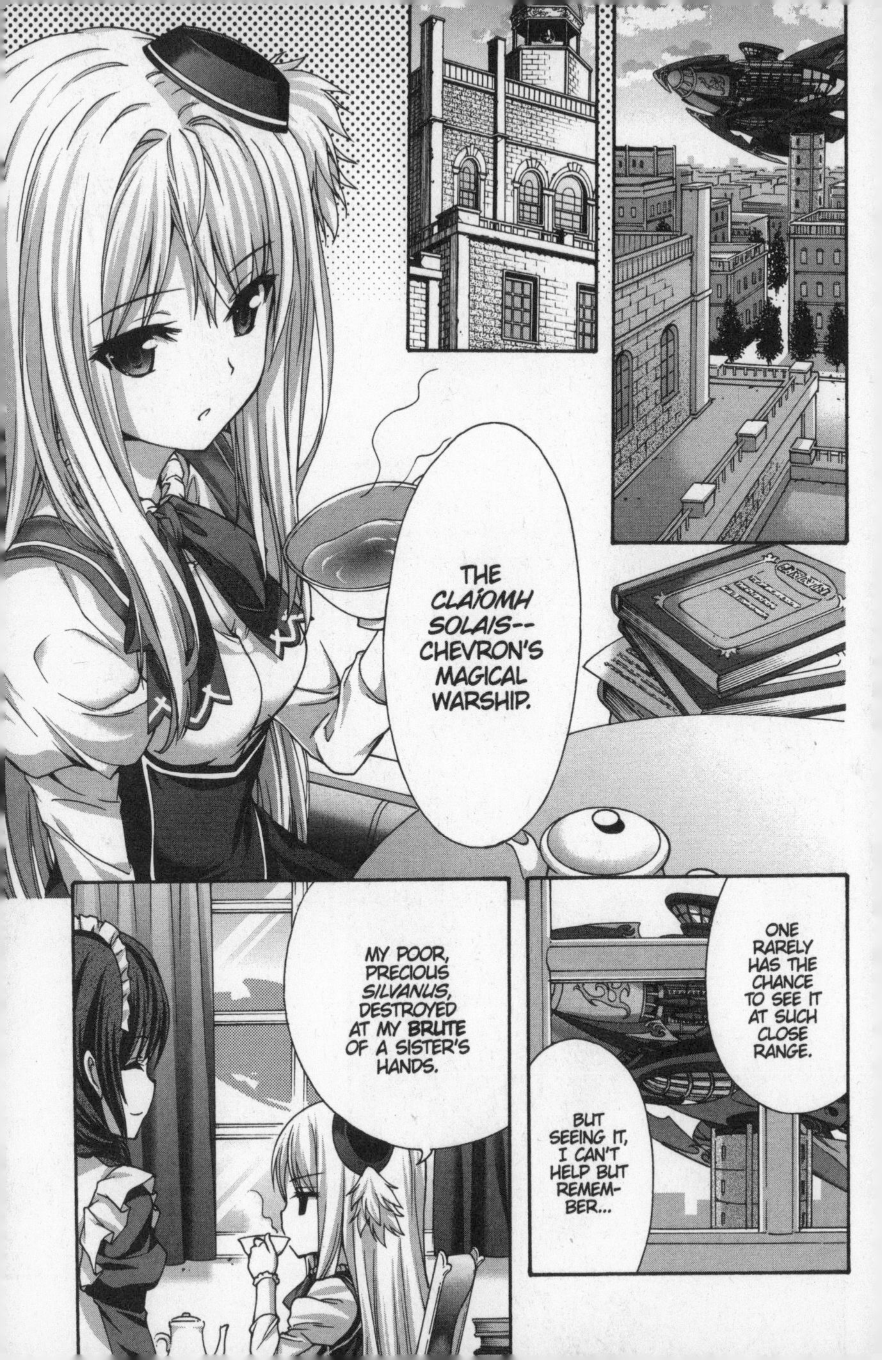
THE CLAÍOMH SOLAIS-- CHEVRON'S MAGICAL WARSHIP.
ONE RARELY HAS THE CHANCE TO SEE IT AT SUCH CLOSE RANGE.
BUT SEEING IT, I CAN'T HELP BUT REMEM-BER...
MY POOR, PRECIOUS SILVANUS, DESTROYED AT MY BRUTE OF A SISTER'S HANDS.

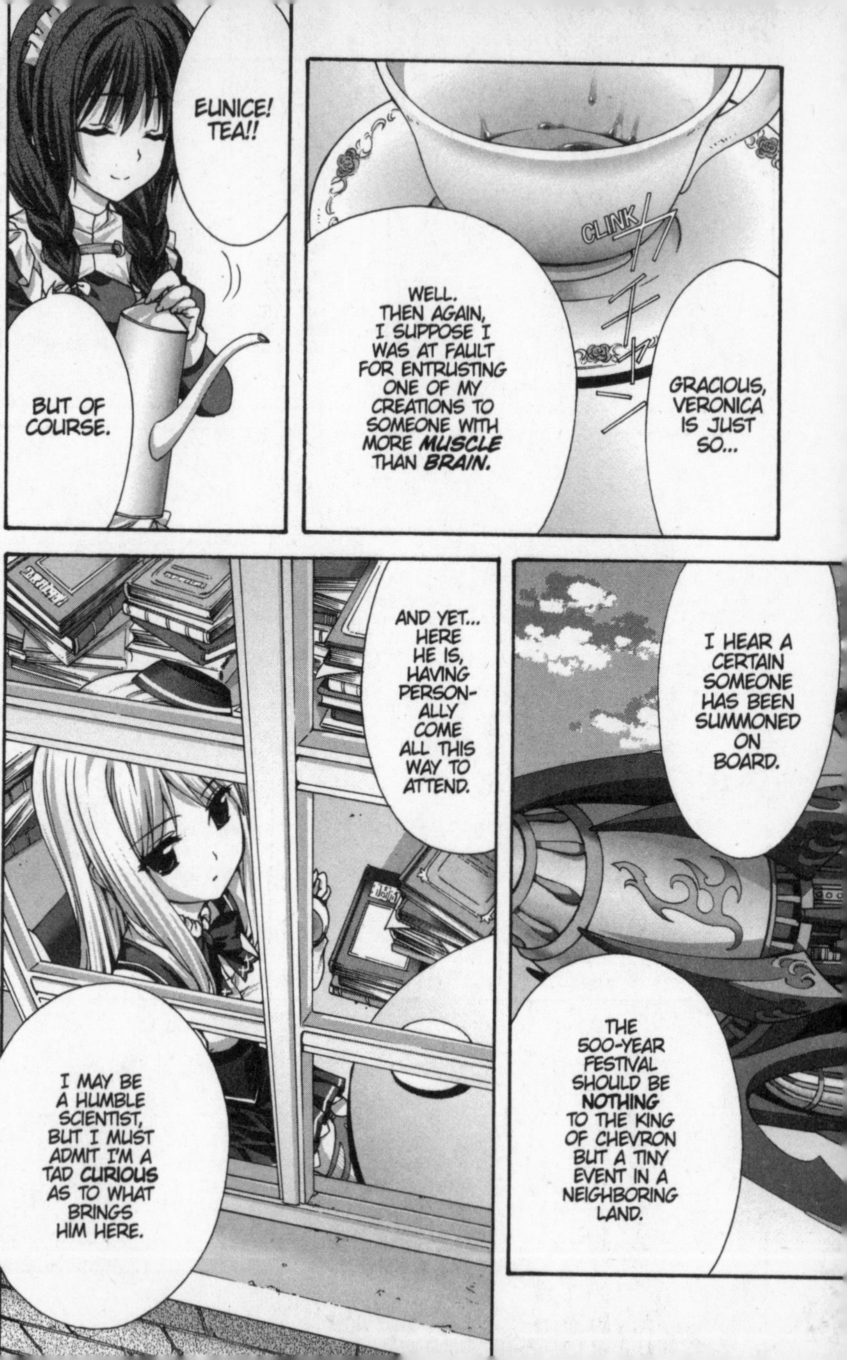
GRACIOUS, VERONICA IS JUST SO...
CLINK
WELL. THEN AGAIN, I SUPPOSE I WAS AT FAULT FOR ENTRUSTING ONE OF MY CREATIONS TO SOMEONE WITH MORE *MUSCLE* THAN *BRAIN.*
EUNICE! TEA!!
BUT OF COURSE.
I HEAR A CERTAIN SOMEONE HAS BEEN SUMMONED ON BOARD.
THE 500-YEAR FESTIVAL SHOULD BE **NOTHING** TO THE KING OF CHEVRON BUT A TINY EVENT IN A NEIGHBORING LAND.
AND YET... HERE HE IS, HAVING PERSON-ALLY COME ALL THIS WAY TO ATTEND.
I MAY BE A HUMBLE SCIENTIST, BUT I MUST ADMIT I'M A TAD **CURIOUS** AS TO WHAT BRINGS HIM HERE.

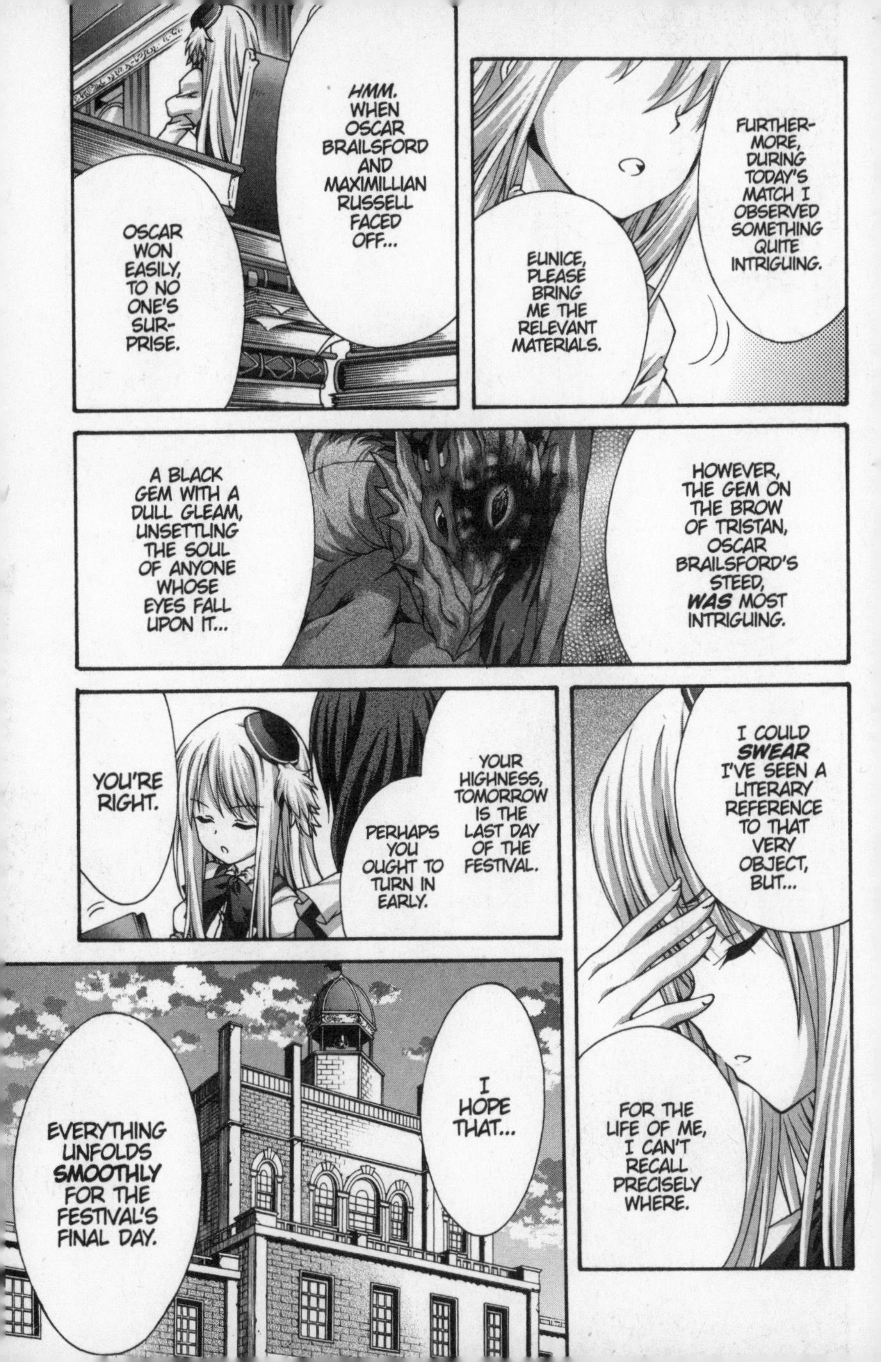
FURTHER-MORE, DURING TODAY'S MATCH I OBSERVED SOMETHING QUITE INTRIGUING.
EUNICE, PLEASE BRING ME THE RELEVANT MATERIALS.
HMM. WHEN OSCAR BRAILSFORD AND MAXIMILLIAN RUSSELL FACED OFF...
OSCAR WON EASILY, TO NO ONE'S SUR-PRISE.
HOWEVER, THE GEM ON THE BROW OF TRISTAN, OSCAR BRAILSFORD'S STEED, ***WAS*** MOST INTRIGUING.
A BLACK GEM WITH A DULL GLEAM, UNSETTLING THE SOUL OF ANYONE WHOSE EYES FALL UPON IT...
I COULD ***SWEAR*** I'VE SEEN A LITERARY REFERENCE TO THAT VERY OBJECT, BUT...
FOR THE LIFE OF ME, I CAN'T RECALL PRECISELY WHERE.
YOUR HIGHNESS, TOMORROW IS THE LAST DAY OF THE FESTIVAL.
PERHAPS YOU OUGHT TO TURN IN EARLY.
YOU'RE RIGHT.
I HOPE THAT...
EVERYTHING UNFOLDS **SMOOTHLY** FOR THE FESTIVAL'S FINAL DAY.

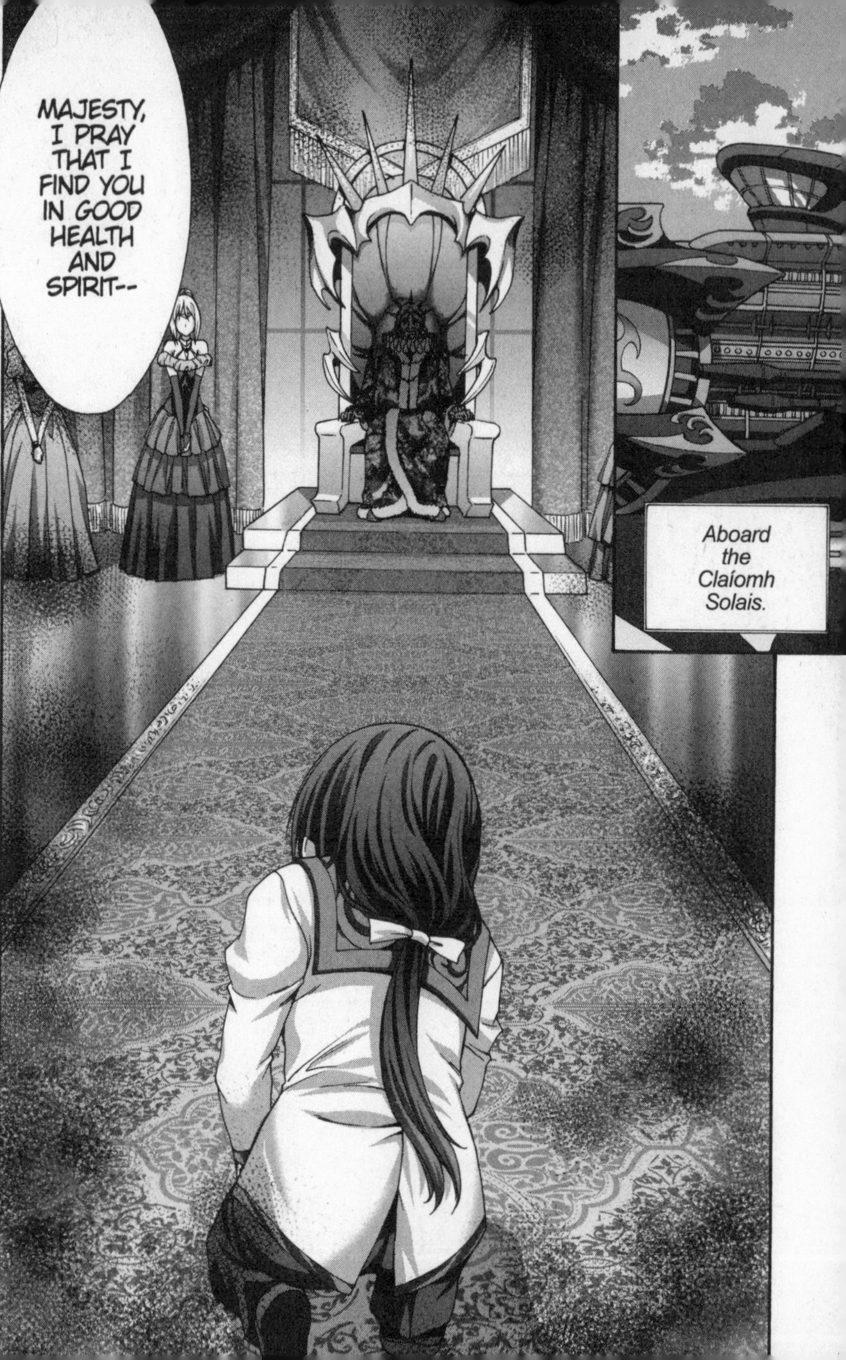
Aboard the Claíomh Solais.
MAJESTY, I PRAY THAT I FIND YOU IN GOOD HEALTH AND SPIRIT--

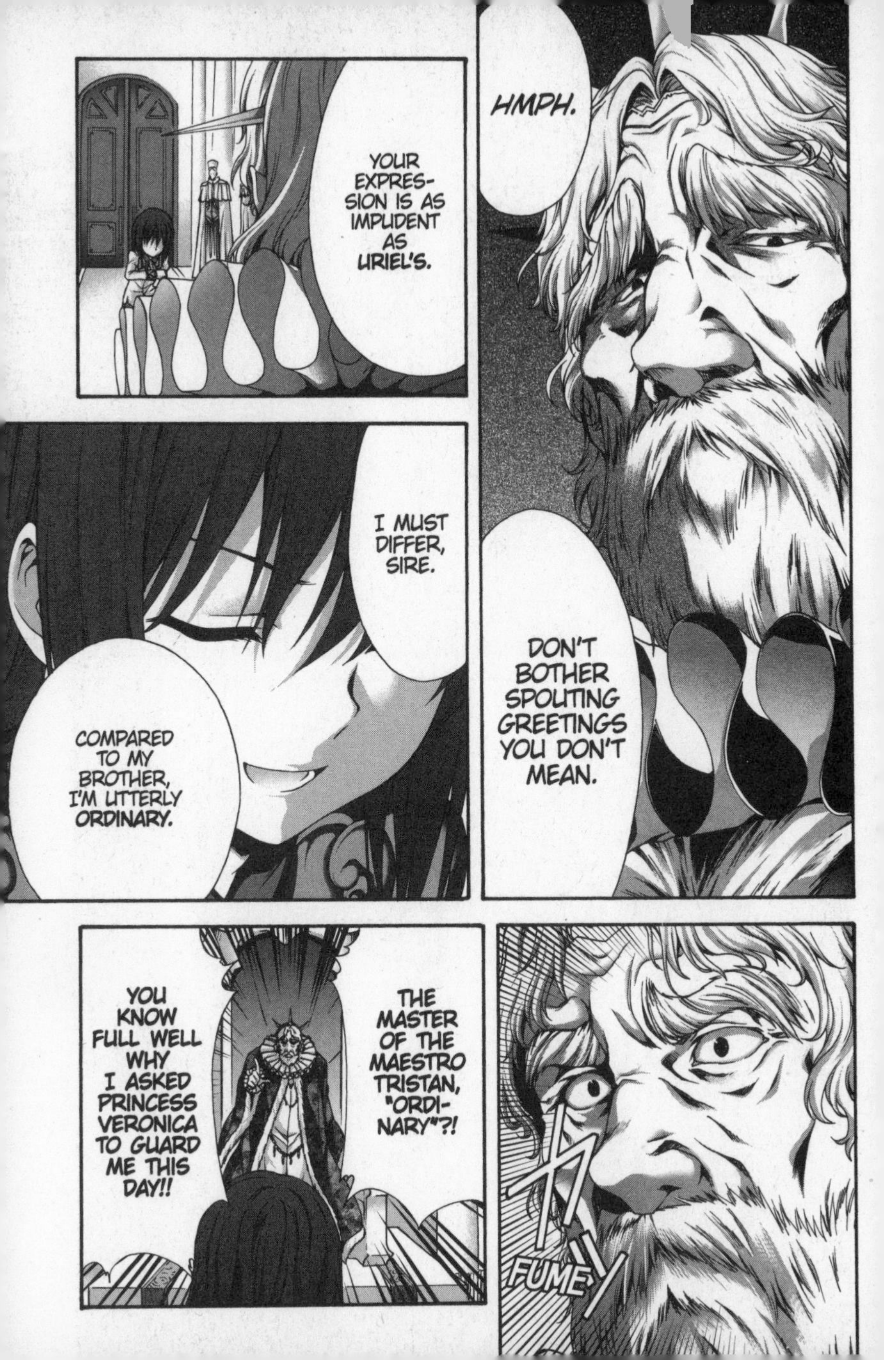
HMPH.
DON'T BOTHER SPOUTING GREETINGS YOU DON'T MEAN.
YOUR EXPRES-SION IS AS IMPUDENT AS URIEL'S.
I MUST DIFFER, SIRE.
COMPARED TO MY BROTHER, I'M UTTERLY ORDINARY.
FUME
THE MASTER OF THE MAESTRO TRISTAN, "ORDI-NARY"?!
YOU KNOW FULL WELL WHY I ASKED PRINCESS VERONICA TO GUARD ME THIS DAY!!

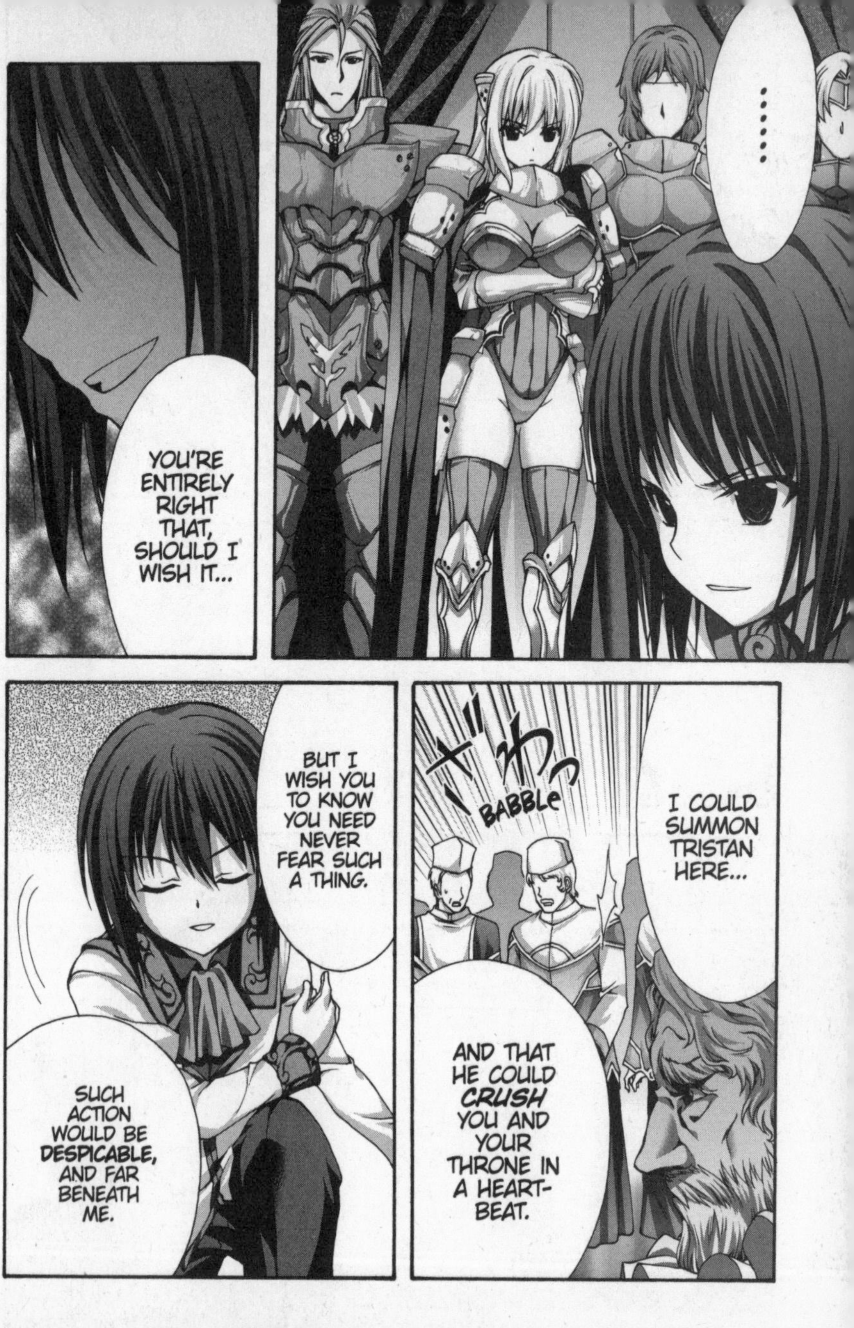
......
YOU'RE ENTIRELY RIGHT THAT, SHOULD I WISH IT...
I COULD SUMMON TRISTAN HERE...
BABBLE
AND THAT HE COULD CRUSH YOU AND YOUR THRONE IN A HEART-BEAT.
BUT I WISH YOU TO KNOW YOU NEED NEVER FEAR SUCH A THING.
SUCH ACTION WOULD BE DESPICABLE, AND FAR BENEATH ME.

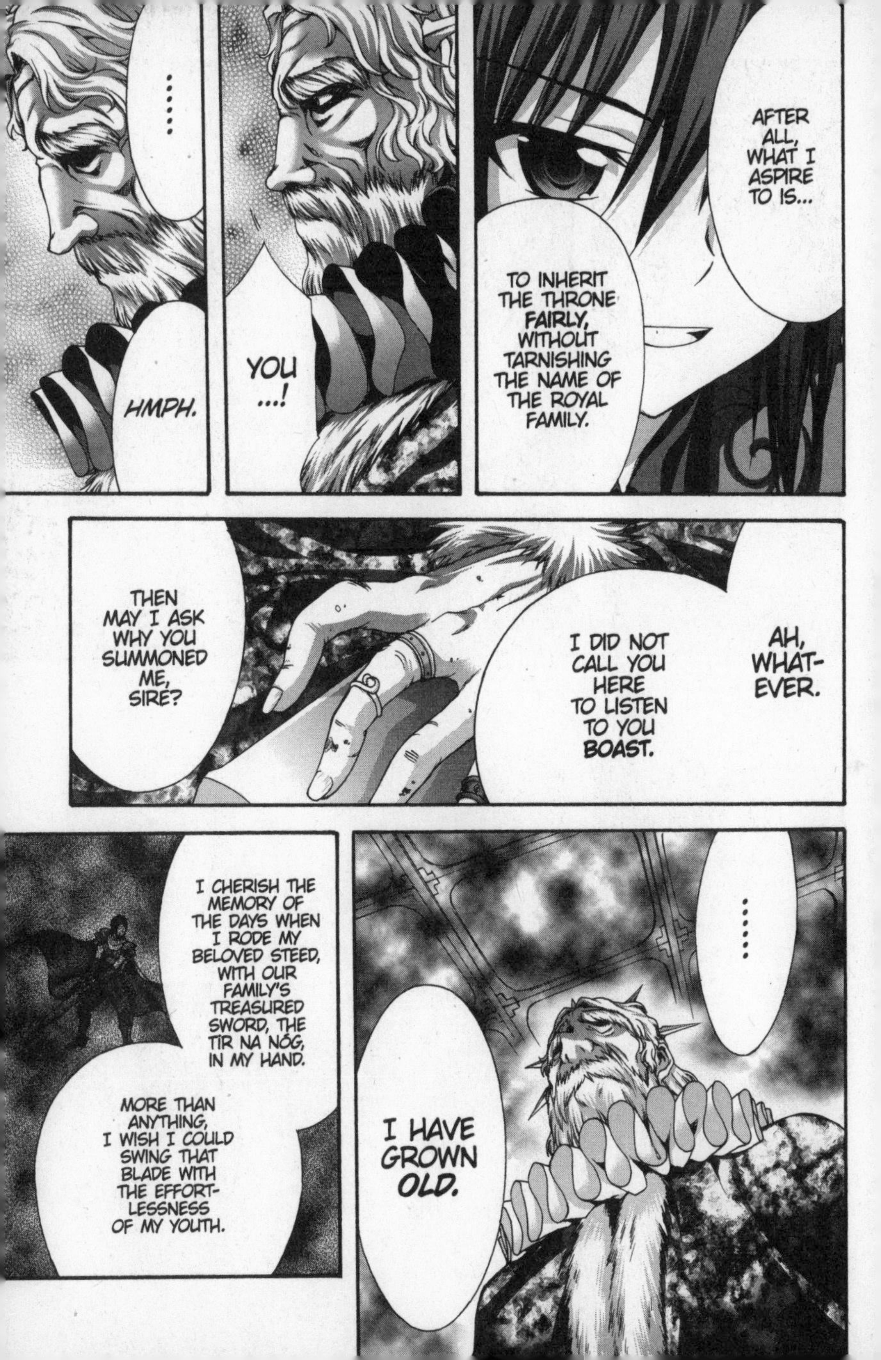
AFTER ALL, WHAT I ASPIRE TO IS...
TO INHERIT THE THRONE FAIRLY, WITHOUT TARNISHING THE NAME OF THE ROYAL FAMILY.
YOU ...!
......
HMPH.
AH, WHATEVER.
I DID NOT CALL YOU HERE TO LISTEN TO YOU BOAST.
THEN MAY I ASK WHY YOU SUMMONED ME, SIRE?
......
I HAVE GROWN OLD.
I CHERISH THE MEMORY OF THE DAYS WHEN I RODE MY BELOVED STEED, WITH OUR FAMILY'S TREASURED SWORD, THE TIR NA NÓG, IN MY HAND.
MORE THAN ANYTHING, I WISH I COULD SWING THAT BLADE WITH THE EFFORTLESSNESS OF MY YOUTH.

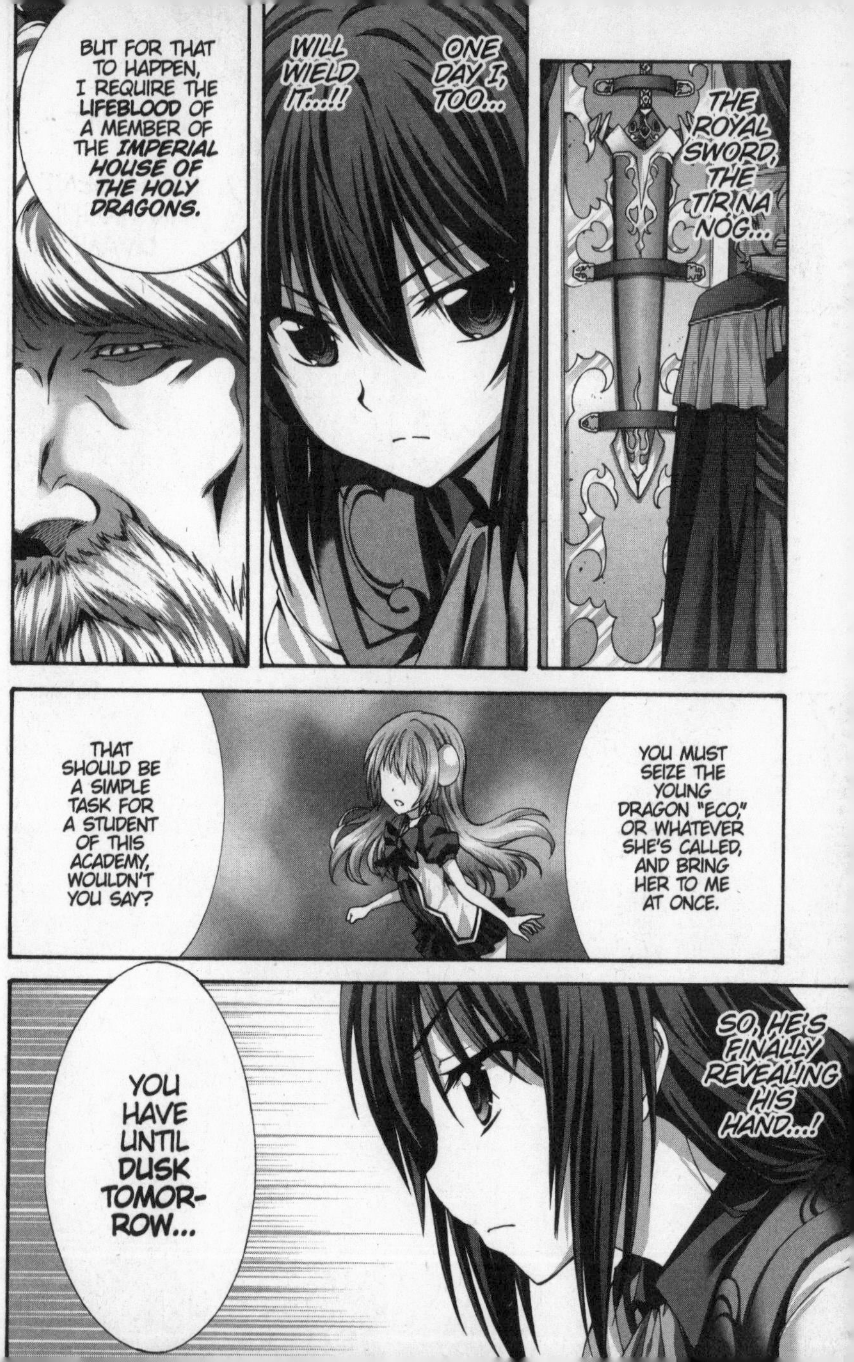
THE ROYAL SWORD, THE TIR NA NÓG...
ONE DAY I, TOO...
WILL WIELD IT...!!
BUT FOR THAT TO HAPPEN, I REQUIRE THE LIFEBLOOD OF A MEMBER OF THE IMPERIAL HOUSE OF THE HOLY DRAGONS.
YOU MUST SEIZE THE YOUNG DRAGON "ECO," OR WHATEVER SHE'S CALLED, AND BRING HER TO ME AT ONCE.
THAT SHOULD BE A SIMPLE TASK FOR A STUDENT OF THIS ACADEMY, WOULDN'T YOU SAY?
SO, HE'S FINALLY REVEALING HIS HAND...!
YOU HAVE UNTIL DUSK TOMORROW...

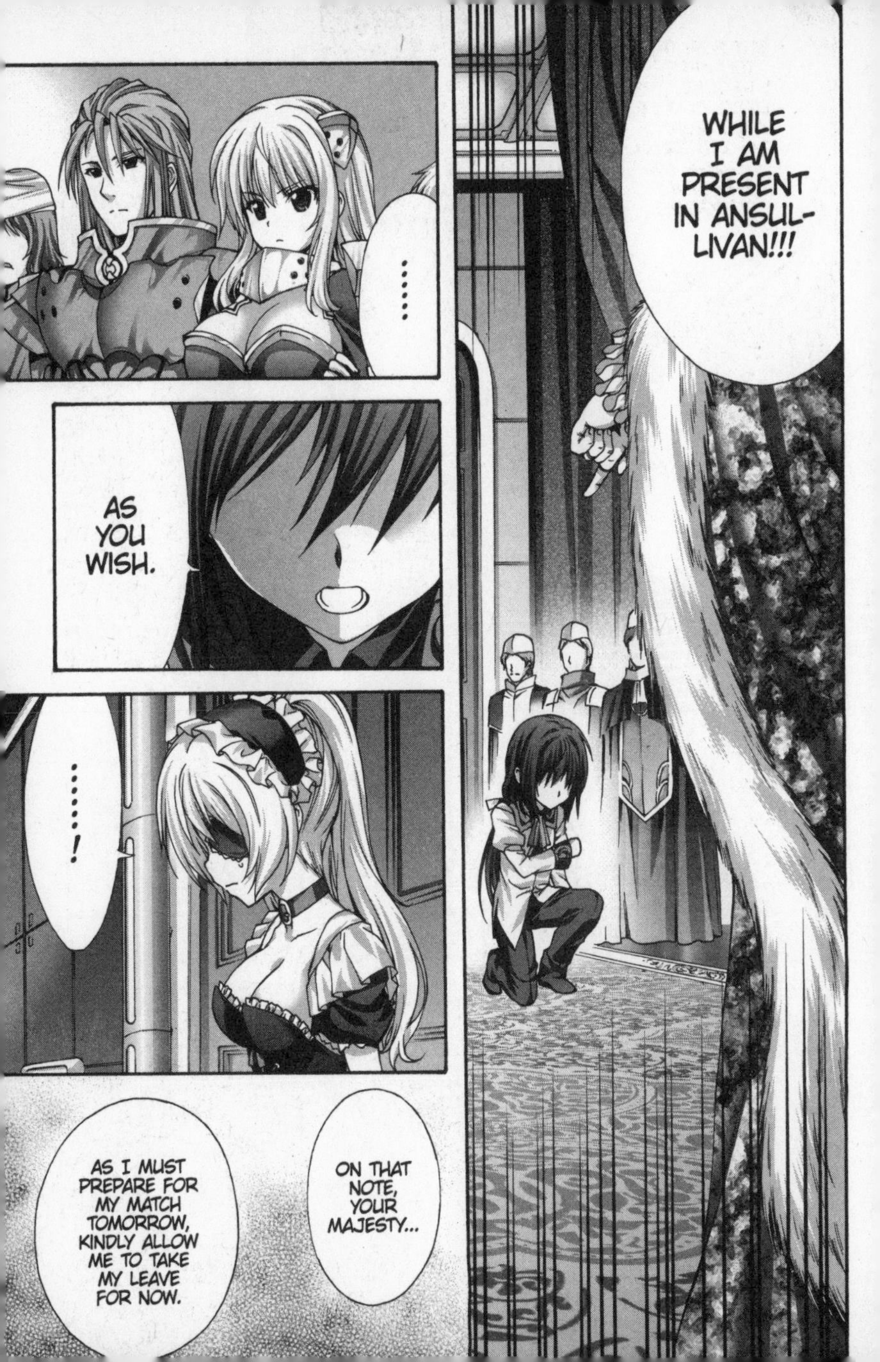
WHILE I AM PRESENT IN ANSUL-LIVAN!!!
……
AS YOU WISH.
……!
ON THAT NOTE, YOUR MAJESTY…
AS I MUST PREPARE FOR MY MATCH TOMORROW, KINDLY ALLOW ME TO TAKE MY LEAVE FOR NOW.

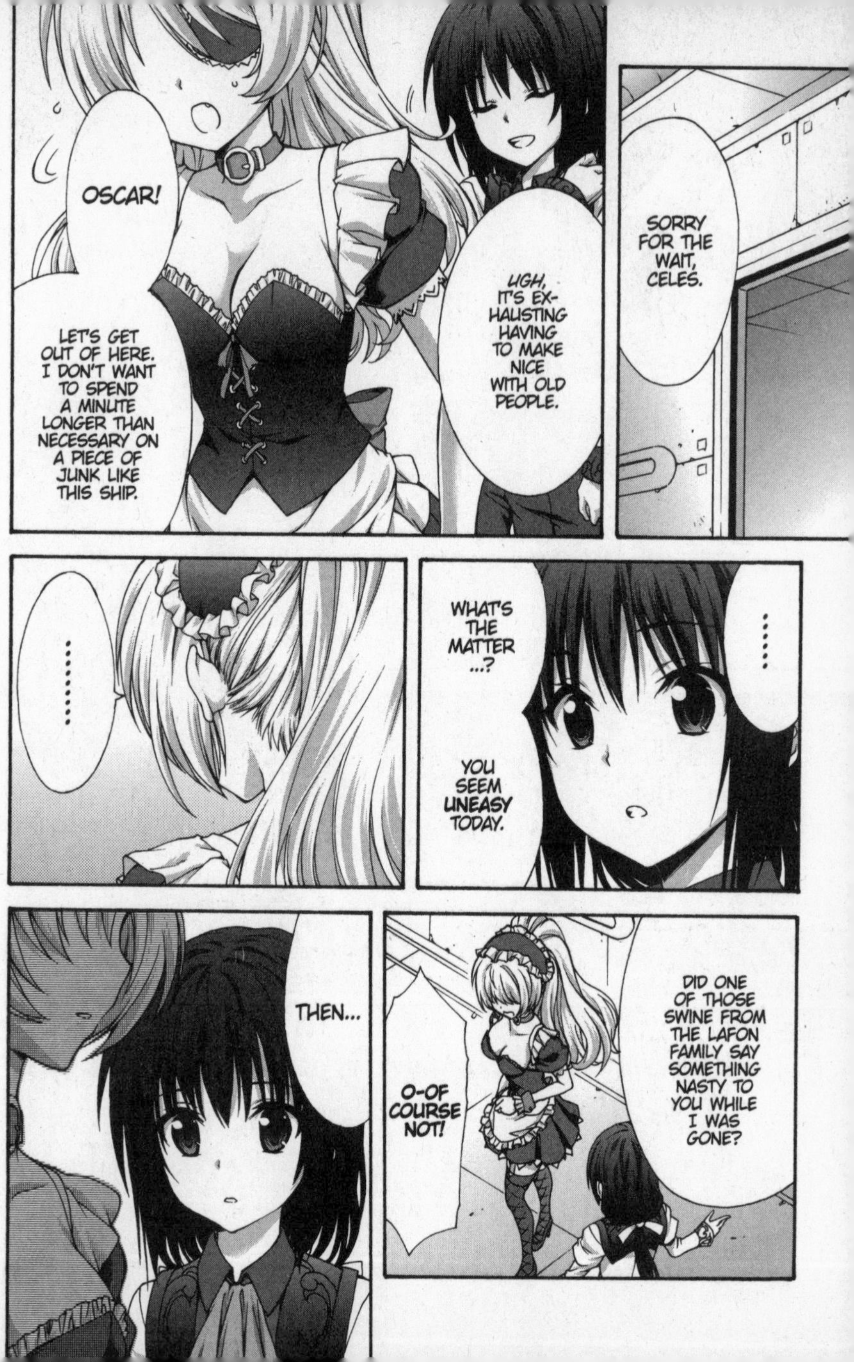
SORRY FOR THE WAIT, CELES.
UGH, IT'S EX-HAUSTING HAVING TO MAKE NICE WITH OLD PEOPLE.
OSCAR!
LET'S GET OUT OF HERE. I DON'T WANT TO SPEND A MINUTE LONGER THAN NECESSARY ON A PIECE OF JUNK LIKE THIS SHIP.
......
WHAT'S THE MATTER ...?
YOU SEEM UNEASY TODAY.
......
DID ONE OF THOSE SWINE FROM THE LAFON FAMILY SAY SOMETHING NASTY TO YOU WHILE I WAS GONE?
O-OF COURSE NOT!
THEN...

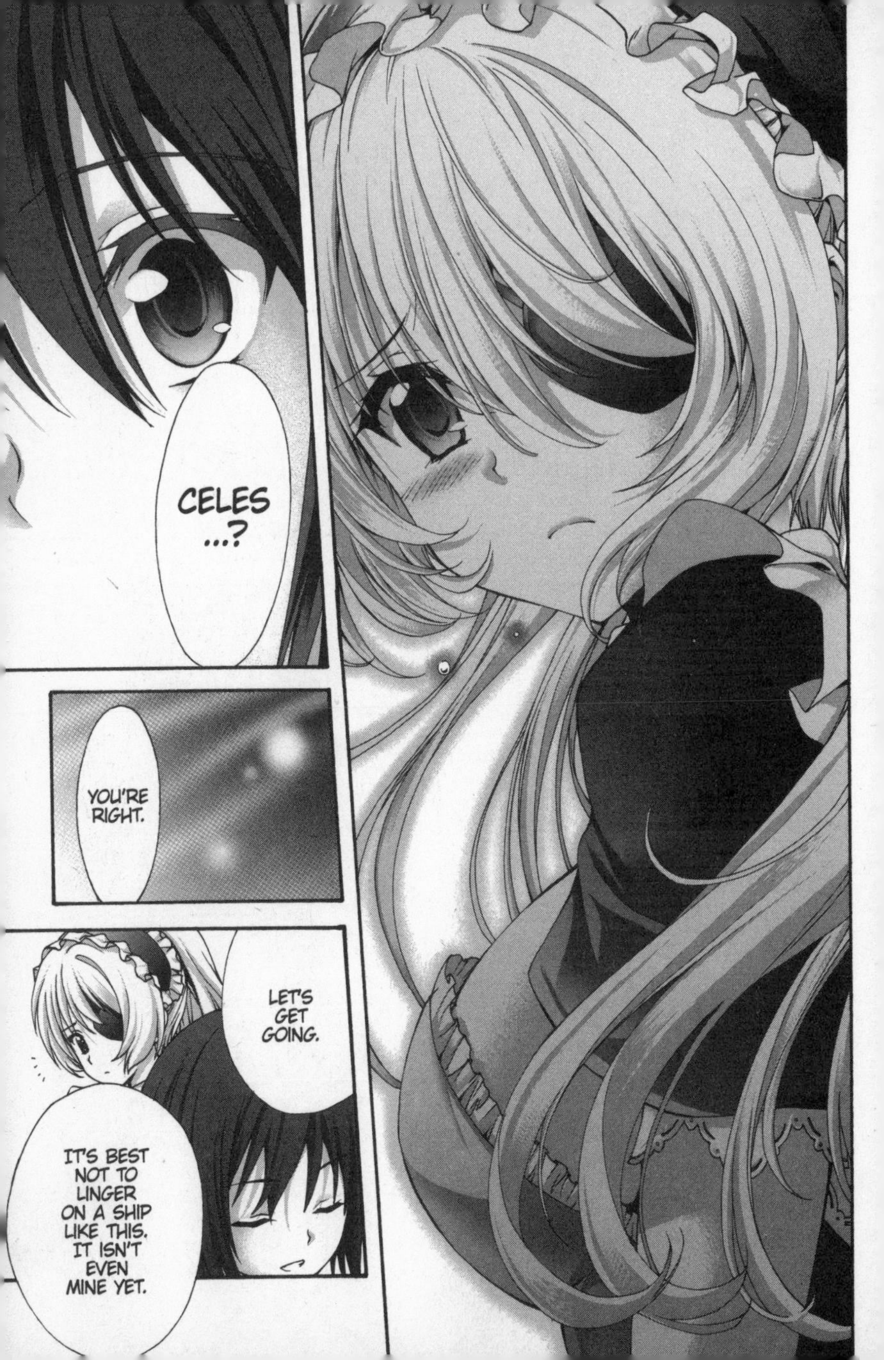
CELES ...?
YOU'RE RIGHT.
LET'S GET GOING.
IT'S BEST NOT TO LINGER ON A SHIP LIKE THIS. IT ISN'T EVEN MINE YET.

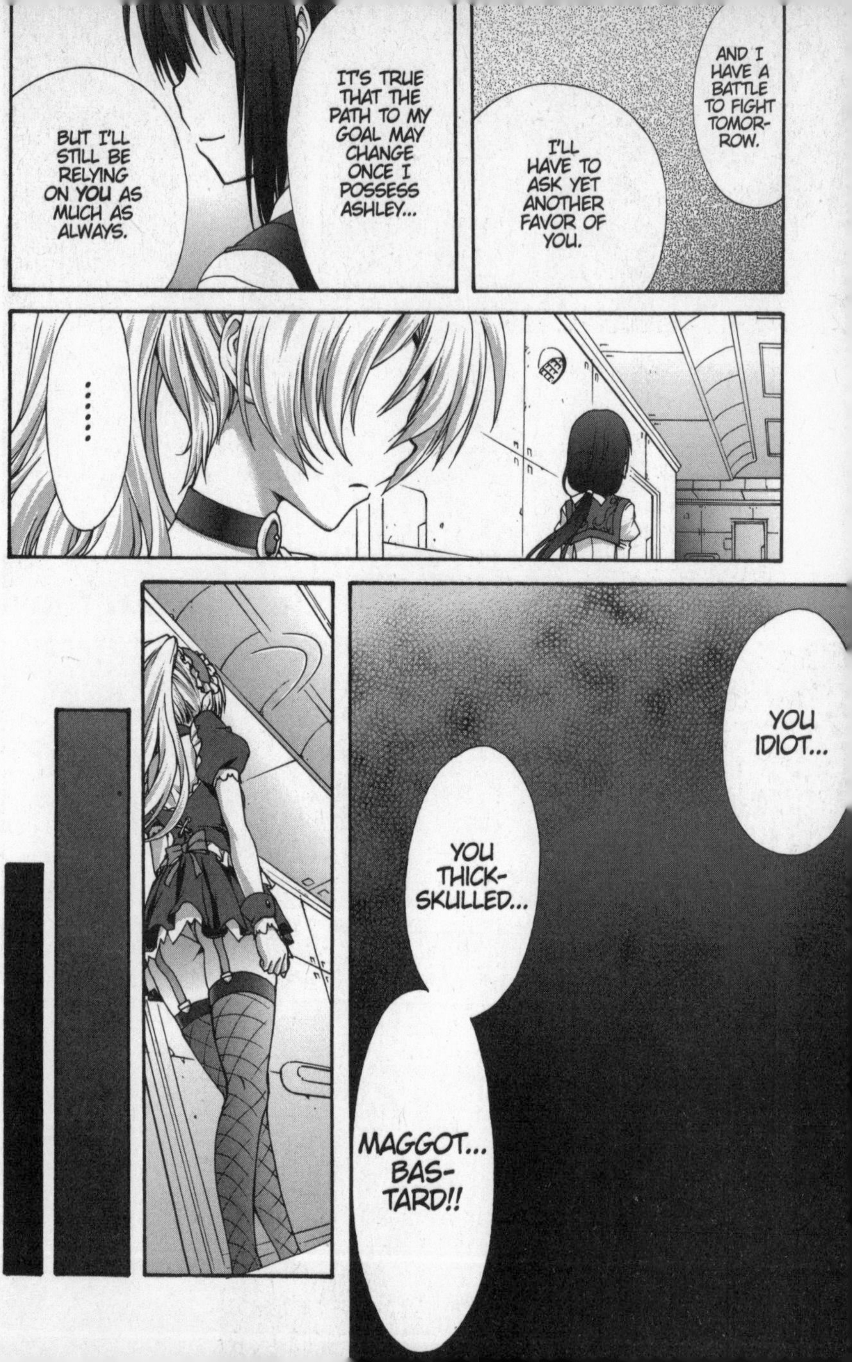
AND I HAVE A BATTLE TO FIGHT TOMOR-ROW.
I'LL HAVE TO ASK YET ANOTHER FAVOR OF YOU.
IT'S TRUE THAT THE PATH TO MY GOAL MAY CHANGE ONCE I POSSESS ASHLEY...
BUT I'LL STILL BE RELYING ON YOU AS MUCH AS ALWAYS.
......
YOU IDIOT...
YOU THICK-SKULLED...
MAGGOT... BAS-TARD!!

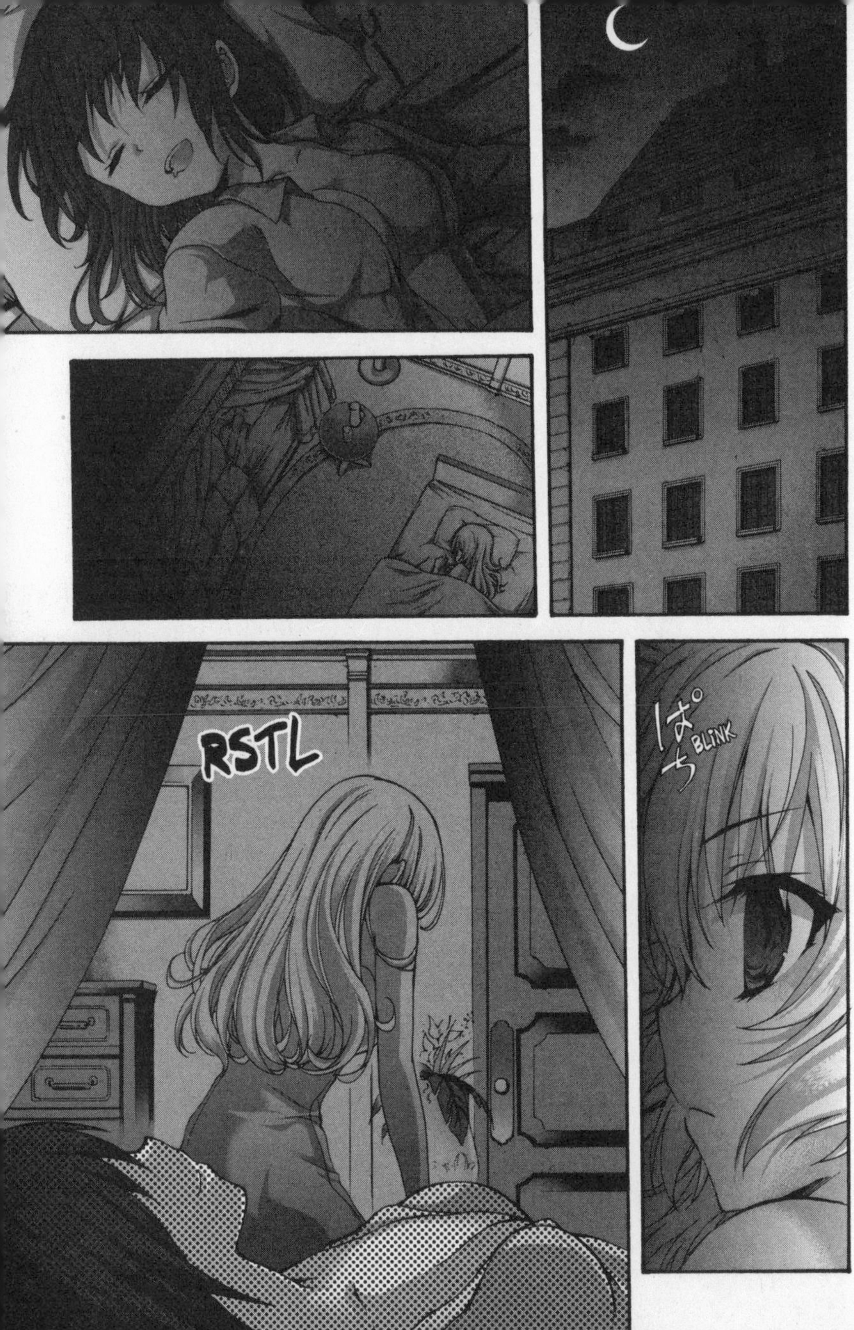
ぱち
BLINK
RSTL

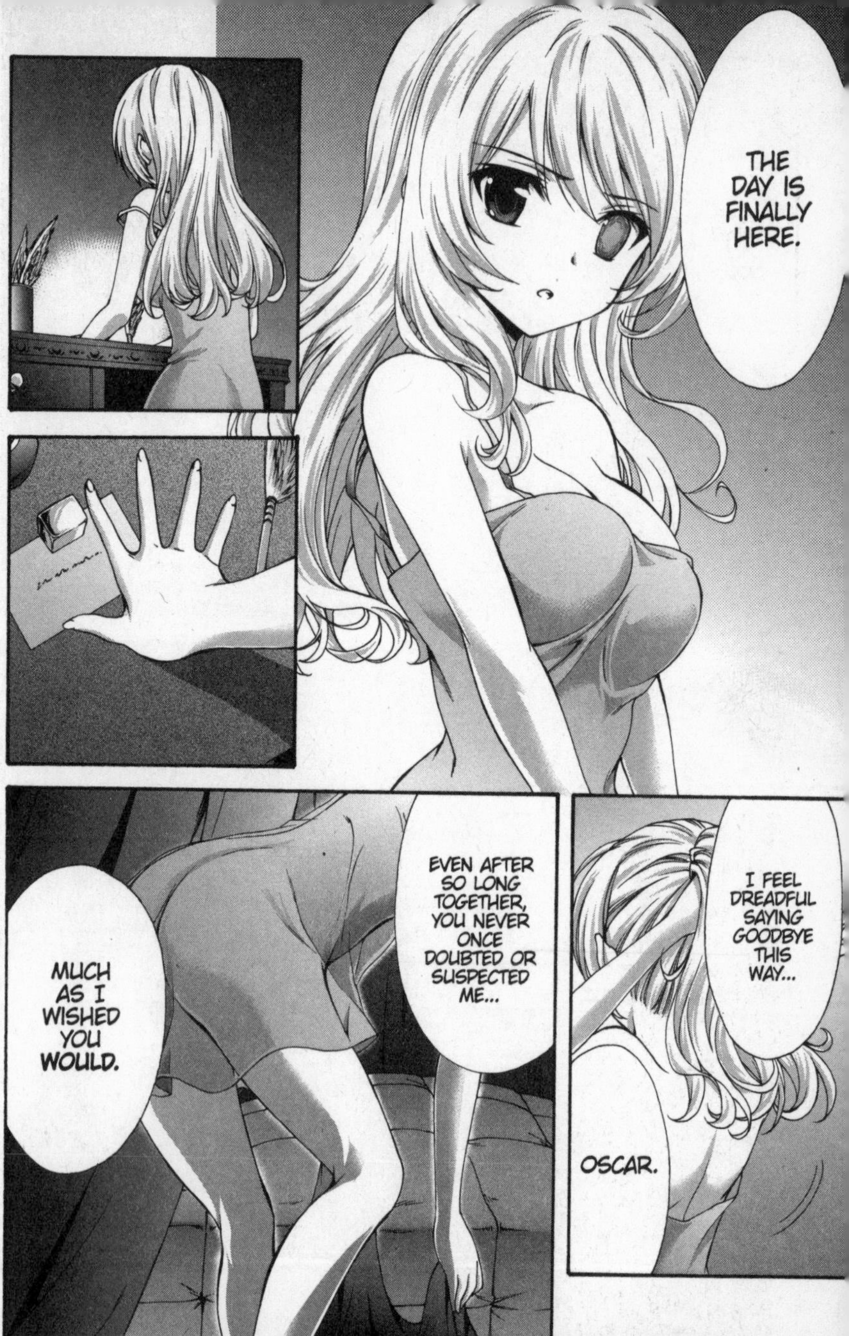
THE DAY IS FINALLY HERE.
I FEEL DREADFUL SAYING GOODBYE THIS WAY...
OSCAR.
EVEN AFTER SO LONG TOGETHER, YOU NEVER ONCE DOUBTED OR SUSPECTED ME...
MUCH AS I WISHED YOU WOULD.

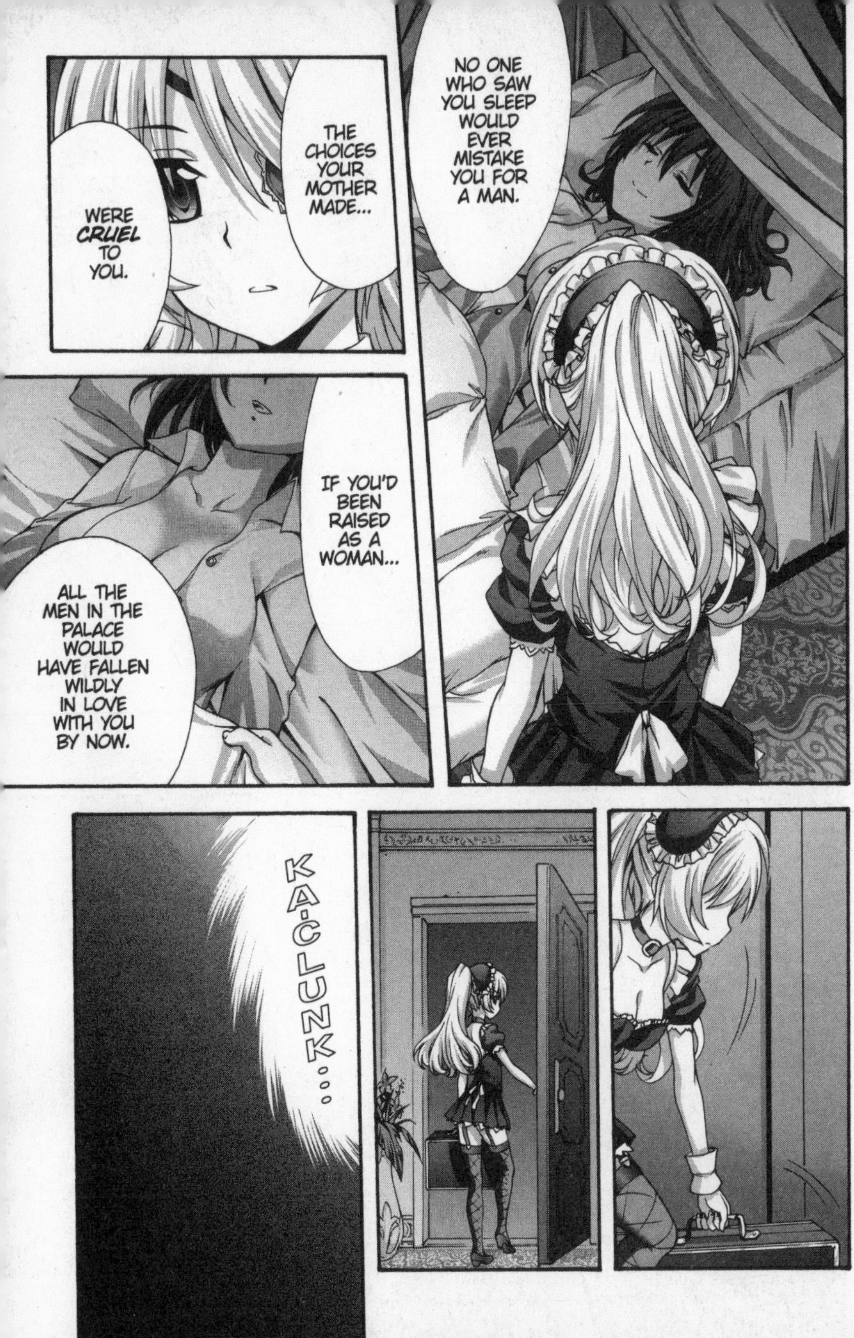
NO ONE WHO SAW YOU SLEEP WOULD EVER MISTAKE YOU FOR A MAN.
THE CHOICES YOUR MOTHER MADE...
WERE **CRUEL** TO YOU.
IF YOU'D BEEN RAISED AS A WOMAN...
ALL THE MEN IN THE PALACE WOULD HAVE FALLEN WILDLY IN LOVE WITH YOU BY NOW.
KA-CLUNK...

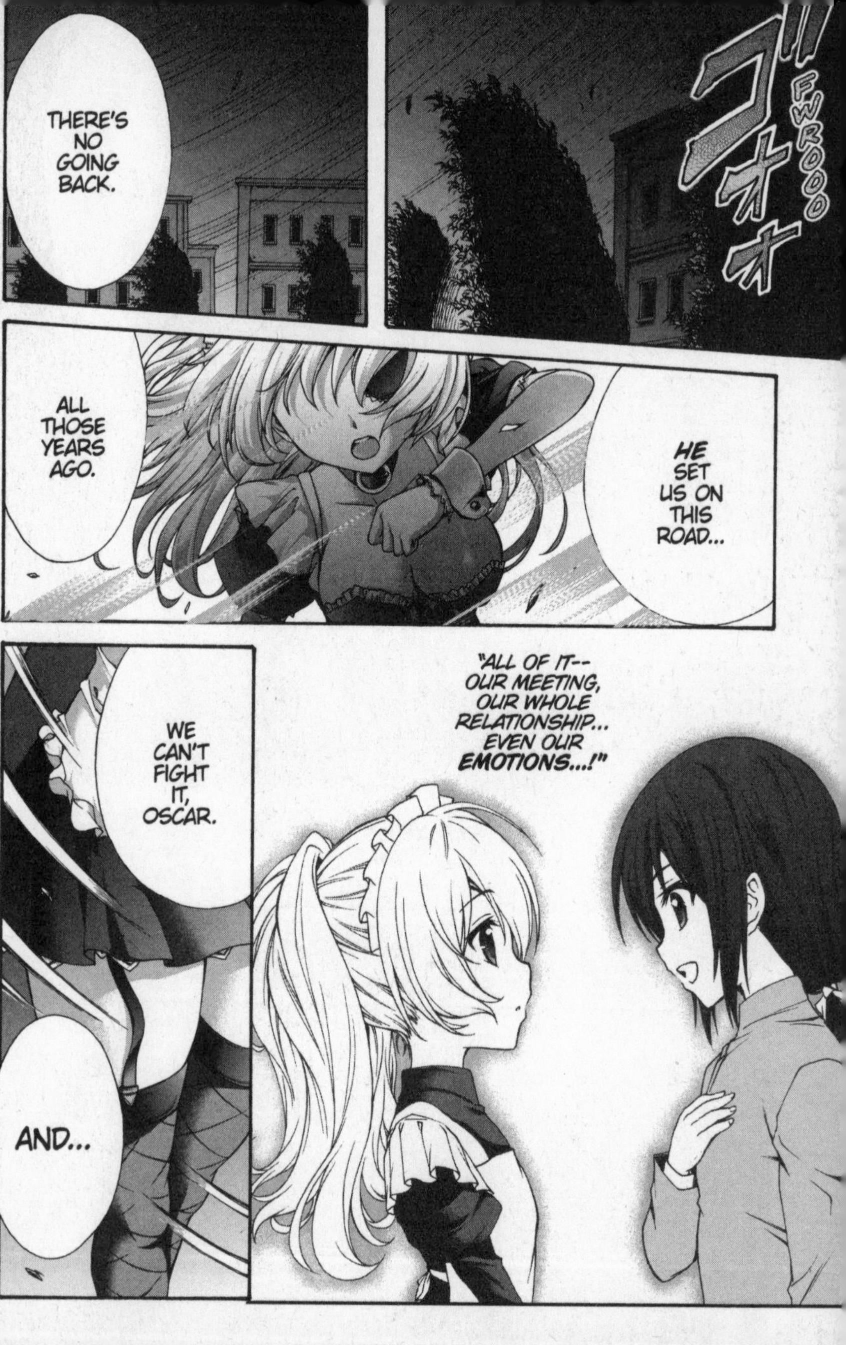
FWROOO
THERE'S NO GOING BACK.
HE SET US ON THIS ROAD...
ALL THOSE YEARS AGO.
"ALL OF IT-- OUR MEETING, OUR WHOLE RELATIONSHIP... EVEN OUR EMOTIONS...!"
WE CAN'T FIGHT IT, OSCAR.
AND...

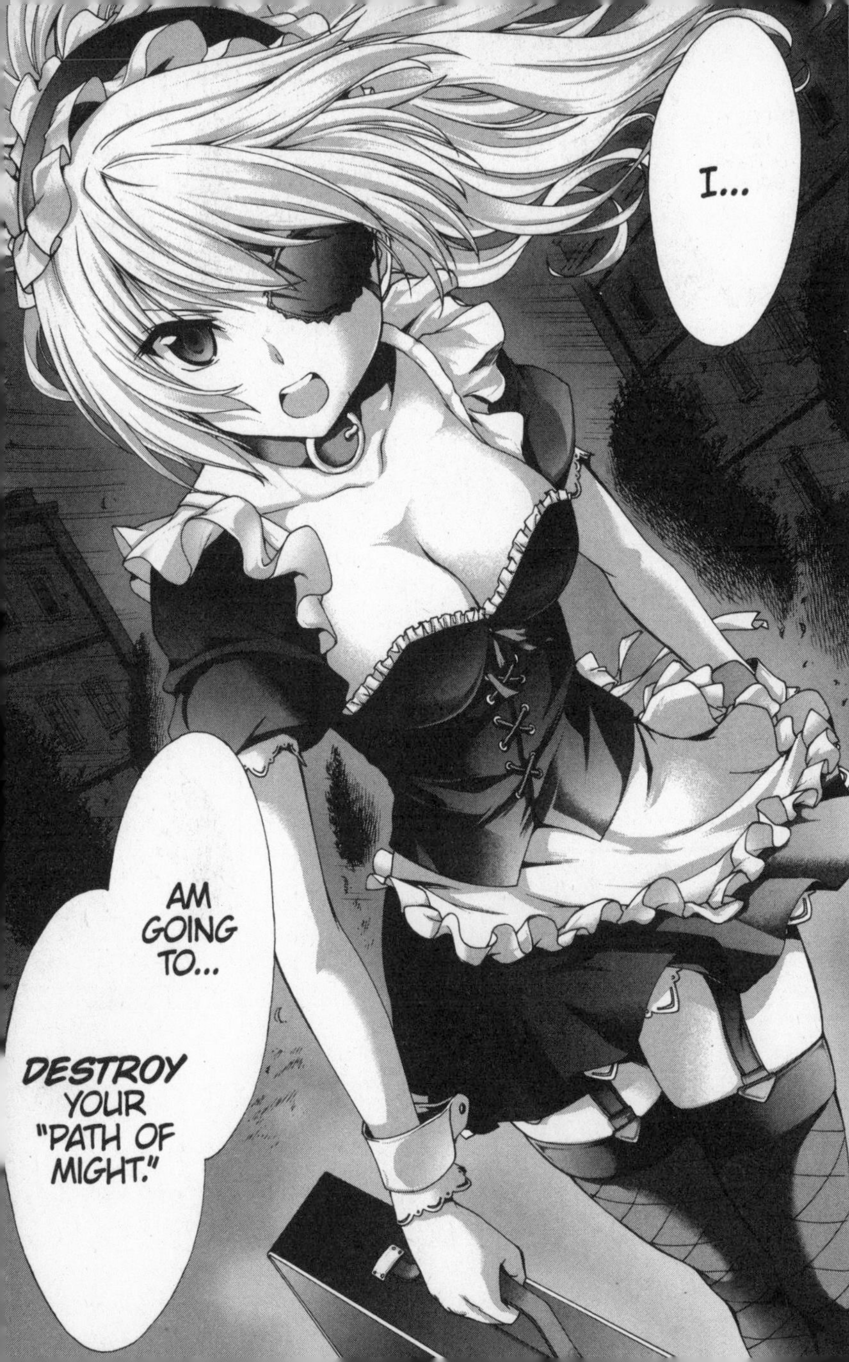
I...
AM GOING TO...
DESTROY YOUR "PATH OF MIGHT."

DRAGONAR
ACADEMY

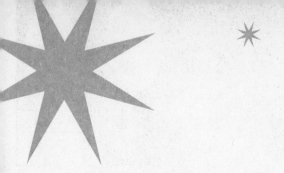

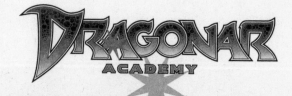

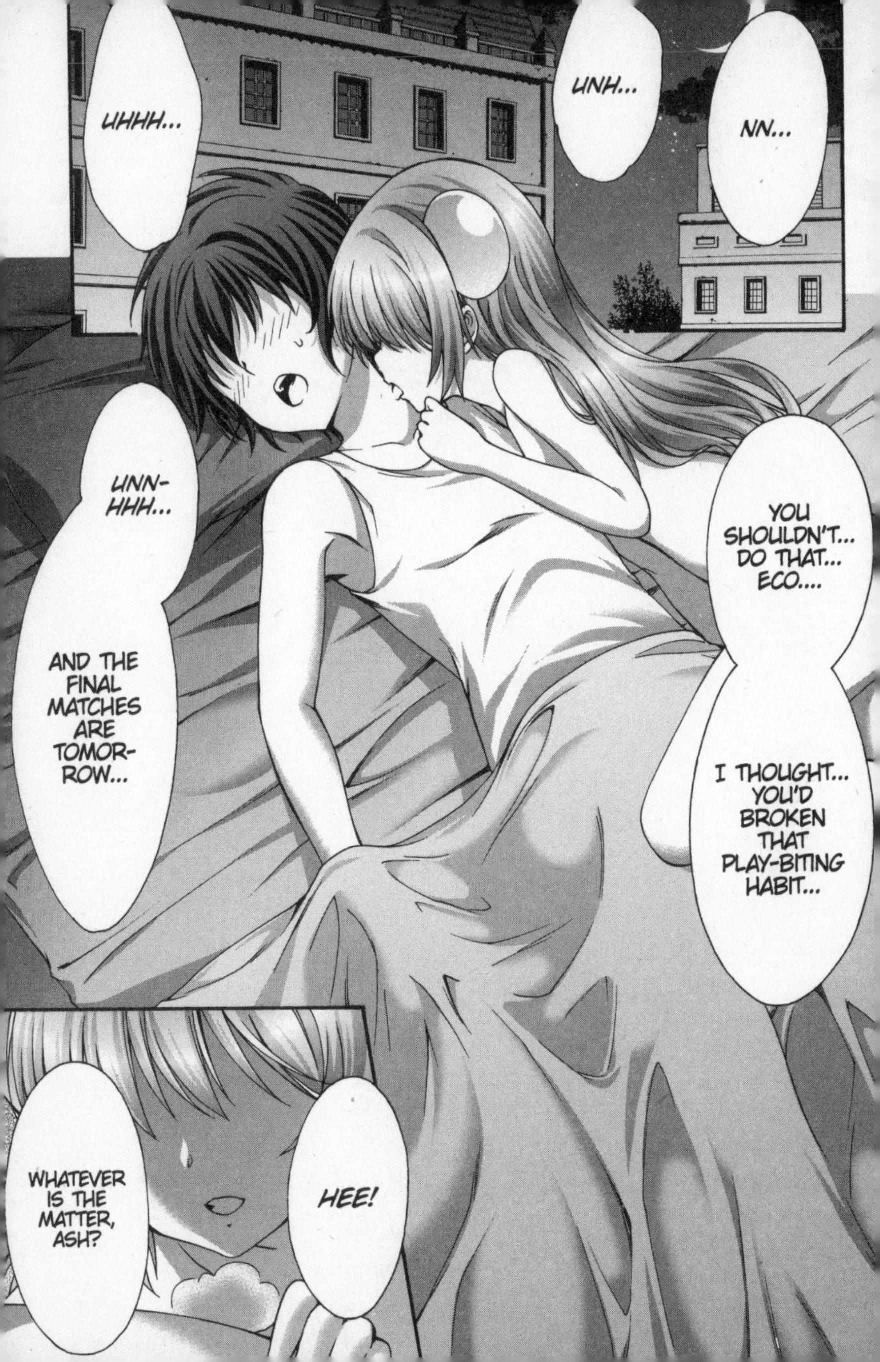
NN...
UNH...
UHHH...
YOU SHOULDN'T... DO THAT... ECO....
I THOUGHT... YOU'D BROKEN THAT PLAY-BITING HABIT...
UNN-HHH...
AND THE FINAL MATCHES ARE TOMORROW...
HEE!
WHATEVER IS THE MATTER, ASH?

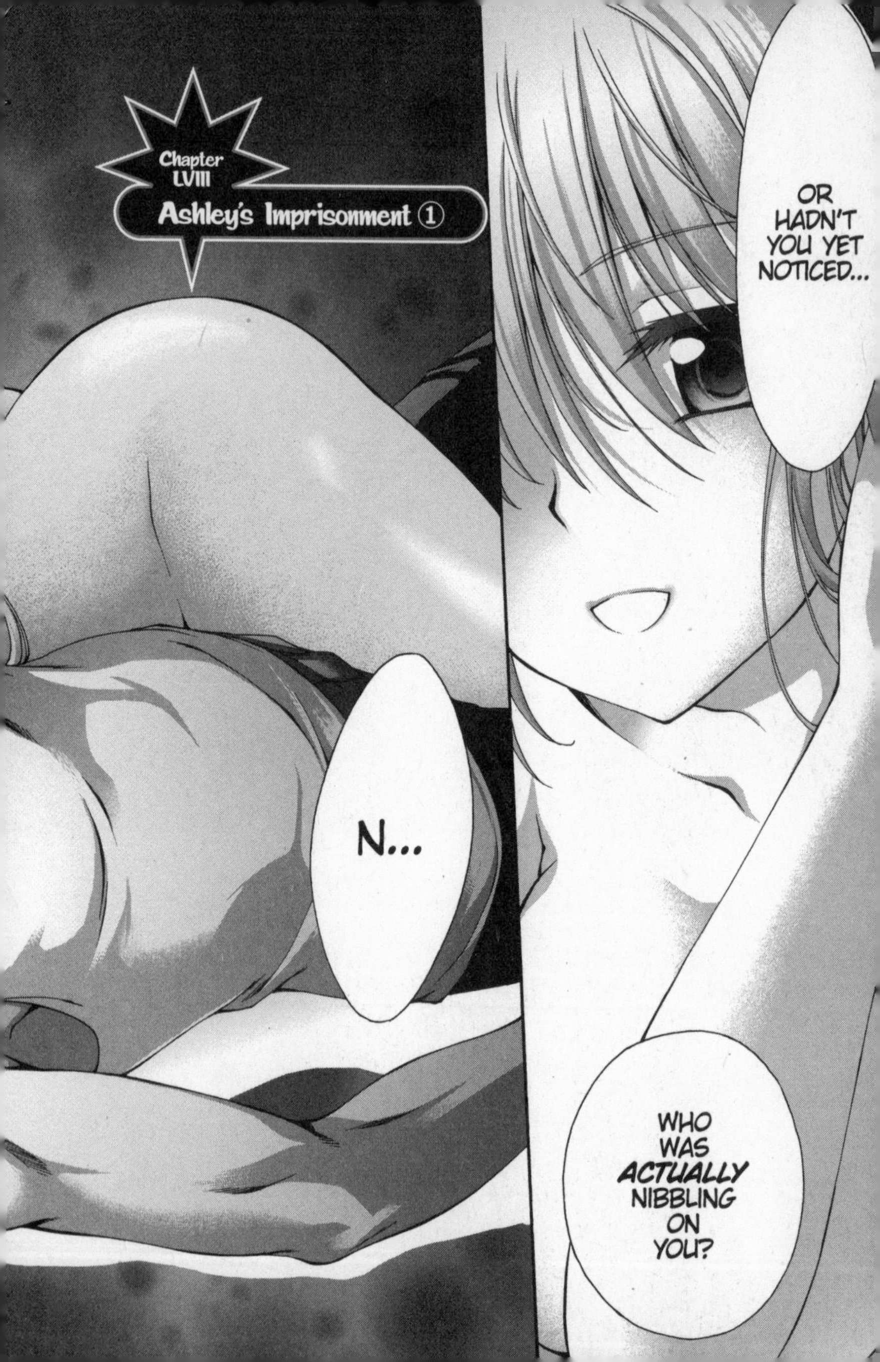
OR HADN'T YOU YET NOTICED...
WHO WAS *ACTUALLY* NIBBLING ON YOU?
Chapter LVIII
Ashley's Imprisonment ①
N...

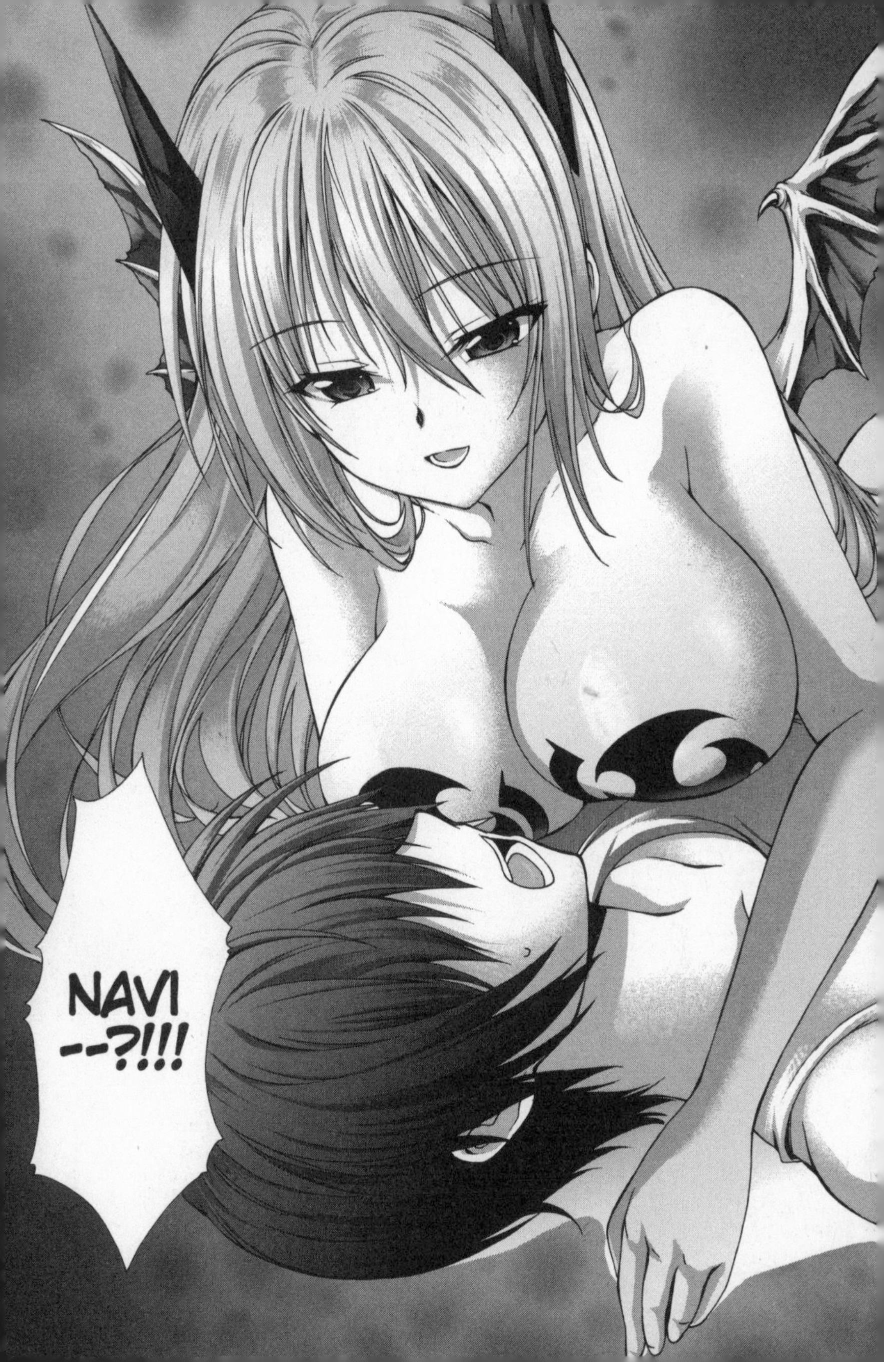
NAVI
--?!!!

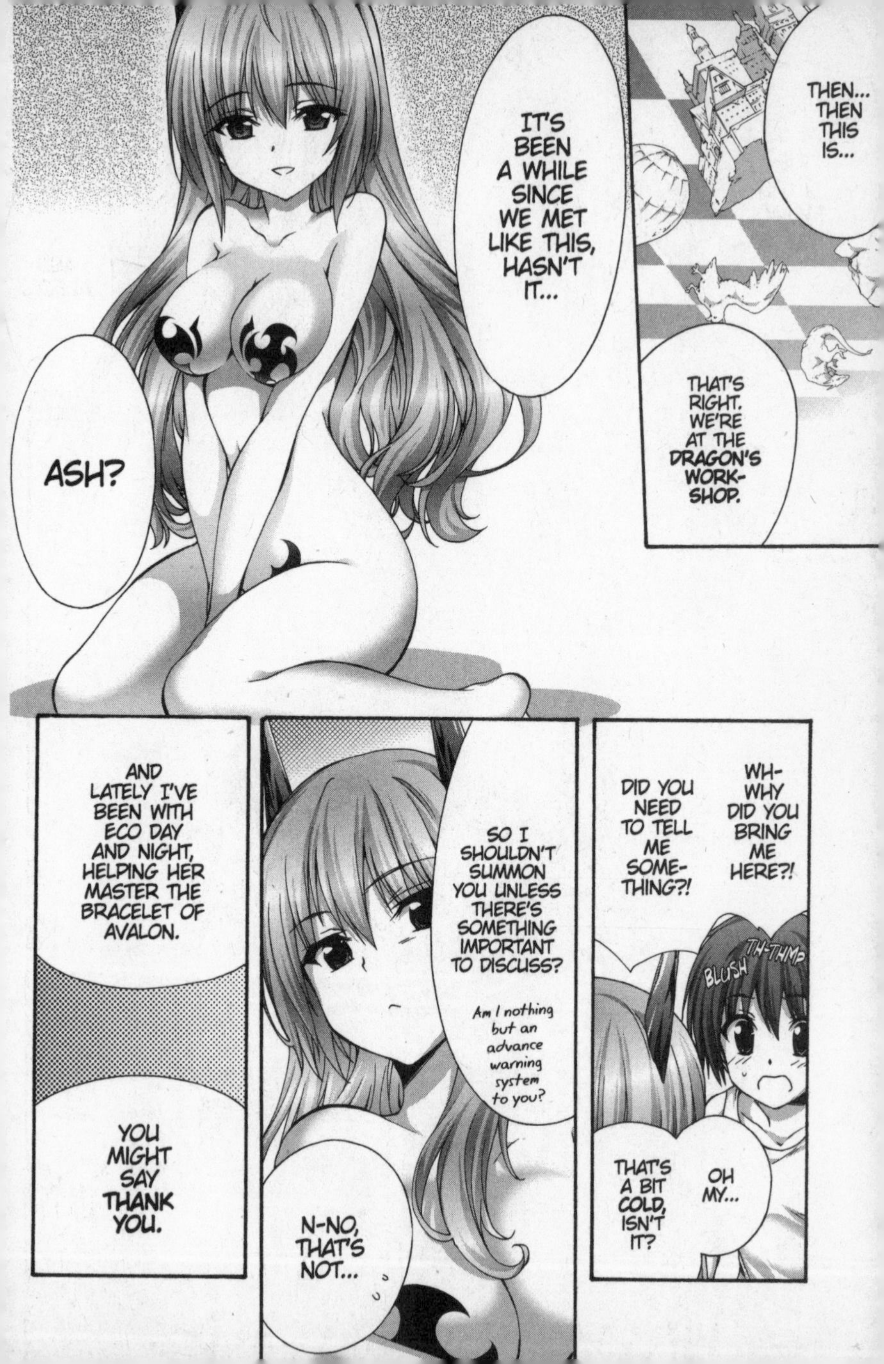
THEN... THEN THIS IS...
THAT'S RIGHT. WE'RE AT THE DRAGON'S WORK-SHOP.
IT'S BEEN A WHILE SINCE WE MET LIKE THIS, HASN'T IT...
ASH?
WH-WHY DID YOU BRING ME HERE?!
DID YOU NEED TO TELL ME SOME-THING?!
TH-THUMP
BLUSH
OH MY...
THAT'S A BIT COLD, ISN'T IT?
SO I SHOULDN'T SUMMON YOU UNLESS THERE'S SOMETHING IMPORTANT TO DISCUSS?
Am I nothing but an advance warning system to you?
N-NO, THAT'S NOT...
AND LATELY I'VE BEEN WITH ECO DAY AND NIGHT, HELPING HER MASTER THE BRACELET OF AVALON.
YOU MIGHT SAY THANK YOU.

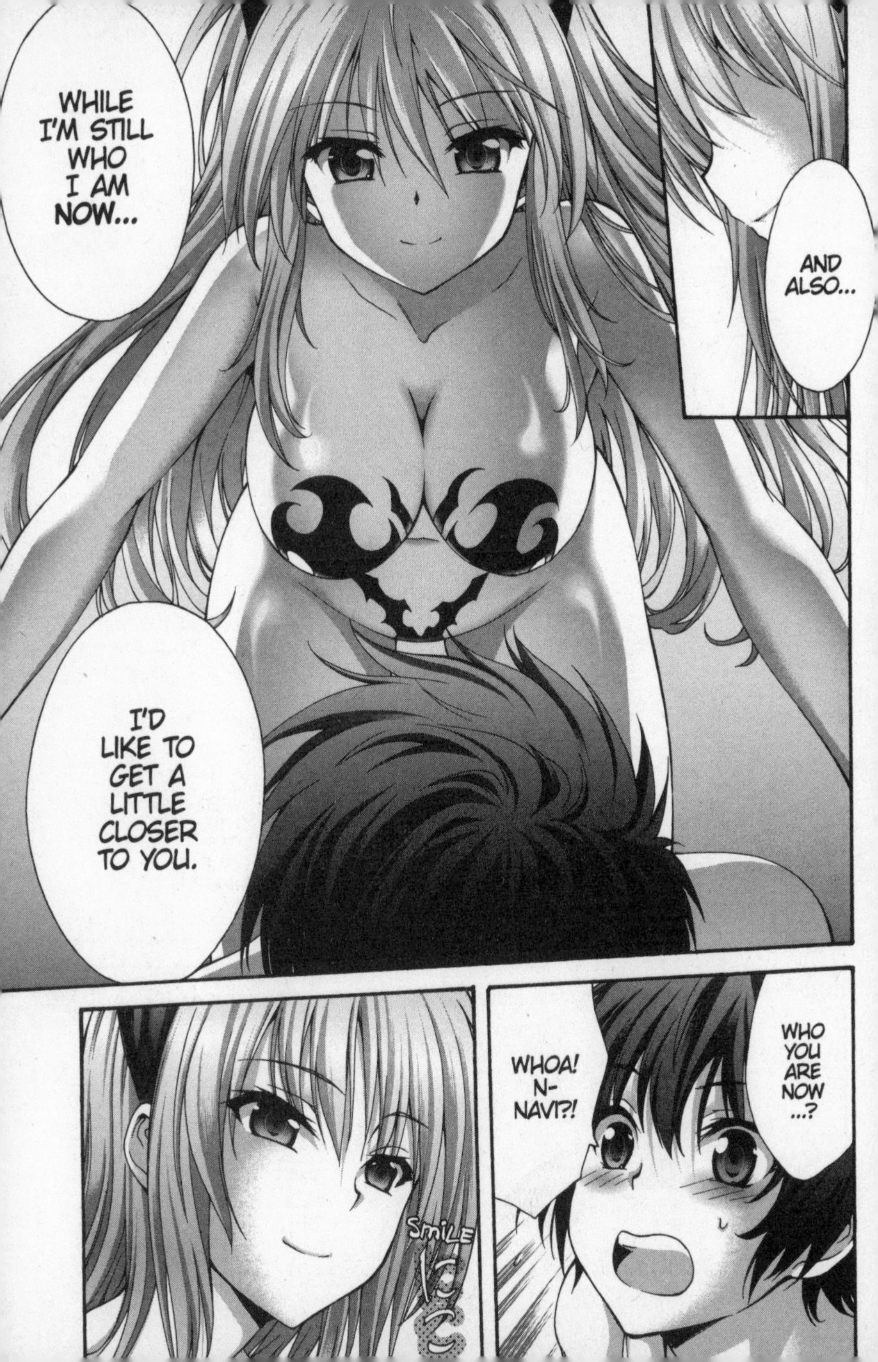
AND ALSO...
WHILE I'M STILL WHO I AM NOW...
I'D LIKE TO GET A LITTLE CLOSER TO YOU.
WHO YOU ARE NOW ...?
WHOA! N-NAVI?!
SMILE

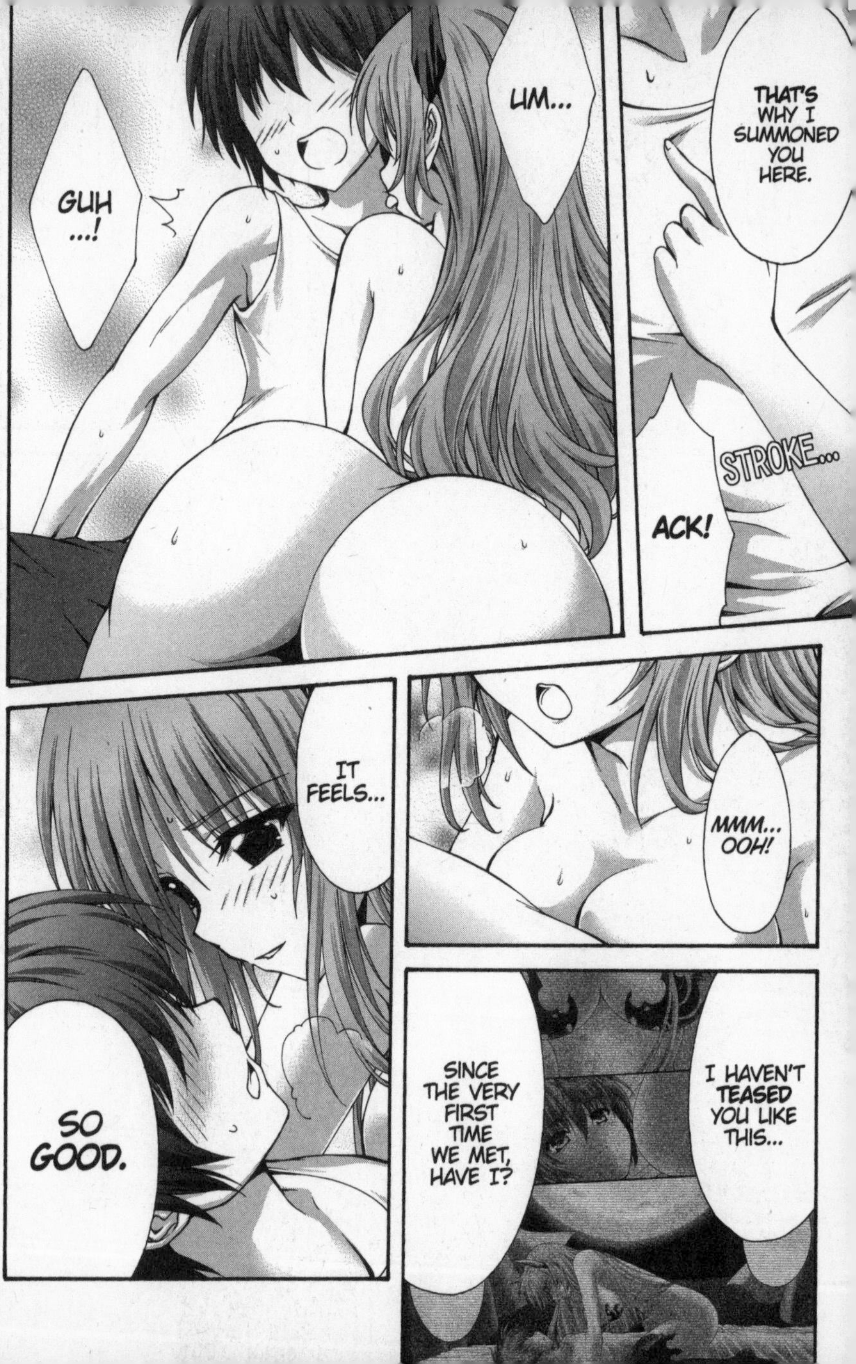
THAT'S WHY I SUMMONED YOU HERE.
STROKE...
ACK!
UM...
GUH ...!
MMM... OOH!
I HAVEN'T TEASED YOU LIKE THIS...
SINCE THE VERY FIRST TIME WE MET, HAVE I?
IT FEELS...
SO GOOD.

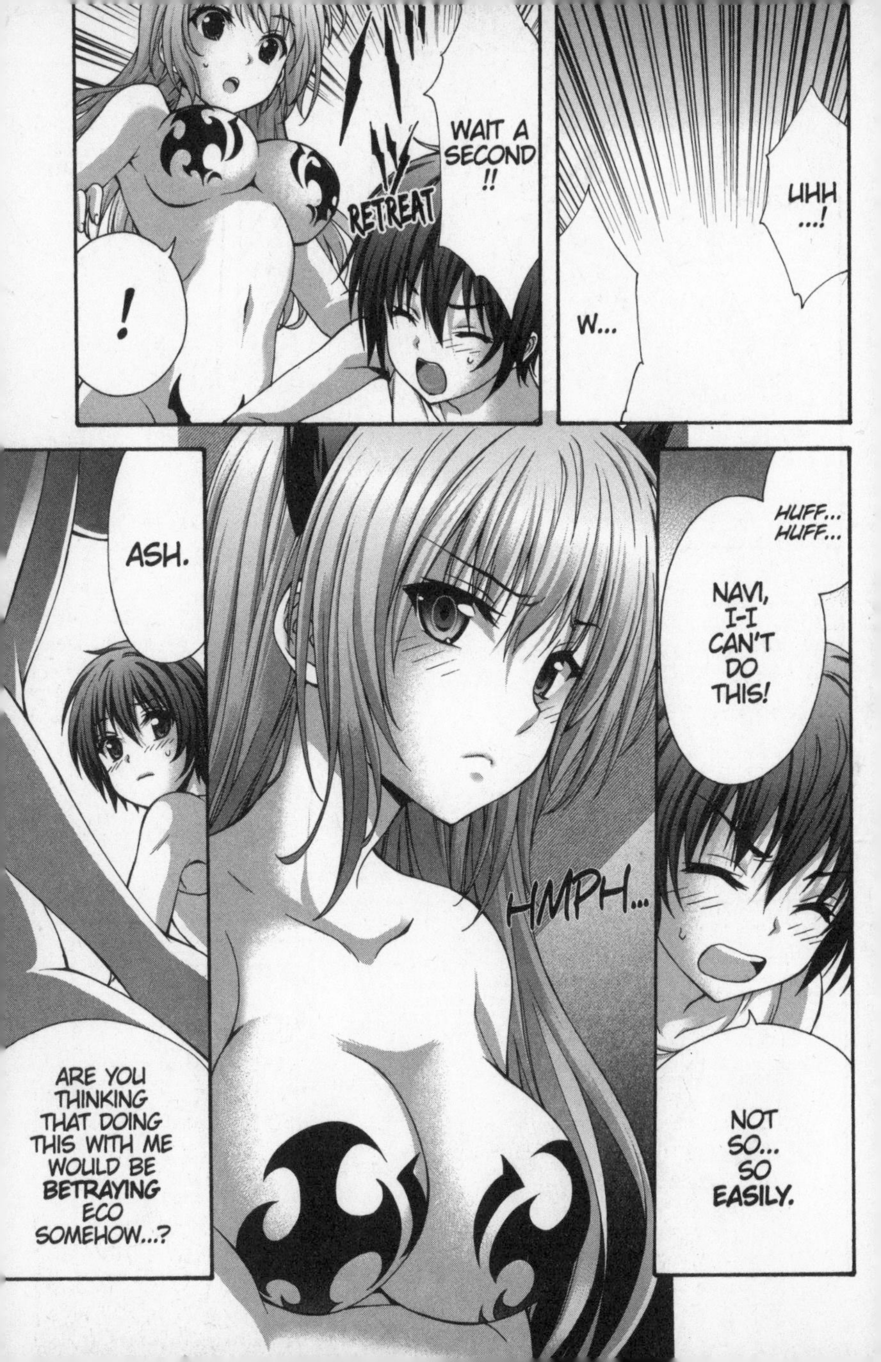
UHH ...!
W...
WAIT A SECOND !!
RETREAT
!
HUFF... HUFF...
NAVI, I-I CAN'T DO THIS!
NOT SO... SO EASILY.
HMPH...
ASH.
ARE YOU THINKING THAT DOING THIS WITH ME WOULD BE BETRAYING ECO SOMEHOW...?

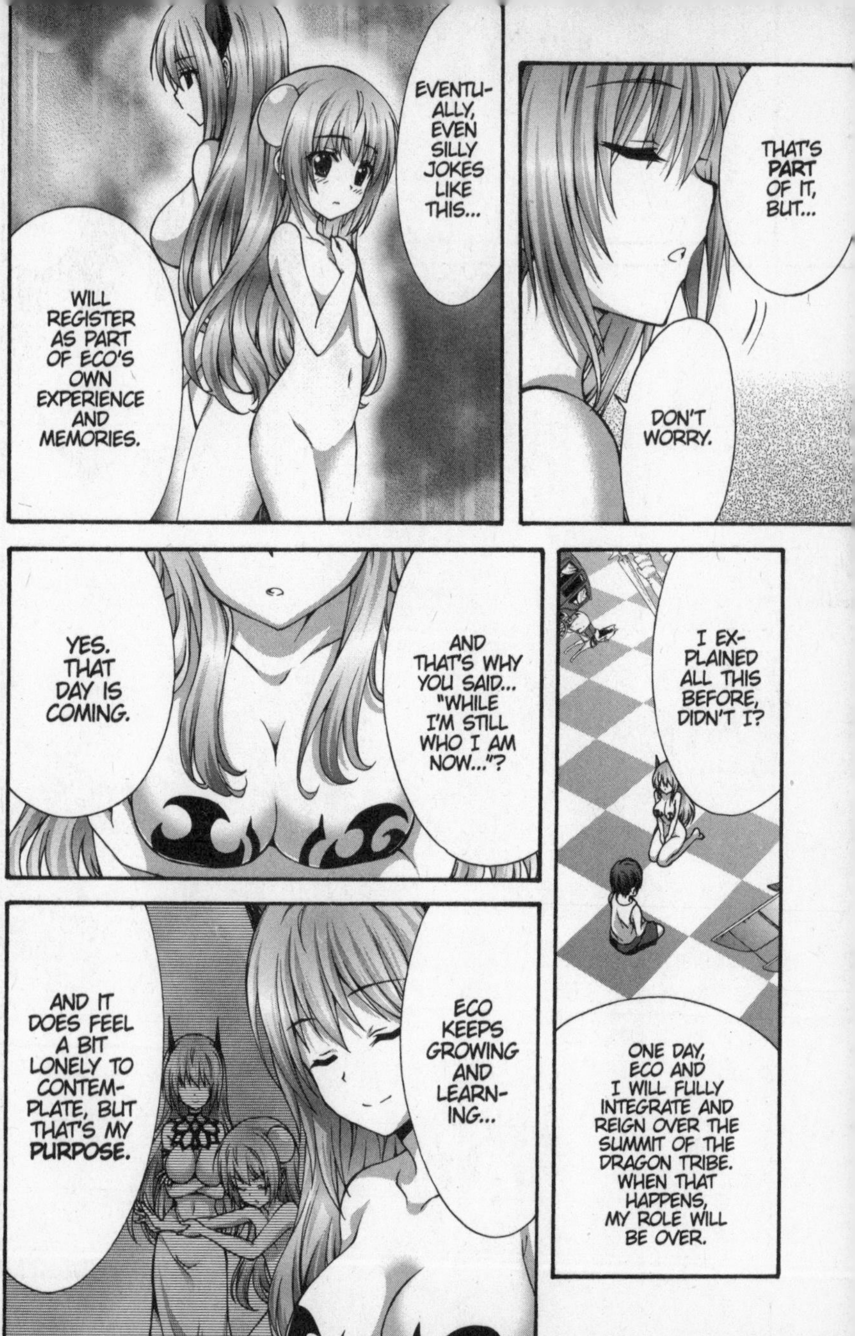
THAT'S PART OF IT, BUT...
DON'T WORRY.
EVENTU-ALLY, EVEN SILLY JOKES LIKE THIS...
WILL REGISTER AS PART OF ECO'S OWN EXPERIENCE AND MEMORIES.
I EX-PLAINED ALL THIS BEFORE, DIDN'T I?
ONE DAY, ECO AND I WILL FULLY INTEGRATE AND REIGN OVER THE SUMMIT OF THE DRAGON TRIBE. WHEN THAT HAPPENS, MY ROLE WILL BE OVER.
AND THAT'S WHY YOU SAID... "WHILE I'M STILL WHO I AM NOW..."?
YES. THAT DAY IS COMING.
ECO KEEPS GROWING AND LEARN-ING...
AND IT DOES FEEL A BIT LONELY TO CONTEM-PLATE, BUT THAT'S MY **PURPOSE.**

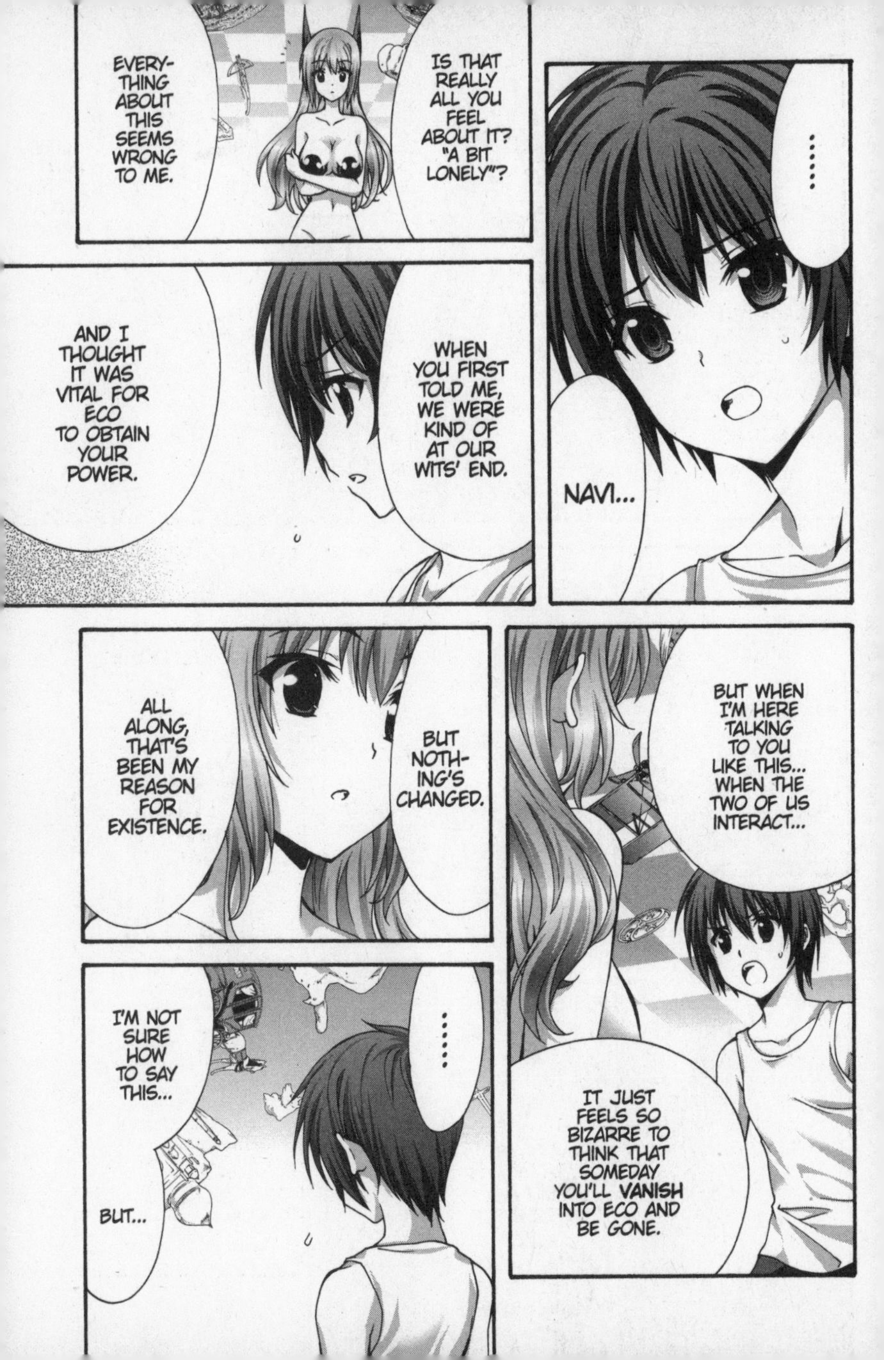
......
NAVI...
IS THAT REALLY ALL YOU FEEL ABOUT IT? "A BIT LONELY"?
EVERY-THING ABOUT THIS SEEMS WRONG TO ME.
WHEN YOU FIRST TOLD ME, WE WERE KIND OF AT OUR WITS' END.
AND I THOUGHT IT WAS VITAL FOR ECO TO OBTAIN YOUR POWER.
BUT WHEN I'M HERE TALKING TO YOU LIKE THIS... WHEN THE TWO OF US INTERACT...
IT JUST FEELS SO BIZARRE TO THINK THAT SOMEDAY YOU'LL **VANISH** INTO ECO AND BE GONE.
BUT NOTH-ING'S CHANGED.
ALL ALONG, THAT'S BEEN MY REASON FOR EXISTENCE.
......
I'M NOT SURE HOW TO SAY THIS...
BUT...

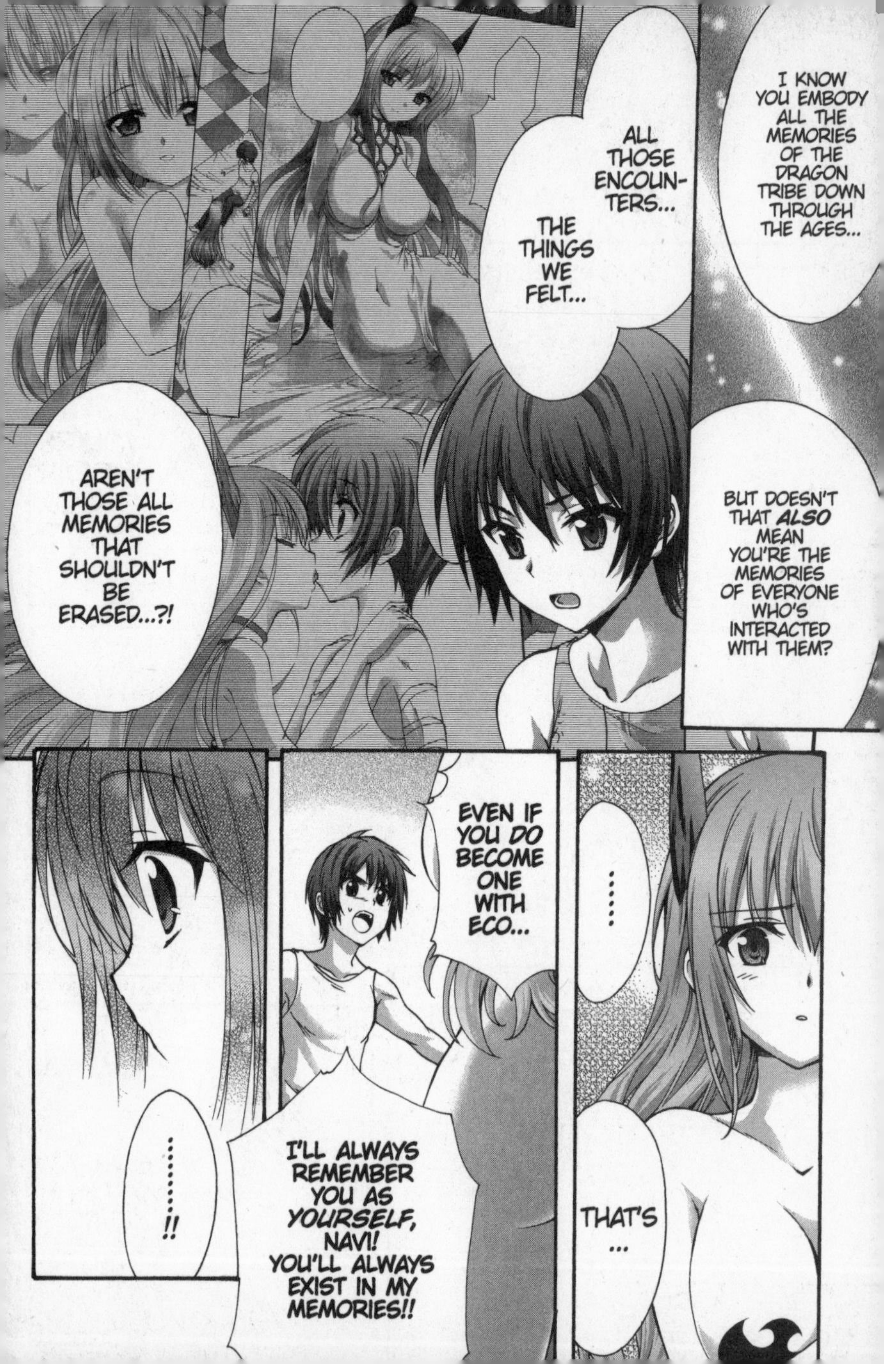
I KNOW YOU EMBODY ALL THE MEMORIES OF THE DRAGON TRIBE DOWN THROUGH THE AGES...
ALL THOSE ENCOUN-TERS...
THE THINGS WE FELT...
BUT DOESN'T THAT *ALSO* MEAN YOU'RE THE MEMORIES OF EVERYONE WHO'S INTERACTED WITH THEM?
AREN'T THOSE ALL MEMORIES THAT SHOULDN'T BE ERASED...?!
......
THAT'S ...
EVEN IF YOU *DO* BECOME ONE WITH ECO...
I'LL ALWAYS REMEMBER YOU AS *YOURSELF*, NAVI! YOU'LL ALWAYS EXIST IN MY MEMORIES!!
......!!

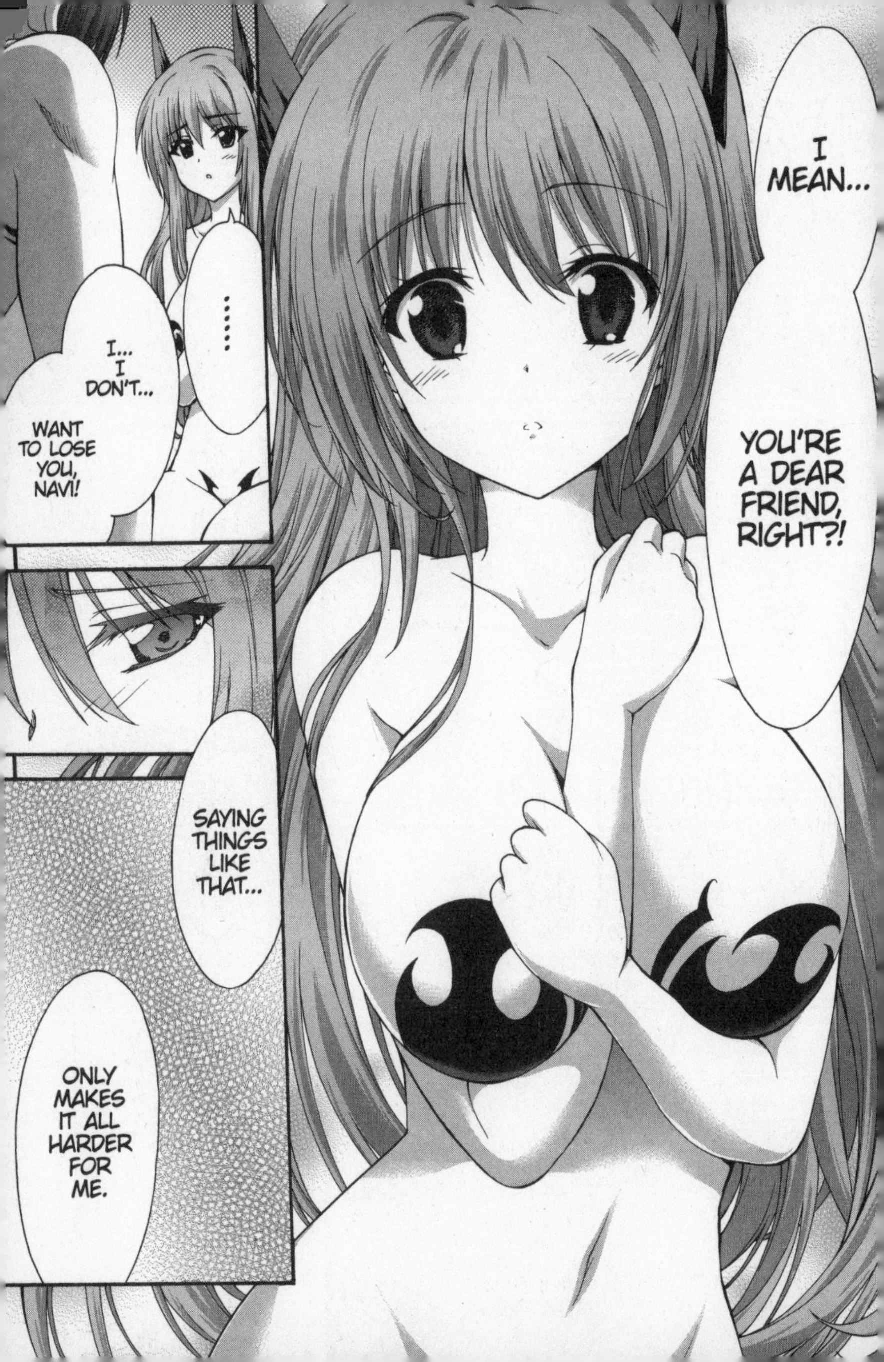
I MEAN...
YOU'RE A DEAR FRIEND, RIGHT?!
......
I... I DON'T...
WANT TO LOSE YOU, NAVI!
SAYING THINGS LIKE THAT...
ONLY MAKES IT ALL HARDER FOR ME.

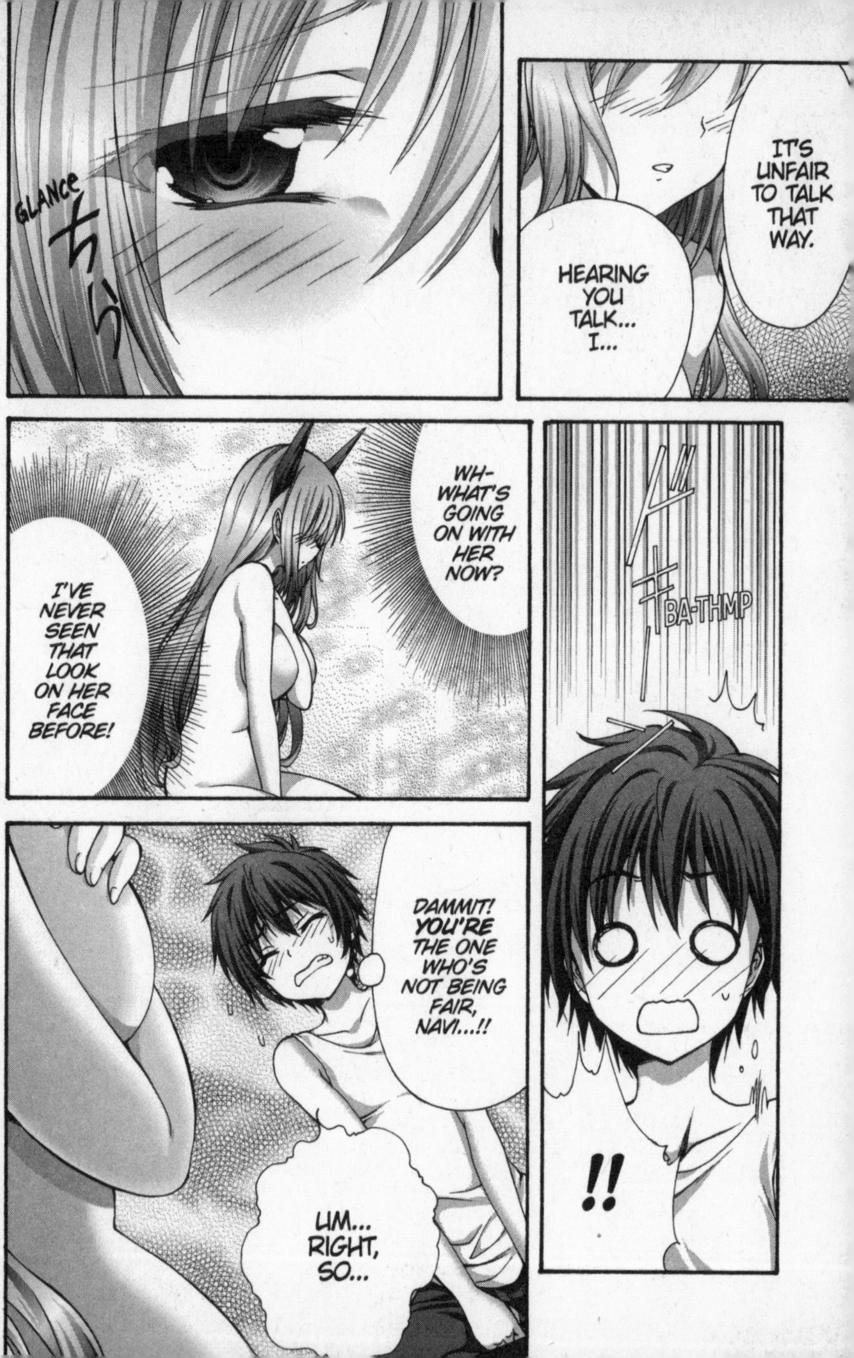
IT'S UNFAIR TO TALK THAT WAY.
HEARING YOU TALK... I...
GLANCE
ちら
BA-THMP
WH-WHAT'S GOING ON WITH HER NOW?
I'VE NEVER SEEN THAT LOOK ON HER FACE BEFORE!
!!
DAMMIT! YOU'RE THE ONE WHO'S NOT BEING FAIR, NAVI...!!
UM... RIGHT, SO...

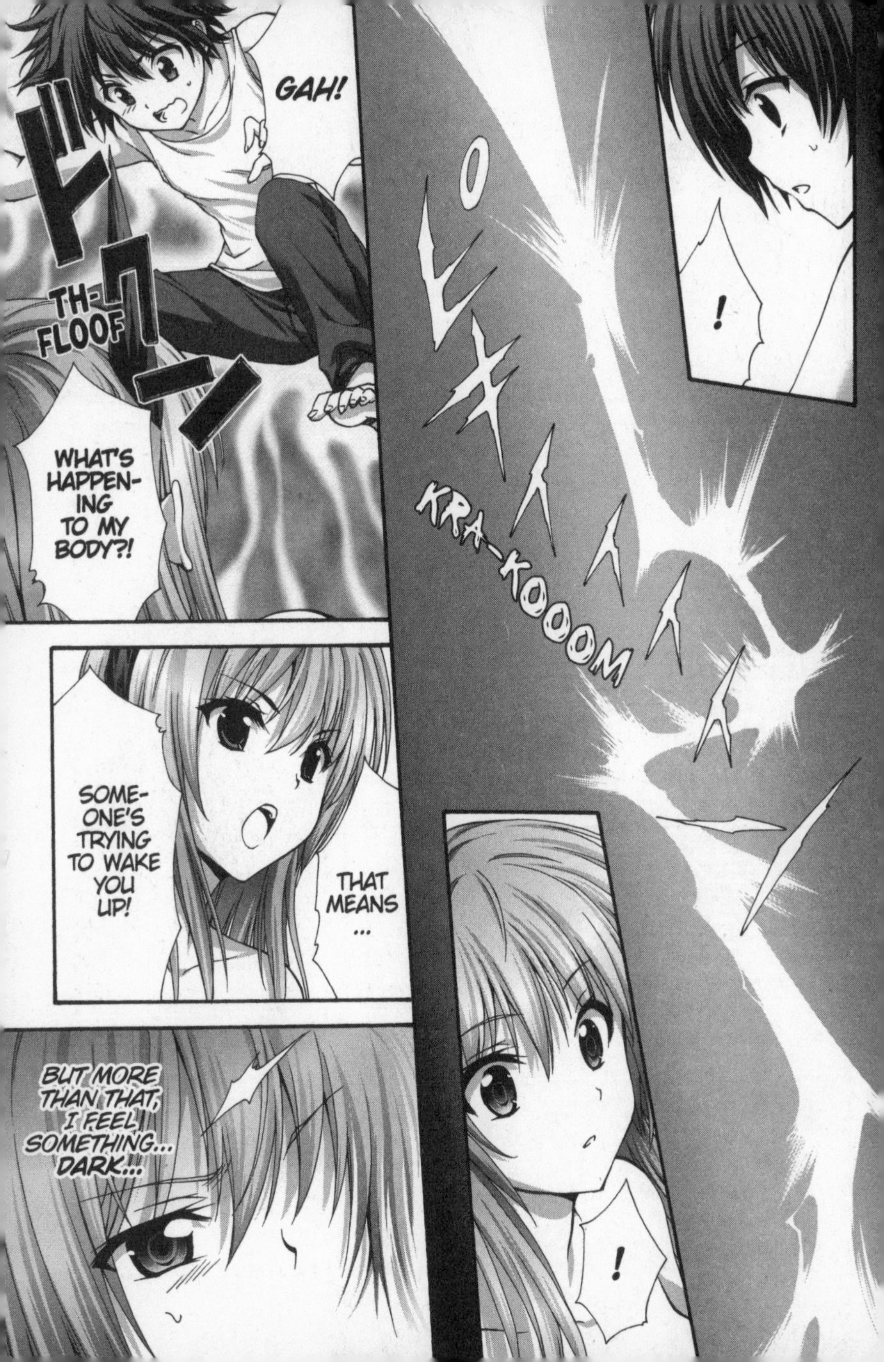
!
KRA-KOOOM
!
GAH!
TH-FLOOF
WHAT'S HAPPEN-ING TO MY BODY?!
SOME-ONE'S TRYING TO WAKE YOU UP!
THAT MEANS ...
BUT MORE THAN THAT, I FEEL SOMETHING... DARK...

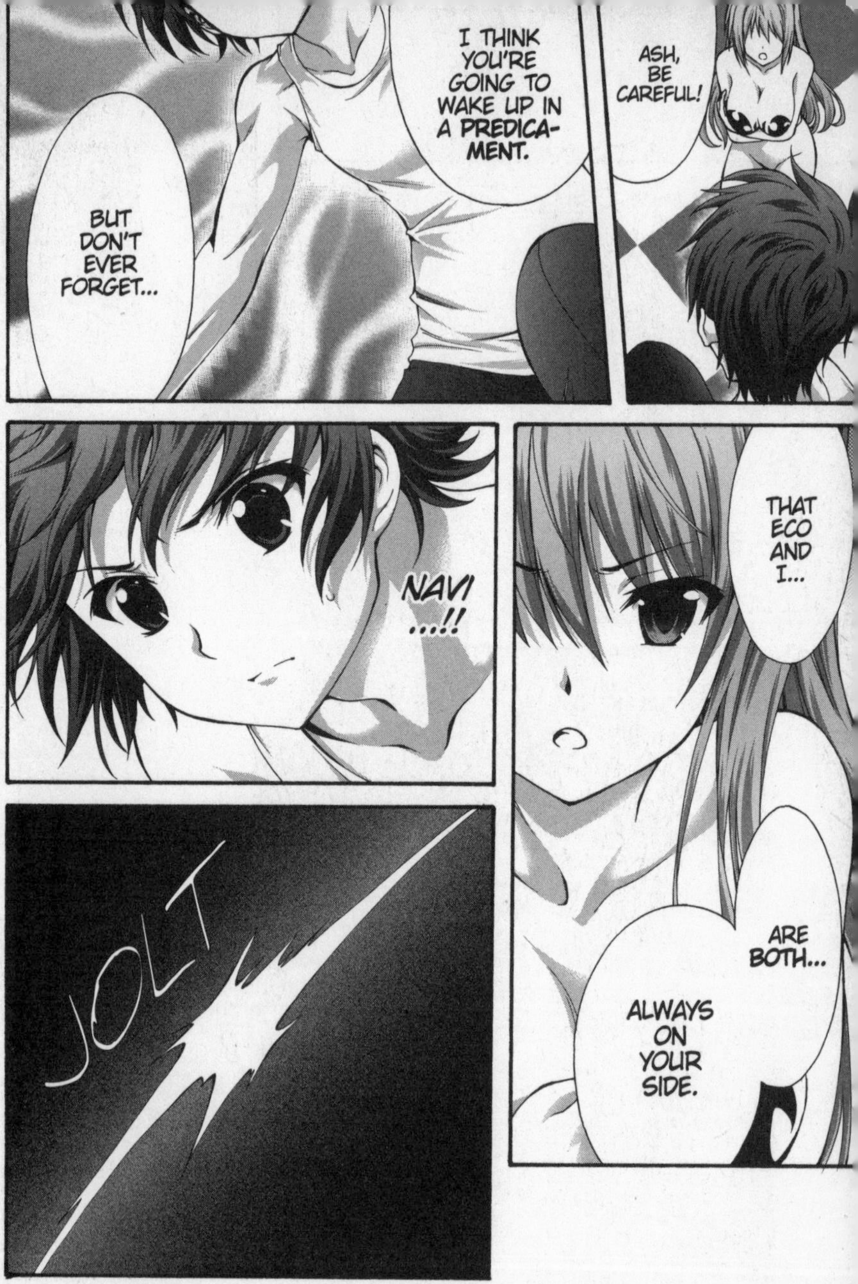
ASH, BE CAREFUL!
I THINK YOU'RE GOING TO WAKE UP IN A PREDICAMENT.
BUT DON'T EVER FORGET...
THAT ECO AND I...
ARE BOTH...
ALWAYS ON YOUR SIDE.
NAVI ...!!
JOLT

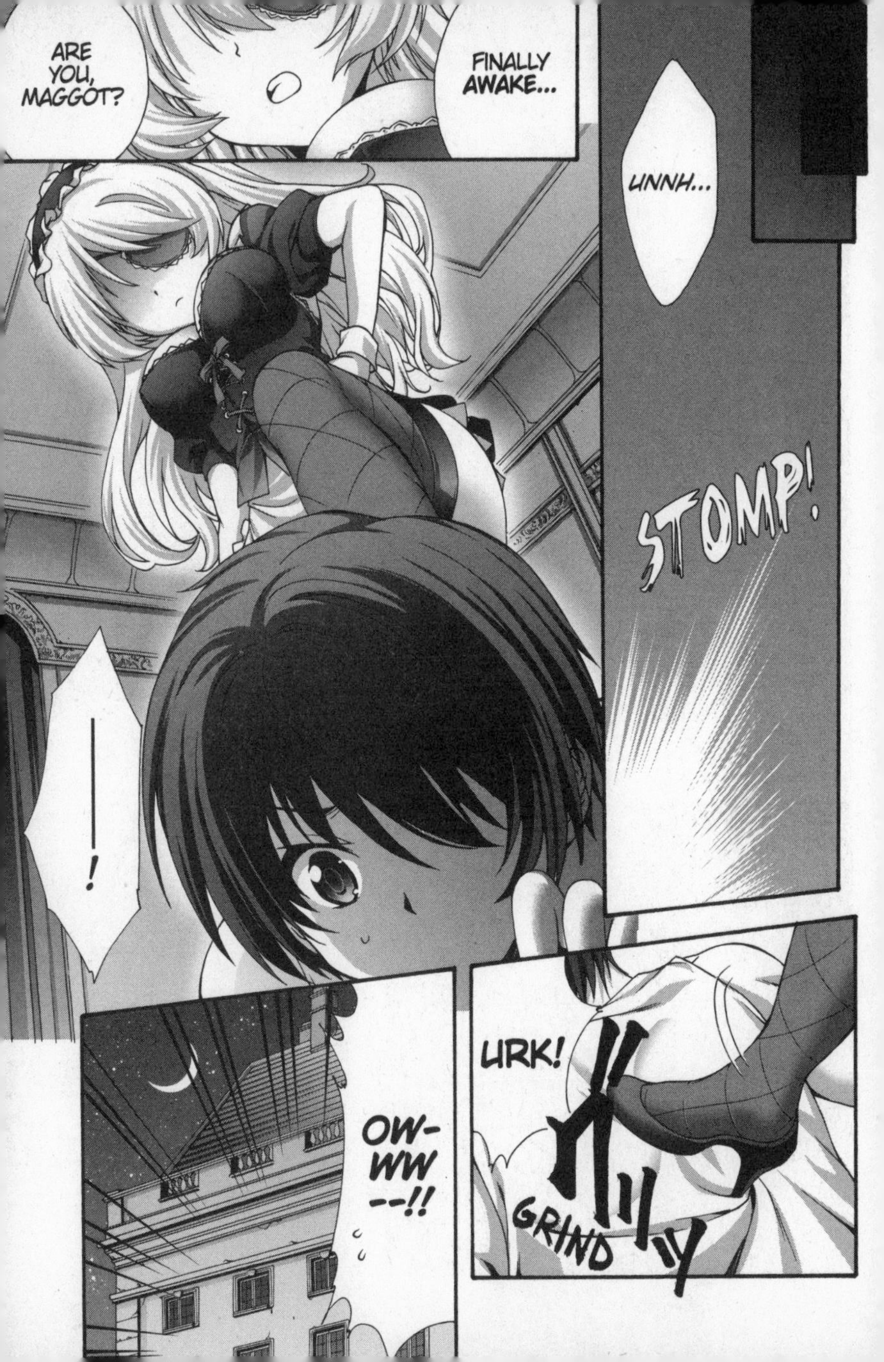
UNNH...
STOMP!
FINALLY AWAKE...
ARE YOU, MAGGOT?
——!
URK!
GRIND
OW-WW--!!

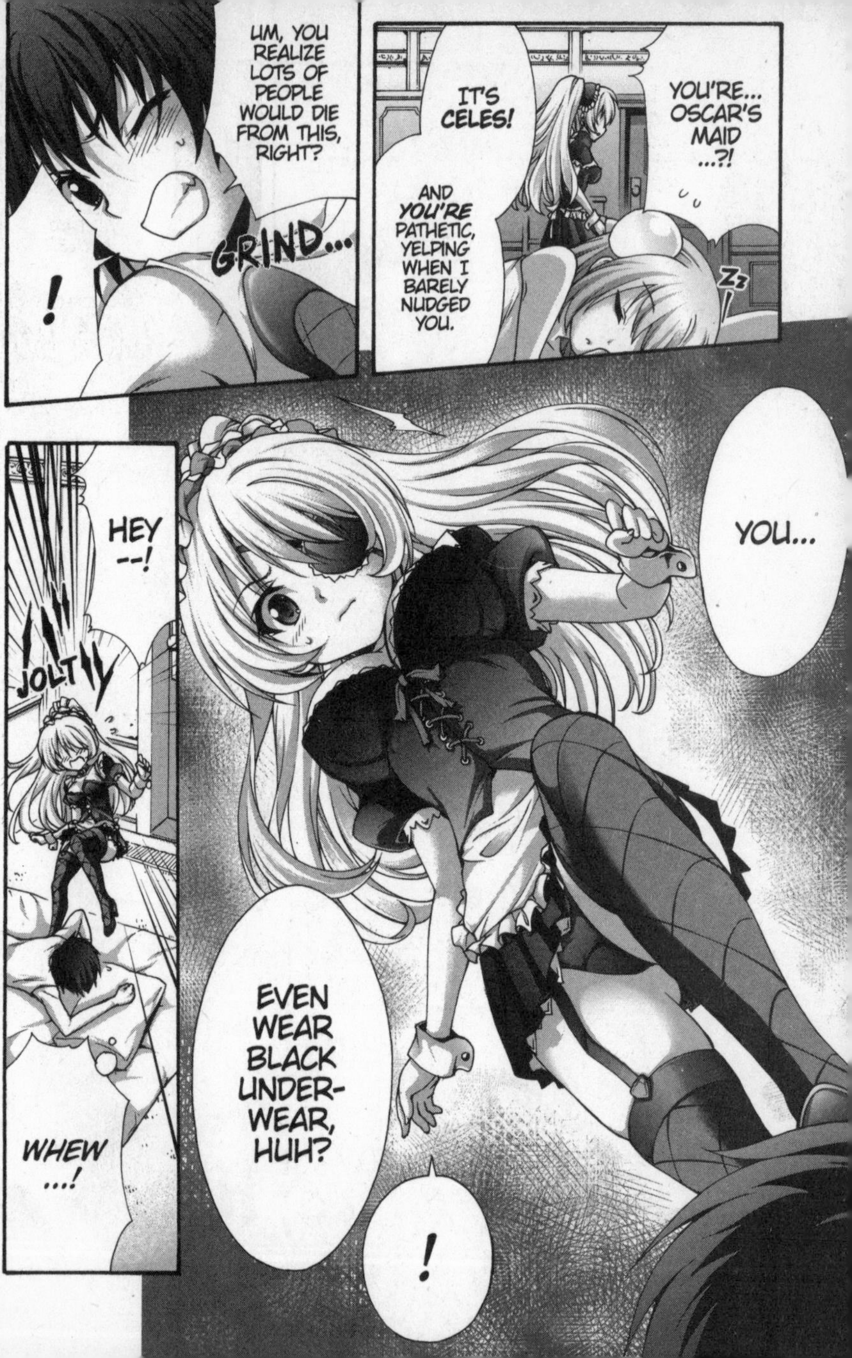
YOU'RE... OSCAR'S MAID ...?!
IT'S CELES!
AND *YOU'RE* PATHETIC, YELPING WHEN I BARELY NUDGED YOU.
Zz
UM, YOU REALIZE LOTS OF PEOPLE WOULD DIE FROM THIS, RIGHT?
GRIND...
!
YOU...
EVEN WEAR BLACK UNDER-WEAR, HUH?
!
HEY --!
JOLT
WHEW ...!

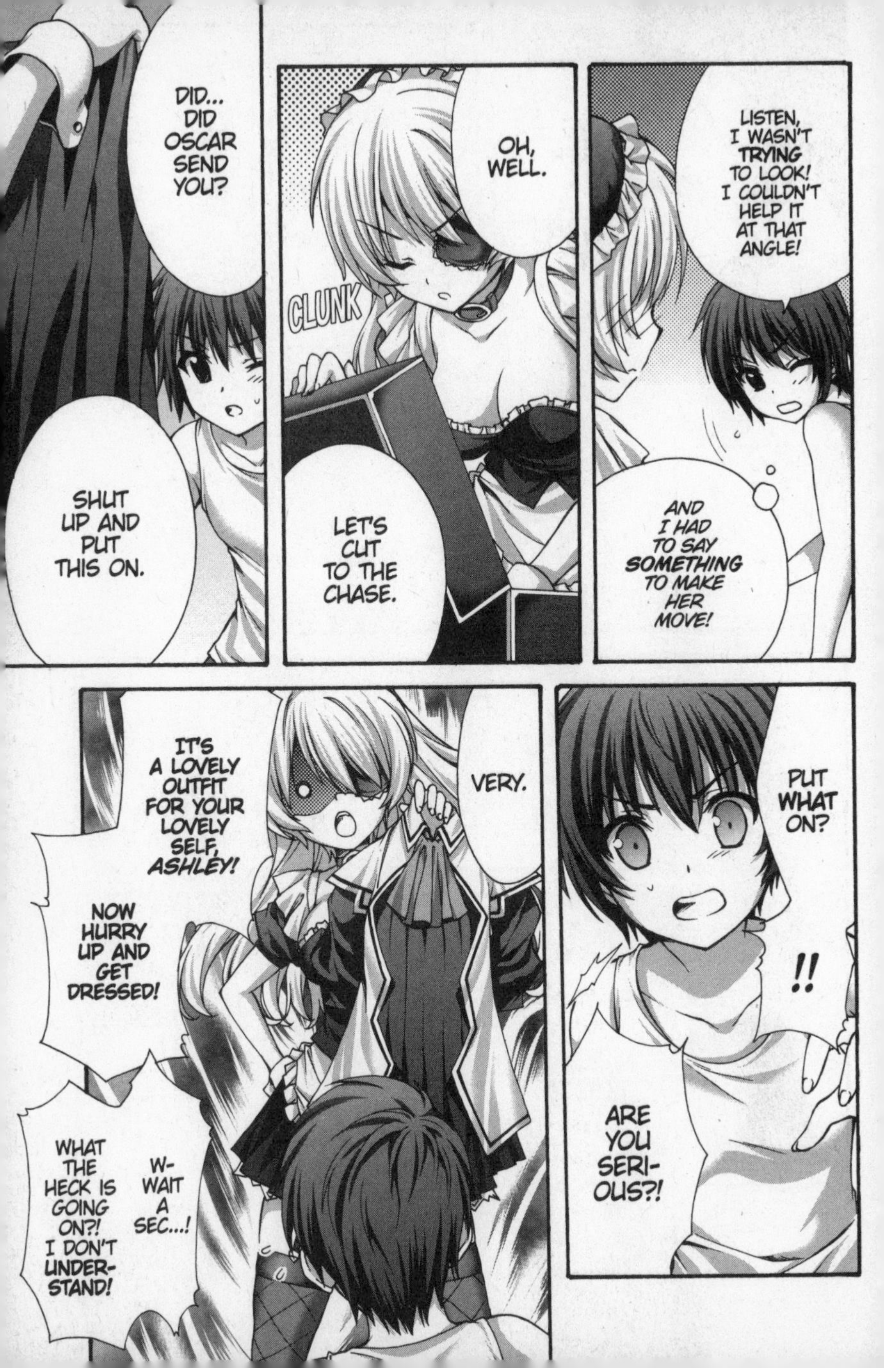
LISTEN, I WASN'T TRYING TO LOOK! I COULDN'T HELP IT AT THAT ANGLE!
AND I HAD TO SAY SOMETHING TO MAKE HER MOVE!
OH, WELL.
CLUNK
LET'S CUT TO THE CHASE.
DID... DID OSCAR SEND YOU?
SHUT UP AND PUT THIS ON.
PUT WHAT ON?
!!
ARE YOU SERI-OUS?!
VERY.
IT'S A LOVELY OUTFIT FOR YOUR LOVELY SELF, ASHLEY!
NOW HURRY UP AND GET DRESSED!
W-WAIT A SEC...!
WHAT THE HECK IS GOING ON?! I DON'T UNDER-STAND!

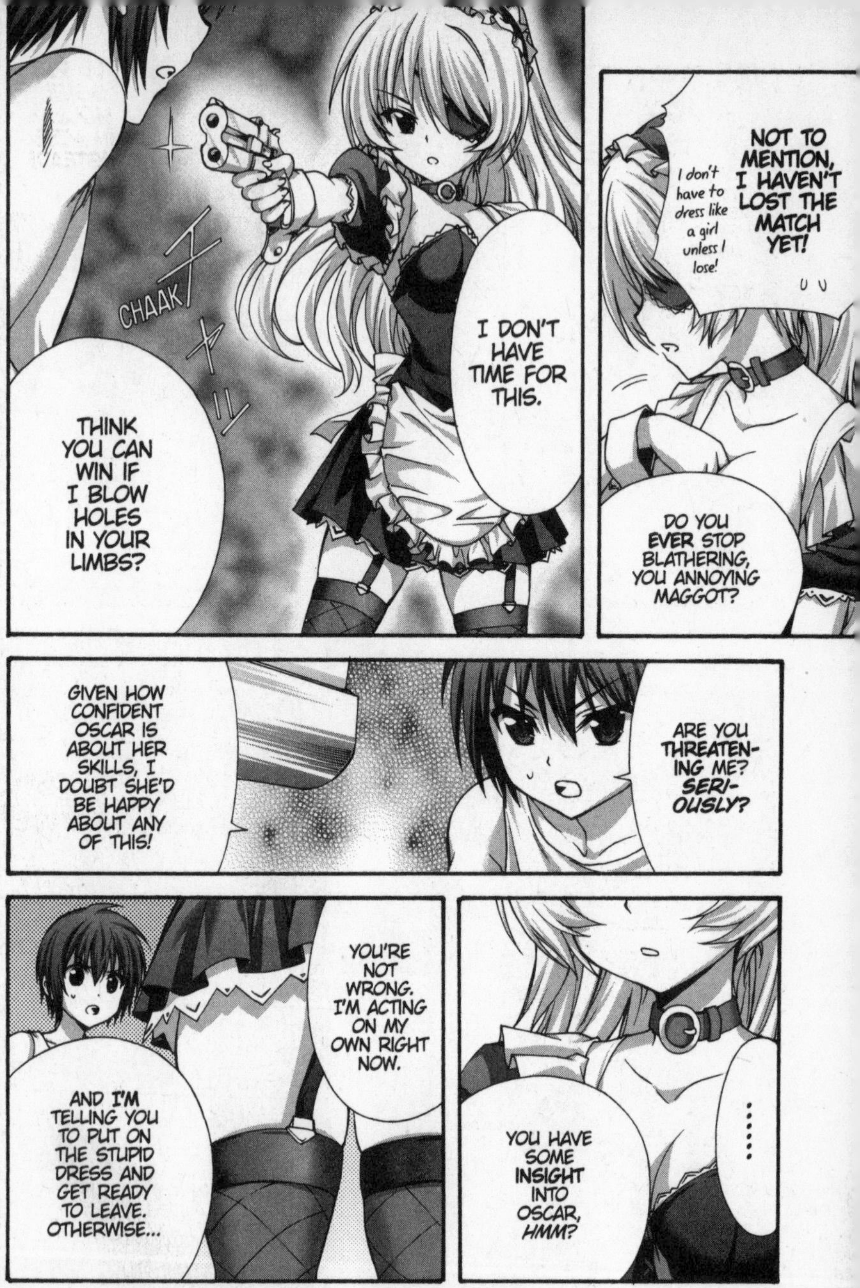
NOT TO MENTION, I HAVEN'T LOST THE MATCH YET!
I don't have to dress like a girl unless I lose!
DO YOU EVER STOP BLATHERING, YOU ANNOYING MAGGOT?
I DON'T HAVE TIME FOR THIS.
CHAAK
THINK YOU CAN WIN IF I BLOW HOLES IN YOUR LIMBS?
ARE YOU THREATENING ME? SERIOUSLY?
GIVEN HOW CONFIDENT OSCAR IS ABOUT HER SKILLS, I DOUBT SHE'D BE HAPPY ABOUT ANY OF THIS!
......
YOU HAVE SOME INSIGHT INTO OSCAR, HMM?
YOU'RE NOT WRONG. I'M ACTING ON MY OWN RIGHT NOW.
AND I'M TELLING YOU TO PUT ON THE STUPID DRESS AND GET READY TO LEAVE. OTHERWISE...

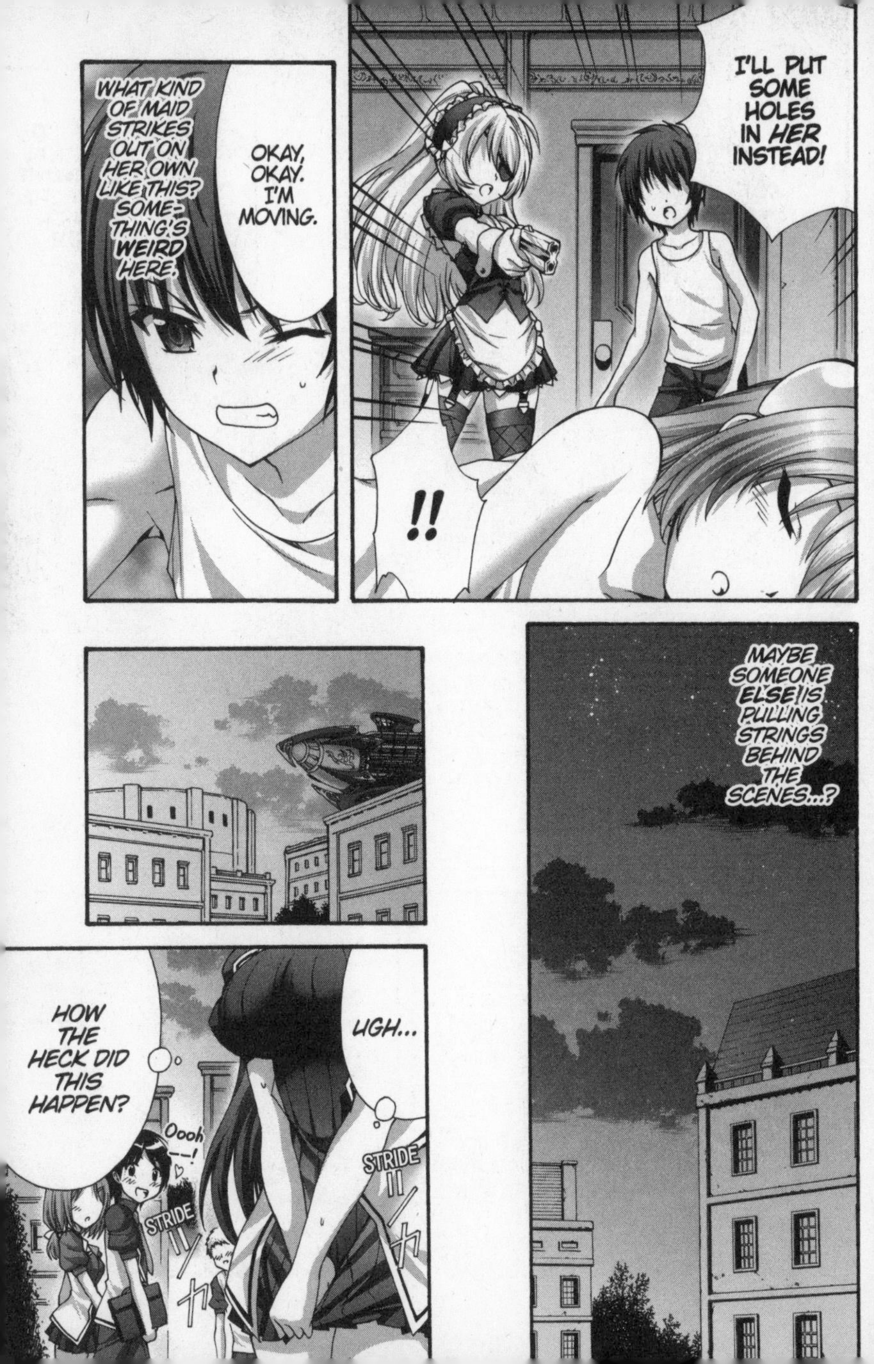
I'LL PUT SOME HOLES IN HER INSTEAD!
!!
OKAY, OKAY. I'M MOVING.
WHAT KIND OF MAID STRIKES OUT ON HER OWN LIKE THIS? SOME-THING'S WEIRD HERE.
MAYBE SOMEONE ELSE IS PULLING STRINGS BEHIND THE SCENES...?
UGH...
HOW THE HECK DID THIS HAPPEN?
STRIDE
Oooh—!
STRIDE

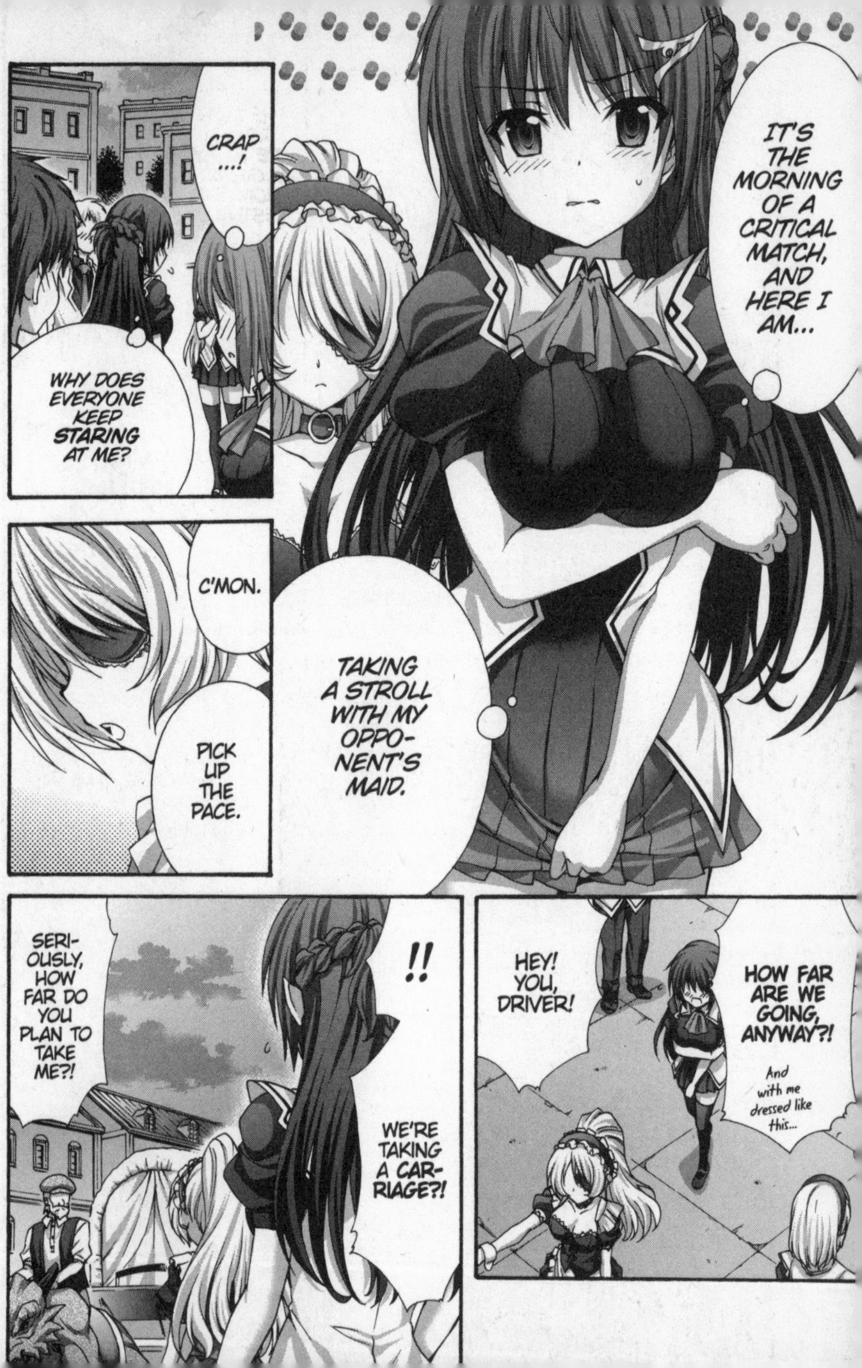

IT'S THE MORNING OF A CRITICAL MATCH, AND HERE I AM...
TAKING A STROLL WITH MY OPPONENT'S MAID.
CRAP ...!
WHY DOES EVERYONE KEEP STARING AT ME?
C'MON.
PICK UP THE PACE.
HOW FAR ARE WE GOING, ANYWAY?!
And with me dressed like this...
HEY! YOU, DRIVER!
SERI-OUSLY, HOW FAR DO YOU PLAN TO TAKE ME?!
!!
WE'RE TAKING A CAR-RIAGE?!

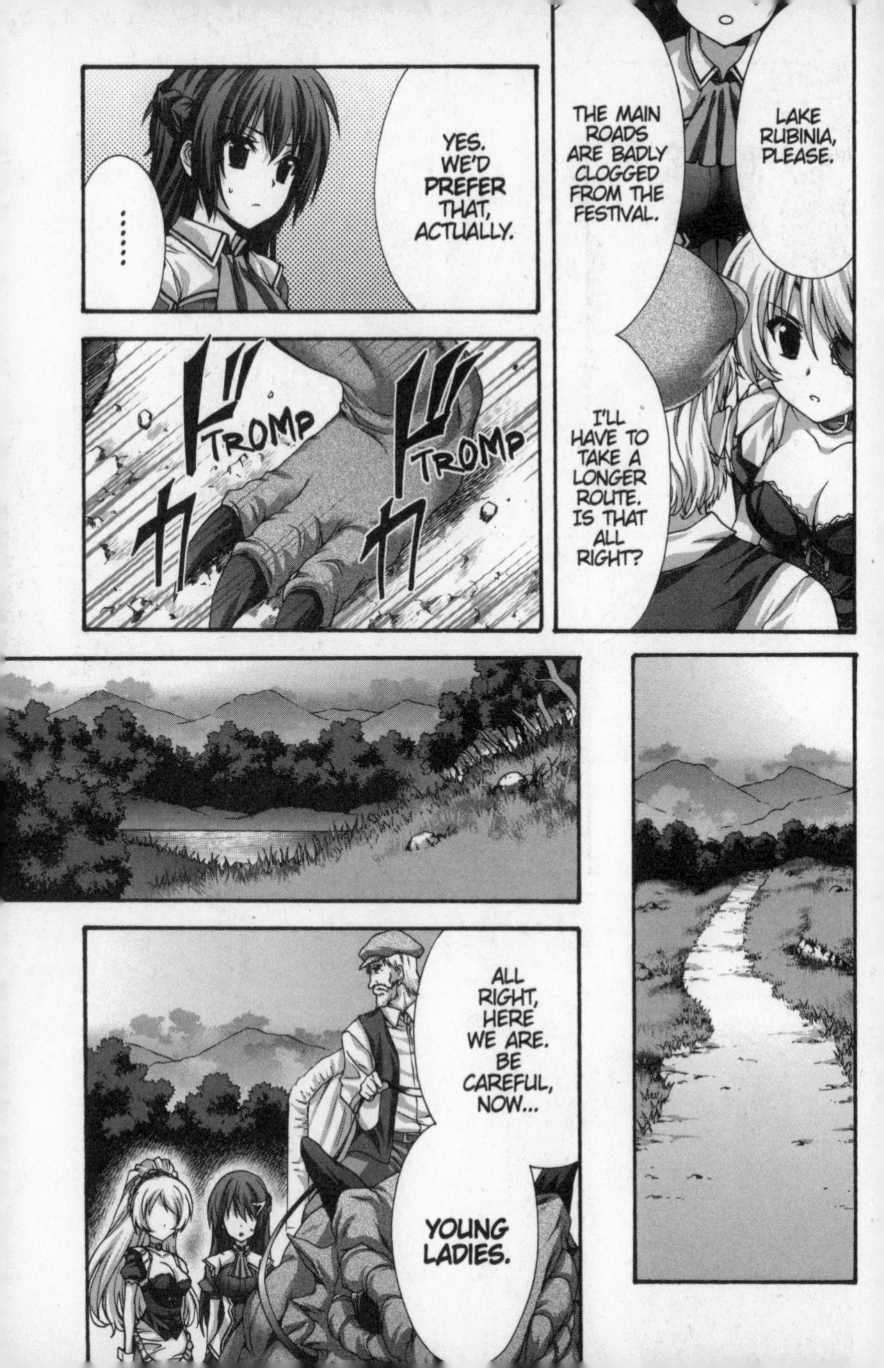
LAKE RUBINIA, PLEASE.
THE MAIN ROADS ARE BADLY CLOGGED FROM THE FESTIVAL.
I'LL HAVE TO TAKE A LONGER ROUTE. IS THAT ALL RIGHT?
YES. WE'D PREFER THAT, ACTUALLY.
......
ドカ
TROMP
ドカ
TROMP
ALL RIGHT, HERE WE ARE. BE CAREFUL, NOW...
YOUNG LADIES.

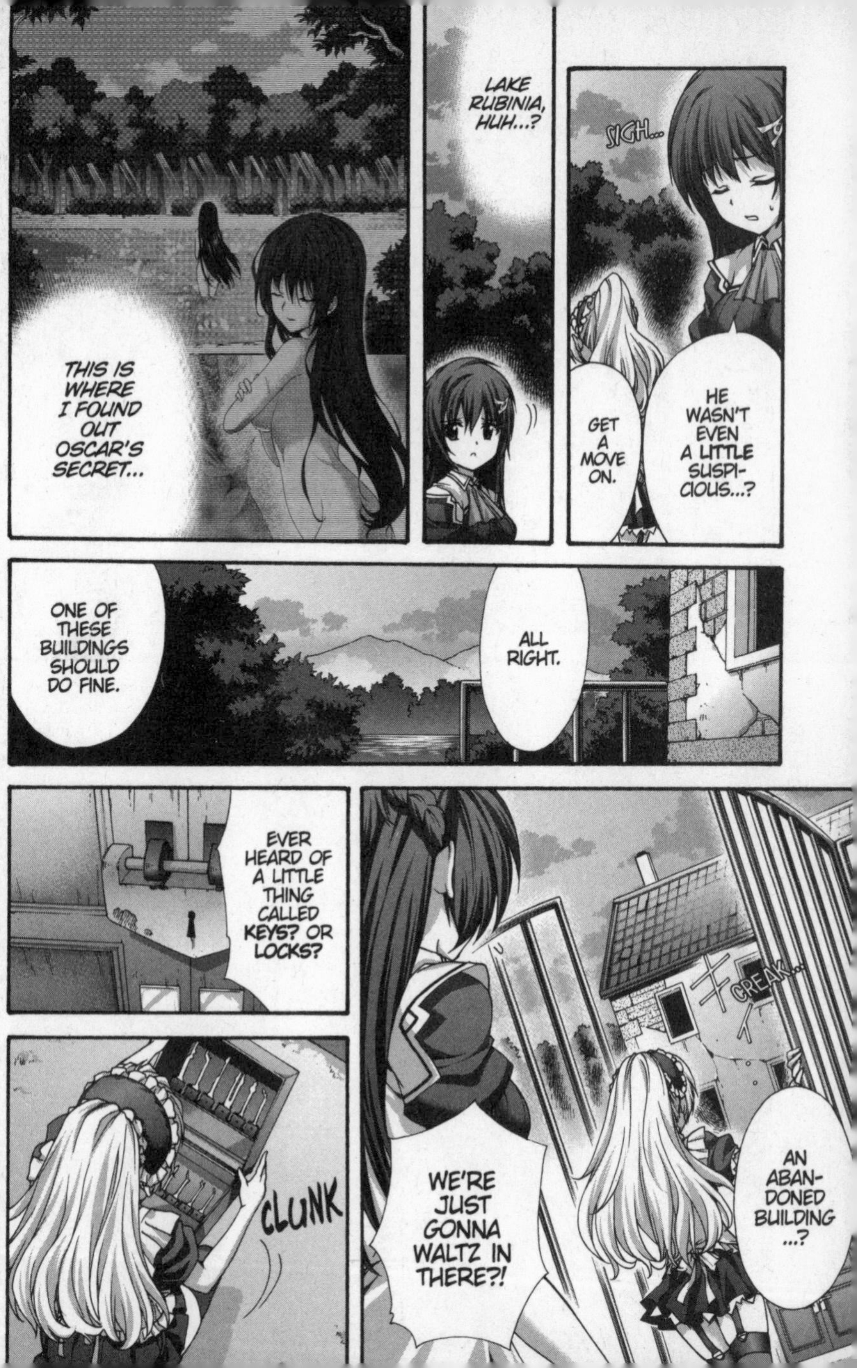
SIGH...
HE WASN'T EVEN A LITTLE SUSPICIOUS...?
GET A MOVE ON.
LAKE RUBINIA, HUH...?
THIS IS WHERE I FOUND OUT OSCAR'S SECRET...
ALL RIGHT.
ONE OF THESE BUILDINGS SHOULD DO FINE.
CREAK...
AN ABANDONED BUILDING...?
WE'RE JUST GONNA WALTZ IN THERE?!
EVER HEARD OF A LITTLE THING CALLED KEYS? OR LOCKS?
CLUNK

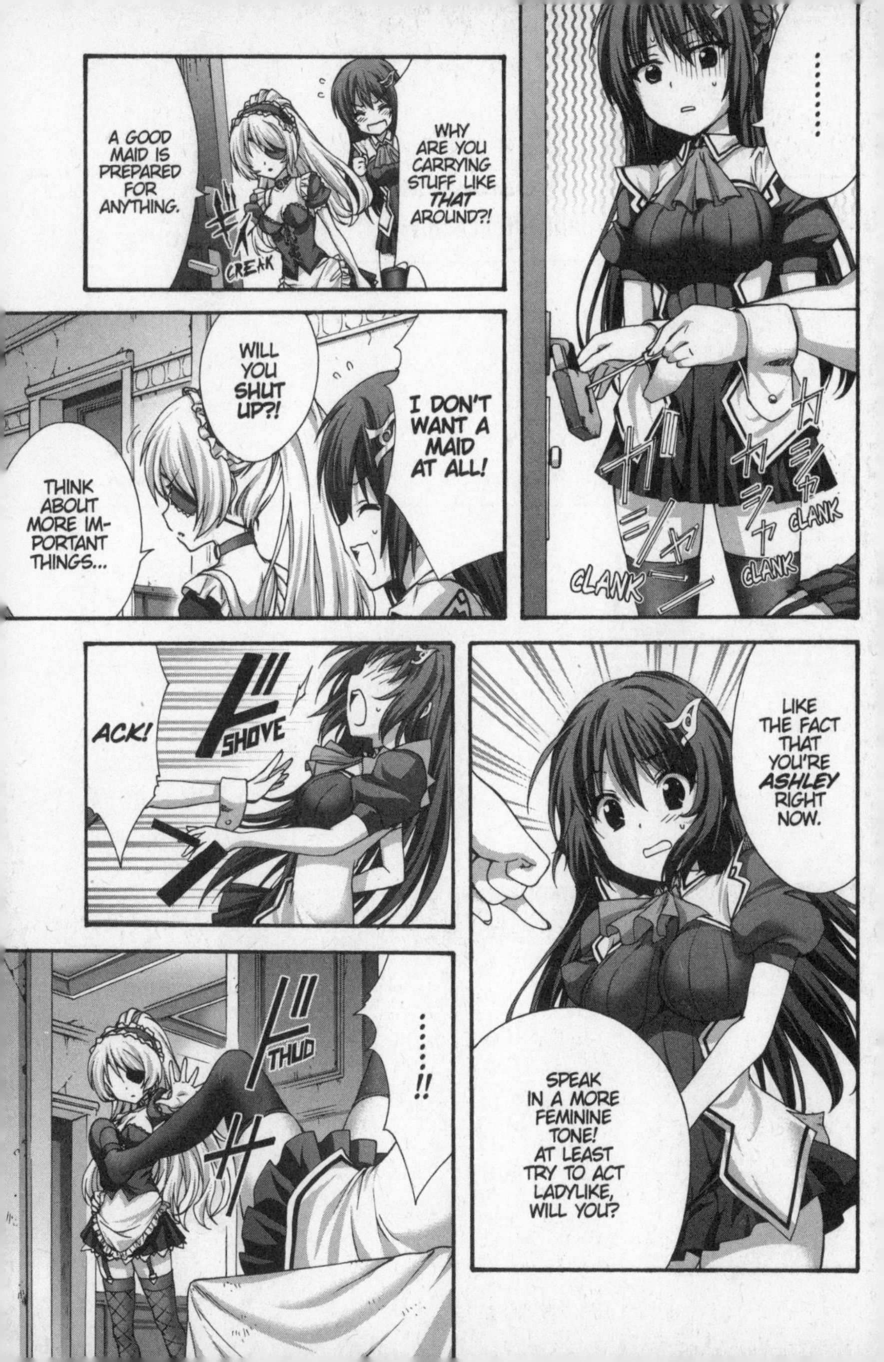

......
CLANK
CLANK
CLANK
WHY ARE YOU CARRYING STUFF LIKE *THAT* AROUND?!
A GOOD MAID IS PREPARED FOR ANYTHING.
CREAK
I DON'T WANT A MAID AT ALL!
WILL YOU SHUT UP?!
THINK ABOUT MORE IM-PORTANT THINGS...
LIKE THE FACT THAT YOU'RE *ASHLEY* RIGHT NOW.
SHOVE
ACK!
SPEAK IN A MORE FEMININE TONE! AT LEAST TRY TO ACT LADYLIKE, WILL YOU?
......!!
THUD

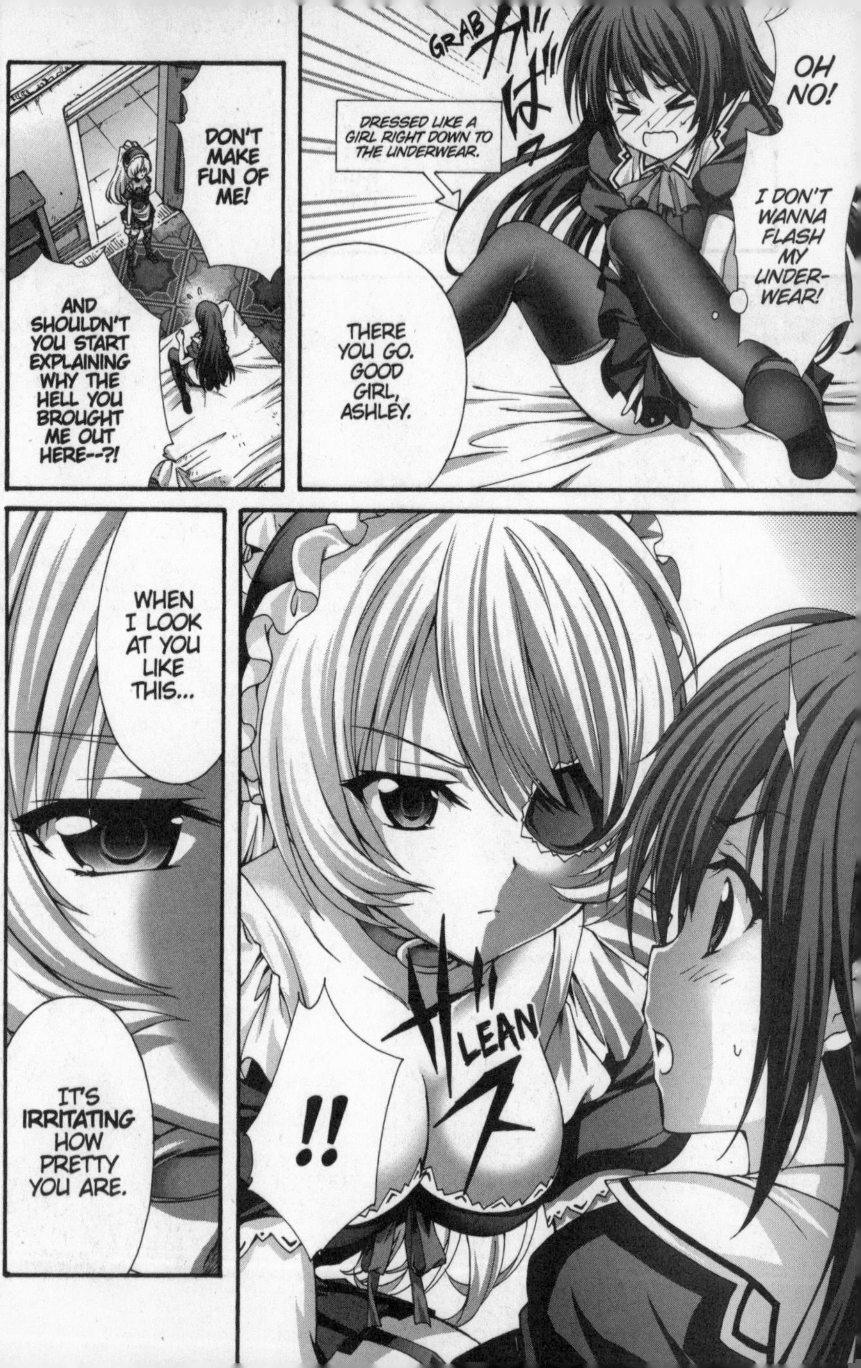
GRAB
OH NO!
I DON'T WANNA FLASH MY UNDER-WEAR!
DRESSED LIKE A GIRL RIGHT DOWN TO THE UNDERWEAR.
THERE YOU GO. GOOD GIRL, ASHLEY.
DON'T MAKE FUN OF ME!
AND SHOULDN'T YOU START EXPLAINING WHY THE HELL YOU BROUGHT ME OUT HERE--?!
LEAN
!!
WHEN I LOOK AT YOU LIKE THIS...
IT'S IRRITATING HOW PRETTY YOU ARE.

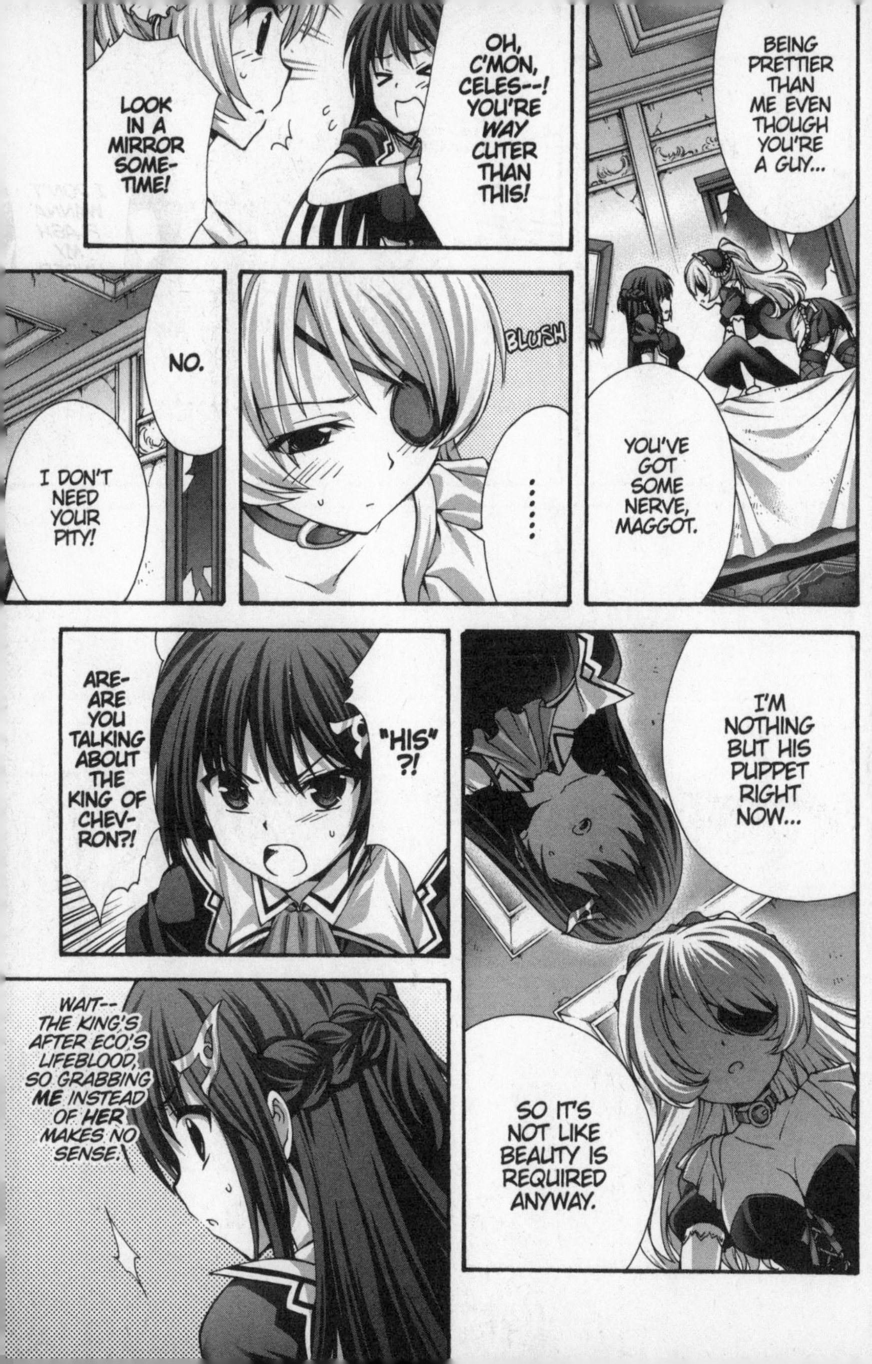
BEING PRETTIER THAN ME EVEN THOUGH YOU'RE A GUY...
YOU'VE GOT SOME NERVE, MAGGOT.
OH, C'MON, CELES--! YOU'RE *WAY* CUTER THAN THIS!
LOOK IN A MIRROR SOME-TIME!
BLUSH
......
NO.
I DON'T NEED YOUR PITY!
I'M NOTHING BUT HIS PUPPET RIGHT NOW...
SO IT'S NOT LIKE BEAUTY IS REQUIRED ANYWAY.
"HIS" ?!
ARE-ARE YOU TALKING ABOUT THE KING OF CHEV-RON?!
*WAIT-- THE KING'S AFTER ECO'S LIFEBLOOD, SO GRABBING **ME** INSTEAD OF **HER** MAKES NO SENSE.*

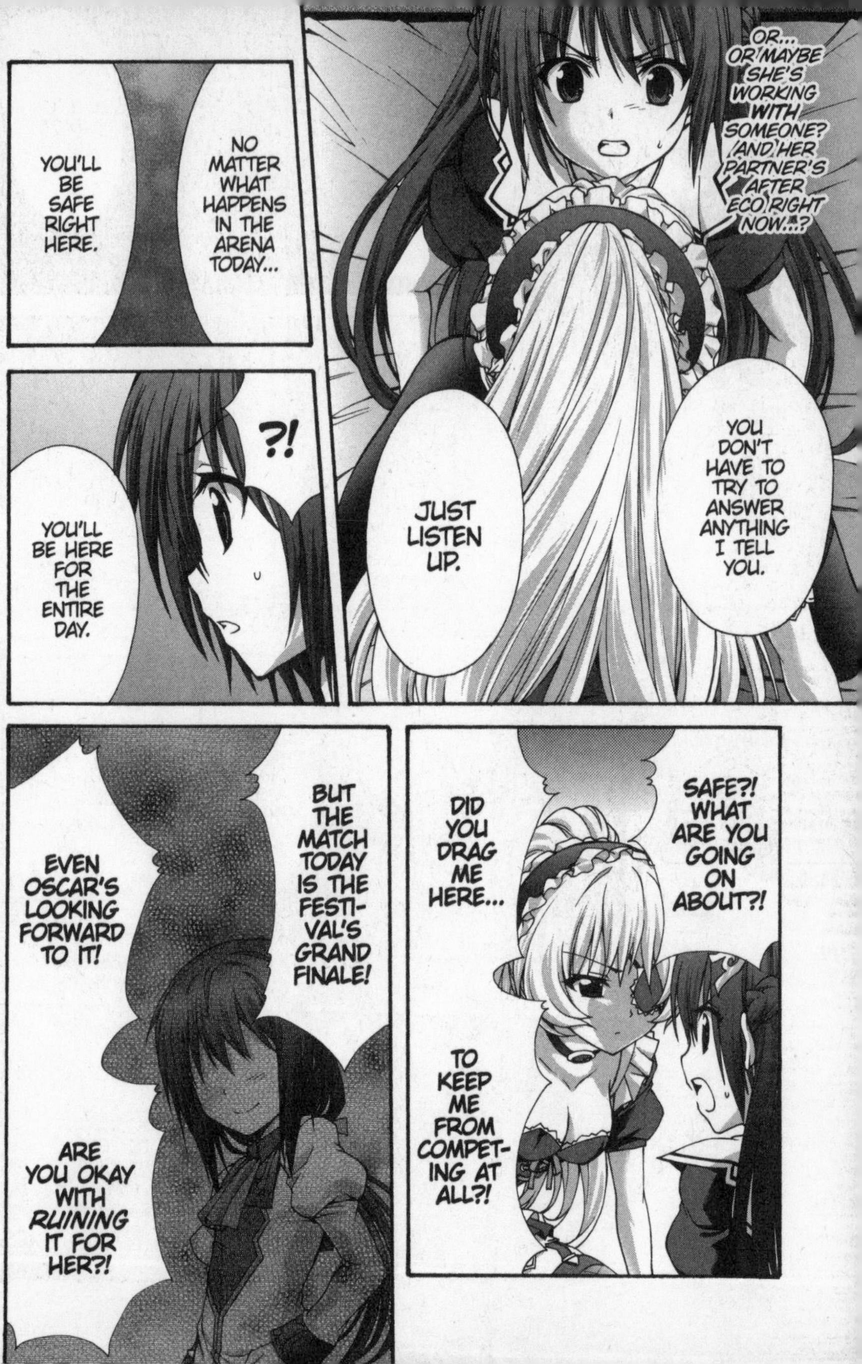
OR... OR MAYBE SHE'S WORKING WITH SOMEONE? AND HER PARTNER'S AFTER ECO RIGHT NOW...?
YOU DON'T HAVE TO TRY TO ANSWER ANYTHING I TELL YOU.
JUST LISTEN UP.
NO MATTER WHAT HAPPENS IN THE ARENA TODAY...
YOU'LL BE SAFE RIGHT HERE.
?!
YOU'LL BE HERE FOR THE ENTIRE DAY.
SAFE?! WHAT ARE YOU GOING ON ABOUT?!
DID YOU DRAG ME HERE...
TO KEEP ME FROM COMPET-ING AT ALL?!
BUT THE MATCH TODAY IS THE FESTI-VAL'S GRAND FINALE!
EVEN OSCAR'S LOOKING FORWARD TO IT!
ARE YOU OKAY WITH *RUINING* IT FOR HER?!

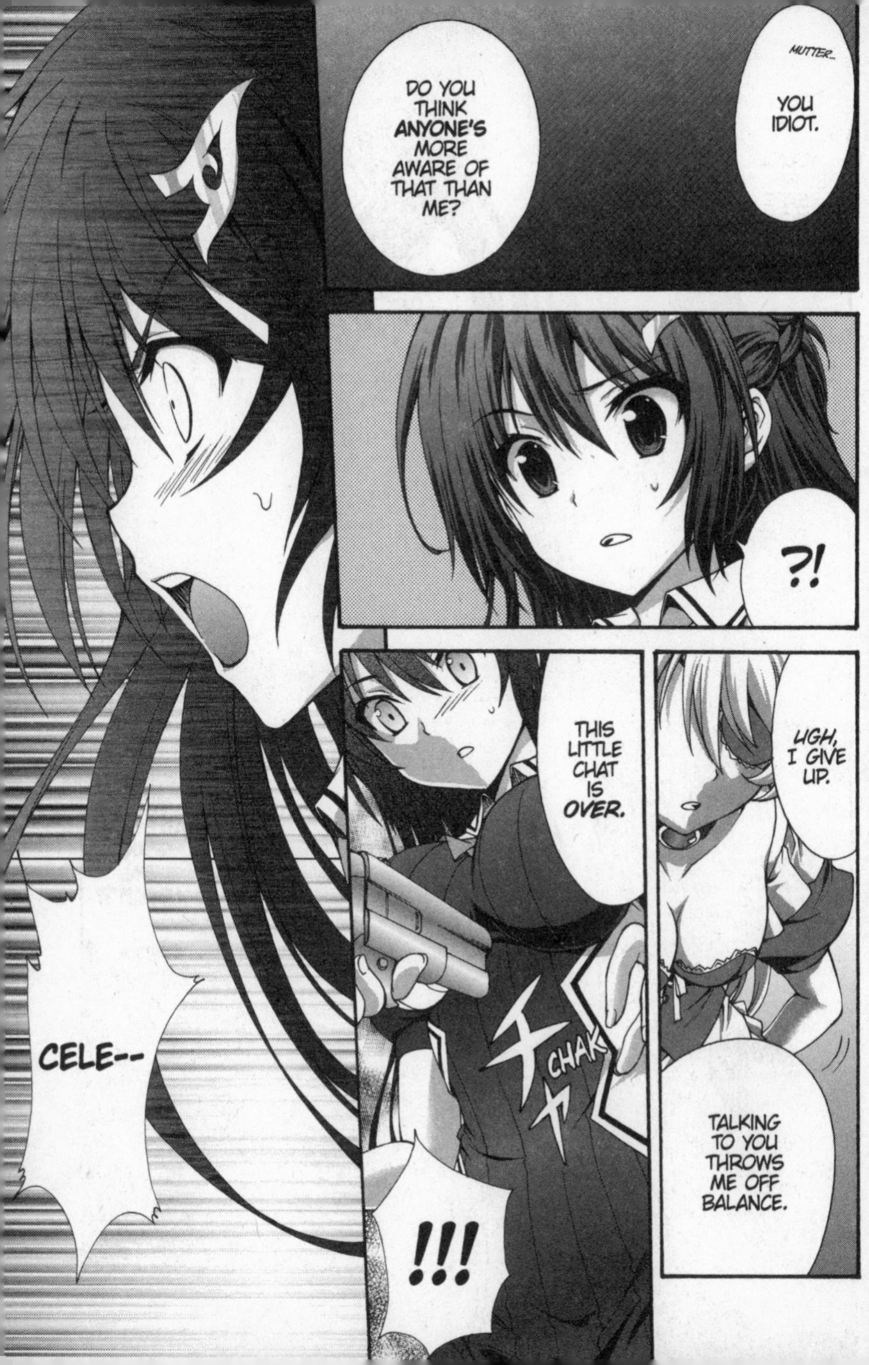
MUTTER...
YOU IDIOT.
DO YOU THINK ANYONE'S MORE AWARE OF THAT THAN ME?
?!
UGH, I GIVE UP.
TALKING TO YOU THROWS ME OFF BALANCE.
THIS LITTLE CHAT IS OVER.
CHAK
!!!
CELE--

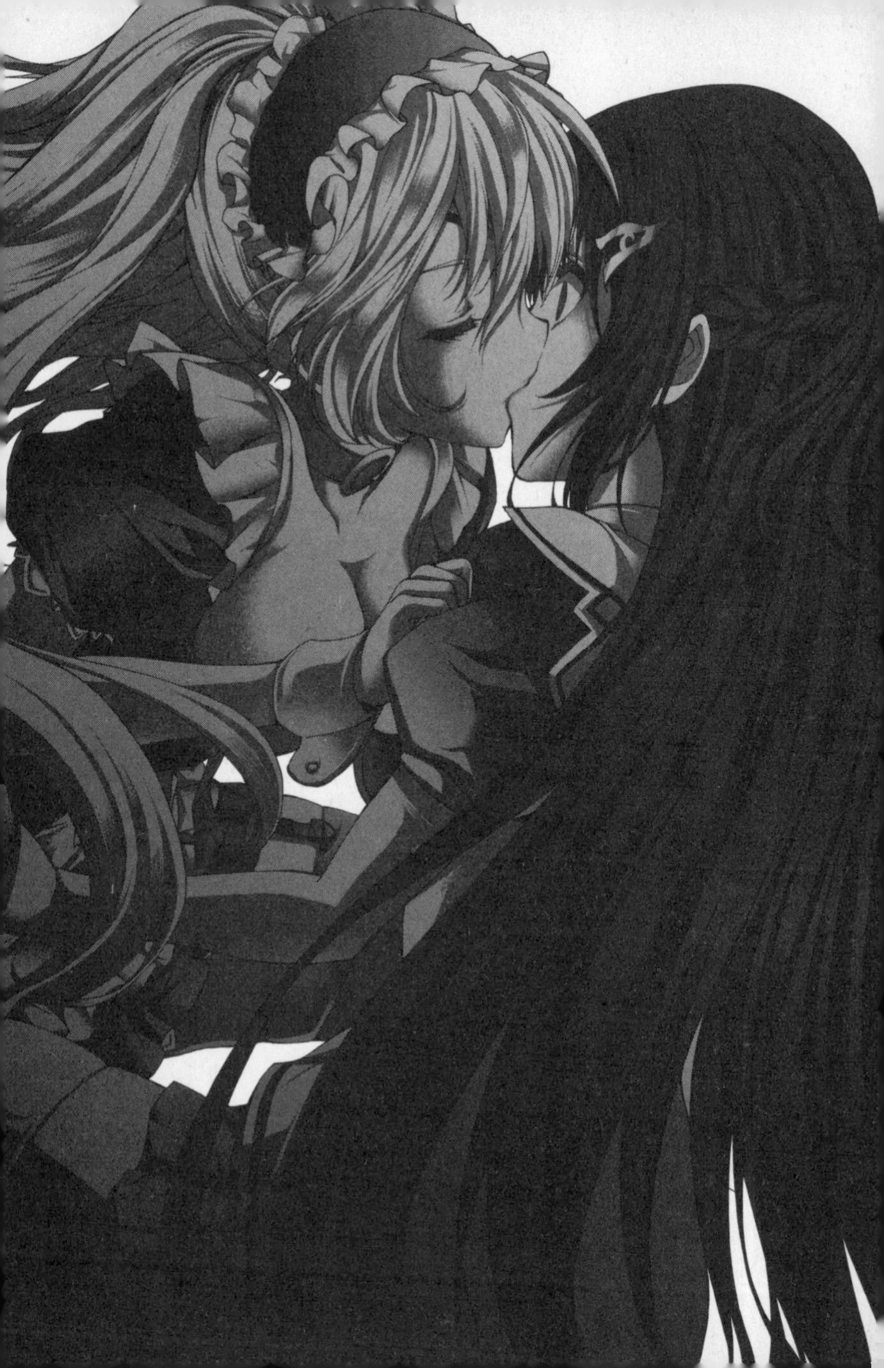

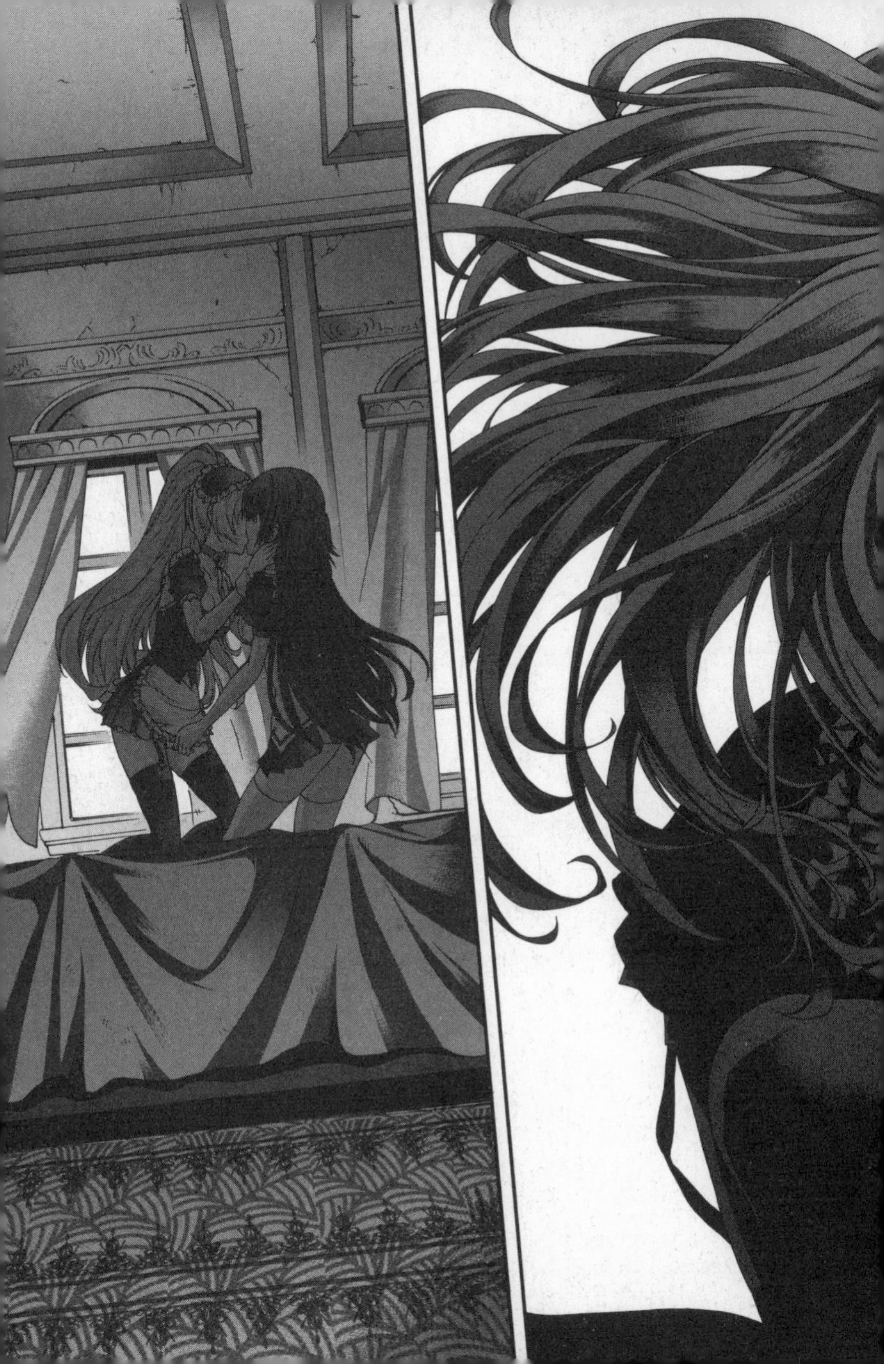

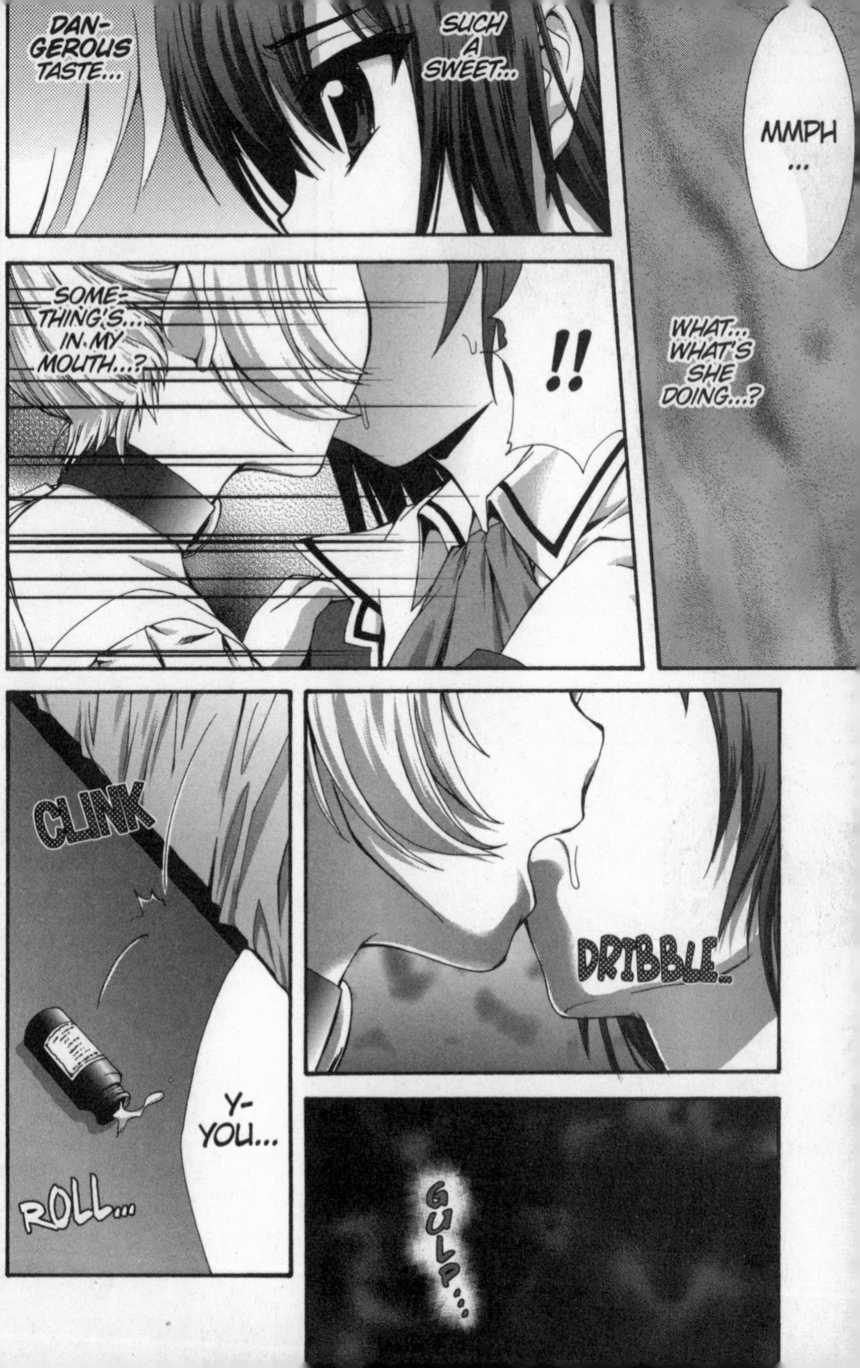
MMPH...
WHAT... WHAT'S SHE DOING...?
SUCH A SWEET...
DAN-GEROUS TASTE...
!!
SOME-THING'S... IN MY MOUTH...?
DRIBBLE...
GULP...
CLINK
Y-YOU...
ROLL...

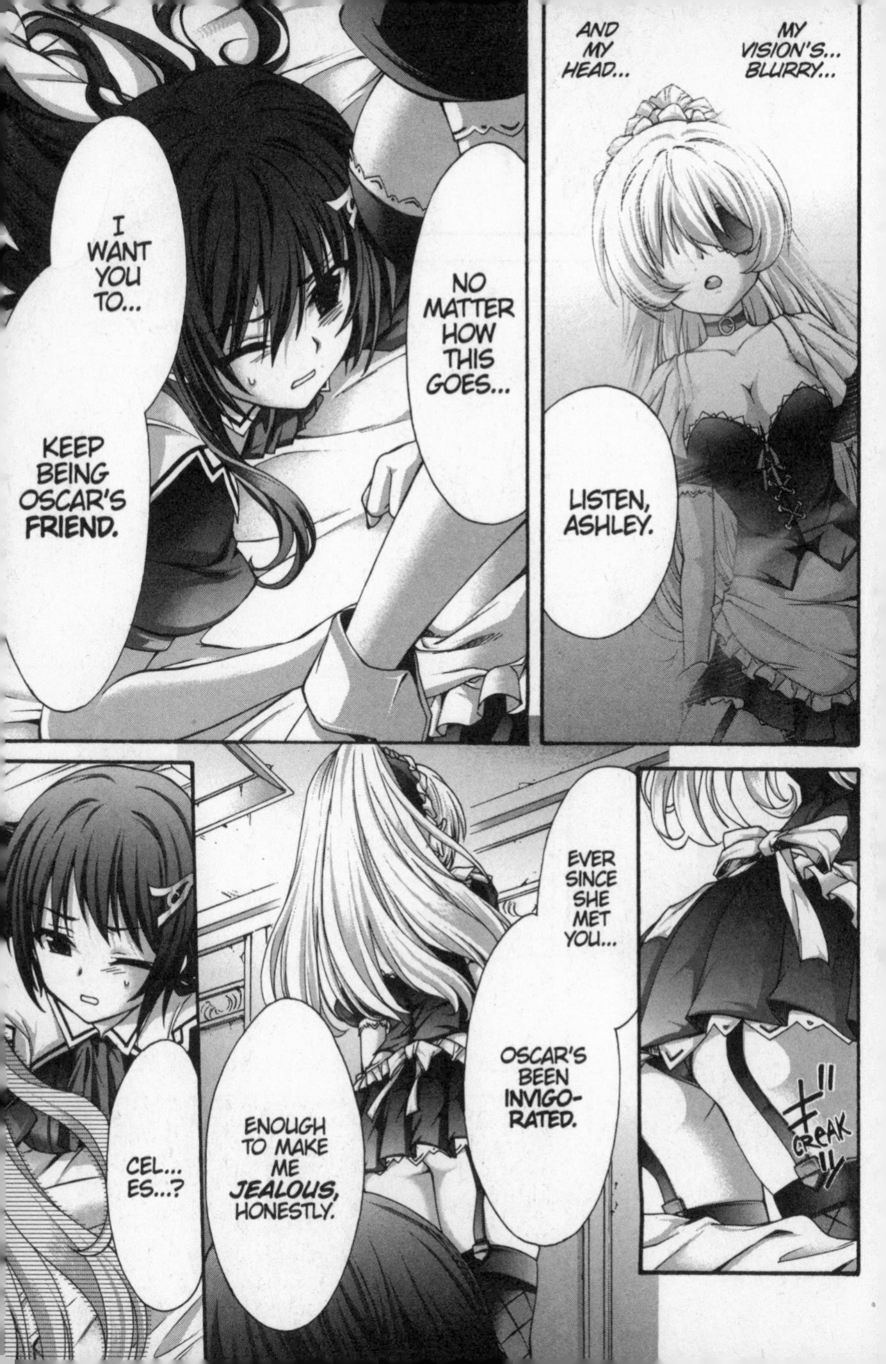
MY VISION'S... BLURRY...
AND MY HEAD...
LISTEN, ASHLEY.
NO MATTER HOW THIS GOES...
I WANT YOU TO...
KEEP BEING OSCAR'S FRIEND.
EVER SINCE SHE MET YOU...
OSCAR'S BEEN INVIGO-RATED.
CREAK
ENOUGH TO MAKE ME *JEALOUS*, HONESTLY.
CEL... ES...?

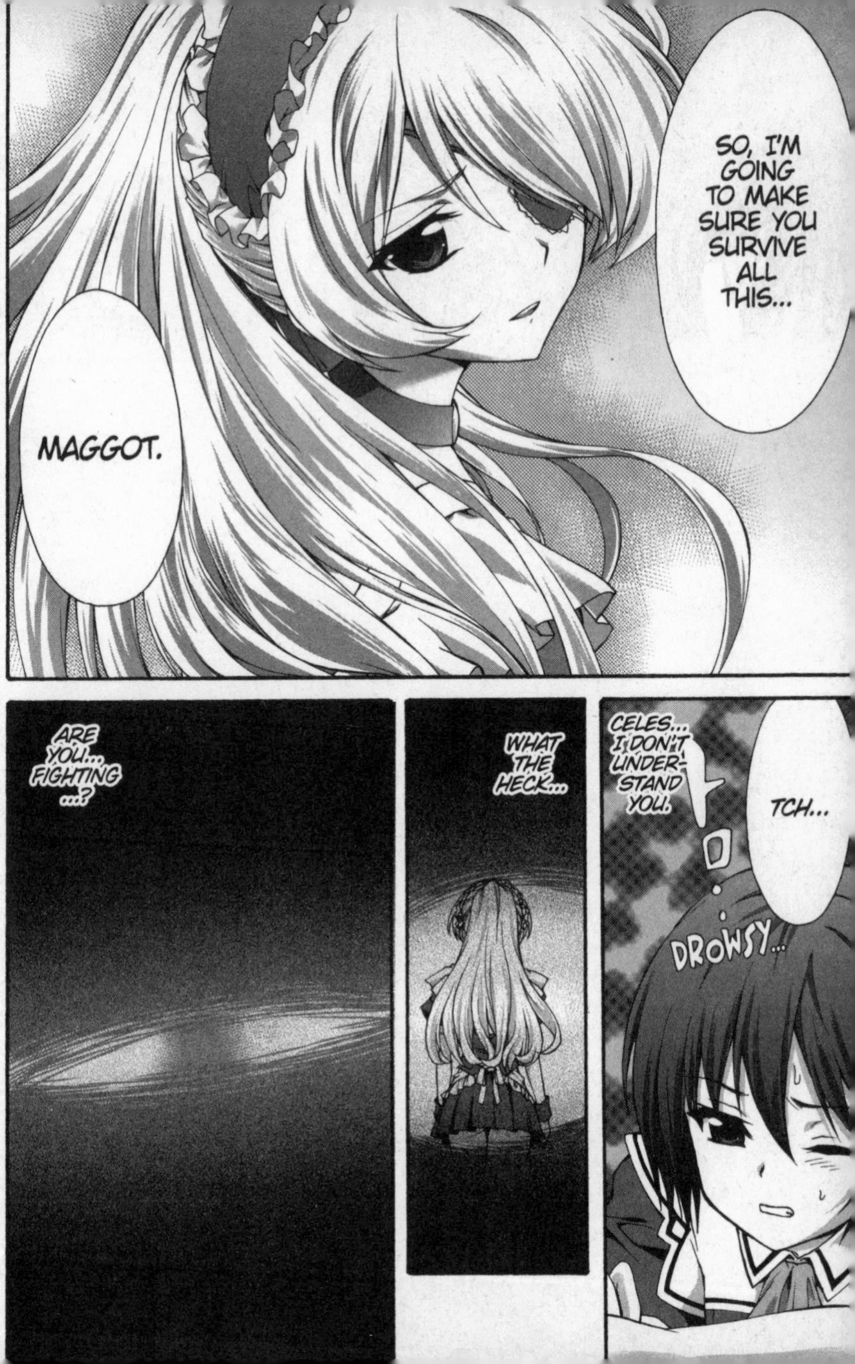
SO, I'M GOING TO MAKE SURE YOU SURVIVE ALL THIS...
MAGGOT.
TCH...
CELES... I DON'T UNDER-STAND YOU.
DROWSY...
WHAT THE HECK...
ARE YOU... FIGHTING ...?

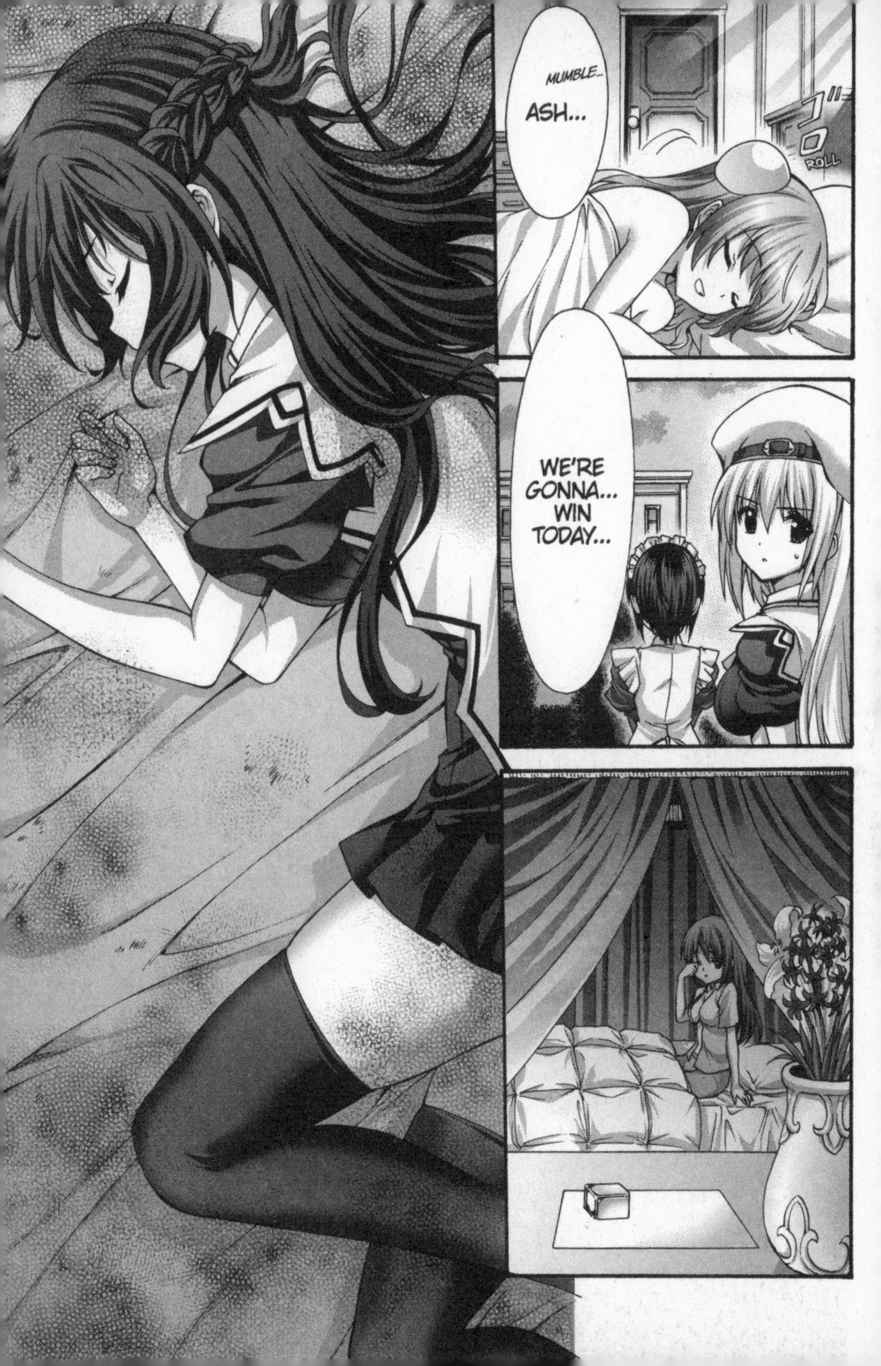
MUMBLE...
ASH...
ゴロ
ROLL
WE'RE GONNA... WIN TODAY...

DRAGONAR ACADEMY

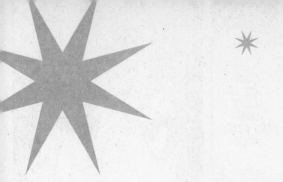

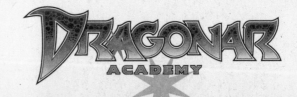

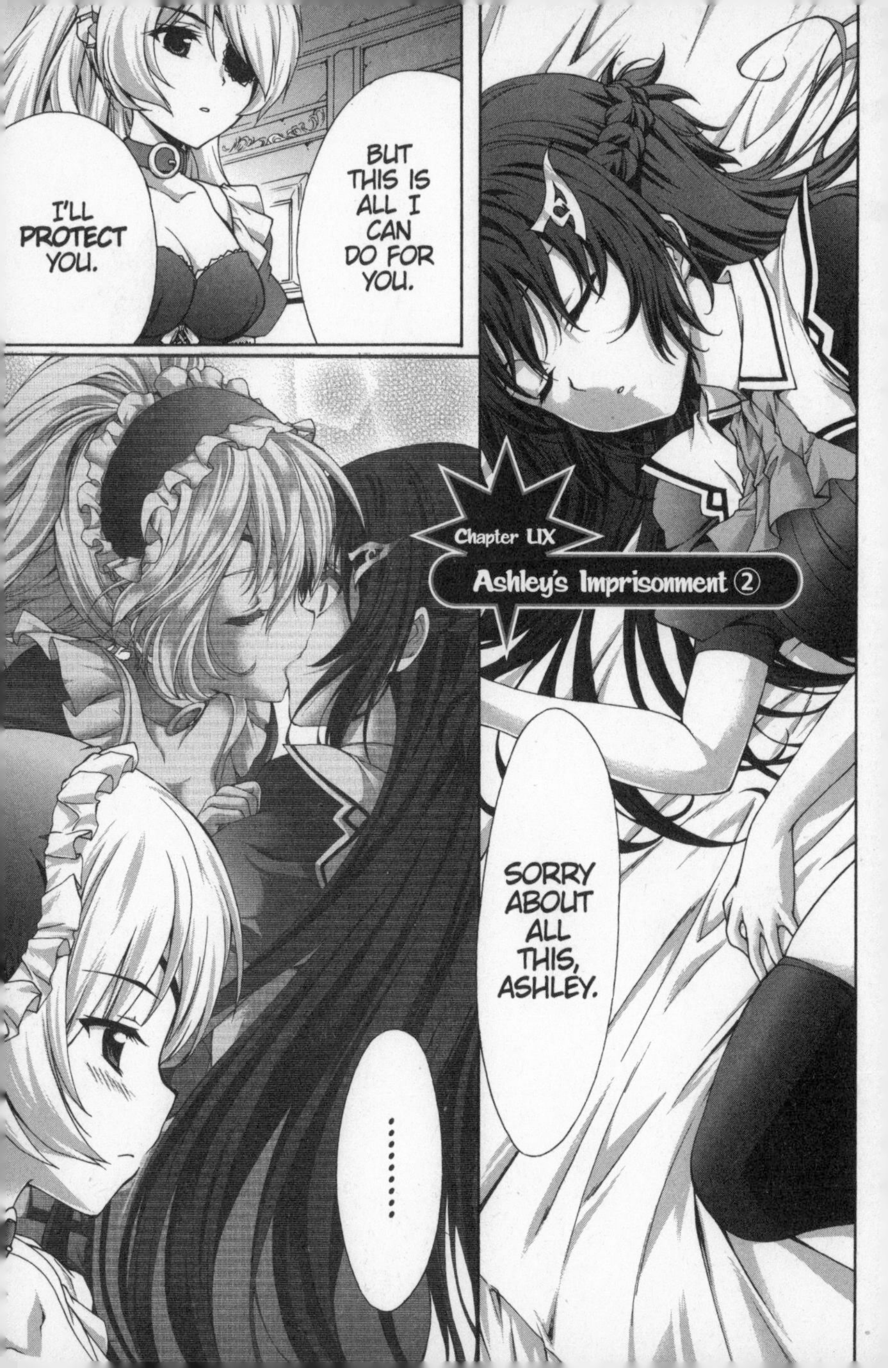
Chapter LIX
Ashley's Imprisonment ②
SORRY ABOUT ALL THIS, ASHLEY.
BUT THIS IS ALL I CAN DO FOR YOU.
I'LL PROTECT YOU.
....

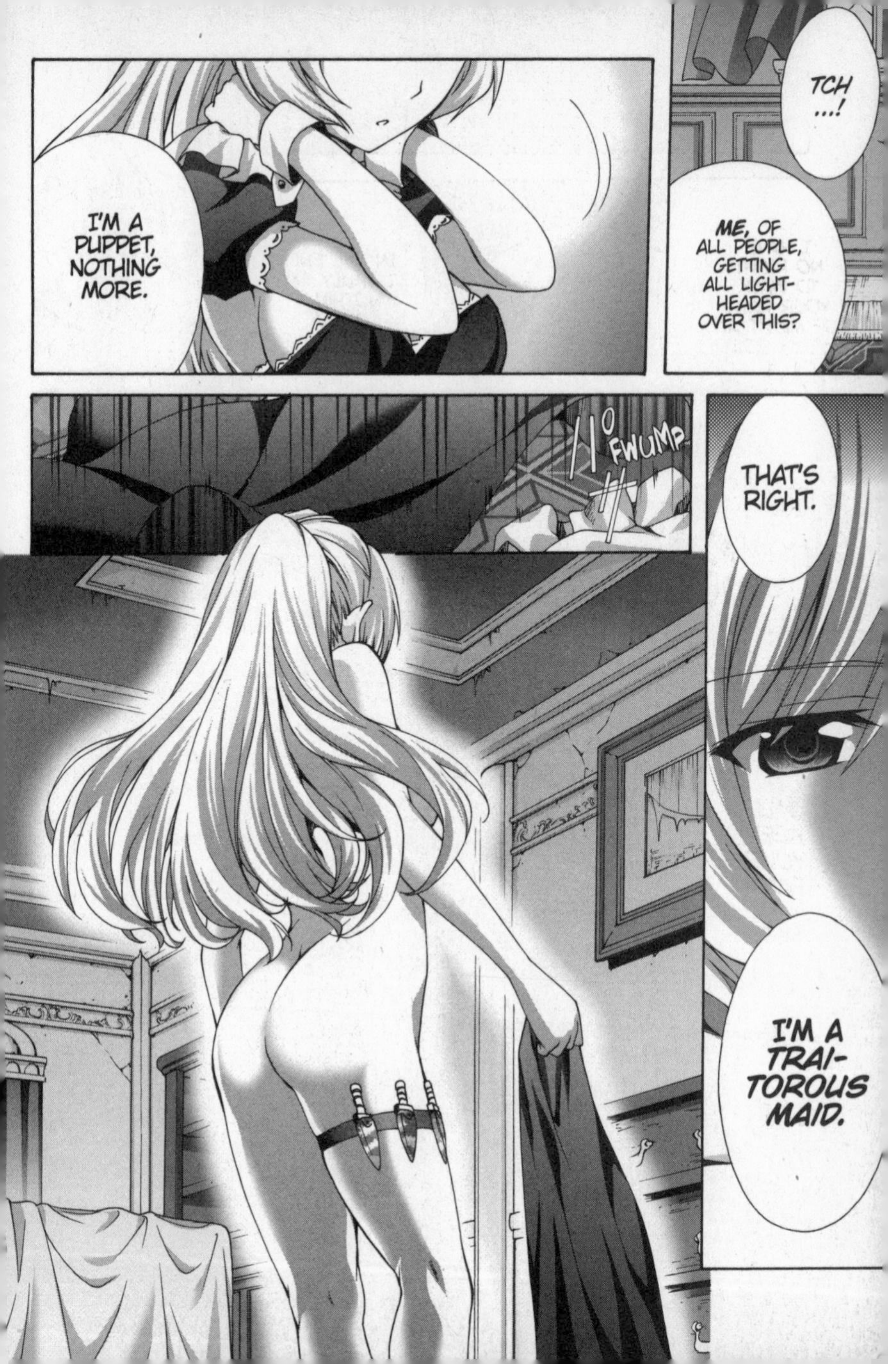
TCH ...!
ME, OF ALL PEOPLE, GETTING ALL LIGHT-HEADED OVER THIS?
I'M A PUPPET, NOTHING MORE.
THAT'S RIGHT.
I'M A TRAI-TOROUS MAID.
FWUMP

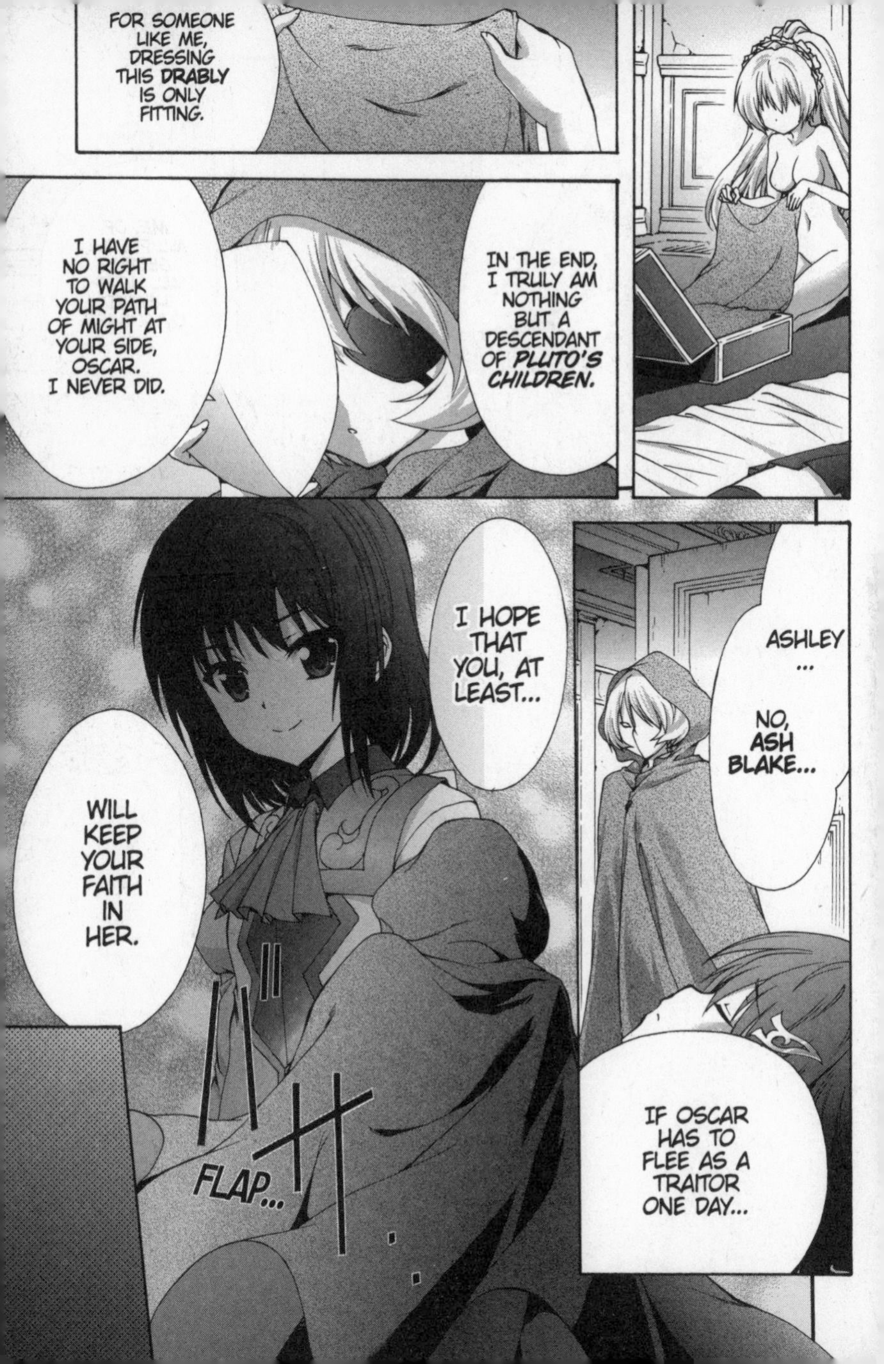
FOR SOMEONE LIKE ME, DRESSING THIS DRABLY IS ONLY FITTING.
IN THE END, I TRULY AM NOTHING BUT A DESCENDANT OF PLUTO'S CHILDREN.
I HAVE NO RIGHT TO WALK YOUR PATH OF MIGHT AT YOUR SIDE, OSCAR. I NEVER DID.
ASHLEY ...
NO, ASH BLAKE...
IF OSCAR HAS TO FLEE AS A TRAITOR ONE DAY...
I HOPE THAT YOU, AT LEAST...
WILL KEEP YOUR FAITH IN HER.
FLAP...

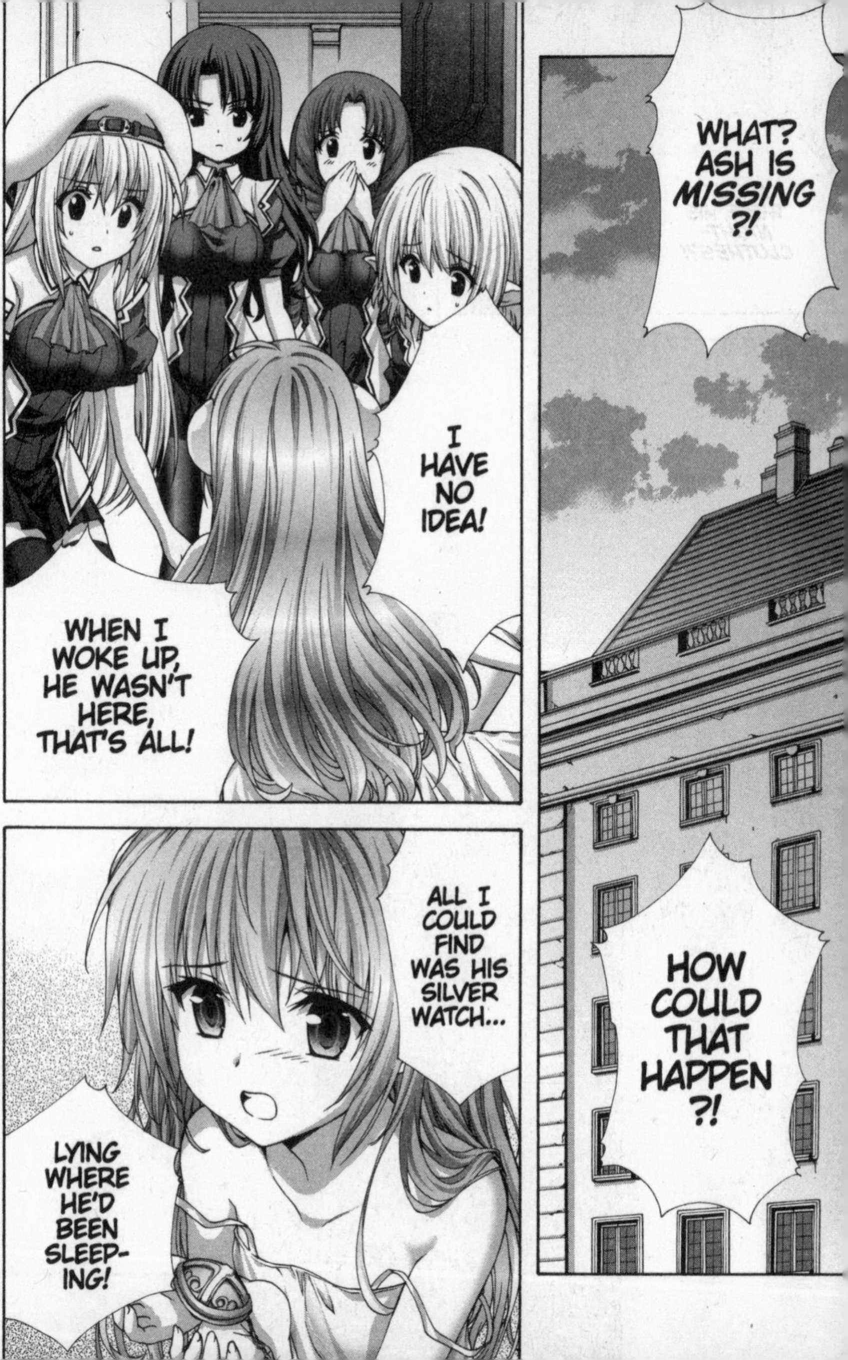
WHAT? ASH IS MISSING ?!
HOW COULD THAT HAPPEN ?!
I HAVE NO IDEA!
WHEN I WOKE UP, HE WASN'T HERE, THAT'S ALL!
ALL I COULD FIND WAS HIS SILVER WATCH...
LYING WHERE HE'D BEEN SLEEP-ING!

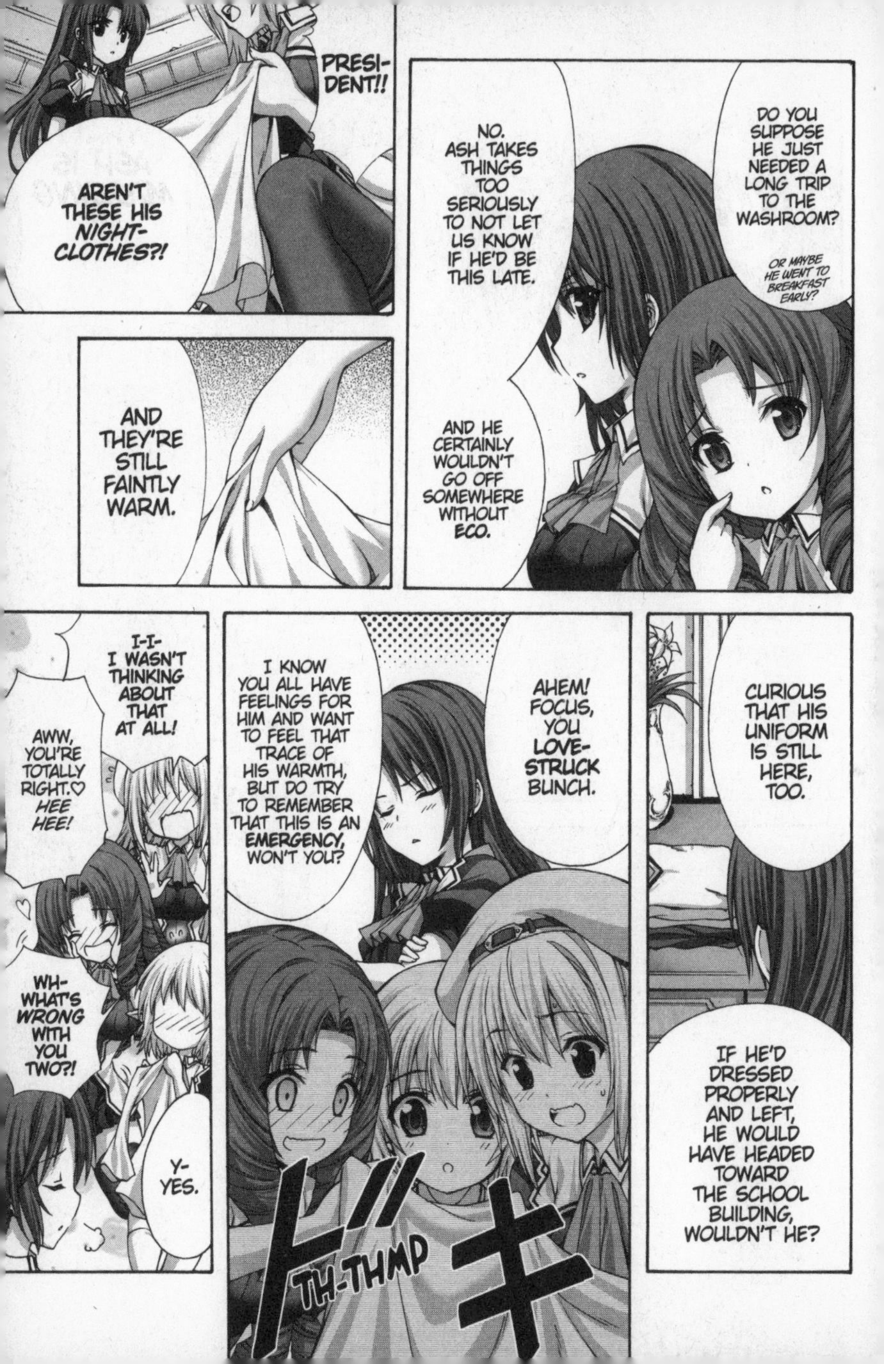

DO YOU SUPPOSE HE JUST NEEDED A LONG TRIP TO THE WASHROOM?
OR MAYBE HE WENT TO BREAKFAST EARLY?
NO. ASH TAKES THINGS TOO SERIOUSLY TO NOT LET US KNOW IF HE'D BE THIS LATE.
AND HE CERTAINLY WOULDN'T GO OFF SOMEWHERE WITHOUT ECO.
PRESIDENT!!
AREN'T THESE HIS NIGHT-CLOTHES?!
AND THEY'RE STILL FAINTLY WARM.
CURIOUS THAT HIS UNIFORM IS STILL HERE, TOO.
IF HE'D DRESSED PROPERLY AND LEFT, HE WOULD HAVE HEADED TOWARD THE SCHOOL BUILDING, WOULDN'T HE?
AHEM! FOCUS, YOU LOVE-STRUCK BUNCH.
I KNOW YOU ALL HAVE FEELINGS FOR HIM AND WANT TO FEEL THAT TRACE OF HIS WARMTH, BUT DO TRY TO REMEMBER THAT THIS IS AN EMERGENCY, WON'T YOU?
TH-THMP
I-I- I WASN'T THINKING ABOUT THAT AT ALL!
AWW, YOU'RE TOTALLY RIGHT.♡ HEE HEE!
WH-WHAT'S WRONG WITH YOU TWO?!
Y-YES.

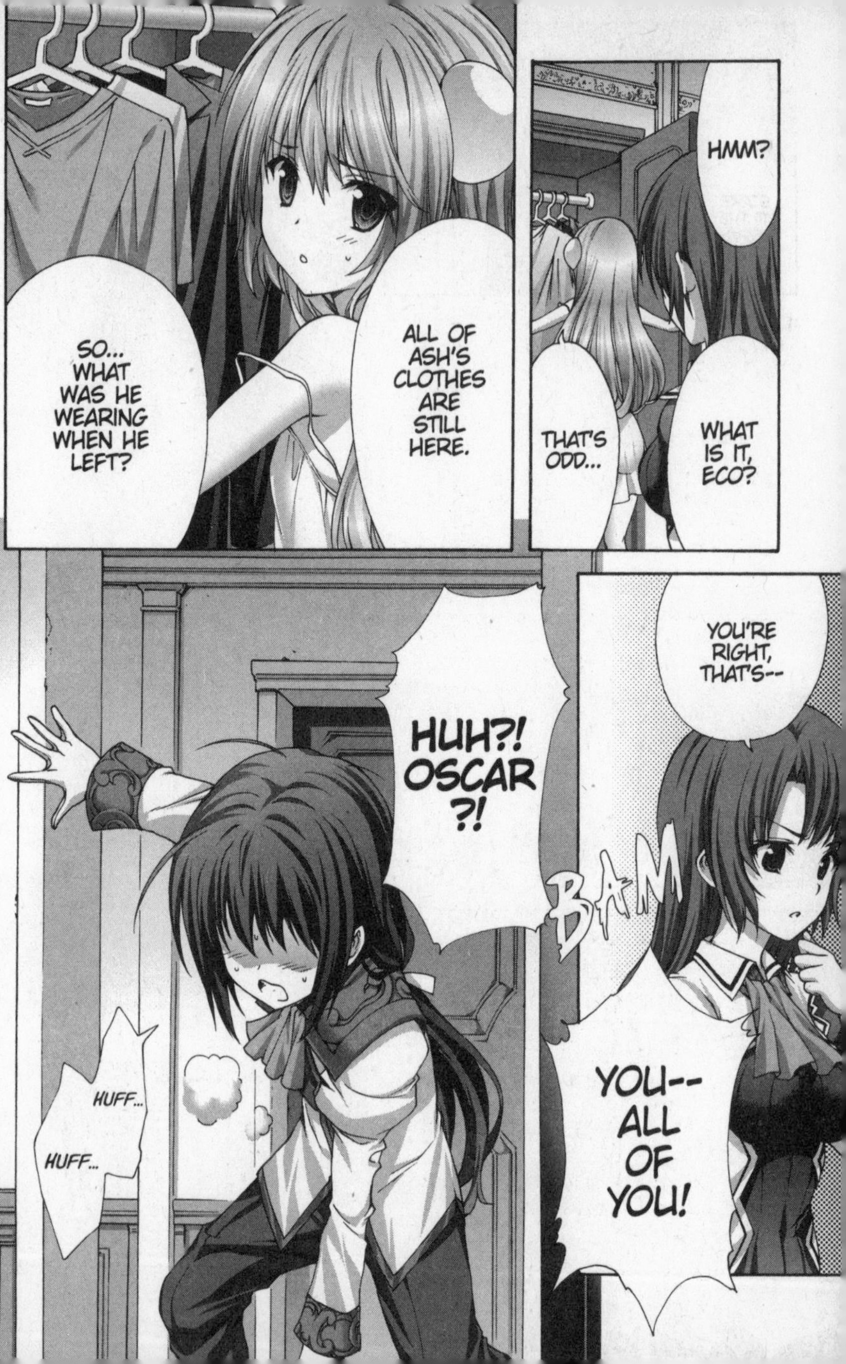
HMM?
WHAT IS IT, ECO?
THAT'S ODD...
ALL OF ASH'S CLOTHES ARE STILL HERE.
SO... WHAT WAS HE WEARING WHEN HE LEFT?
YOU'RE RIGHT, THAT'S--
HUH?! OSCAR?!
BAM
YOU-- ALL OF YOU!
HUFF...
HUFF...

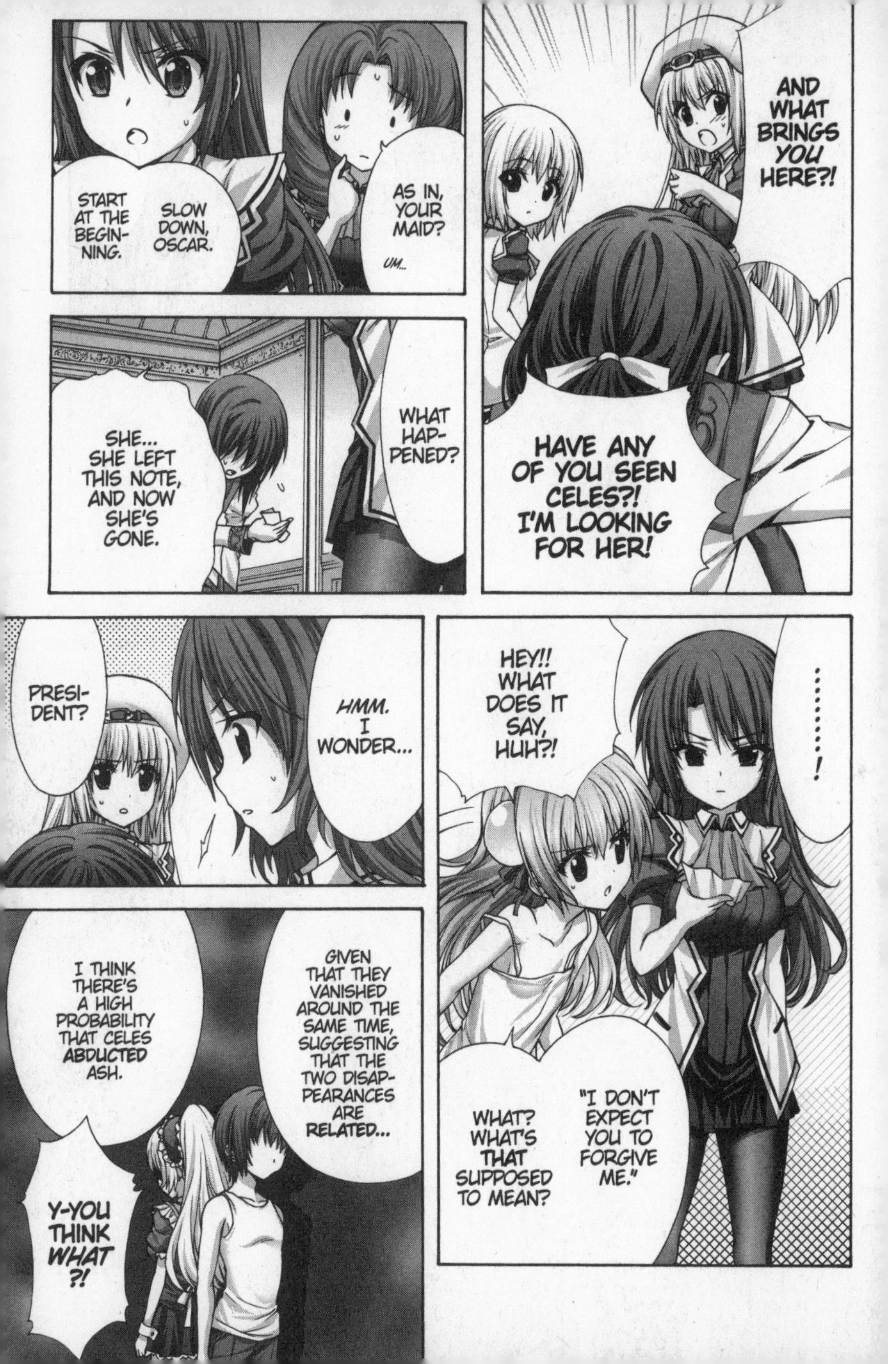
AND WHAT BRINGS YOU HERE?!
HAVE ANY OF YOU SEEN CELES?! I'M LOOKING FOR HER!
AS IN, YOUR MAID?
UM...
SLOW DOWN, OSCAR.
START AT THE BEGINNING.
WHAT HAPPENED?
SHE... SHE LEFT THIS NOTE, AND NOW SHE'S GONE.
......!
HEY!! WHAT DOES IT SAY, HUH?!
"I DON'T EXPECT YOU TO FORGIVE ME."
WHAT? WHAT'S THAT SUPPOSED TO MEAN?
HMM. I WONDER...
PRESIDENT?
GIVEN THAT THEY VANISHED AROUND THE SAME TIME, SUGGESTING THAT THE TWO DISAPPEARANCES ARE RELATED...
I THINK THERE'S A HIGH PROBABILITY THAT CELES ABDUCTED ASH.
Y-YOU THINK WHAT?!

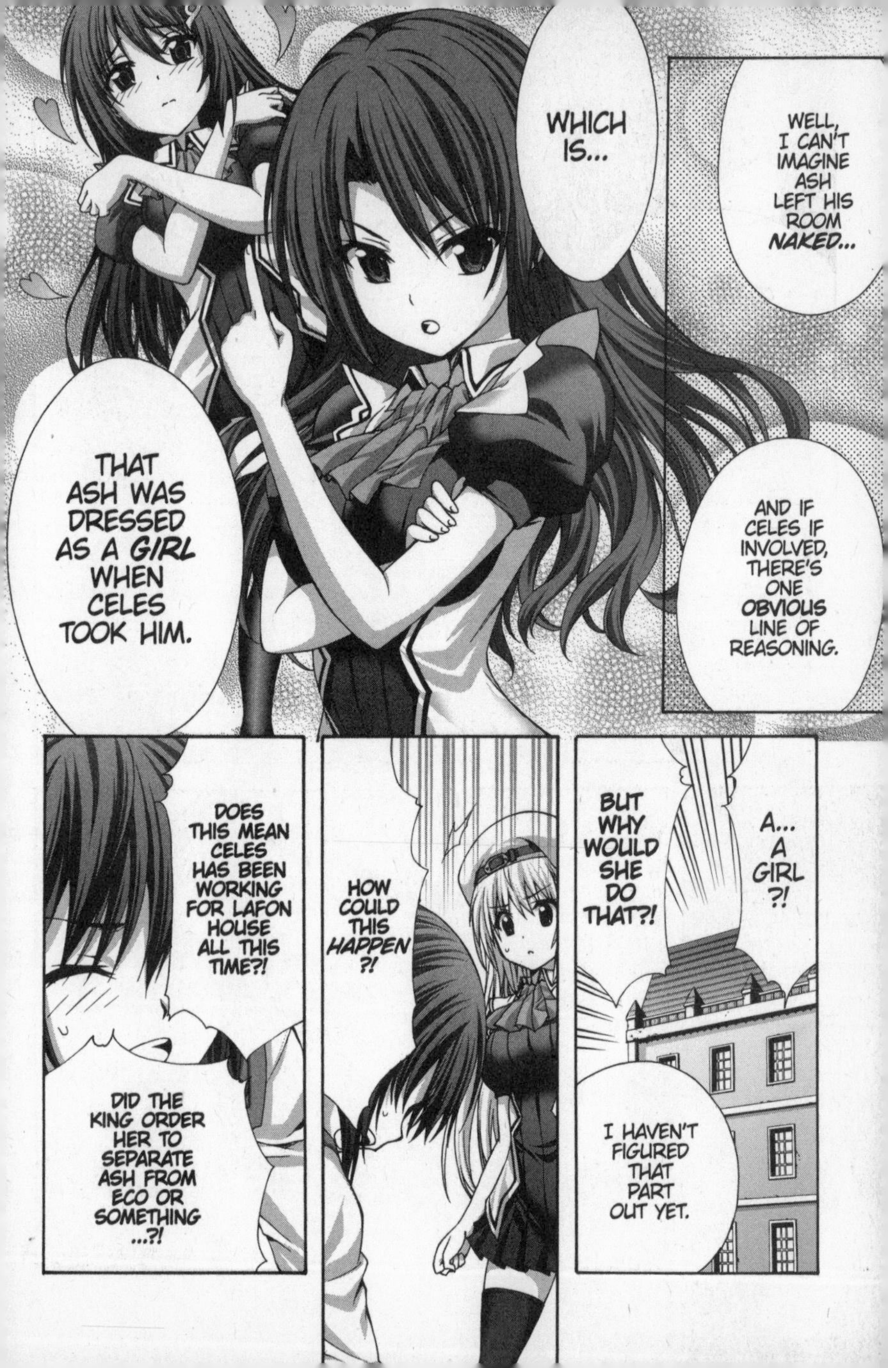
WELL, I CAN'T IMAGINE ASH LEFT HIS ROOM NAKED...
AND IF CELES IF INVOLVED, THERE'S ONE OBVIOUS LINE OF REASONING.
WHICH IS...
THAT ASH WAS DRESSED AS A GIRL WHEN CELES TOOK HIM.
A... A GIRL?!
BUT WHY WOULD SHE DO THAT?!
I HAVEN'T FIGURED THAT PART OUT YET.
HOW COULD THIS HAPPEN?!
DOES THIS MEAN CELES HAS BEEN WORKING FOR LAFON HOUSE ALL THIS TIME?!
DID THE KING ORDER HER TO SEPARATE ASH FROM ECO OR SOMETHING...?!

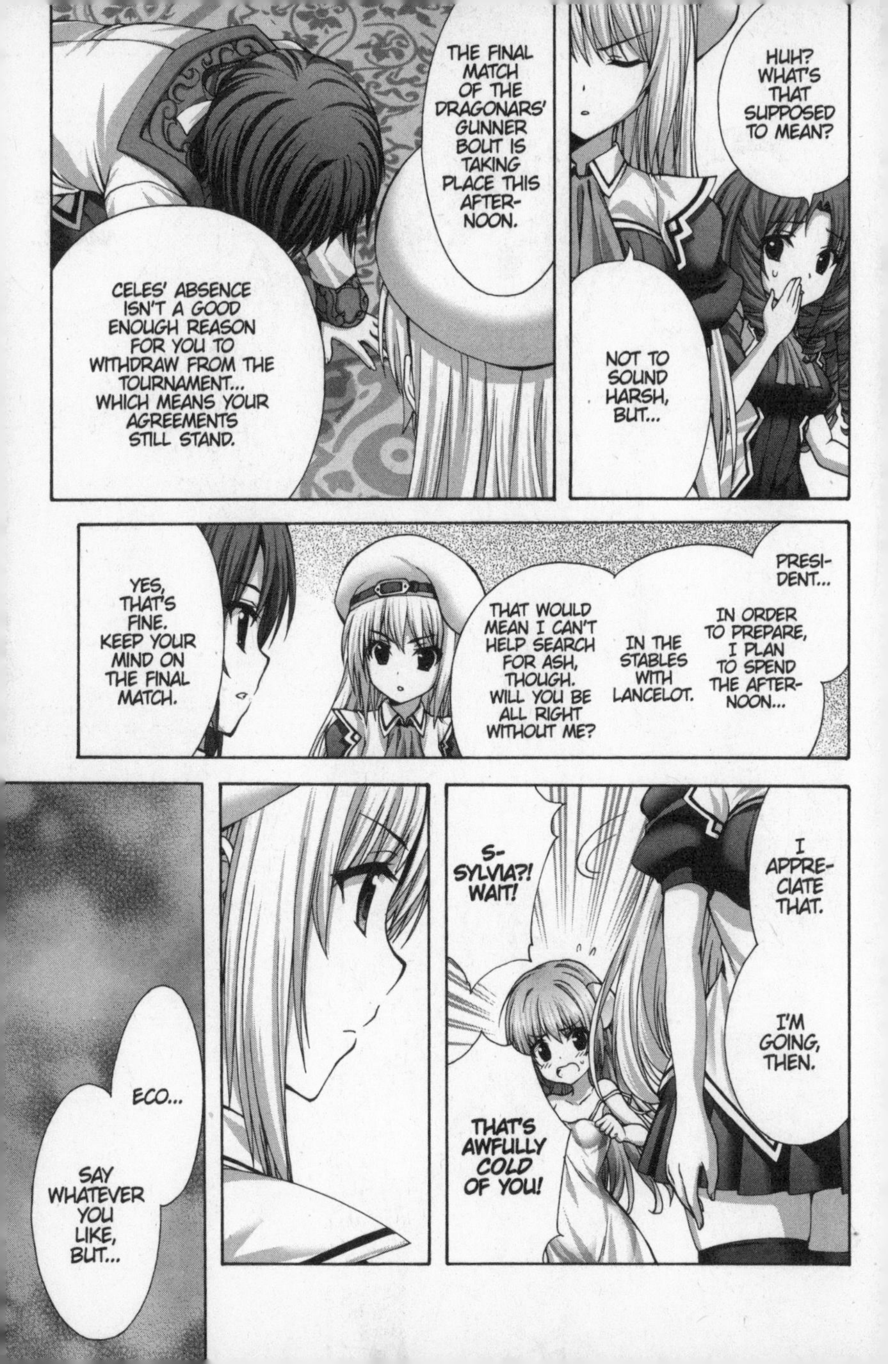
HUH? WHAT'S THAT SUPPOSED TO MEAN?
NOT TO SOUND HARSH, BUT...
THE FINAL MATCH OF THE DRAGONARS' GUNNER BOUT IS TAKING PLACE THIS AFTER-NOON.
CELES' ABSENCE ISN'T A GOOD ENOUGH REASON FOR YOU TO WITHDRAW FROM THE TOURNAMENT... WHICH MEANS YOUR AGREEMENTS STILL STAND.
PRESI-DENT...
IN ORDER TO PREPARE, I PLAN TO SPEND THE AFTER-NOON...
IN THE STABLES WITH LANCELOT.
THAT WOULD MEAN I CAN'T HELP SEARCH FOR ASH, THOUGH. WILL YOU BE ALL RIGHT WITHOUT ME?
YES, THAT'S FINE. KEEP YOUR MIND ON THE FINAL MATCH.
I APPRE-CIATE THAT.
I'M GOING, THEN.
S-SYLVIA?! WAIT!
THAT'S AWFULLY COLD OF YOU!
ECO...
SAY WHATEVER YOU LIKE, BUT...

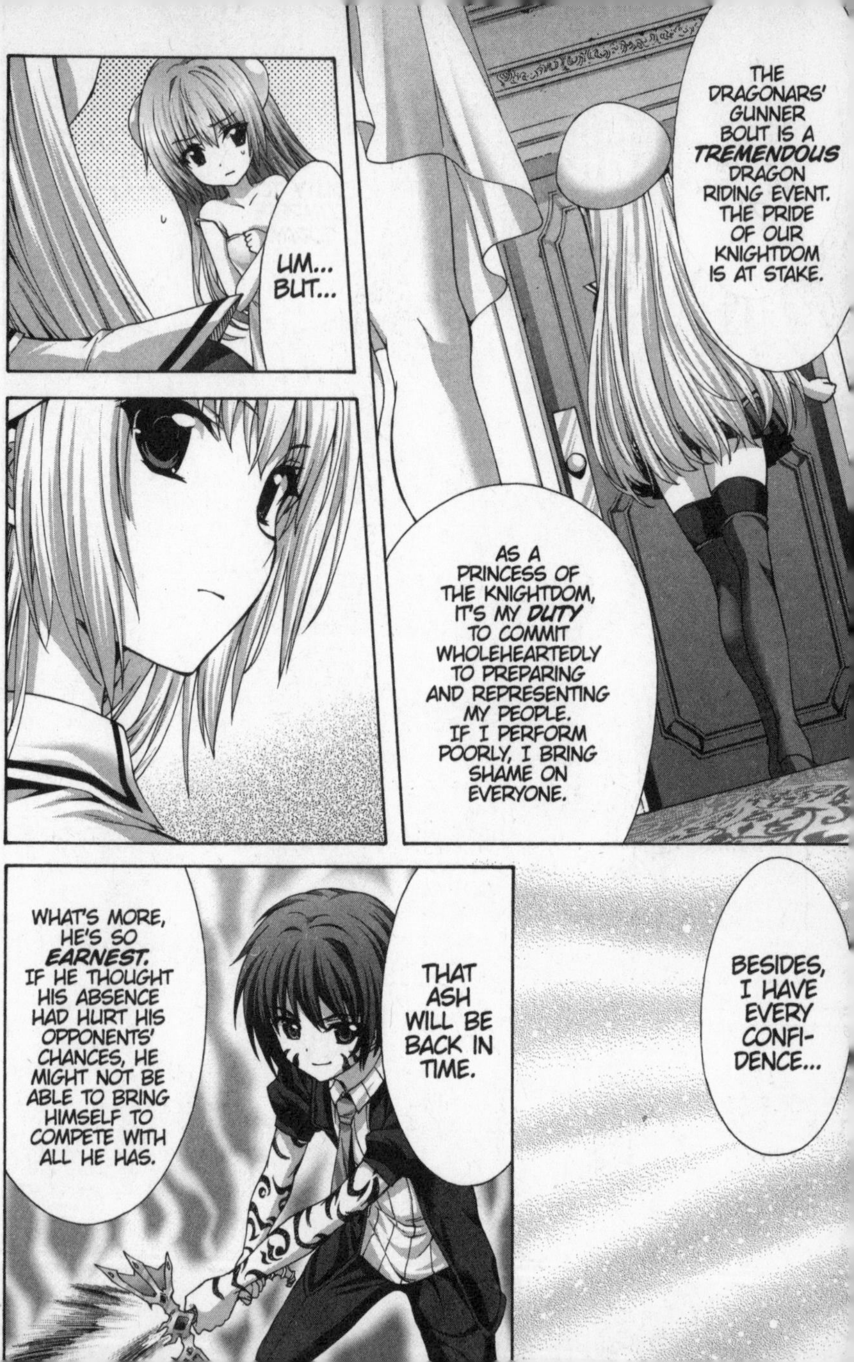
THE DRAGONARS' GUNNER BOUT IS A ***TREMENDOUS*** DRAGON RIDING EVENT. THE PRIDE OF OUR KNIGHTDOM IS AT STAKE.
AS A PRINCESS OF THE KNIGHTDOM, IT'S MY ***DUTY*** TO COMMIT WHOLEHEARTEDLY TO PREPARING AND REPRESENTING MY PEOPLE. IF I PERFORM POORLY, I BRING SHAME ON EVERYONE.
UM... BUT...
BESIDES, I HAVE EVERY CONFIDENCE...
THAT ASH WILL BE BACK IN TIME.
WHAT'S MORE, HE'S SO ***EARNEST.*** IF HE THOUGHT HIS ABSENCE HAD HURT HIS OPPONENTS' CHANCES, HE MIGHT NOT BE ABLE TO BRING HIMSELF TO COMPETE WITH ALL HE HAS.

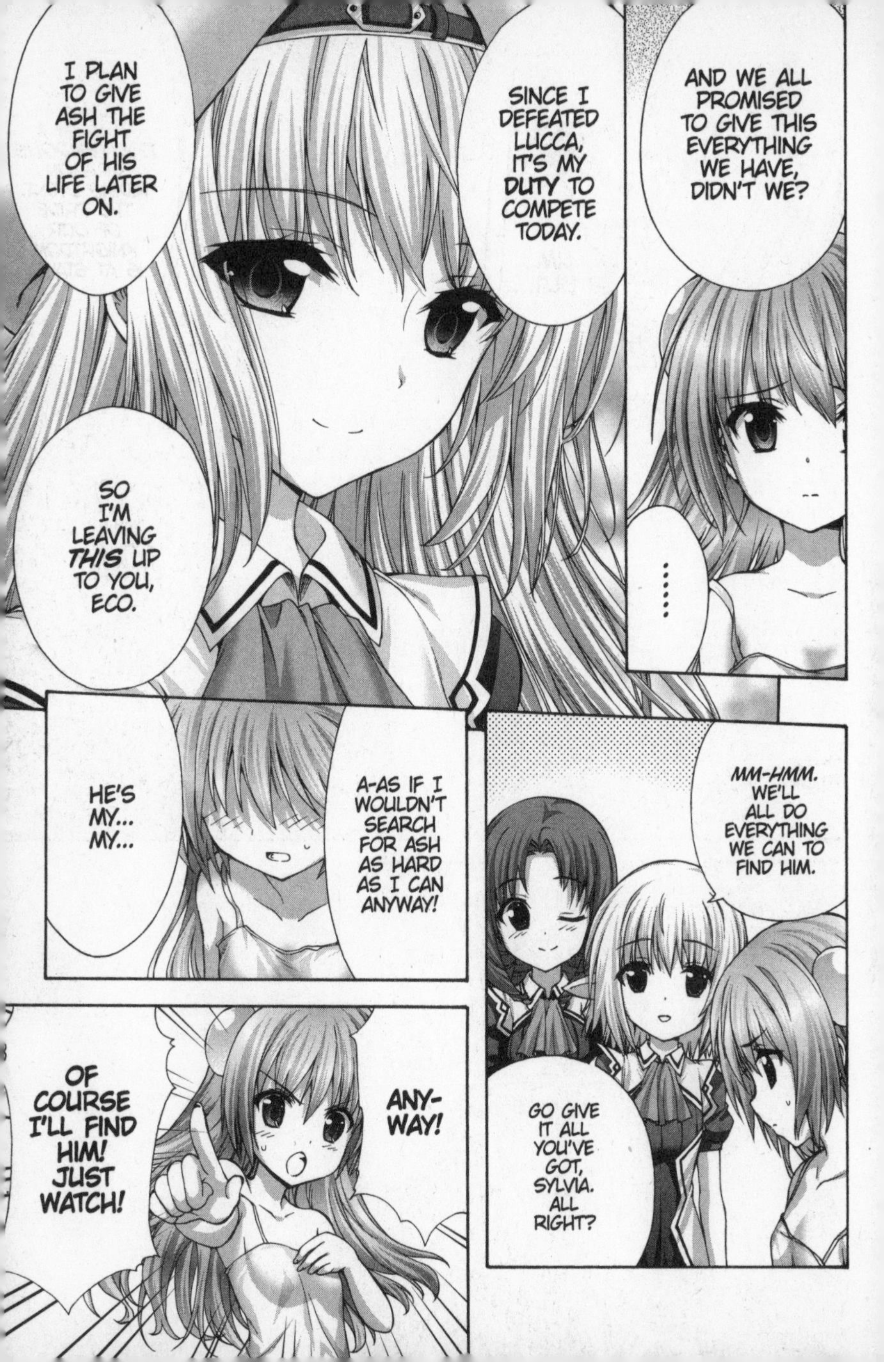
AND WE ALL PROMISED TO GIVE THIS EVERYTHING WE HAVE, DIDN'T WE?
......
SINCE I DEFEATED LUCCA, IT'S MY DUTY TO COMPETE TODAY.
I PLAN TO GIVE ASH THE FIGHT OF HIS LIFE LATER ON.
SO I'M LEAVING THIS UP TO YOU, ECO.
MM-HMM. WE'LL ALL DO EVERYTHING WE CAN TO FIND HIM.
GO GIVE IT ALL YOU'VE GOT, SYLVIA. ALL RIGHT?
A-AS IF I WOULDN'T SEARCH FOR ASH AS HARD AS I CAN ANYWAY!
HE'S MY... MY...
ANY-WAY!
OF COURSE I'LL FIND HIM! JUST WATCH!

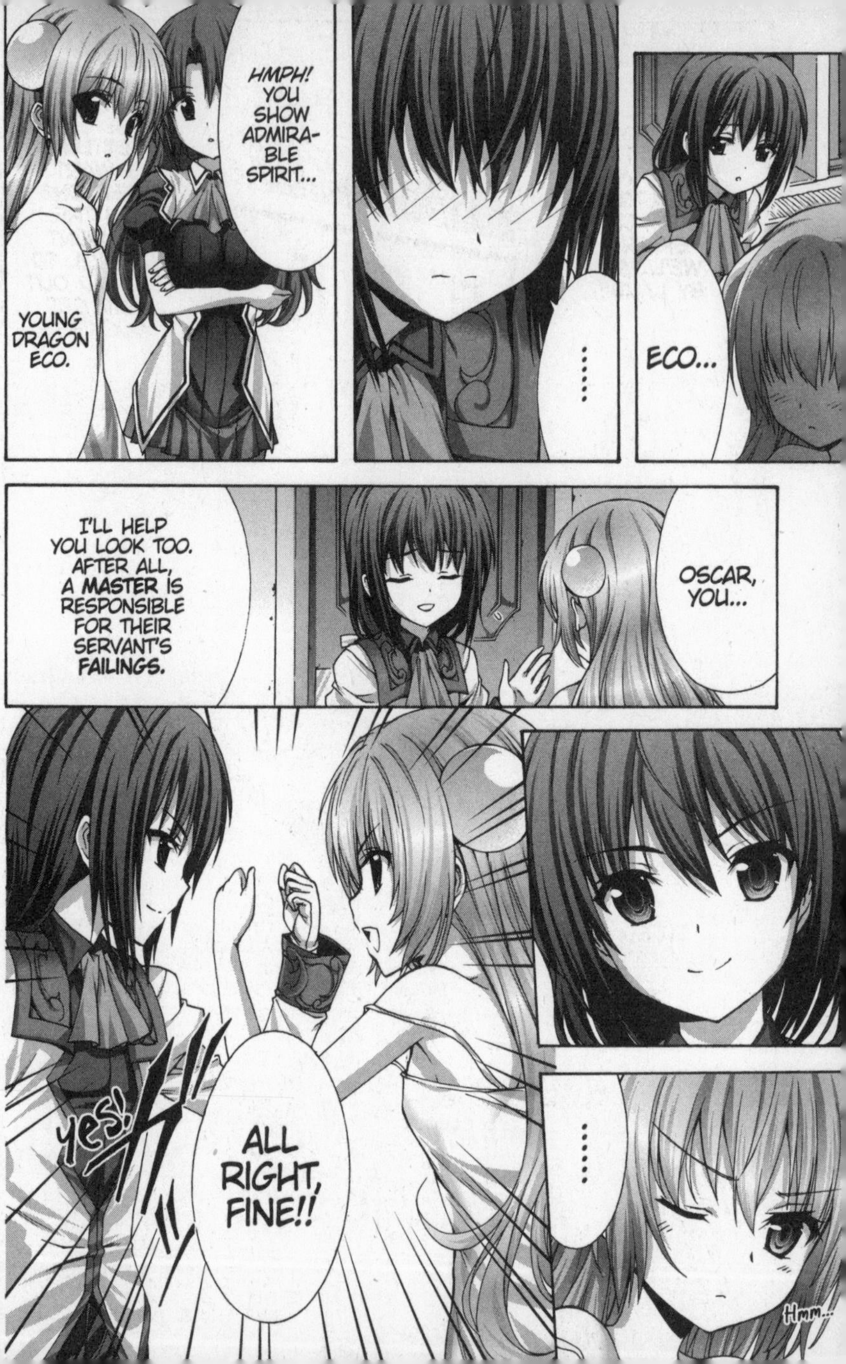
ECO...
......
HMPH! YOU SHOW ADMIRA-BLE SPIRIT...
YOUNG DRAGON ECO.
OSCAR, YOU...
I'LL HELP YOU LOOK TOO. AFTER ALL, A MASTER IS RESPONSIBLE FOR THEIR SERVANT'S FAILINGS.
......
Hmm...
ALL RIGHT, FINE!!
yes!

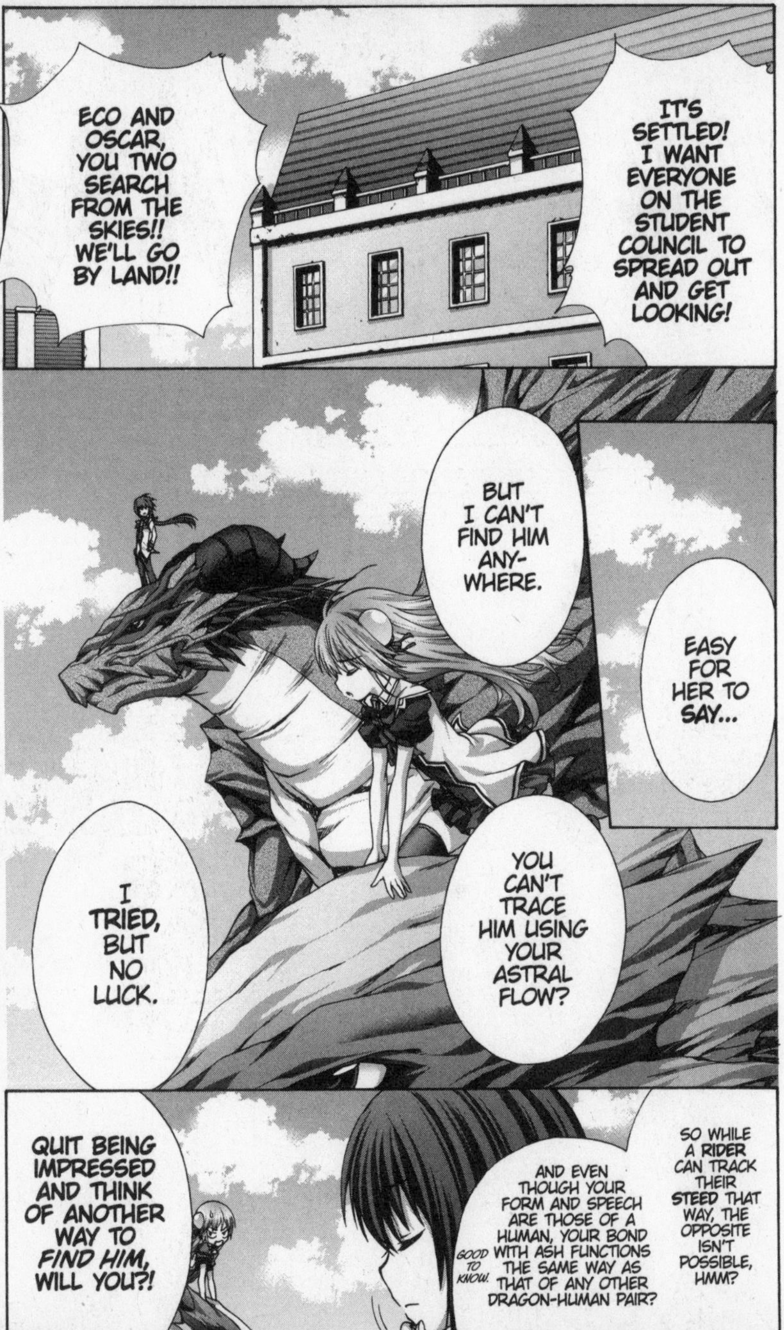
IT'S SETTLED! I WANT EVERYONE ON THE STUDENT COUNCIL TO SPREAD OUT AND GET LOOKING!
ECO AND OSCAR, YOU TWO SEARCH FROM THE SKIES!! WE'LL GO BY LAND!!
BUT I CAN'T FIND HIM ANY-WHERE.
EASY FOR HER TO SAY...
YOU CAN'T TRACE HIM USING YOUR ASTRAL FLOW?
I TRIED, BUT NO LUCK.
SO WHILE A RIDER CAN TRACK THEIR STEED THAT WAY, THE OPPOSITE ISN'T POSSIBLE, HMM?
AND EVEN THOUGH YOUR FORM AND SPEECH ARE THOSE OF A HUMAN, YOUR BOND WITH ASH FUNCTIONS THE SAME WAY AS THAT OF ANY OTHER DRAGON-HUMAN PAIR?
GOOD TO KNOW.
QUIT BEING IMPRESSED AND THINK OF ANOTHER WAY TO *FIND HIM*, WILL YOU?!

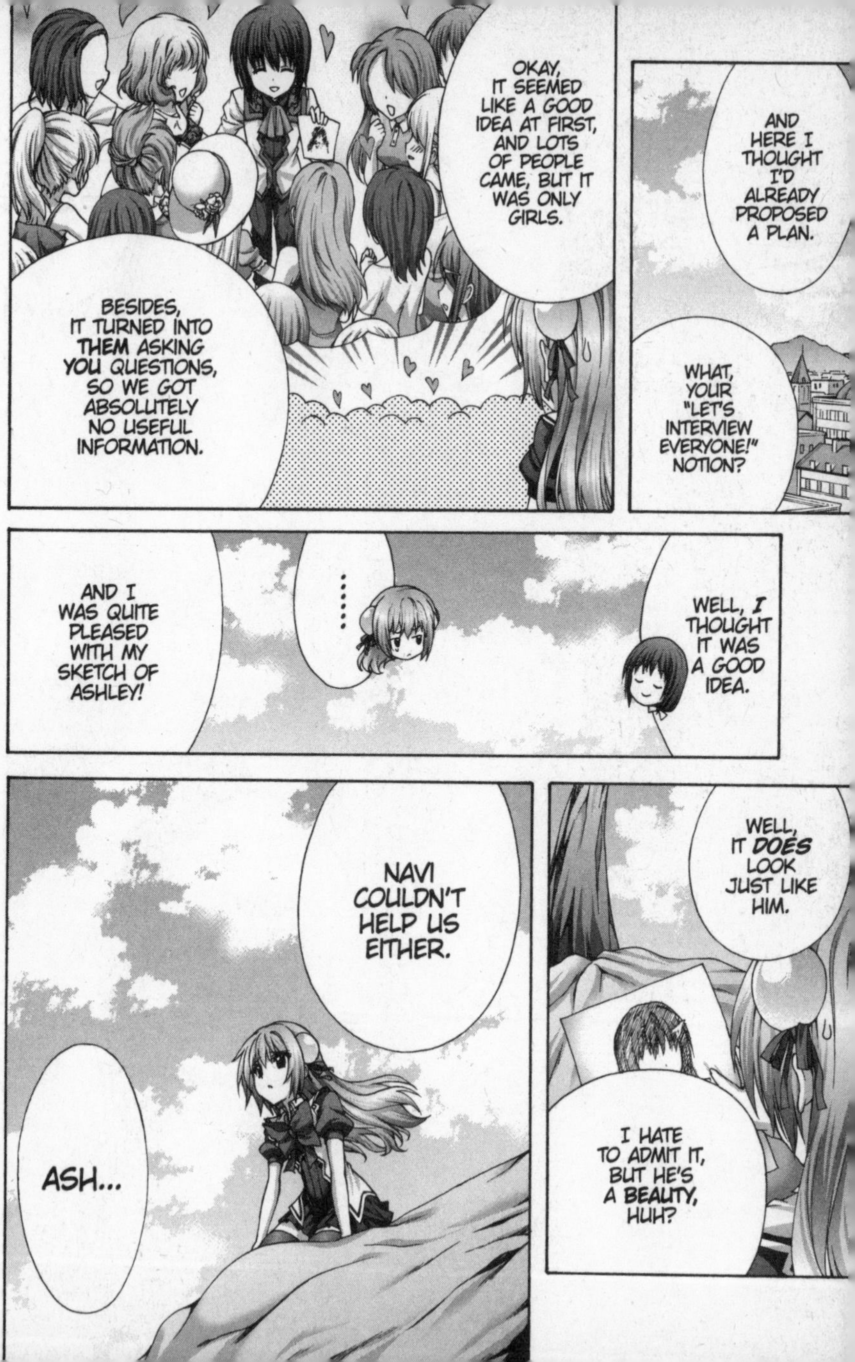
AND HERE I THOUGHT I'D ALREADY PROPOSED A PLAN.
WHAT, YOUR "LET'S INTERVIEW EVERYONE!" NOTION?
OKAY, IT SEEMED LIKE A GOOD IDEA AT FIRST, AND LOTS OF PEOPLE CAME, BUT IT WAS ONLY GIRLS.
BESIDES, IT TURNED INTO **THEM** ASKING **YOU** QUESTIONS, SO WE GOT ABSOLUTELY NO USEFUL INFORMATION.
WELL, *I* THOUGHT IT WAS A GOOD IDEA.
......
AND I WAS QUITE PLEASED WITH MY SKETCH OF ASHLEY!
WELL, IT ***DOES*** LOOK JUST LIKE HIM.
I HATE TO ADMIT IT, BUT HE'S A **BEAUTY**, HUH?
NAVI COULDN'T HELP US EITHER.
ASH...

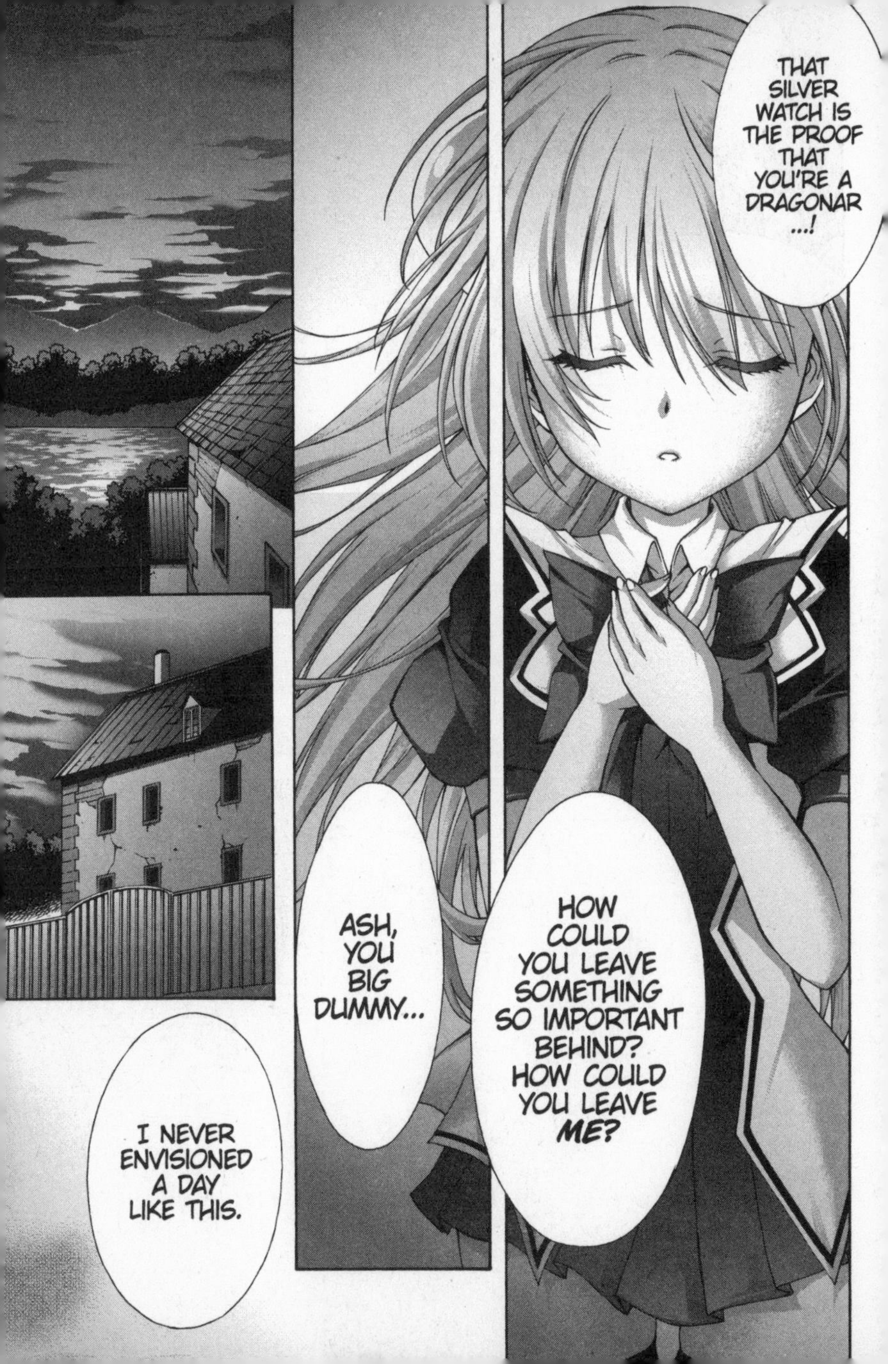
THAT SILVER WATCH IS THE PROOF THAT YOU'RE A DRAGONAR ...!
HOW COULD YOU LEAVE SOMETHING SO IMPORTANT BEHIND? HOW COULD YOU LEAVE *ME*?
ASH, YOU BIG DUMMY...
I NEVER ENVISIONED A DAY LIKE THIS.

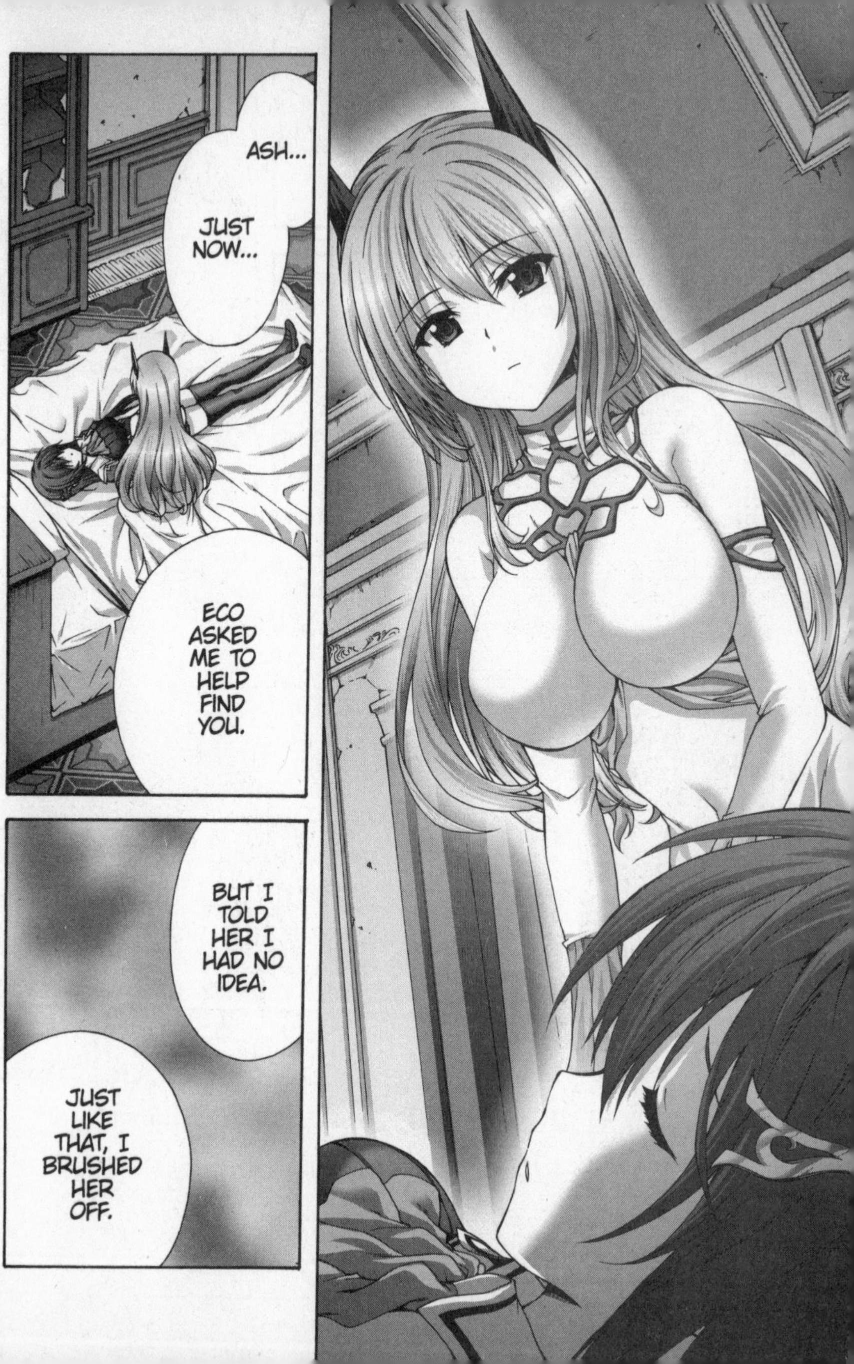
ASH...
JUST NOW...
ECO ASKED ME TO HELP FIND YOU.
BUT I TOLD HER I HAD NO IDEA.
JUST LIKE THAT, I BRUSHED HER OFF.

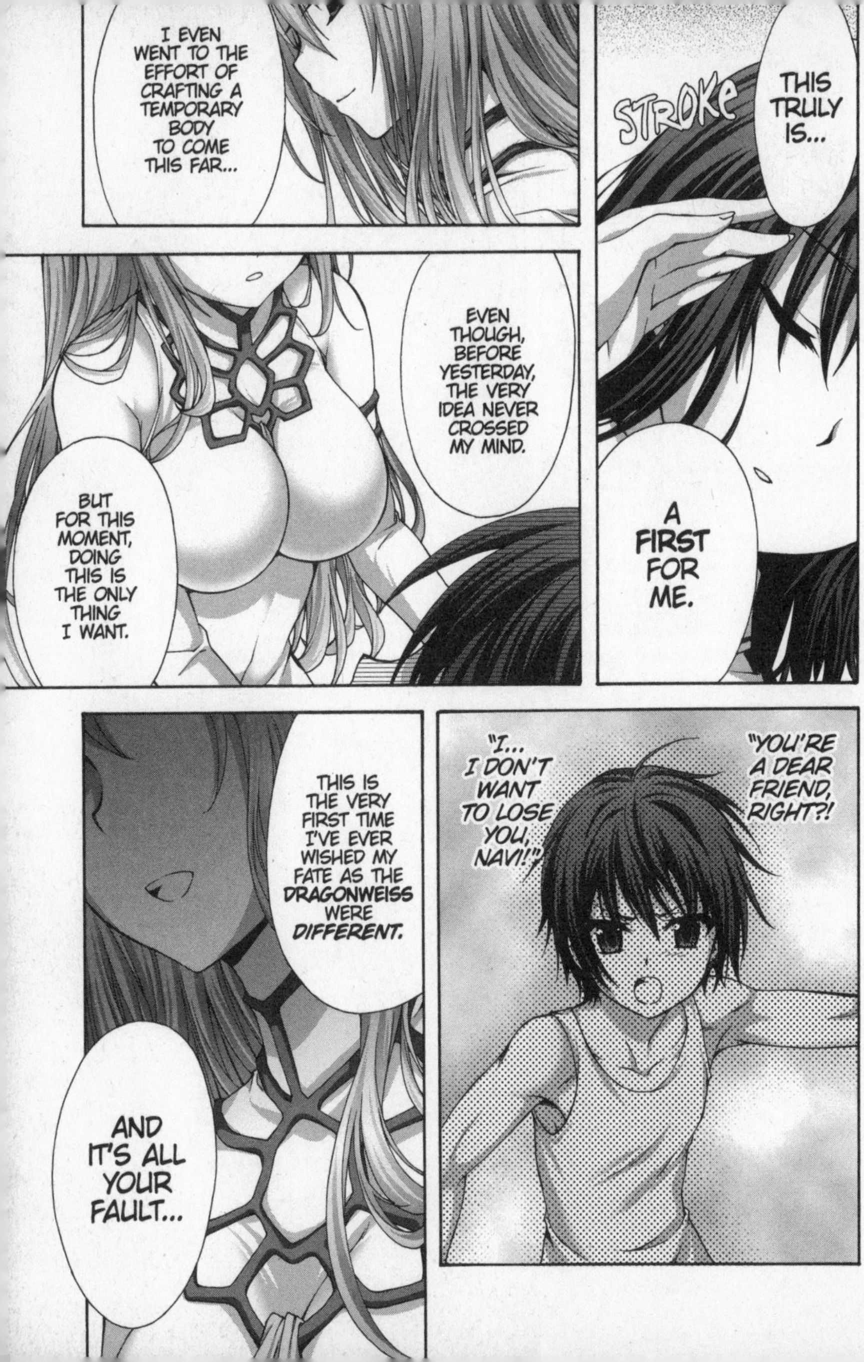
THIS TRULY IS...
STROKE
A FIRST FOR ME.
I EVEN WENT TO THE EFFORT OF CRAFTING A TEMPORARY BODY TO COME THIS FAR...
EVEN THOUGH, BEFORE YESTERDAY, THE VERY IDEA NEVER CROSSED MY MIND.
BUT FOR THIS MOMENT, DOING THIS IS THE ONLY THING I WANT.
"YOU'RE A DEAR FRIEND, RIGHT?!
"I... I DON'T WANT TO LOSE YOU, NAVI!"
THIS IS THE VERY FIRST TIME I'VE EVER WISHED MY FATE AS THE DRAGONWEISS WERE DIFFERENT.
AND IT'S ALL YOUR FAULT...

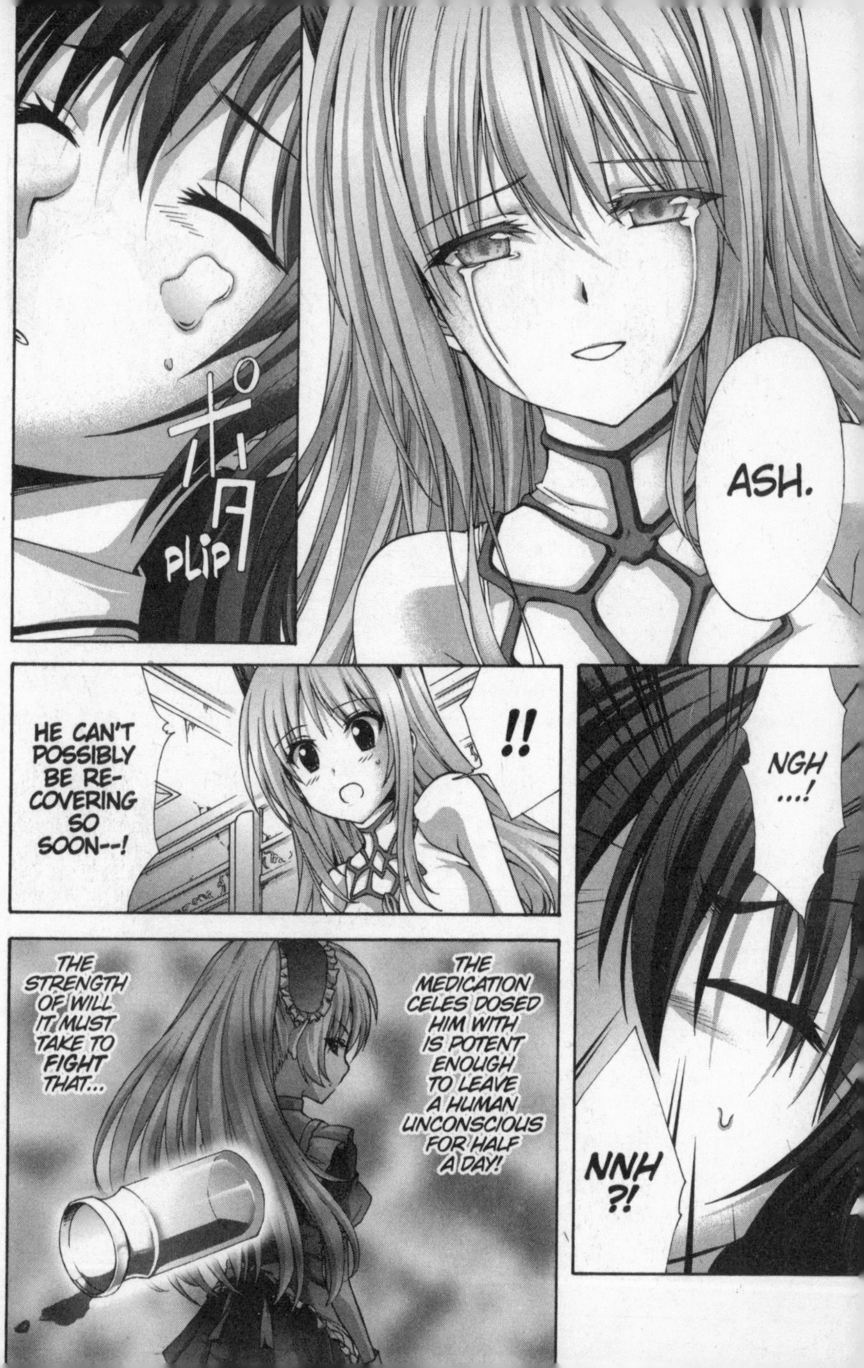
ASH.
ポタ
PLIP
NGH ...!
NNH ?!
!!
HE CAN'T POSSIBLY BE RE-COVERING SO SOON--!
THE MEDICATION CELES DOSED HIM WITH IS POTENT ENOUGH TO LEAVE A HUMAN UNCONSCIOUS FOR HALF A DAY!
THE STRENGTH OF WILL IT MUST TAKE TO FIGHT THAT...

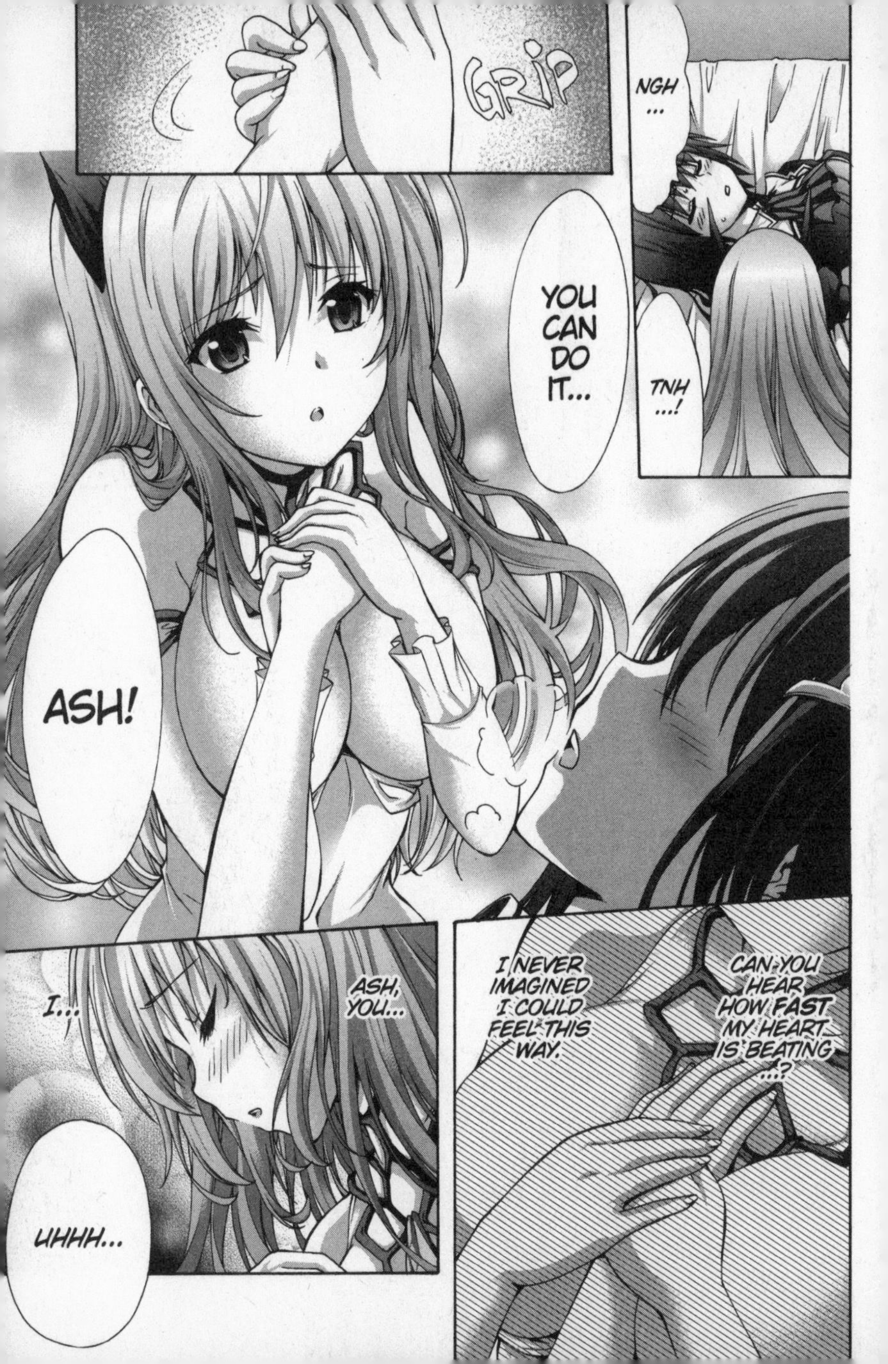
NGH...
TNH...!
GRIP
YOU CAN DO IT...
ASH!
CAN YOU HEAR HOW FAST MY HEART IS BEATING...?
I NEVER IMAGINED I COULD FEEL THIS WAY.
ASH, YOU...
I...
UHHH...

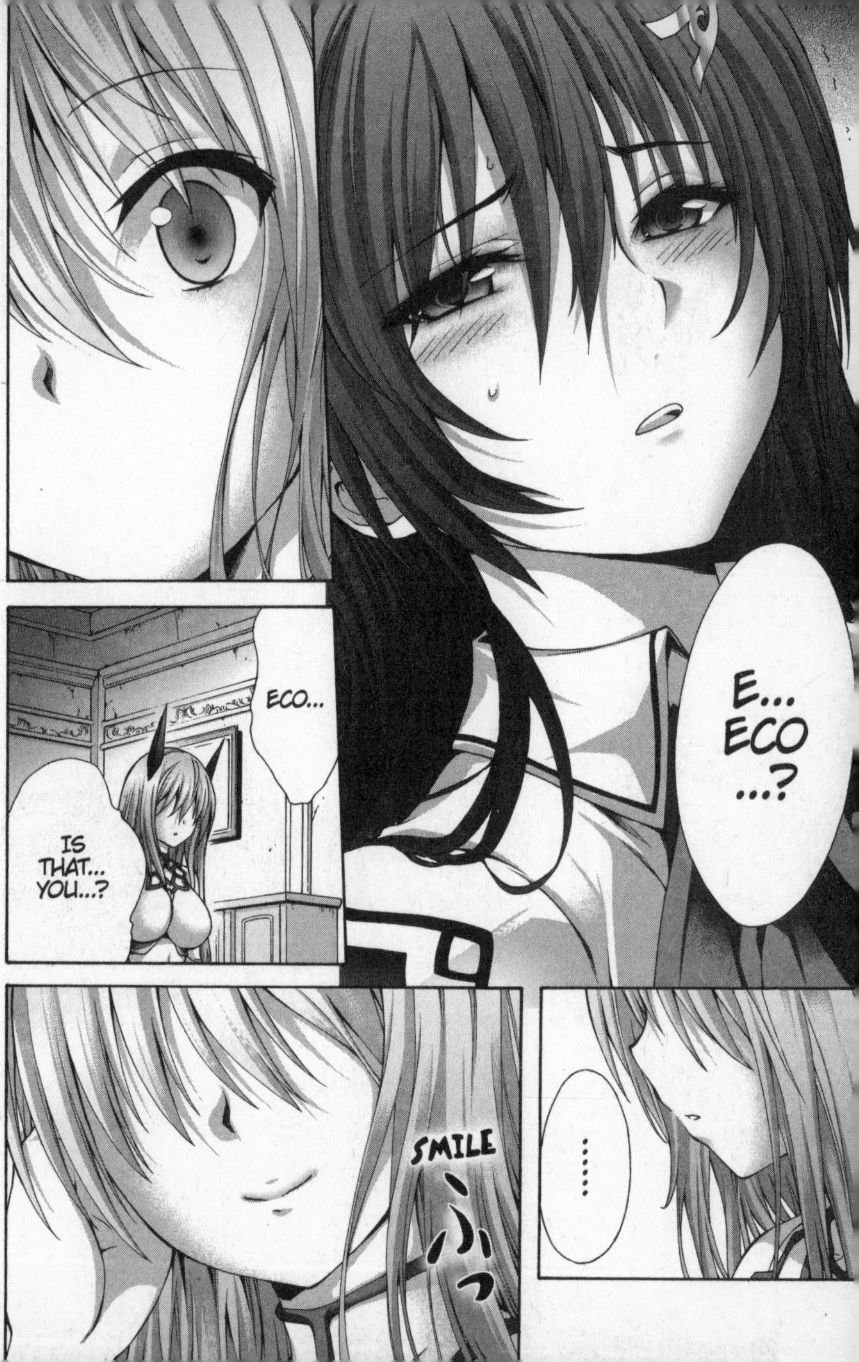
E... ECO ...?
ECO...
IS THAT... YOU...?
......
SMILE
ふっ

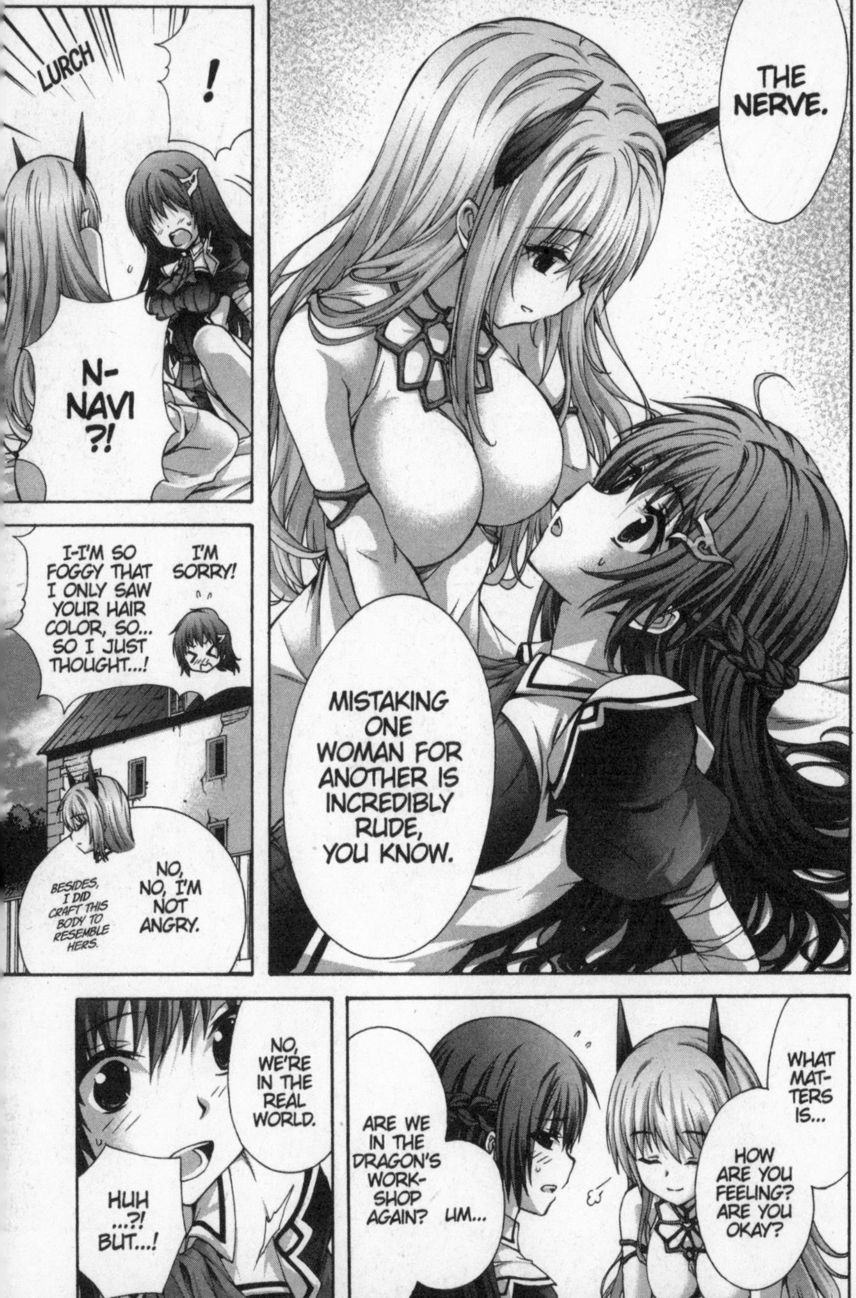
THE NERVE.
MISTAKING ONE WOMAN FOR ANOTHER IS INCREDIBLY RUDE, YOU KNOW.
LURCH
!
N-NAVI?!
I'M SORRY!
I-I'M SO FOGGY THAT I ONLY SAW YOUR HAIR COLOR, SO... SO I JUST THOUGHT...!
NO, NO, I'M NOT ANGRY.
BESIDES, I DID CRAFT THIS BODY TO RESEMBLE HERS.
WHAT MATTERS IS...
HOW ARE YOU FEELING? ARE YOU OKAY?
ARE WE IN THE DRAGON'S WORKSHOP AGAIN?
UM...
NO, WE'RE IN THE REAL WORLD.
HUH...?! BUT...!

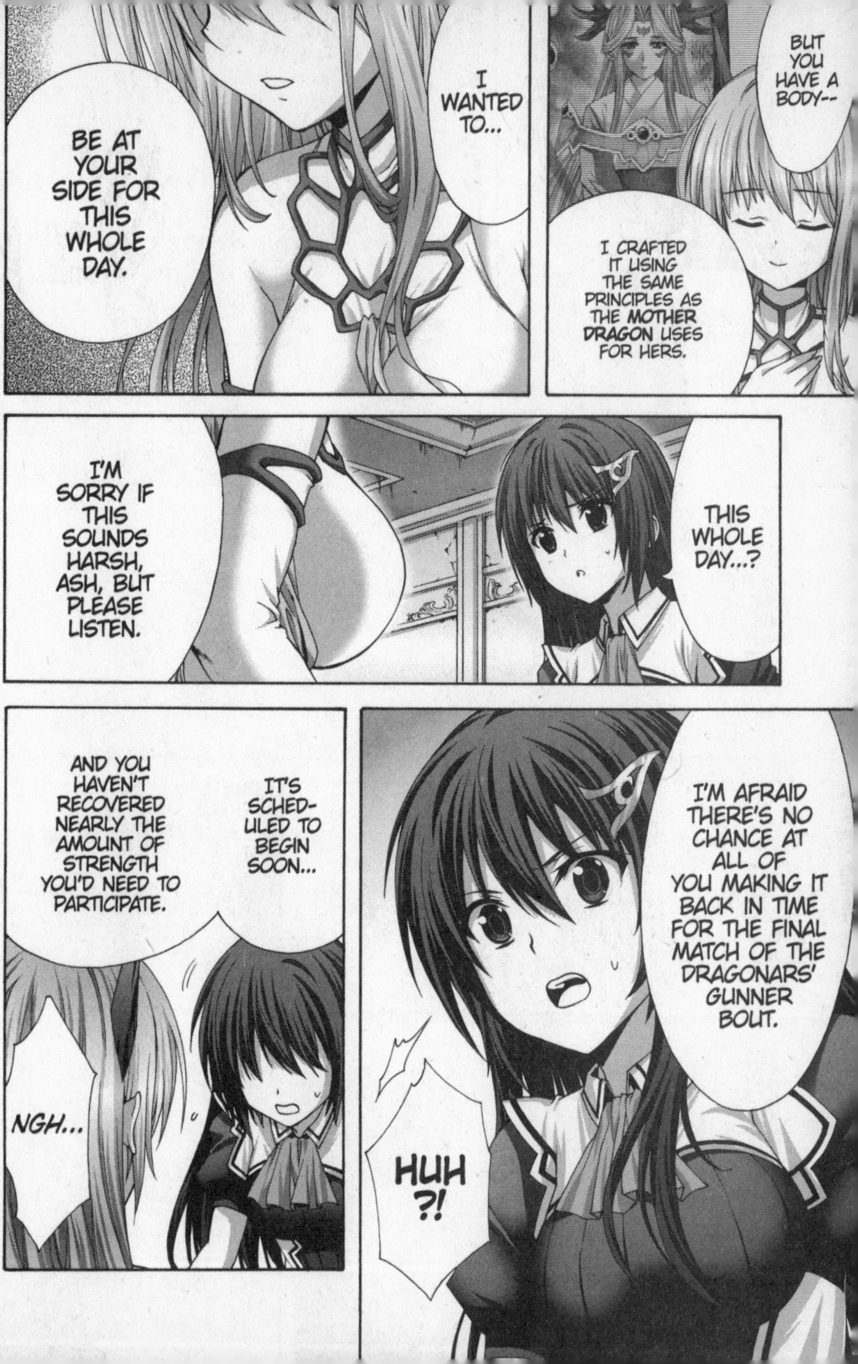

BUT YOU HAVE A BODY--
I CRAFTED IT USING THE SAME PRINCIPLES AS THE MOTHER DRAGON USES FOR HERS.
I WANTED TO...
BE AT YOUR SIDE FOR THIS WHOLE DAY.
THIS WHOLE DAY...?
I'M SORRY IF THIS SOUNDS HARSH, ASH, BUT PLEASE LISTEN.
I'M AFRAID THERE'S NO CHANCE AT ALL OF YOU MAKING IT BACK IN TIME FOR THE FINAL MATCH OF THE DRAGONARS' GUNNER BOUT.
HUH ?!
IT'S SCHED-ULED TO BEGIN SOON...
AND YOU HAVEN'T RECOVERED NEARLY THE AMOUNT OF STRENGTH YOU'D NEED TO PARTICIPATE.
NGH...

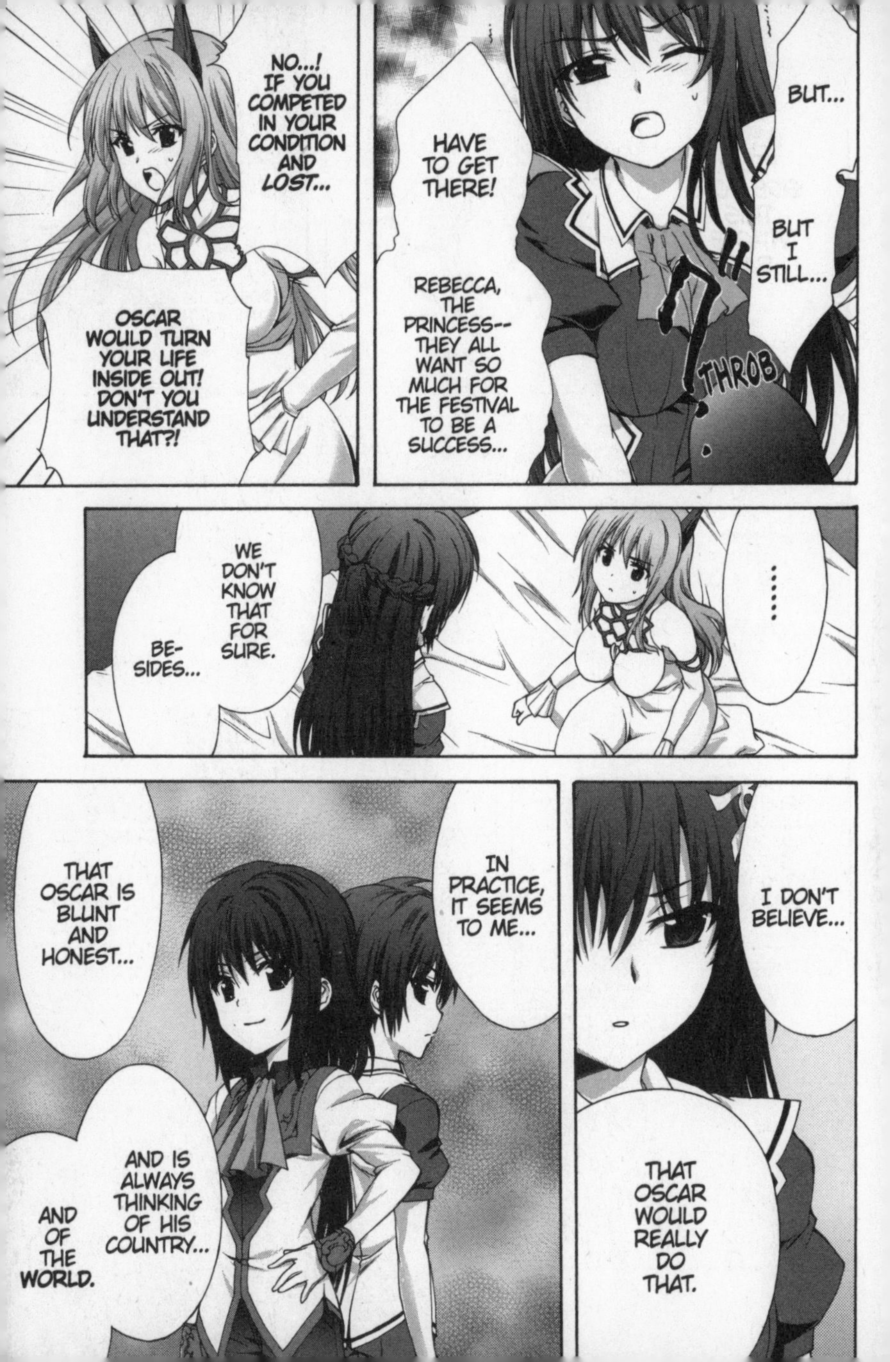
BUT...
REBECCA, THE PRINCESS-- THEY ALL WANT SO MUCH FOR THE FESTIVAL TO BE A SUCCESS...
BUT I STILL...
THROB
HAVE TO GET THERE!
NO...! IF YOU COMPETED IN YOUR CONDITION AND LOST...
OSCAR WOULD TURN YOUR LIFE INSIDE OUT! DON'T YOU UNDERSTAND THAT?!
......
WE DON'T KNOW THAT FOR SURE.
BE-SIDES...
I DON'T BELIEVE...
THAT OSCAR WOULD REALLY DO THAT.
IN PRACTICE, IT SEEMS TO ME...
THAT OSCAR IS BLUNT AND HONEST...
AND IS ALWAYS THINKING OF HIS COUNTRY...
AND OF THE WORLD.

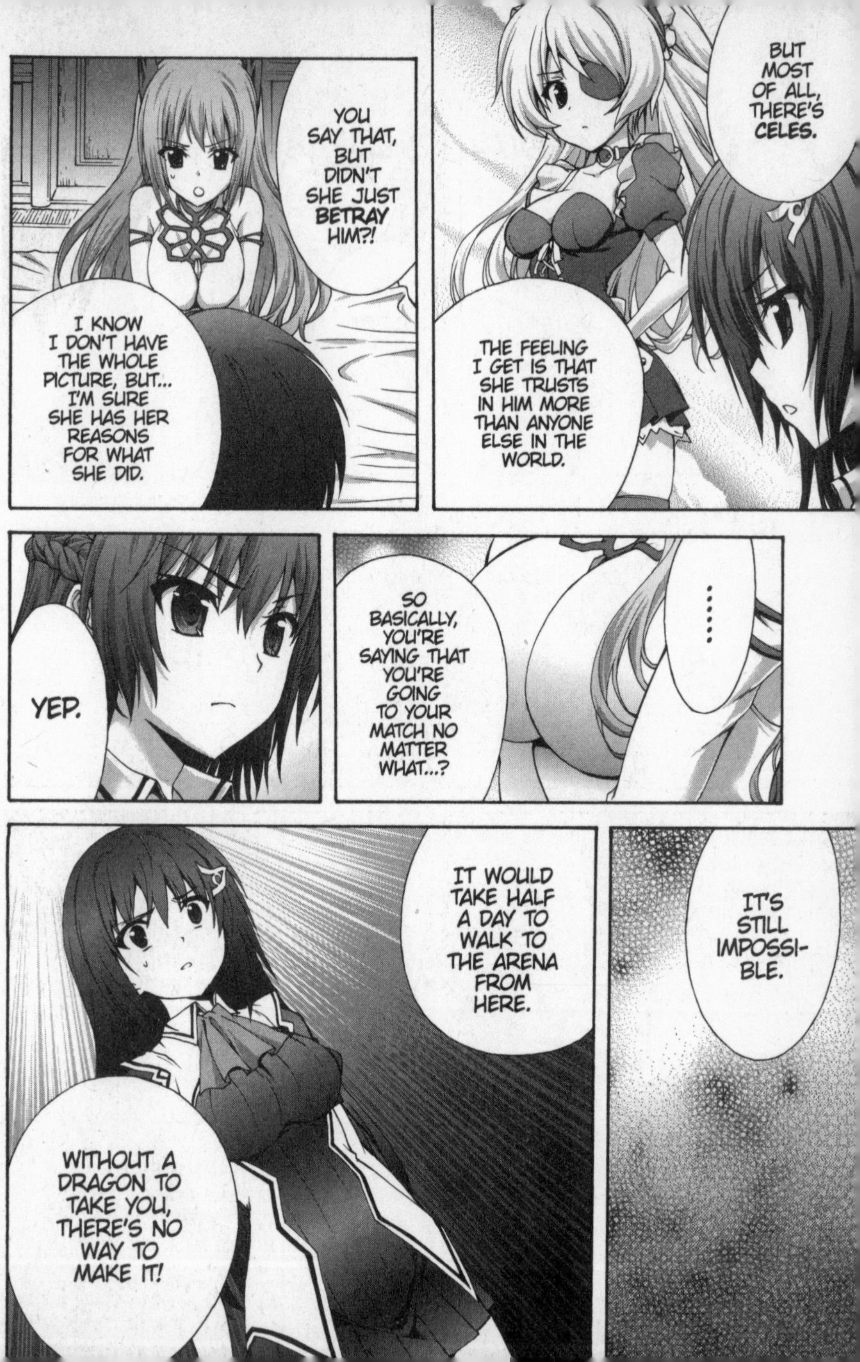
BUT MOST OF ALL, THERE'S CELES.
THE FEELING I GET IS THAT SHE TRUSTS IN HIM MORE THAN ANYONE ELSE IN THE WORLD.
YOU SAY THAT, BUT DIDN'T SHE JUST BETRAY HIM?!
I KNOW I DON'T HAVE THE WHOLE PICTURE, BUT... I'M SURE SHE HAS HER REASONS FOR WHAT SHE DID.
......
SO BASICALLY, YOU'RE SAYING THAT YOU'RE GOING TO YOUR MATCH NO MATTER WHAT...?
YEP.
IT'S STILL IMPOSSI-BLE.
IT WOULD TAKE HALF A DAY TO WALK TO THE ARENA FROM HERE.
WITHOUT A DRAGON TO TAKE YOU, THERE'S NO WAY TO MAKE IT!

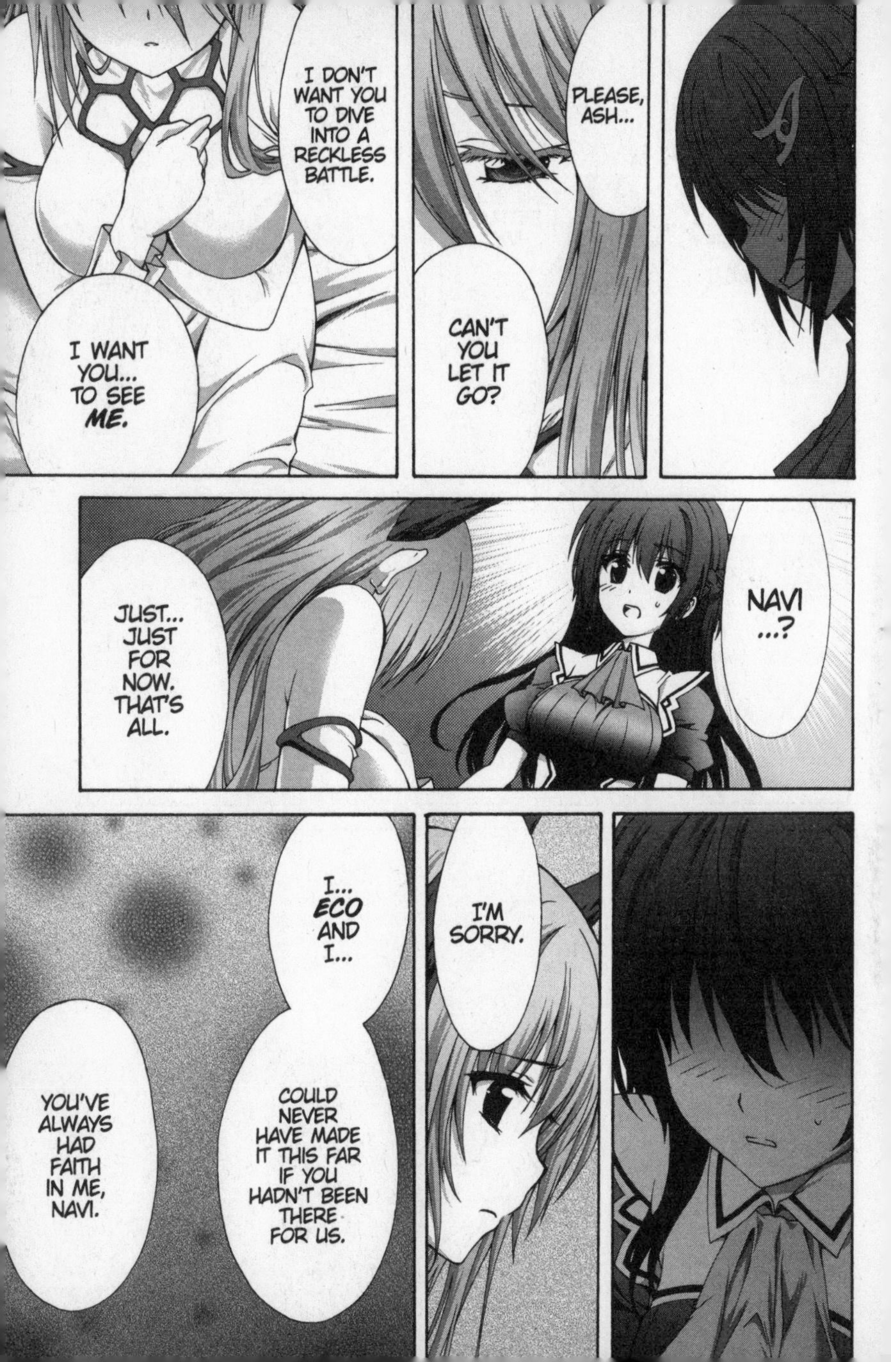
PLEASE, ASH...
CAN'T YOU LET IT GO?
I DON'T WANT YOU TO DIVE INTO A RECKLESS BATTLE.
I WANT YOU... TO SEE *ME.*
NAVI ...?
JUST... JUST FOR NOW. THAT'S ALL.
I'M SORRY.
I... *ECO* AND I...
COULD NEVER HAVE MADE IT THIS FAR IF YOU HADN'T BEEN THERE FOR US.
YOU'VE ALWAYS HAD FAITH IN ME, NAVI.

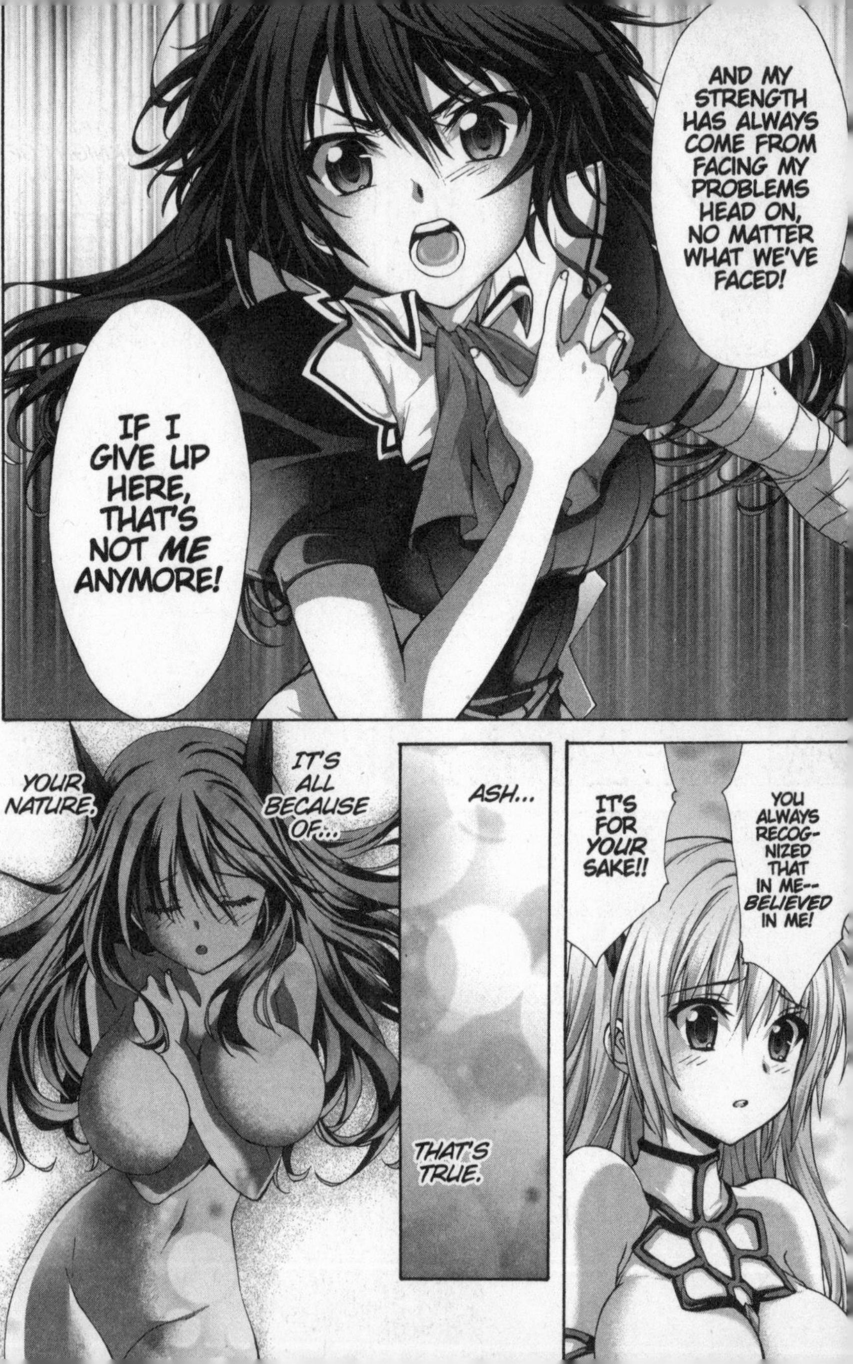
AND MY STRENGTH HAS ALWAYS COME FROM FACING MY PROBLEMS HEAD ON, NO MATTER WHAT WE'VE FACED!
IF I GIVE UP HERE, THAT'S NOT *ME* ANYMORE!
YOU ALWAYS RECOG-NIZED THAT IN ME-- *BELIEVED* IN ME!
IT'S FOR *YOUR* SAKE!!
ASH...
THAT'S TRUE.
IT'S ALL BECAUSE OF...
YOUR NATURE.

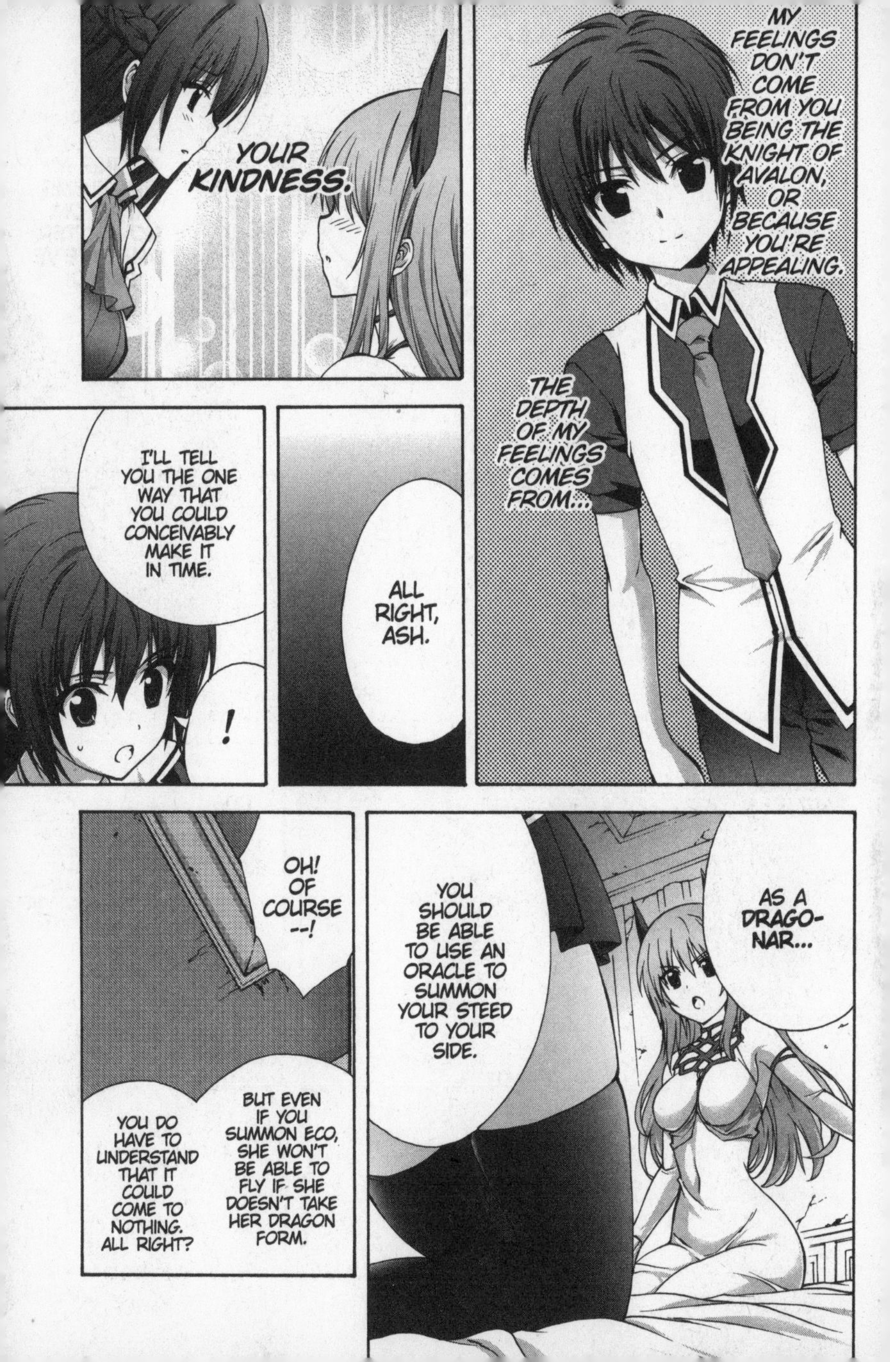
MY FEELINGS DON'T COME FROM YOU BEING THE KNIGHT OF AVALON, OR BECAUSE YOU'RE APPEALING.
THE DEPTH OF MY FEELINGS COMES FROM...
YOUR KINDNESS.
ALL RIGHT, ASH.
I'LL TELL YOU THE ONE WAY THAT YOU COULD CONCEIVABLY MAKE IT IN TIME.
!
AS A DRAGONAR...
YOU SHOULD BE ABLE TO USE AN ORACLE TO SUMMON YOUR STEED TO YOUR SIDE.
OH! OF COURSE --!
BUT EVEN IF YOU SUMMON ECO, SHE WON'T BE ABLE TO FLY IF SHE DOESN'T TAKE HER DRAGON FORM.
YOU DO HAVE TO UNDERSTAND THAT IT COULD COME TO NOTHING. ALL RIGHT?

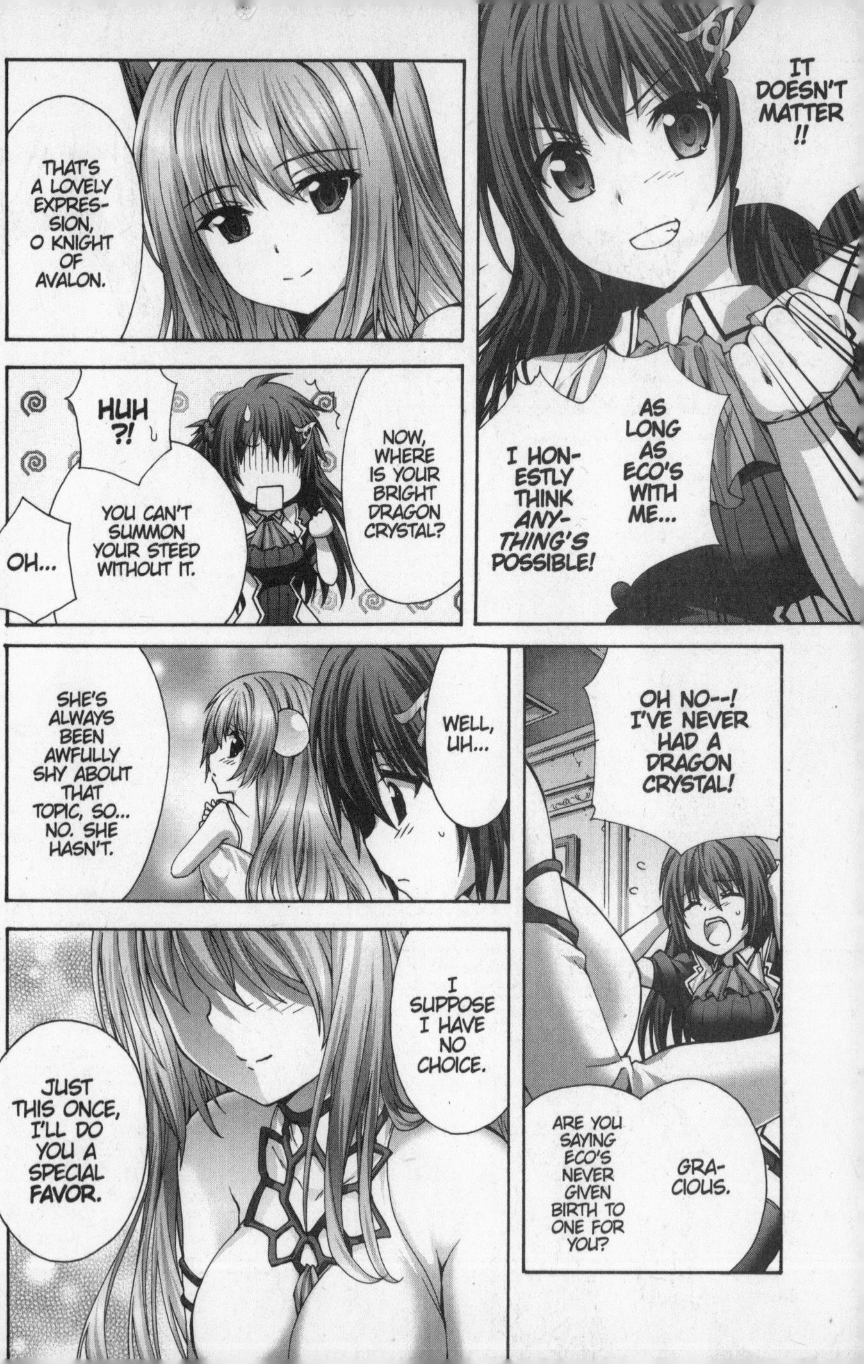
IT DOESN'T MATTER!!
AS LONG AS ECO'S WITH ME...
I HONESTLY THINK ANYTHING'S POSSIBLE!
THAT'S A LOVELY EXPRESSION, O KNIGHT OF AVALON.
NOW, WHERE IS YOUR BRIGHT DRAGON CRYSTAL?
HUH?!
YOU CAN'T SUMMON YOUR STEED WITHOUT IT.
OH...
OH NO--! I'VE NEVER HAD A DRAGON CRYSTAL!
GRACIOUS.
ARE YOU SAYING ECO'S NEVER GIVEN BIRTH TO ONE FOR YOU?
WELL, UH...
SHE'S ALWAYS BEEN AWFULLY SHY ABOUT THAT TOPIC, SO... NO. SHE HASN'T.
I SUPPOSE I HAVE NO CHOICE.
JUST THIS ONCE, I'LL DO YOU A SPECIAL FAVOR.

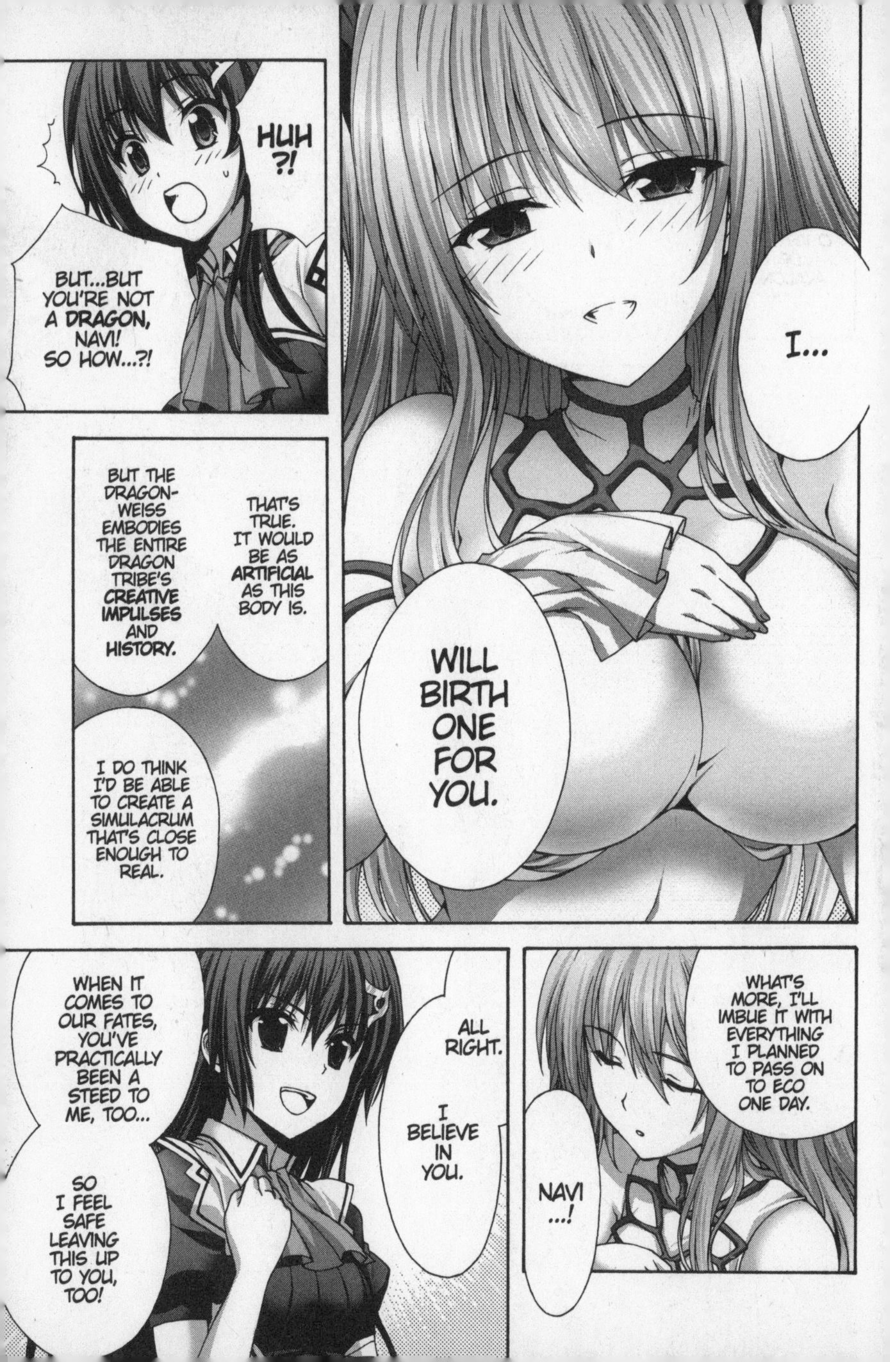
I...
WILL BIRTH ONE FOR YOU.
HUH ?!
BUT...BUT YOU'RE NOT A DRAGON, NAVI! SO HOW...?!
THAT'S TRUE. IT WOULD BE AS ARTIFICIAL AS THIS BODY IS.
BUT THE DRAGON-WEISS EMBODIES THE ENTIRE DRAGON TRIBE'S CREATIVE IMPULSES AND HISTORY.
I DO THINK I'D BE ABLE TO CREATE A SIMULACRUM THAT'S CLOSE ENOUGH TO REAL.
WHAT'S MORE, I'LL IMBUE IT WITH EVERYTHING I PLANNED TO PASS ON TO ECO ONE DAY.
NAVI ...!
ALL RIGHT.
I BELIEVE IN YOU.
WHEN IT COMES TO OUR FATES, YOU'VE PRACTICALLY BEEN A STEED TO ME, TOO...
SO I FEEL SAFE LEAVING THIS UP TO YOU, TOO!

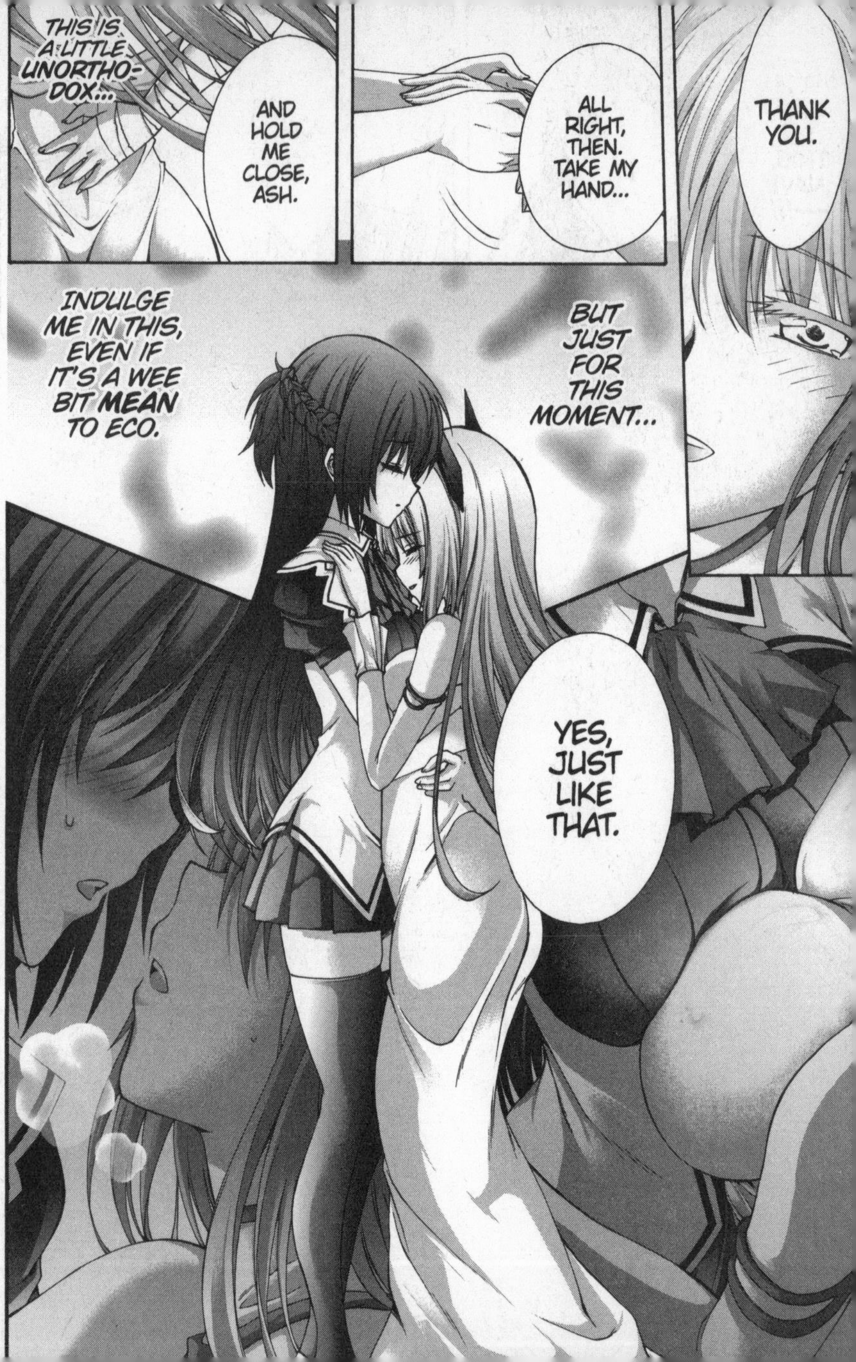
THANK YOU.
ALL RIGHT, THEN. TAKE MY HAND...
THIS IS A LITTLE UNORTHODOX...
AND HOLD ME CLOSE, ASH.
BUT JUST FOR THIS MOMENT...
INDULGE ME IN THIS, EVEN IF IT'S A WEE BIT MEAN TO ECO.
YES, JUST LIKE THAT.

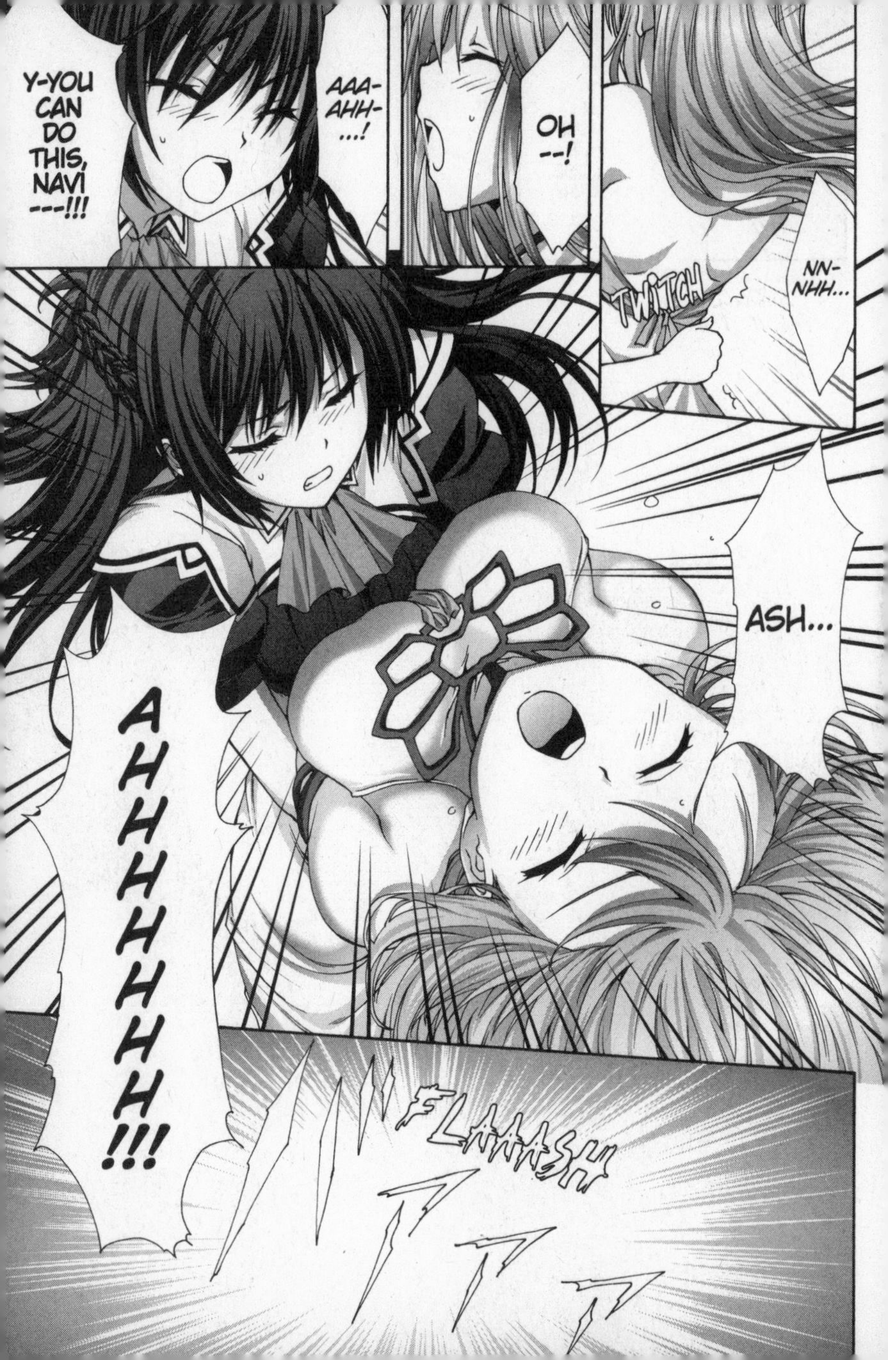
NN-NHH...
TWITCH
OH --!
AAA-AHH-...!
Y-YOU CAN DO THIS, NAVI ---!!!
ASH...
AHHHHHHH!!!
FLAAASH

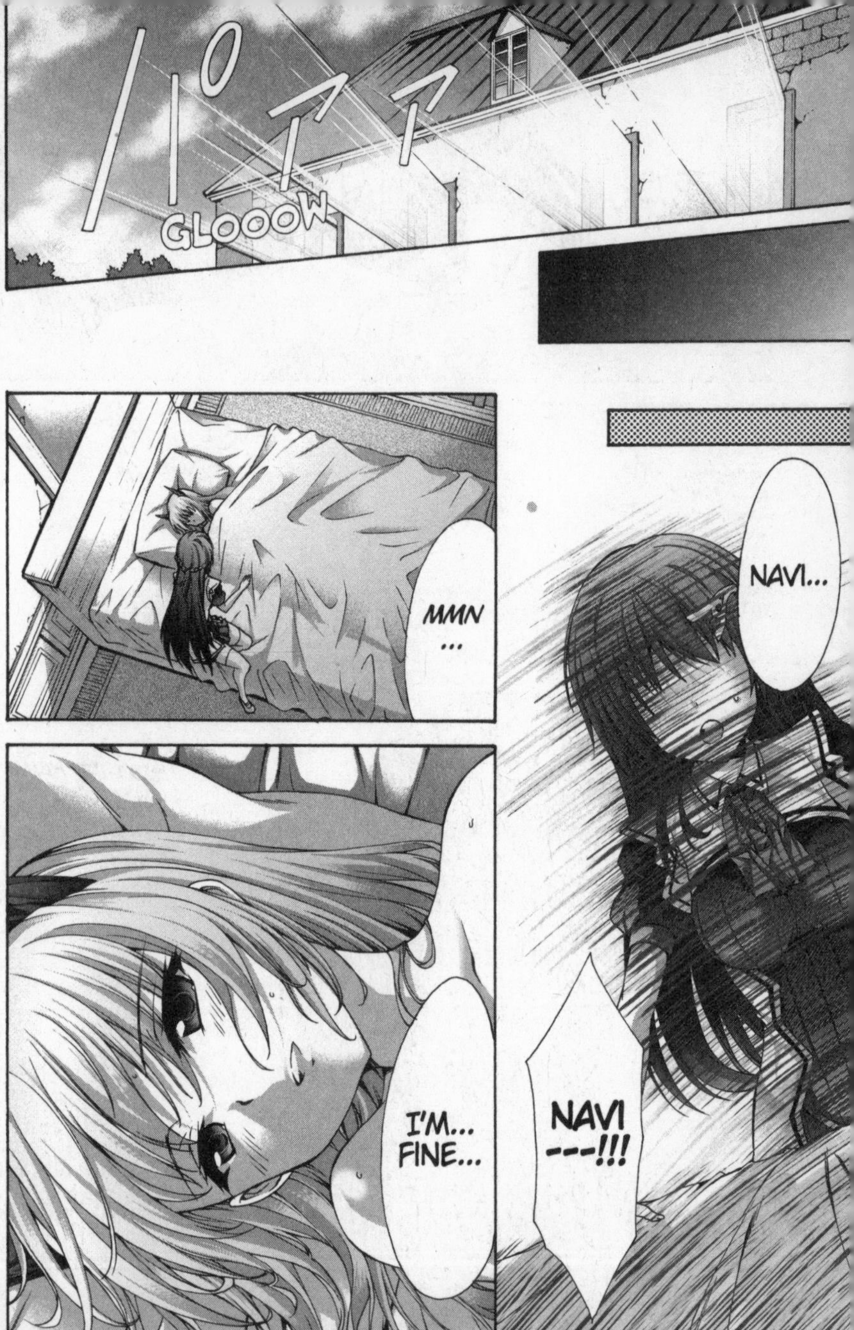
GLOOOW
NAVI...
NAVI---!!!
MMN...
I'M... FINE...

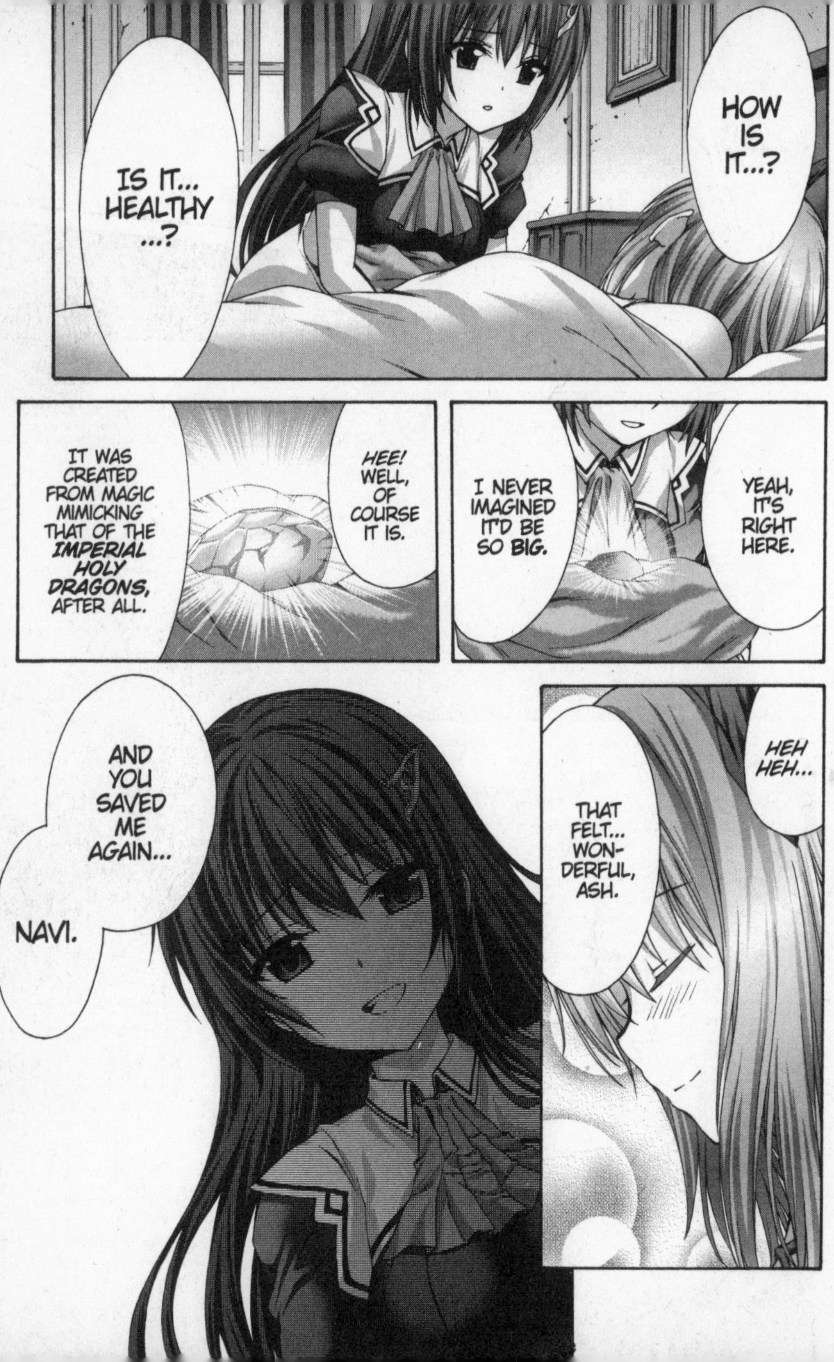
HOW IS IT...?
IS IT... HEALTHY ...?
YEAH, IT'S RIGHT HERE.
I NEVER IMAGINED IT'D BE SO BIG.
HEE! WELL, OF COURSE IT IS.
IT WAS CREATED FROM MAGIC MIMICKING THAT OF THE IMPERIAL HOLY DRAGONS, AFTER ALL.
HEH HEH...
THAT FELT... WON-DERFUL, ASH.
AND YOU SAVED ME AGAIN...
NAVI.

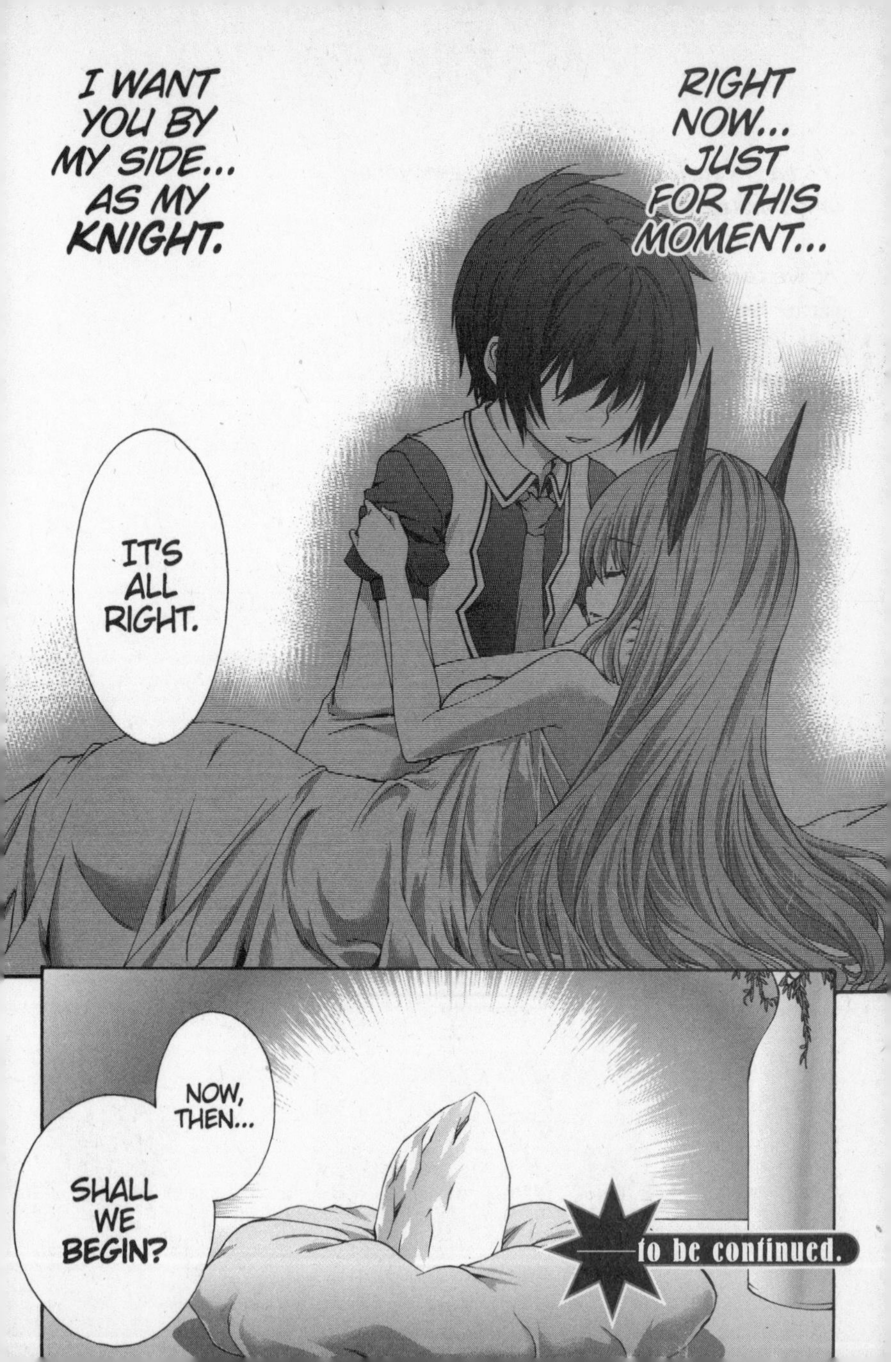
RIGHT NOW... JUST FOR THIS MOMENT...
I WANT YOU BY MY SIDE... AS MY KNIGHT.
IT'S ALL RIGHT.
NOW, THEN...
SHALL WE BEGIN?
——to be continued.

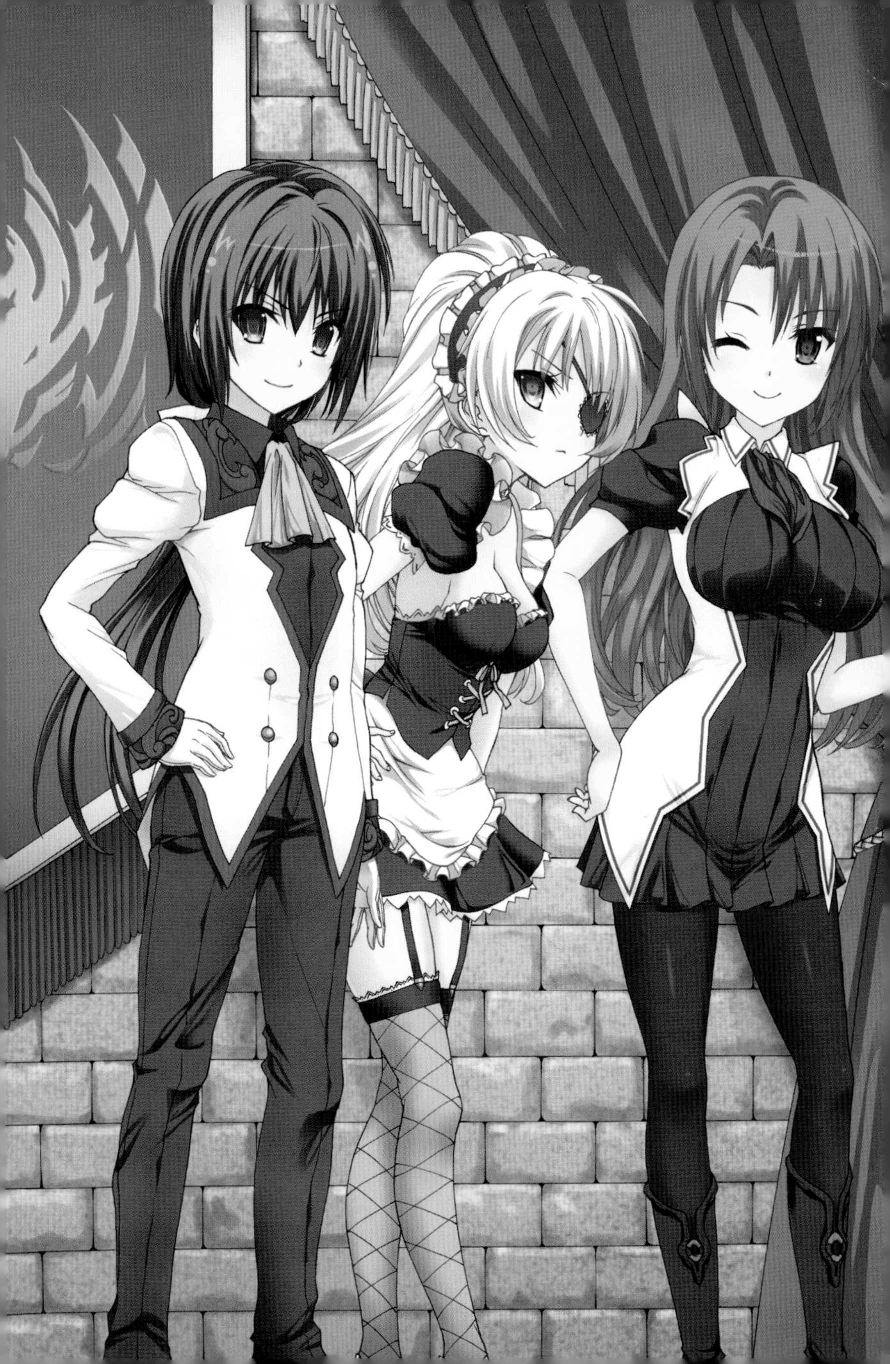

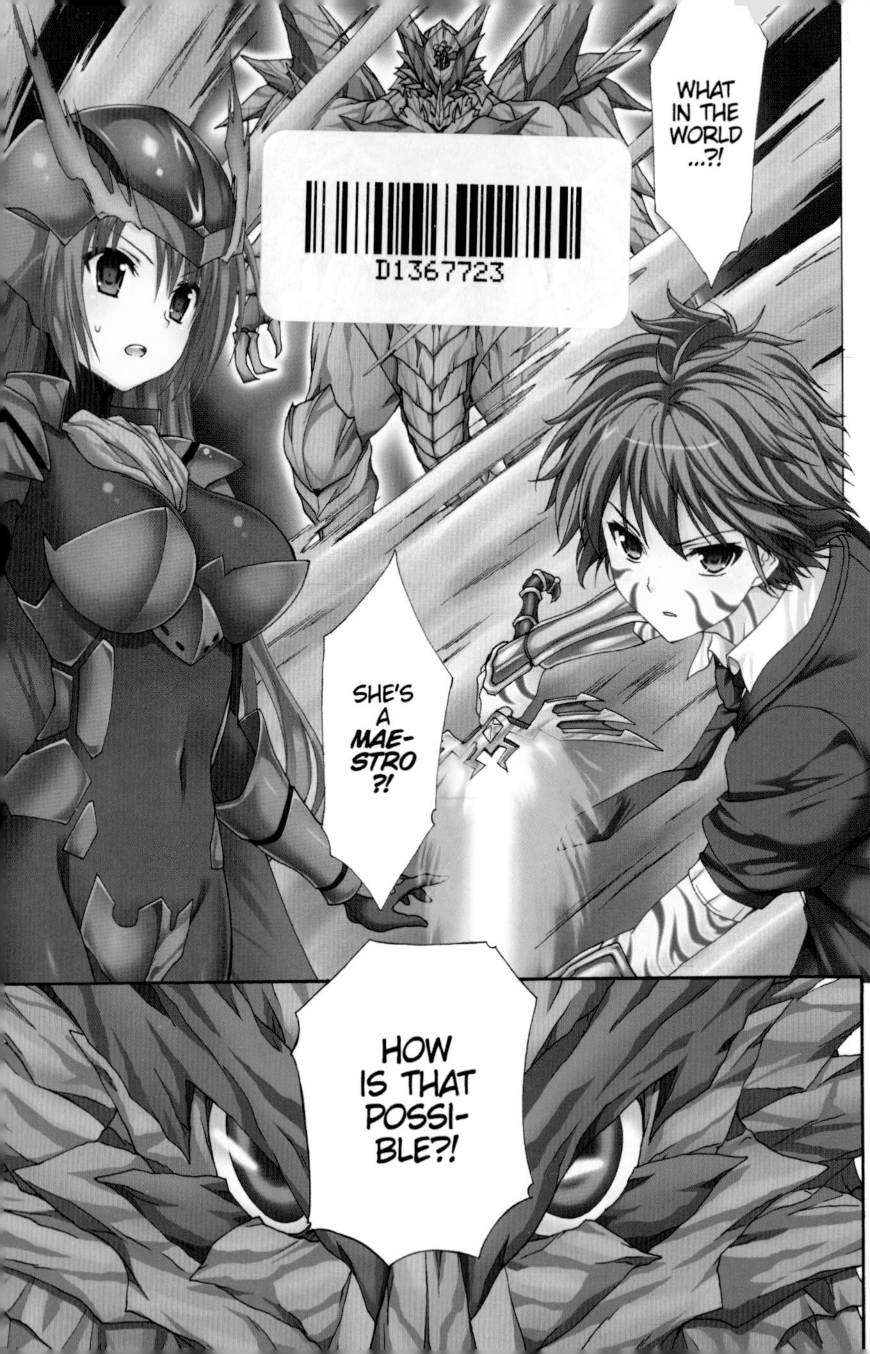
WHAT IN THE WORLD ...?!
SHE'S A MAESTRO?!
HOW IS THAT POSSIBLE?!

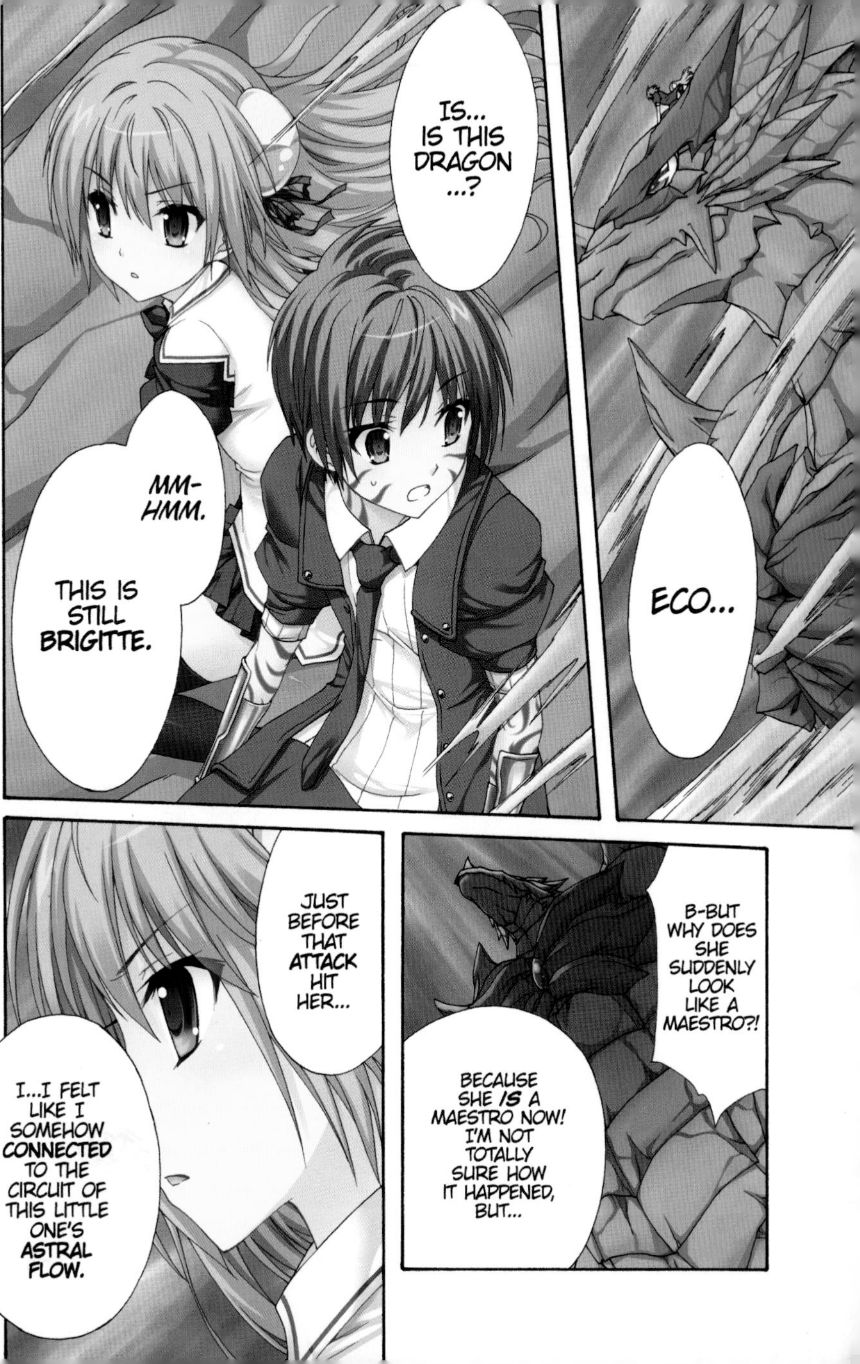
ECO...
IS... IS THIS DRAGON ...?
MM-HMM.
THIS IS STILL BRIGITTE.
B-BUT WHY DOES SHE SUDDENLY LOOK LIKE A MAESTRO?!
BECAUSE SHE *IS* A MAESTRO NOW! I'M NOT TOTALLY SURE HOW IT HAPPENED, BUT...
JUST BEFORE THAT ATTACK HIT HER...
I...I FELT LIKE I SOMEHOW CONNECTED TO THE CIRCUIT OF THIS LITTLE ONE'S ASTRAL FLOW.

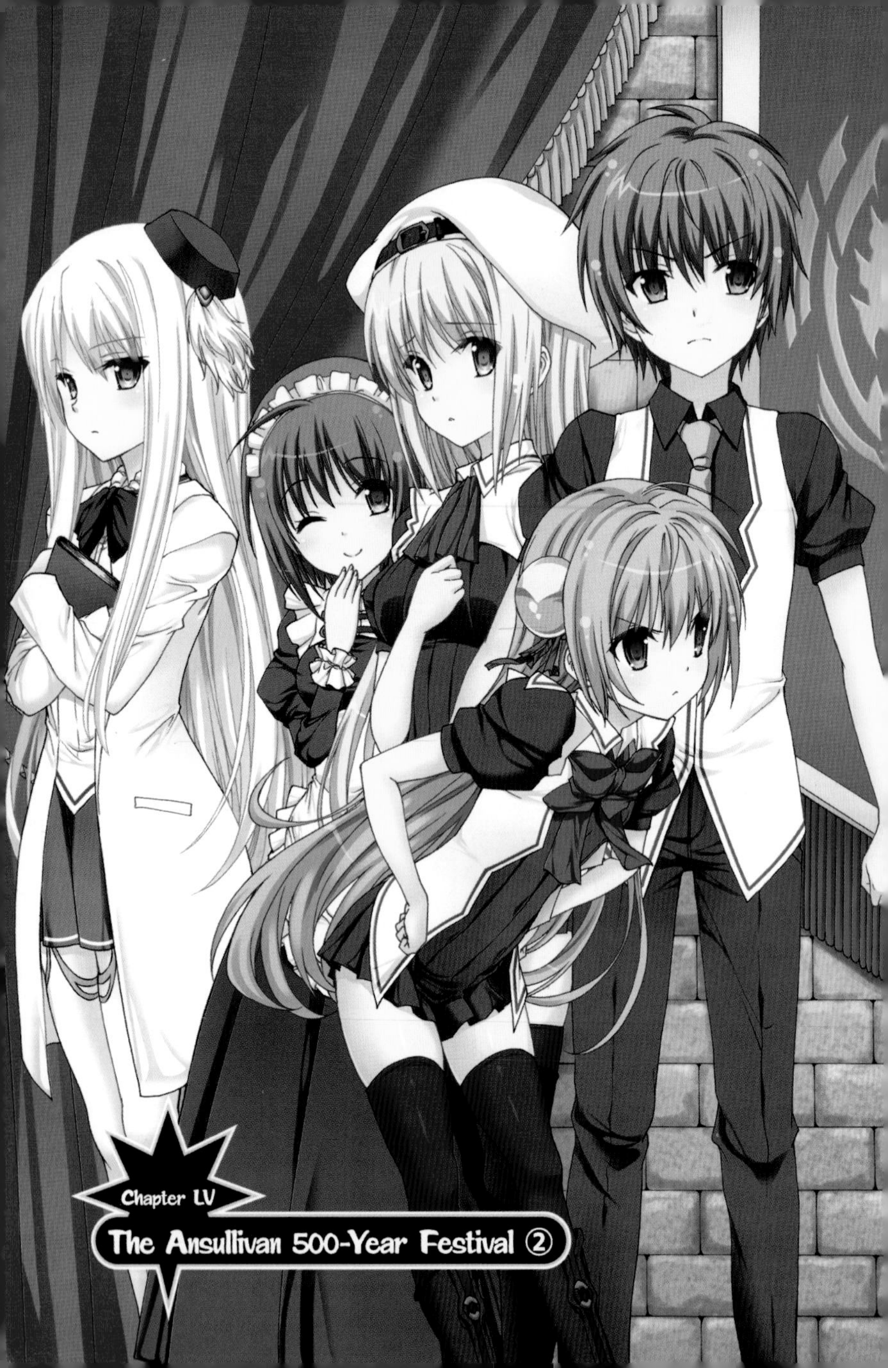
Chapter LV
The Ansullivan 500-Year Festival ②